UPHEAVAL

UPHEAVAL

How Nations Cope with

Crisis and Change

JARED DIAMOND

ALLEN LANE
an imprint of
PENGUIN BOOKS

ALLEN LANE

UK | USA | Canada | Ireland | Australia
India | New Zealand | South Africa

Allen Lane is part of the Penguin Random House group of companies
whose addresses can be found at global.penguinrandomhouse.com

First published in the United States of America by Little, Brown and Company 2019
First published in Great Britain by Allen Lane 2019
002

Printed and bound in Great Britain by Clays Ltd, Elcograf S.p.A.

A CIP catalogue record for this book is available from the British Library

ISBN: 978–0–241–00339–8

www.greenpenguin.co.uk

MIX
Paper from
responsible sources
FSC® C018179

Penguin Random House is committed to a
sustainable future for our business, our readers
and our planet. This book is made from Forest
Stewardship Council® certified paper.

I dedicate this book
to the memory of my parents
Louis and Flora Diamond,
and
to the future
of my wife Marie Cohen
and of my sons Max and Joshua Diamond

Contents

CONTENTS

UPHEAVAL

LEGACIES OF COCOANUT GROVE

Two stories — What's a crisis? —
Individual and national crises — What this book is
and isn't — Plan of the book

A t one or more times during our lives, most of us undergo a personal upheaval or crisis, which may or may not get resolved successfully through our making personal changes. Similarly, nations undergo national crises, which also may or may not get resolved successfully through national changes. There is a large body of research and anecdotal information, built up by therapists, about the resolution of personal crises. Could the resulting conclusions help us understand the resolution of national crises?

To illustrate personal and national crises, I'll begin this book with two stories from my own life. It's said that a child's earliest datable firm memories are laid down from around the age of four years, although children also retain indistinct memories of earlier events. That generalization does apply to me, because the earliest memory that I can date is of Boston's Cocoanut Grove fire, which happened just after my fifth birthday. Although (fortunately) I was not at the fire myself, I experienced it second-hand through the frightening accounts of my physician father.

On November 28, 1942, a fire broke out and spread rapidly through an overcrowded Boston nightclub called Cocoanut Grove (the owner's spelling), whose sole exit became blocked. A total of 492 people died, and hundreds of others were injured, by suffocation, smoke inhalation, or being trampled or burned (Plate 0.1). Boston physicians and hospitals were overwhelmed — not just by the wounded and dying victims of the fire itself, but also by the fire's psychological victims: relatives, distraught that their husbands or wives or children or siblings had died in a horrible way; and the fire's survivors, traumatized by guilt, because they had survived while hundreds of other guests had died. Until 10:15 P.M., their lives had been normal, and focused on celebrating the Thanksgiving holiday weekend, a football game, and wartime leaves of soldiers. By 11:00 P.M., most of the victims were already dead, and the lives of their relatives and of the survivors were in crisis. Their expected life trajectories had been derailed. They felt ashamed that they were alive while a dear one was dead. The relatives had lost someone central to their identity. Not only for the fire's survivors but also for Bostonians remote from the fire (including me as a five-year-old), the fire shook our faith in a world of justice. Those punished weren't naughty boys and evil people: they were ordinary people, killed through no fault of their own.

Some of those survivors and relatives remained traumatized for the rest of their lives. A few committed suicide. But most of them, after an intensely painful several weeks during which they could not accept their loss, began a slow process of grieving, reappraising their values, rebuilding their lives, and discovering that not everything in their world was ruined. Many who had lost spouses went on to remarry. Even in the best cases, though, decades later they

4

remained mosaics of their new identities formed after the Cocoanut Grove fire, and of their old identities established before the fire.
We shall have frequent opportunity throughout this book to apply
that metaphor of "mosaic" to individuals and nations in whom or in
which disparate elements coexist uneasily.

Cocoanut Grove provides an extreme example of a personal
crisis. But it was extreme only in that bad things befell a large number of victims simultaneously — in fact, so many victims that the
fire also provoked a crisis demanding new solutions in the field of
psychotherapy itself, as we'll see in Chapter 1. Many of us experience individual tragedy first-hand in our own lives, or second-hand
through the experiences of a relative or a friend. Yet such tragedies
that strike only one victim are as painful to that victim, and to his
or her circle of friends, as Cocoanut Grove was to the circles of its
492 victims.

Now, for comparison, here is an example of a national crisis. I
lived in Britain in the late 1950's and early 1960's, at a time when it
was undergoing a slow national crisis, although neither my British
friends nor I fully appreciated it then. Britain was world-leading in
science, blessed with a rich cultural history, proudly and uniquely
British, and still basking in memories of having had the world's
largest fleet, the greatest wealth, and the most far-flung empire in
history. Unfortunately, by the 1950's Britain was bleeding economically, losing its empire and its power, conflicted about its role in
Europe, and struggling with long-standing class differences and
recent waves of immigrants. Things came to a head between 1956
and 1961, when Britain scrapped all of its remaining battleships,
experienced its first race riots, had to begin granting independence
to its African colonies, and saw the Suez Crisis expose the humiliating loss of its ability to act independently as a world power. My
British friends struggled to make sense of those events, and to
explain them to me as an American visitor. Those blows intensified

5

discussions, among the British people and British politicians, about Britain's identity and role.

Today, 60 years later, Britain is a mosaic of its new self and its old self. Britain has shed its empire, become a multi-ethnic society, and adopted a welfare state and high-quality government-run schools to reduce class differences. Britain never regained its naval and economic dominance over the world, and it remains notoriously conflicted ("Brexit") about its role in Europe. But Britain is still among the world's six richest nations, is still a parliamentary democracy under a figurehead monarch, is still a world leader in science and technology, and still maintains as its currency the pound sterling rather than the euro.

Those two stories illustrate this book's theme. Crises, and pressures for change, confront individuals and their groups at all levels, ranging from single people, to teams, to businesses, to nations, to the whole world. Crises may arise from external pressures, such as a person being deserted or widowed by his or her spouse, or a nation being threatened or attacked by another nation. Alternatively, crises may arise from internal pressures, such as a person becoming sick, or a nation enduring civil strife. Successful coping with either external or internal pressures requires *selective* change. That's as true of nations as of individuals.

The key word here is "selective." It's neither possible nor desirable for individuals or nations to change completely, and to discard everything of their former identities. The challenge, for nations as for individuals in crisis, is to figure out which parts of their identities are already functioning well and don't need changing, and which parts are no longer working and do need changing. Individuals or nations under pressure must take honest stock of their abilities and values. They must decide what of themselves still works, remains appropriate even under the new changed circumstances, and thus can be retained. Conversely, they need the courage to recognize what must be changed in order to deal with the new situation. That requires the individuals or nations to find new solutions compatible with their abilities and with the rest of their being. At the same time, they have to draw a line and stress the elements so fundamental to their identities that they refuse to change them.

Those are among the parallels between individuals and nations with respect to crises. But there are also glaring differences that we shall acknowledge.

———

How do we define a "crisis"? A convenient starting point is the derivation of the English word "crisis" from the Greek noun "krisis" and verb "krino," which have several related meanings: "to separate," "to decide," "to draw a distinction," and "turning point." Hence one can think of a crisis as a moment of truth: a turning point, when conditions before and after that "moment" are "much more" different from one another than before and after "most" other moments. I put the words "moment," "much more," and "most" in quotes, because it's a practical problem to decide how brief should be the moment, how different should be the changed conditions, and how much rarer than most other moments should a turning point be for us to label it as a "crisis," rather than just as another small event blip or a gradual natural evolution of changes.

The turning point represents a challenge. It creates pressure to devise new coping methods, when former coping methods have proved inadequate to resolve the challenge. If an individual or nation does devise new and better coping methods, then we say that the crisis has been resolved successfully. But we'll see in Chapter 1 that the difference between success and failure in resolving a crisis is often not sharp — that success may just be partial, may not last forever, and the same problem may return. (Think of the

7

United Kingdom "resolving" its world role by entering the European Union in 1973, and then voting in 2017 to leave the European Union.)

Let's now illustrate that practical problem: how brief, how major, and how infrequent must a turning point be, to warrant applying the term "crisis"? How often in an individual's lifetime, or in a millennium of regional history, is it useful to label what happens as a "crisis"? Those questions have alternative answers; different answers prove useful for different purposes.

One extreme answer restricts the term "crisis" to long intervals and rare, dramatic upheavals: e.g., just a few times in a lifetime for an individual, and just every few centuries for a nation. As one example, a historian of ancient Rome might apply the word "crisis" to only three events after the foundation of the Roman Republic around 509 BC: the first two wars against Carthage (264–241 and 218–201 BC), the replacement of republican government by the empire (around 23 BC), and the barbarian invasions leading to the Western Roman Empire's fall (around AD 476). Of course, such a Roman historian doesn't consider everything else in Roman history between 509 BC and AD 476 as trivial; he just reserves the term "crisis" for those three exceptional events.

At the opposite extreme, my UCLA colleague David Rigby and his associates Pierre-Alexandre Balland and Ron Boschma published a fine study of "technological crises" in American cities, which they defined operationally as periods of sustained downturn in patent applications, with the word "sustained" defined mathematically. According to those definitions, they found that an American city undergoes a technological crisis on average about every 12 years, that the average such crisis lasts for four years, and that an average American city finds itself in a state of technological crisis for about three years in every decade. They found that definition to be fruitful for understanding a question of much practical interest:

what enables some but not other American cities to avoid technological crises defined in that way? But a Roman historian would
dismiss the events studied by David and his colleagues as ephemeral bagatelles, while David and his colleagues would counter that
the Roman historian is neglecting everything that happened in 985
years of Roman history except for three events.

My point is that one can define "crisis" in different ways, according to different frequencies, different durations, and different scales
of impact. One can usefully study either rare big crises or frequent
small crises. In this book the time scale that I adopt ranges from a
few decades to a century. All of the countries that I discuss have
experienced what I consider as a "major crisis" during my lifetime.
That isn't to deny that all of them also experienced more frequent
smaller turning points.

Both for individual crises and for national crises, we often focus
on a single moment of truth: for instance, the day when a wife tells
her husband that she is filing for divorce; or (for Chilean history)
the date September 11, 1973, when the Chilean military overthrew
Chile's democratic government, whose president committed suicide. A few crises do indeed arrive out of the blue with no anteced-
ents, such as the December 26, 2004 Sumatra tsunami that
suddenly killed 200,000 people, or my cousin's death in the prime
of his life when his car was crushed by a train at a railroad crossing,
leaving his wife widowed and his four children orphaned. But most
individual as well as national crises are the culmination of evolutionary changes extending over many years: for example, the
divorcing couple's prolonged marital difficulties, or Chile's political
and economic difficulties. The "crisis" is a sudden realization of, or
a sudden acting on, pressures that have been building up for a long
time. This truth was acknowledged explicitly by Australia's Prime
Minister Gough Whitlam, who (as we'll see in Chapter 7) devised a
whirlwind program of apparently major changes in 19 days of

December 1972, but who downplayed his own reforms as a "recognition of what has already happened."

———

Nations aren't individuals writ large: they differ from individuals in many obvious ways. Why is it nevertheless illuminating to view national crises through the lens of individual crises? What are the advantages of this approach?

One advantage, which I often encounter in discussing national crises with friends and students, is that individual crises are more familiar and understandable to non-historians. Hence the perspective of individual crises makes it easier for lay readers to "relate to" national crises, and to make sense of their complexities.

Another advantage is that study of individual crises has yielded a road-map of a dozen factors that help us to understand the varying outcomes. Those factors provide a useful starting point for devising a corresponding map of factors to understand the varying outcomes of national crises. We shall see that some factors translate straightforwardly from individual crises to national crises. For instance, individuals in crisis often receive help from friends, just as nations in crisis may recruit help from allied nations. Individuals in crisis may model their solutions on ways in which they see other individuals addressing similar crises; nations in crisis may borrow and adapt solutions already devised by other nations facing similar problems. Individuals in crisis may derive self-confidence from having survived previous crises; so do nations.

Those are among the straightforward parallels. But we'll also see that some factors illuminating outcomes of individual crises, while not straightforwardly transferable to national crises, still serve as useful metaphors suggesting factors relevant to national crises. For instance, therapists have found it helpful to define a quality of individuals termed "ego strength." While nations don't have psychological ego strength,

10

that concept suggests a related concept important for nations, namely, "national identity." Similarly, individuals often find their freedom of choice in resolving a crisis limited by practical constraints, such as child-care responsibilities and job demands. Of course nations aren't limited by child-care responsibilities and job demands. But we'll see that nations do experience limitations on their freedom of choice for other reasons, such as geopolitical constraints and national wealth.

Comparison with individual crises also brings into sharper relief those features of national crises lacking analogues for individual crises. Among those distinctive features, nations have leaders but individuals don't, so questions about the role of leadership arise regularly for national crises but not for personal crises. Among historians, there has been a long and still on-going debate about whether unusual leaders really changed the course of history (often termed the "Great-Man" view of history), or whether history's outcome would have been similar under any other likely leader. (For instance, would World War Two have broken out if a car accident that came close to killing Hitler in 1930 actually had killed him?) Nations have their own political and economic institutions; individuals don't. Resolution of national crises always involves group interactions and decision-making within the nation; but individuals can often make decisions by themselves. National crises may be resolved either by violent revolution (e.g., Chile in 1973) or by peaceful evolution (e.g., Australia after World War Two); but lone individuals don't commit violent revolutions.

Those similarities, metaphors, and differences are why I have found comparisons of national crises and individual crises useful in helping my UCLA students to understand national crises.

———

Readers and reviewers of a book often gradually discover, as they read, that the book's coverage and approach aren't what they

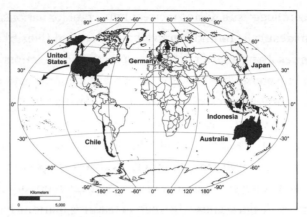

FIG. 1 *Map of the World*

expected or wanted. What are this book's coverage and approach, and which coverages and approaches do I not include?

This book is: a comparative, narrative, exploratory study of crisis and selective change operating over many decades in seven modern nations, of all of which I have much personal experience, and viewed from the perspective of selective change in personal crises. Those nations are Finland, Japan, Chile, Indonesia, Germany, Australia, and the United States.

Let's consider, one by one, each of these words and phrases.

This is a *comparative* book. It doesn't devote its pages to discussing just one nation. Instead, it divides those pages among seven nations, so that those nations can be compared. Non-fiction authors have to choose between presenting single case studies and comparing multiple cases. Each approach has different advantages and different limitations. In a given length of text, single case studies can of course provide far more detail about that single case, but comparative studies can offer perspectives and detect issues that wouldn't emerge from studying just a single case.

Historical comparisons force one to ask questions that are unlikely to emerge from a case study: why did a certain type of event produce result R_1 in one country, when it produced a very different result R_2 in another country? For example, one-volume histories of the American Civil War, which I love reading, can devote six pages to the second day of the Battle of Gettysburg, but can't explore why the American Civil War, unlike the Spanish and Finnish Civil Wars, ended with the victors sparing the lives of the defeated. Authors of single case studies often decry comparative studies as oversimplified and superficial, while authors of comparative studies equally often decry single case studies as unable to address broad questions. The latter view is expressed in the quip "Those who study just one country end up understanding no country." This book is a comparative study, with its resulting advantages and limitations.

Because this book divides its pages among seven nations, I'm painfully aware that my account of each nation has to be concise. As I sit at my desk and turn my head, I see behind me, on my study's floor, a dozen piles of books and papers, each up to five feet high, one pile for the material of each chapter. It was agonizing for me to contemplate condensing five vertical feet of material on post-war Germany into one chapter of 11,000 words. So much had to be omitted! But conciseness has its compensations: it helps readers to compare major issues between post-war Germany and other nations, without becoming distracted and overwhelmed by fascinating details, exceptions, if's, and but's. For readers who want to go on to learn more fascinating details, the concluding bibliography of this book lists books and articles devoted to single case studies.

This book's style of presentation is *narrative:* that is, the traditional style of historians, going all the way back to the foundation of history as a discipline developed by the Greek authors Herodotus and Thucydides over 2,400 years ago. "Narrative style" means that arguments are developed by prose reasoning, without equations, tables of numbers, graphs, or statistical tests of significance, and with only a small number of cases studied. That style may be contrasted with a powerful new quantitative approach in modern social science research, making heavy use of equations, explicit testable hypotheses, tables of data, graphs, and large sample sizes (i.e., many cases studied) that permit statistical tests of significance.

I've learned to appreciate the power of modern quantitative methods. I used them in a statistical study of deforestation on 73 Polynesian islands,[1] in order to reach conclusions that could never have been extracted convincingly from a narrative account of deforestation on a few islands. I also co-edited a book[2] in which some of my co-authors ingeniously used quantitative methods to resolve questions previously debated endlessly and without resolution by narrative historians: for example, whether Napoleon's military conquests and political upheavals were good or bad for the subsequent economic development of Europe.

I had initially hoped to incorporate modern quantitative methods into this book. I devoted months to that effort, only to reach the conclusion that it would have to remain a task for a separate future project. That's because this book instead had to accomplish the task of identifying, by a narrative study, hypotheses and variables for a subsequent quantitative study to test. My sample of just seven nations is too small for extracting statistically significant conclusions. It will take much further work to "operationalize" my narrative qualitative concepts such as "successful crisis resolution" and "honest self-appraisal": i.e., to translate those verbal concepts into things that can be measured as numbers. Therefore, this book is a narrative *exploration*, which I hope will stimulate quantitative testing.

---

1   Barry Rolett and Jared Diamond. Environmental predictors of pre-European deforestation on Pacific islands. *Nature* 431: 443–446 (2004).
2   Jared Diamond and James Robinson, eds. *Natural Experiments of History.* (Harvard University Press, Cambridge, MA, 2010).

Among the world's more than 210 nations, this book discusses only *seven* familiar to me. I've made repeated visits to all seven. I've lived for extended periods, beginning as long as 70 years ago, in six of them. I speak or formerly spoke the languages of those six. I like and admire all of those nations, happily revisit all of them, have visited all within the last two years, and seriously considered moving permanently to two of them. As a result, I can write sympathetically and knowledgeably about them, on the basis of my own first-hand experiences and those of my long-term friends living there. My and my friends' experiences encompass a sufficiently long period of time for us to have witnessed major changes. Among my seven nations, Japan is the one of which my first-hand experience is more limited, because I don't speak the language and have made only briefer visits extending back in time for only 21 years. In compensation, though, for Japan I have been able to draw on the lifelong experiences of my Japanese relatives by marriage, and of my Japanese friends and students.

Of course, the seven nations that I selected on the basis of those personal experiences aren't a random sample of the world's nations. Five are rich industrialized nations, one is modestly affluent, and only one is a poor developing nation. None is African; two are European, two are Asian, and one each is North American, South American, or Australian. It remains for other authors to test to what extent my conclusions derived from this non-random sample of nations apply to other nations. I accepted that limitation and chose those seven because of what seemed to me the overwhelming advantage of only discussing nations that I understand on the basis of long and intense personal experience, friendships, and (in six cases) familiarity with the language.

This book is almost entirely about *modern* national crises that occurred within my lifetime, permitting me to write from the perspective of my own contemporary experience. The outlier, for which I discuss changes before my lifetime, again involves Japan, to which I devote two chapters. One of those chapters discusses Japan today, but the other discusses Japan of the Meiji Era (1868–1912). I included that chapter on Meiji Japan because it constitutes such a striking example of conscious selective change, because it is still in the recent past, and because the memories and issues of Meiji Japan remain prominent in modern Japan.

Of course, national crises and changes have also occurred in the past, and posed similar questions. Though I can't address questions of the past from personal experience, such past crises have been the subject of a large literature. Well-known examples include the decline and fall of the Western Roman Empire in the fourth and fifth centuries of the Christian Era; the rise and fall of southern Africa's Zulu state in the 19th century; the 1789 French Revolution and subsequent reorganization of France; and Prussia's catastrophic defeat at the Battle of Jena in 1806, its conquest by Napoleon, and its subsequent social, administrative, and military reforms. Several years after I began to write this book, I discovered that a book whose title refers to similar themes (*Crisis, Choice, and Change*) had already been published by my own American publisher (Little, Brown) in 1973![3] That book differs from mine in including several case studies from the past, as well as in other basic respects. (It was a multi-authored edited volume using a framework called "system functionalism.")

Research by professional historians emphasizes *archival studies*, i.e., the analysis of preserved written primary documents. Each new history book justifies itself by exploiting previously unutilized or underutilized archival sources, or by reinterpreting archival sources

---

3   Gabriel Almond, Scott Flanagan, and Robert Mundt, eds. *Crisis, Choice, and Change: Historical Studies of Political Development.* (Little, Brown, Boston, 1973).

already utilized by other historians. Unlike most of the numerous books cited in my bibliography, my book is not based on archival studies. Instead, its contribution depends on a new framework derived from personal crises, an explicitly comparative approach, and a perspective drawn from my own life experiences and those of my friends.

———

This is not a magazine article about current affairs, intended to be read for a few weeks after its publication, and then to fall out-of-date. Instead, this is a book expected to remain in print for many decades. I state that obvious fact just to explain why you might otherwise be astonished to find nothing whatsoever in this book about the specific policies of the current Trump administration in the U.S., nor about President Trump's leadership, nor about the current Brexit negotiations in Britain. Anything that I could write today about those fast-moving issues would become embarrassingly superseded by the time that this book is published, and would be useless a few decades from now. Readers interested in President Trump, his policies, and Brexit will find abundant published discussions elsewhere. But my Chapters 9 and 10 do have a lot to say about major U.S. issues that have been operating for the past two decades, that are now claiming even more attention under the current administration, and that are likely to continue to operate for at least the next decade.

———

Now, here is a road-map to my book itself. In my first chapter I shall discuss personal crises, before devoting the rest of this book to national crises. We've all seen, by living through our own crises and witnessing the crises of our relatives and friends, that there is much variation among crisis outcomes. In the best cases, people succeed in figuring out new and better coping methods, and they emerge stronger. In the saddest cases, they become overwhelmed and revert to their old ways, or else they adopt new but worse coping methods. Some people in crisis even commit suicide. Therapists have identified many factors, of which I'll discuss a dozen in Chapter 1, influencing the likelihood that a personal crisis will be successfully resolved. Those are the factors for which I'll explore parallel factors influencing the outcomes of national crises.

To anyone who groans in dismay, "A dozen factors are a lot to remember, why don't you reduce them to just a few?" — I reply: it would be absurd to think that the outcomes of people's lives, or of nations' histories, could be usefully reduced to just a few catchwords. If you should have the misfortune to pick up a book claiming to achieve that, throw it away without reading any further. Conversely, if you have the misfortune to pick up a book proposing to discuss all 76 factors influencing crisis resolution, throw that book away also: it's the job of a book's author, not of a book's readers, to digest and prioritize life's infinite complexity into a useful framework. I found that using a dozen factors offers an acceptable compromise between those two extremes: detailed enough to explain much of reality, without being so detailed as to constitute a laundry list useful for tracking laundry but not for understanding the world.

That introductory chapter is followed by three pairs of chapters, each pair on a different kind of national crisis. The first pair concerns crises in two countries (Finland and Japan) that exploded in a sudden upheaval, provoked by shocks from another country. The second pair is also about crises that exploded suddenly, but due to internal explosions (in Chile and Indonesia). The last pair describes crises that did not explode with a bang, but that instead unfolded gradually (in Germany and Australia), especially due to stresses unleashed by World War Two.

Finland's crisis (Chapter 2) exploded with the Soviet Union's massive attack upon Finland on November 30, 1939. In the resulting Winter War, Finland was virtually abandoned by all of its potential allies and sustained heavy losses, but nevertheless succeeded in preserving its independence against the Soviet Union, whose population outnumbered Finland's by 40 to 1. I spent a summer in Finland 20 years later, hosted by veterans and widows and orphans of the Winter War. The war's legacy was conspicuous selective change that made Finland an unprecedented mosaic, a mixture of contrasting elements: an affluent small liberal democracy, pursuing a foreign policy of doing everything possible to earn the trust of the impoverished giant reactionary Soviet dictatorship. That policy was considered shameful and denounced as "Finlandization" by many non-Finns who failed to understand the historical reasons for its adoption. One of the most intense moments of my summer in Finland unfolded when I ignorantly expressed similar views to a Winter War veteran, who replied by politely explaining to me the bitter lessons that Finns had learned from being denied help by other nations.

The other of the two crises provoked by an external shock involved Japan, whose long-held policy of isolation from the outside world was ended on July 8, 1853, when a fleet of American warships sailed into Tokyo Bay's entrance, demanding a treaty and rights for U.S. ships and sailors (Chapter 3). The eventual result was the overthrow of Japan's previous system of government, a consciously adopted program of drastic wide-ranging change, and an equally conscious program of retention of many traditional features that leave Japan today as the world's most distinctive rich industrialized nation. Japan's transformation during the decades following the U.S. fleet's arrival, the so-called Meiji Era, strikingly illustrates at the national level many of the factors influencing personal crises. The decision-making processes and resulting military successes of

Meiji Japan help us by contrast to understand why Japan made different decisions in the 1930's, leading to its crushing military defeat in World War Two.

Chapter 4 concerns Chile, the first of the pair of countries whose crises were internal explosions resulting from a breakdown of political compromise among their citizens. On September 11, 1973, after years of political stalemate, Chile's democratically elected government under President Allende was overturned by a military coup whose leader, General Pinochet, remained in power for almost 17 years. Neither the coup itself, nor the world records for sadistic tortures smashed by Pinochet's government, had been foreseen by my Chilean friends while I was living in Chile several years before the coup. In fact, they had proudly explained to me Chile's long democratic traditions, so unlike those of other South American countries. Today, Chile is once again a democratic outlier in South America, but selectively changed, incorporating parts of Allende's and parts of Pinochet's models. To U.S. friends who commented on my book manuscript, this Chilean chapter was the most frightening chapter of my book, because of the speed and completeness with which a democracy turned into a sadistic dictatorship.

Paired with that chapter on Chile is Chapter 5 on Indonesia, whose breakdown of political compromise among its citizens also resulted in the internal explosion of a coup attempt, in this case on October 1, 1965. The coup's outcome was opposite to that of Chile's coup: a counter-coup led to genocidal elimination of the faction presumed to have supported the coup attempt. Indonesia stands in further contrast to all of the other nations discussed in this book: it is the poorest, least industrialized, and least Westernized of my seven nations; and it has the youngest national identity, cemented only during the 40 years that I have been working there.

The next two chapters (Chapters 6 and 7) discuss German and Australian national crises that seemingly unfolded gradually instead of exploding with a bang. Some readers may hesitate to apply the term "crisis" or "upheaval" to such gradual developments. But even if one prefers to apply a different term to them, I have still found it useful to view them within the same framework that I use to discuss more abrupt transitions, because they pose the same questions of selective change and illustrate the same factors influencing outcomes. In addition, the difference between "explosive crises" and "gradual change" is arbitrary rather than sharp: they grade into each other. Even in the cases of apparently abrupt transitions, such as Chile's coup, decades of gradually growing tension led to the coup, and decades of gradual changes followed it. I describe the crises of Chapters 6 and 7 as only "seemingly" unfolding gradually, because in fact post-war Germany's crisis began with the most traumatic devastation experienced by any of the countries discussed in this book: Germany's ruined condition as of the date of its surrender in World War Two on May 8, 1945. Similarly, while post-war Australia's crisis unfolded gradually, it began with three shocking military defeats within the space of less than three months.

The first of my two nations illustrating non-explosive crises is post–World War Two Germany (Chapter 6), which was simultaneously confronted with the issues of its Nazi-era legacies, of disagreements about its society's hierarchal organization, and of the trauma of political division between West and East Germany. Within my comparative framework, distinctive features of crisis resolution in post-war Germany include exceptionally violent clashes between generations, strong geopolitical constraints, and the process of reconciliation with nations that had been victims of German wartime atrocities.

My other example of non-explosive crises is Australia (Chapter 7), which has remodeled its national identity during the 55 years that I have been visiting it. When I first arrived in 1964, Australia seemed like a remote British outpost in the Pacific Ocean, still looking to Britain for its identity, and still practicing a White Australia policy that limited or excluded non-European immigrants. But Australia was facing an identity crisis, because that white and British identity conflicted increasingly with Australia's geographic location, foreign policy needs, defense strategy, economy, and population make-up. Today, Australia's trade and politics are oriented towards Asia, Australian city streets and university campuses are crowded with Asians, and Australian voters only narrowly defeated a referendum to remove the Queen of England as Australia's head of state. However, as in Meiji Japan and Finland, those changes have been selective: Australia is still a parliamentary democracy, its national language is still English, and a large majority of Australians are still British by ancestry.

All of these national crises discussed so far are well recognized, and have been resolved (or at least resolutions are already long underway), with the result that we can evaluate their outcomes. The last four chapters describe present and future crises, whose outcomes are still unknown. I begin this section with Japan (Chapter 8), already the subject of Chapter 3. Japan today faces numerous fundamental problems, some of which are widely recognized and acknowledged by the Japanese people and government, while others are not recognized or even are widely denied by the Japanese. At present, these problems are not clearly moving towards solution; Japan's future is truly up for grabs, in the hands of its own people. Will the memories of how Meiji Japan courageously and successfully overcame its crisis help modern Japan to succeed?

The next two chapters (Chapters 9 and 10) concern my own country, the United States. I identify four growing crises that hold the potential to undermine American democracy and American strength within the next decade, as already happened in Chile. Of course, these are not discoveries of mine: there is open discussion of all four among many Americans, and a sense of crisis is widespread in the U.S. today. It appears to me that all four problems are not currently moving towards solution, but are instead getting worse. Yet the U.S., like Meiji Japan, has its own memories of overcoming crises, notably our long and lacerating Civil War, and our suddenly being dragged out of political isolation into World War Two. Will those memories now help my country to succeed?

Finally comes the whole world (Chapter 11). While one could assemble an infinite list of problems facing the world, I focus on four for which it seems to me that trends already underway will, if they continue, undermine living standards worldwide within the next several decades. Unlike Japan and the U.S., both of which have long histories of national identity, self-government, and memories of successful collective action, the whole world lacks such a history. Without such memories to inspire us, will the world succeed, now that for the first time in history we are confronted with problems that are potentially fatal worldwide?

This book concludes with an epilogue that examines our studies of seven nations and of the world, in the light of our dozen factors. I ask whether nations require crises to galvanize them into undertaking big changes. It required the shock of the Cocoanut Grove fire to transform short-term psychotherapy: can nations decide to transform themselves without the shock of a Cocoanut Grove? I consider whether leaders have decisive effects on history; I propose directions for future studies; and I suggest types of lessons that might realistically be gained from examining history. If people, or even just their leaders, choose to reflect on past crises, then understanding of the past might help us to resolve our present and future crises.

PART 1

INDIVIDUALS

CHAPTER 1

PERSONAL CRISES

A personal crisis — Trajectories —
Dealing with crises — Factors related to
outcomes — National crises

At the age of 21, I experienced the most severe crisis of my professional life. I had grown up in Boston as the oldest child of educated parents, my father a Harvard professor and my mother a
linguist and pianist and teacher, who encouraged my love of learning. I attended a great secondary school (Roxbury Latin School),
then a great college (Harvard College). I thrived in school, did well
in all of my courses, completed and published two laboratory
research projects while still in college, and graduated at the top of
my class. Influenced by the example of my physician father, and by
my happy and successful experiences of undergraduate research, I
decided to pursue a PhD in the laboratory science of physiology.
For graduate study I moved in September 1958 to the University of
Cambridge in England, at that time a world leader in physiology.
Additional attractions of my moving to Cambridge included my
first opportunities to live far from home, to travel in Europe, and to

speak foreign languages, of which by then I had already learned six from books.

Graduate study in England soon proved far more difficult for me than had been my Roxbury Latin and Harvard courses, or even than my undergraduate research experience. My PhD mentor at Cambridge, whose laboratory and office I shared, was a great physiologist about to study electricity generation in electric eels. He wanted me to measure movements of charged particles (sodium and potassium ions) across the eels' electricity-generating membranes. That required me to design the necessary equipment. But I had never been good with my hands. I hadn't even been able to complete unassisted a high school assignment of building a simple radio. I certainly had no idea how to design a chamber to study eel membranes, no less to do anything remotely complicated involving electricity.

I had come to Cambridge highly recommended by my Harvard University research advisor. But it was now as obvious to me as it was to my Cambridge advisor that I was a disappointment to him. I was useless to him as a research collaborator. He transferred me to a separate lab of my own, where I could figure out a research project for myself.

In an effort to find a project better suited to my technological ineptitude, I latched onto the idea of studying sodium and water transport by the gallbladder, a simple sac-like organ. The required technology was elementary: just suspend a fluid-filled fish gallbladder every 10 minutes from an accurate scale, and weigh the water contained in the gallbladder. Even I could do that! The gallbladder itself isn't so important, but it belongs to a class of tissues called epithelia that include much more important organs, such as the kidneys and intestines. At that time in 1959, all known epithelial tissues that transported ions and water, as did the gallbladder, developed voltages associated with their transport of the charged ions. But whenever I tried to measure a voltage across the gallbladder, I recorded zero. In those days that was considered strong evidence either that I hadn't mastered even the simple technology that would have sufficed to detect a voltage across the gallbladder if there had been any, or that I had somehow killed the tissue and it wasn't functioning. In either case, I was chalking up another failure as a laboratory physiologist.

My demoralization increased when I attended in June 1959 the first congress of the International Biophysical Society at Cambridge. Hundreds of scientists from around the world presented papers on their research; I had no results to present. I felt humiliated. I had been used to being always at the top of my class; now, I was a nobody.

I began to develop philosophical doubts about pursuing a career of scientific research at all. I read and re-read Thoreau's famous book *Walden*. I felt shaken by what I saw as its message for me: that the real motive for pursuing science was the egotistical one of getting recognition from other scientists. (Yes, that really is a big motive for most scientists!) But Thoreau persuasively dismissed such motives as empty pretense. *Walden*'s core message was: I should figure out what I really want in my life, and not be seduced by the vanity of recognition. Thoreau reinforced my doubts about whether to continue in scientific research at Cambridge. But a moment of decision was approaching: my second year of graduate school would begin at the end of the summer, and I would have to re-enroll if I wanted to continue.

At the end of June I went off to spend a month's vacation in Finland, a wonderful and profound experience that I'll discuss in the next chapter. In Finland for the first time, I had the experience of learning a language, the difficult and beautiful Finnish language, not from books but just by listening and talking to people. I loved it. It was as satisfying and successful as my physiological research was depressing and unsuccessful.

By the end of my month in Finland, I was seriously considering abandoning a career in science, or indeed in any academic discipline. Instead, I thought of going to Switzerland, indulging my love for and ability in languages, and becoming a simultaneous translator of languages at the United Nations. That would mean turning my back on the life of research, creative thought, and academic fame that I had imagined for myself, and that my professor father exemplified. As a translator, I would not be well paid. But at least I would be doing something that I thought I'd enjoy and would be good at — so it seemed to me then.

My crisis came to a head on my return from Finland, when I met my parents (whom I hadn't seen in a year) for a week in Paris. I told them of my practical and philosophical doubts about pursuing a research career, and my thoughts of becoming a translator. It must have been agonizing for my parents to witness my confusion and misery. Bless them, they listened, and they didn't presume to tell me what to do.

The crisis reached resolution one morning while my parents and I were sitting together on a Paris park bench, once again thrashing out the question of whether I should give up on science now or should continue. Finally, my father gently made a suggestion, without pressuring me. Yes, he acknowledged, I had doubts about a scientific research career. But this had been only my first year of graduate school, and I had been trying to study the gallbladder for only a few months. Wasn't it really too early to give up on a planned lifetime career? Why not return to Cambridge, give it another chance, and devote just another half-year to trying to solve gallbladder research problems? If that didn't work out, I could still give it up in the spring of 1960; I didn't have to make an irreversible big decision now.

My father's suggestion felt to me like a life-preserver thrown to a drowning man. I could postpone the big decision for a good reason (to try for another half-year); there was nothing shameful about that. The decision didn't commit me irrevocably to a scientific research career. I still had the option of becoming a simultaneous translator after half-a-year.

That settled it. I did return to Cambridge to begin my second year there. I resumed my gallbladder research. Two young physiology faculty members, to whom I'll be eternally grateful, helped me to solve the technological problems of gallbladder research. In particular, one helped me to realize that my method of measuring voltages across the gallbladder was perfectly adequate; the gallbladder did develop voltages that I could measure (so-called "diffusion potentials" and "streaming potentials") under appropriate conditions. It was just that the gallbladder didn't develop voltages while transporting ions and water, for the remarkable reason that (uniquely among transporting epithelia known at the time) it transported positive and negative ions equally, and so transported no net charge and developed no transport voltage.

My gallbladder results began to interest other physiologists, and to excite even me. As my gallbladder experiments succeeded, my broad philosophical doubts about the vanity of recognition by other scientists faded away. I stayed at Cambridge for four years, completed my PhD, returned to the U.S., got good university jobs doing research and teaching in physiology (first at Harvard and then at UCLA), and became a very successful physiologist.

That was my first major professional crisis, a common type of personal crisis. Of course it wasn't my last life crisis. I later had two much milder professional crises around 1980 and 2000, concerning changes in the direction of my research. Ahead of me still lay severe personal crises about getting married for the first time, and (seven-and-a-half years later) about getting divorced. That first professional crisis was in its specifics unique to me: I doubt that anyone else in world history has ever struggled with a decision about whether to abandon gallbladder physiological research in favor of becoming a simultaneous translator. But, as we'll now see, the broad issues that my 1959 crisis posed were completely typical for personal crises in general.

———

Almost all readers of this book have experienced or will experience an upheaval constituting a personal "crisis," as I did in 1959. When you're in the middle of it, you don't pause to think about academic questions of defining "crisis"; you *know* that you're in one. Later, when the crisis has passed and you have the leisure to reflect on it, you may define it in retrospect as a situation in which you found yourself facing an important challenge that felt insurmountable by your usual methods of coping and problem-solving. You struggled to develop new coping methods. As did I, you questioned your identity, your values, and your view of the world.

Undoubtedly, you've seen how personal crises arise in different forms and from different causes, and follow different trajectories. Some take the form of a single unanticipated shock — such as the sudden death of a loved one, or being fired without warning from your job, or a serious accident, or a natural disaster. The resulting loss may precipitate a crisis not only because of the practical consequences of the loss itself (e.g., you no longer have a spouse), but also because of the emotional pain, and the blow to your belief that the world is fair. That was true for relatives and close friends of the victims of the Cocoanut Grove fire. Other crises instead take the form of a problem building up slowly until it explodes — such as the disintegration of a marriage, chronic serious illness in oneself or in a loved one, or a money-related or career-related problem. Still other crises are developmental ones that tend to unfold at certain major life transitions, such as adolescence, midlife, retirement, and old age. For instance, in a midlife crisis you may feel that the best years of your life are over, and you grapple to identify satisfying goals for the rest of your life.

Those are the different forms of personal crises. Among their commonest specific causes are relationship problems: a divorce, a break-up of a close relationship, or else deep dissatisfaction leading you or your partner to question continuing the relationship. Divorce often drives people to ask themselves: What did I do wrong? Why does he/she want to leave me? Why did I make such a bad choice? What can I do differently next time? Will there ever be a next time for me? If I can't succeed in a relationship even with the person who is closest to me and whom I chose, what good am I at all?

Besides relationship problems, other frequent causes of personal crises include deaths and illnesses of loved ones, and setbacks to one's health, career, or financial security. Still other crises involve religion: lifelong believers in a faith may find themselves plagued by doubt, or (conversely) non-believers may find themselves drawn to a religion. But, shared among all of those types of crisis, whatever their cause, is the sense that something important about one's current approach to life isn't working, and that one has to find a new approach.

My own interest in personal crises, like that of many other people, stemmed initially from the crises that I've experienced myself or that I've seen befalling friends and relatives. For me, that familiar personal motive has been further stimulated by the career of my wife Marie, a clinical psychologist. During the first year of our marriage, Marie trained at a community mental health center, in which a clinic offered short-term psychotherapy for clients in crisis. Clients visited or phoned that clinic in a state of crisis, because they felt overwhelmed by a big challenge that they couldn't solve by themselves. When the door opened or the phone rang at the clinic reception, and the next client walked in or began talking, the counselor didn't know in advance what type of issue that particular person faced. But the counselor knew that that client, like all the previous clients, would be in a state of acute personal crisis, precipitated by their having acknowledged to themselves that their established ways of coping were no longer sufficient.

The outcomes of consultation sessions at health centers offering crisis therapy vary widely. In the saddest cases, some clients attempt or commit suicide. Other clients can't figure out a new coping method that works for them: they revert to their old ways, and may end up crippled by their grief, anger, or frustration. In the best cases, though, the client does discover a new and better way of coping, and emerges from the crisis stronger than before. That outcome is reflected in the Chinese written character translated as "crisis," which is pronounced "wei-ji" and consists of two characters: the Chinese character "wei," meaning "danger," plus the Chinese character "ji," meaning "crucial occasion, critical point, opportunity." The German philosopher Friedrich Nietzsche expressed a similar idea by his quip "What doesn't kill us makes us stronger." Winston Churchill's corresponding quip was "Never let a good crisis go to waste!"

A frequent observation by those helping others in an acute personal crisis is that something happens within a time span of about six weeks. During that short transitional period, we question our cherished beliefs, and we are much more receptive to personal change than during our previous long period of relative stability. We can't live for much longer than that without *some* ways of coping, although we can grieve, suffer, or remain unemployed or angry for much longer. Within about six weeks, either we start to explore a new way of coping that will ultimately prove successful, or we embark on a new maladaptive way of coping, or we revert by default to our old maladaptive ways.

Of course, those observations about acute crises don't imply that our lives conform to an oversimplified model of: (1) receive

shock, set alarm clock for six weeks; (2) acknowledge failure of previous coping methods; (3) explore new coping methods; and (4)
alarm clock goes off: either give up and revert, or else succeed /
crisis solved / live happily ever after. No: many life changes instead
unfold gradually, without an acute phase. We succeed in identifying and solving many impending or growing problems before they
ever become crises and overwhelm us. Even crises with an acute
phase may merge into a long phase of slow rebuilding. That's especially true of midlife crises, when the initial burst of dissatisfaction
and glimmerings of a solution may be acute, but putting a new
solution into effect may take years. A crisis doesn't necessarily stay
solved forever. For instance, a couple that resolves a serious dispute
and avoids divorce may outgrow their solution to the dispute and
have to deal again with the same problem or a similar one. Someone who has dealt with one type of crisis may eventually encounter
a new problem and face a new crisis, as did I. But even those caveats
don't change the fact that many of us do traverse crises with the
approximate course that I described.

———

How does a therapist deal with someone in crisis? Obviously, the
traditional methods of long-term psychotherapy, which often focus
on childhood experiences in order to understand root causes of
current problems, are inappropriate in a crisis because they are
much too slow. Instead, crisis therapy focuses on the immediate
crisis itself. The methods were initially worked out by the psychia-
trist Dr. Erich Lindemann in the immediate aftermath of the
Cocoanut Grove fire, when Boston hospitals were swamped not
only by the medical challenge of trying to save the lives of hundreds of severely wounded and dying people, but also by the psychological challenge of dealing with the grief and the guilt feelings
of the even larger numbers of survivors, relatives, and friends.

Those distraught people were asking themselves why the world had permitted such a thing to happen, and why they were still alive when a loved one had just died a horrible death from burns, trampling, or asphyxiation. For example, one guilt-stricken husband, berating himself for having brought his now-dead wife to Cocoanut Grove, jumped out a window in order to join her in death. While surgeons were helping the fire's burn victims, how could therapists help the fire's psychological victims? That was the crisis that the Cocoanut Grove fire posed to psychotherapy itself. The fire proved to be the birth hour of crisis therapy.

Struggling to assist the huge number of traumatized people, Lindemann began to develop the approach that is now termed "crisis therapy," and that expanded soon from the Cocoanut Grove disaster to the other types of acute crises that I mentioned above. Over the decades since 1942, other therapists have continued to explore methods of crisis therapy, which is now practiced and taught at many clinics such as the one at which Marie trained. Basic to crisis therapy as it has evolved is that it's *short-term*, consisting of only about half-a-dozen sessions spaced out at weekly intervals, spanning the approximate time course of a crisis's acute stage.

Typically when one is first plunged into a state of crisis, one feels overwhelmed by the sense that everything in one's life has gone wrong. As long as one remains thus paralyzed, it's difficult to make progress dealing with one thing at a time. Hence a therapist's immediate goal in the first session — or else the first step if one is dealing with an acknowledged crisis by oneself or with the help of friends — is to overcome that paralysis by means of what is termed "building a fence." That means identifying the specific things that really have gone wrong during the crisis, so that one can say, "Here, inside the fence, are the particular problems in my life, but everything else outside the fence is normal and OK." Often, a person in crisis feels relieved as soon as he or she starts to formulate the problem and to build a fence around it. The therapist can then help the client to explore alternative ways of coping with the specific problem inside the fence. The client thereby embarks on a process of *selective change*, which is possible, rather than remaining paralyzed by the seeming necessity of total change, which would be impossible.

Besides that issue of building a fence that gets addressed in the first session, another issue is also often addressed then: the question "Why now?" That's short-hand for: "Why did you decide to seek help in a crisis center *today*, and why do you feel a sense of crisis *now*, rather than some time earlier, or not at all?" In the case of a crisis arising from a single unanticipated shock, such as the Cocoanut Grove fire, that question needn't be asked because the obvious answer is the shock itself. But the answer is not obvious for a crisis building up slowly until it explodes, or for a developmental crisis associated with an extended life phase such as the teen-age years or middle age.

A typical example is that a woman may say that she came to the crisis center because her husband is having an affair. But it then turns out that she has known for a long time that he has been having the affair. Why did the woman decide to seek help about the affair today, rather than a month ago or a year ago? The immediate impetus may have been a single sentence spoken, or else a detail of the affair that the client held to be the "last straw," or a seemingly trivial event reminding the client of something significant in the client's past. Often the client isn't even conscious of the answer to that question "Why now?" But when the answer is discovered, it may prove helpful to the client, or to the therapist, or to both, in understanding the crisis. In the case of my 1959 career crisis, which had been building for half-a-year, the reason why the first week of August 1959 became "now" was the visit of my parents, and the practical necessity of telling them whether or not I would return next week to the Cambridge Physiological Laboratories for a second year.

Of course, short-term crisis therapy isn't the only approach to dealing with personal crises. My reason for discussing it isn't because of any parallels between the time-limited six-session course of crisis therapy and the course of dealing with national crises. The latter course never involves six national discussions within a short time frame. Instead, I focus on short-term crisis therapy because it's a specialty practiced by therapists who have built up a large body of experience and shared their observations with one another. They spend much time discussing with one another and publishing articles and books about the factors influencing outcomes. I heard a lot about those discussions from Marie, almost every week during her year of training at the crisis therapy center. I found those discussions useful for suggesting factors worth examining as possible influences on outcomes of national crises.

———

Crisis therapists have identified at least a dozen factors that make it more or less likely that an individual will succeed in resolving a personal crisis (Table 1.1). Let's consider those factors, starting with three or four that inevitably are critical at or before the beginning of the course of treatment:

1. **Acknowledgment that one is in crisis**. This is the factor that leads people to enter crisis therapy. Without such an acknowledgment, they would not even present themselves at a crisis therapy clinic, nor (if they didn't go to a clinic) would they begin to deal with the crisis themselves. Until someone admits, "Yes, I do have a problem" — and that admission may take a long time — there can't be any progress towards resolving the problem. My 1959 professional crisis began with my having to acknowledge that I was failing as a laboratory scientist, after a dozen years of uninterrupted successes in school.

Table 1.1. Factors related to the outcomes of personal crises

1. Acknowledgment that one is in crisis
2. Acceptance of one's personal responsibility to do something
3. Building a fence, to delineate one's individual problems needing to be solved
4. Getting material and emotional help from other individuals and groups
5. Using other individuals as models of how to solve problems
6. Ego strength
7. Honest self-appraisal
8. Experience of previous personal crises
9. Patience
10. Flexible personality
11. Individual core values
12. Freedom from personal constraints

2. **Acceptance of personal responsibility**. But it's not enough just to acknowledge "I have a problem." People often then go on to say, "Yes, but — my problem is someone else's fault. Other people or outside forces are what's making my life miserable." Such self-pity, and the tendency to assume the role of victim, are among the commonest excuses that people offer to avoid addressing personal problems. Hence a second hurdle, after a person has acknowledged "I have a problem," is for the person to assume responsibility for solving it. "Yes, there are those outside forces and those other people, but they aren't me. I can't change other people. I'm the only person whose actions I can fully control. If I want those other forces and other people to change, it's my responsibility to do something about it, by changing my own behavior and responses.

Those other people aren't going to change spontaneously if I don't do something myself."

3. Building a fence. Once a person has acknowledged a crisis, accepted responsibility for doing something to resolve it, and presented himself at a crisis therapy center, the first therapy session can focus on the step of "building a fence," i.e., identifying and delineating the problem to be solved. If a person in crisis doesn't succeed in doing that, he sees himself as totally flawed and feels paralyzed. Hence a key question is: what is there of yourself that is already functioning well, and that doesn't need changing, and that you could hold on to? What can and should you discard and replace with new ways? We shall see that that issue of *selective change* is key also to reappraisals by whole nations in crisis.

4. Help from others. Most of us who have successfully gotten through a crisis have discovered the value of material and emotional support from friends, as well as from institutionalized support groups such as those of cancer patients, alcoholics, or drug addicts. Familiar examples of material support include offering a temporary spare bedroom to enable someone whose marriage has just collapsed to move out; thinking clearly, to compensate for the temporarily diminished problem-solving ability of a person in crisis; and providing practical assistance in obtaining information, a new job, new companions, and new child-care arrangements. Emotional support includes being a good listener, helping to clarify issues, and assisting someone who has temporarily lost hope and self-confidence to regain both.

For a client at a crisis therapy clinic, that "call for help" is inevitably among the first factors arising to resolve the crisis: the client came to the center *because* they realized that they needed help. For people in crisis who don't come to a crisis therapy clinic, their call for help may come early, later, or even not at all: some people make things difficult for themselves by trying to solve a crisis entirely without assistance. As a personal example of a call for help outside a crisis therapy center — when my first wife jolted me by (finally) telling me that she wanted a divorce, during the next few days I called four of my closest friends and poured out my heart to them. All four understood and sympathized with my situation, because three had themselves been divorced, and the fourth had managed to rebuild a troubled marriage. While my call for help didn't stave off eventual divorce in my case, it did prove to be the first step in a long process of reexamining my relationships, and eventually making a happy second marriage. Talking to close friends made me feel that I wasn't uniquely flawed, and that I too might eventually gain happiness, as they had.

5. **Other people as models**. Related to that value of other people as sources of help is their value as models of alternative coping methods. Again, as most of us who have weathered a crisis have discovered, it's a big advantage if you know someone who has weathered a similar crisis, and who constitutes a model of successful coping skills that you can try to imitate. Ideally, those models are friends or other people with whom you can talk, and from whom you can learn directly how they solved a problem similar to yours. But the model can also be someone whom you don't know personally, and about whose life and coping methods you have merely read or heard. For example, while few readers of this book could have known Nelson Mandela, Eleanor Roosevelt, or Winston Churchill personally, their biographies or autobiographies have still yielded ideas and inspiration to other people who used them as models for resolving a personal crisis.

6. **Ego strength**. A factor that's important in coping with a crisis, and that differs from person to person, is something that psychologists call "ego strength." That includes self-confidence, but it's much broader. Ego strength means having a sense of yourself, having a sense of purpose, and accepting yourself for who you are, as a proud independent person not dependent on other people for approval or for your survival. Ego strength includes being able to tolerate strong emotions, to keep focused under stress, to express yourself freely, to perceive reality accurately, and to make sound decisions. Those linked qualities are essential for exploring new solutions and overcoming the paralyzing fear that often arises in a crisis. Ego strength begins to develop in childhood, especially from having parents who accept you for who you are, don't expect you to fulfill their dreams, and don't expect you to be older or younger than you actually are. It develops from parents who help you learn to tolerate frustration, by not giving you everything that you want, but also by not depriving you of everything that you want. All of that background goes into the ego strength that helps one work through a crisis.

7. **Honest self-appraisal**. This is related to ego strength but deserves separate mention. For an individual in crisis, fundamental to making good choices is an honest, albeit painful, self-appraisal to assess your strengths and weaknesses, the parts of you that are working, and the parts of you that are not working. Only then can you selectively change in ways that retain your strengths while replacing your weaknesses with new ways of coping. While the importance of honesty in resolving a crisis may seem too obvious to require mention, in fact the reasons why people often are not honest with themselves are legion.

The issue of honest self-appraisal constituted one of the key struggles of my 1959 professional crisis. I overestimated my abilities in one respect, and I underestimated them in another respect. As for my overestimate, my love for languages deluded me into thinking that I had the abilities necessary to becoming a simultaneous translator. But it began to dawn on me that love of languages by itself wouldn't be enough to make me a successful simultaneous translator. Growing up in the U.S., I didn't even begin to learn my first spoken foreign language until I was 11 years old. I didn't live in a non-English-speaking country and become conversationally fluent in any foreign language (German) until I was 23 years old. Because I thus came to speak other languages only relatively late in my schooling, my accents today in even my best foreign languages are still recognizably American accents. It wasn't until my late 70's that I finally became able to switch quickly *between* two languages other than English. But, as a simultaneous translator, I would be competing with Swiss translators who had already developed fluency, accents, and ease of switching in several languages by the age of eight. I eventually had to admit to myself: I was deluding myself if I dreamed that I could ever compete as a linguist with the Swiss.

The other area of self-appraisal with which I struggled in 1959, and in which I underestimated rather than overestimated my abilities, concerned scientific research. I overgeneralized from my inability to solve a technologically challenging problem, namely, how to measure ion fluxes across electric eel membranes. But I was still perfectly capable of measuring water transport in the gallbladder by the simple method of weighing a gallbladder. Even now, 60 years later, I still use only the simplest of technologies to do science. I've learned to recognize important scientific questions that can be addressed with simple technologies. I still can't turn on our home television set with its 47-button remote control; I can do only the simplest things with my recently acquired iPhone; and I depend completely on my secretary and on my wife for anything requiring a computer. Whenever I've wanted to carry out a research project that required complicated technology — cable analysis of epithelial current spread, noise analysis of membrane ion channels, statistical analysis of pairwise bird species distributions — I've been fortunate to find colleagues who were skilled at doing those analyses, and who were willing to collaborate with me.

Thus, I eventually learned to appraise, honestly, what I was or wasn't capable of doing.

8. Experience of previous crises. If you have already had the experience of coping successfully with some different crisis in the past, that gives you more confidence that you can solve the new crisis as well. That contrasts with the sense of helplessness, growing out of previous crises not mastered, that, whatever you do, you won't succeed. The importance of previous experience is a main reason why crises tend to be so much more traumatic for adolescents and young adults than for older people. While the break-up of a close relationship can be devastating at any age, the break-up of one's first close relationship is especially devastating. At the time of later break-ups, no matter how painful, one recalls having gone through and gotten over similar pain before. That was part of the reason why my 1959 crisis was so traumatic to me: it was my first acute life crisis. By comparison, my 1980 and 2000 professional crises were un-traumatic. I did eventually switch career directions from membrane physiology to evolutionary physiology around 1980, and from physiology to geography after 2000. But those decisions weren't painful, because I had come to assume from my previous experience that things would probably turn out OK.

9. Patience. Another consideration is the ability to tolerate uncertainty, ambiguity, or failure at initial attempts to change: in short, patience. It's unlikely that a person in a crisis will figure out a successful way of coping on the first try. Instead, it may take several attempts, testing different ways to see whether they solve the crisis and whether they are compatible with one's personality, until one finally finds a solution that works. People who cannot tolerate uncertainty or failure, and who give up the search early, are less likely to arrive at a compatible new way of coping. That's why my father's gentle advice to me on the park bench in Paris, "Why not devote just another half-year to graduate school in physiology?," felt like a life-saver to me. Dad made patience sound reasonable to me; I hadn't figured that out for myself.

10. Flexibility. An important element in overcoming a crisis through selective change involves the advantage of a flexible personality over a rigid, inflexible personality. "Rigidity" means the pervasive belief that there is only one way. Of course that belief is an obstacle to exploring other ways, and to replacing one's failed old approach with a successful new approach. Rigidity or inflexibility can be the result of a previous history of abuse or trauma, or of an upbringing that offered a child no permission to experiment or to deviate from the family norms. Flexibility can come from the freedom of having been allowed to make one's own choices as one was growing up.

For me, learning to be flexible came later in life, as a result of expeditions that I began at age 26 to study rainforest birds on the tropical island of New Guinea. Detailed plans almost never work out as anticipated in New Guinea. Airplanes, boats, and road vehicles regularly break down, crash, or sink; local people and government officials don't behave as expected and can't be ordered around; bridges and trails prove impassable; mountains prove not to be where maps had shown them to be; and myriad other things go wrong. Almost every one of my New Guinea expeditions has begun with my setting out to do X, arriving in New Guinea, finding X to be impossible, and having to be *flexible:* i.e., to improvise a new plan on the spot. When Marie and I eventually had children, I found my experience of New Guinea bird expeditions to be for me the most useful preparation for being a father — because children are also unpredictable, can't be ordered around, and require flexibility on the part of their parents.

11. <u>Core values</u>. The next-to-last consideration, still related to ego strength, involves what are termed core values: i.e., the beliefs that one considers central to one's identity, and that underlie one's moral code and outlook on life, such as one's religion and one's commitment to one's family. In a crisis you have to figure out where to draw the line in adopting selective change: which core values would you refuse to change because you consider them non-negotiable? At what point do you say to yourself, "I'd rather die, than change THAT"? For instance, many people consider family commitments, religion, and honesty as non-negotiable. We're inclined to admire someone who would refuse to betray his family, lie, recant his religion, or steal in order to get out of a crisis.

But crises can produce gray areas in which values previously considered non-negotiable do come up for reconsideration. To take an obvious example, a husband or wife who sues for divorce does thereby decide to break a family commitment to his or her spouse. The moral commandment "Thou shall not steal" had to be abandoned by prisoners at Nazi concentration camps during World War Two: food rations were so inadequate that it was impossible to survive if one did not steal food. Numerous concentration camp survivors abandoned their religion, because they found the evil of the camps impossible to reconcile with belief in a god. For example, the great Italian Jewish author Primo Levi, who did survive Auschwitz, said afterwards, "The experience of Auschwitz for me was such as to sweep away whatever legacies of my religious education that I had retained. There is Auschwitz, therefore God cannot exist. I haven't found a solution to that dilemma."

Core values may thus make it either easier or harder to resolve a crisis. On the one hand, one's core values can provide clarity, a foundation of strength and certainty from which one can contemplate changing other parts of oneself. On the other hand, clinging to core values even when they reveal themselves as misguided under changed circumstances may prevent one from solving a crisis.

12. **Freedom from constraints**. The remaining factor to mention is the freedom of choice that comes from being unconstrained by practical problems and responsibilities. It's more difficult to experiment with new solutions if you have heavy responsibilities for other people (such as children), or if you have to keep up with a very demanding job, or if you are often exposed to physical dangers. Of course that doesn't mean that it's impossible to work through a crisis when you have those burdens, but they do impose extra challenges. In 1959 I was fortunate that, amidst the personal turmoil of having to figure out whether I still wanted to become a research scientist, I wasn't having to wrestle with any practical constraints. I held a National Science Foundation fellowship that would pay my tuition and living expenses for several more years; the Cambridge Physiology Department wasn't threatening to expel me, nor even requiring me to pass any exams; and nobody was pressing me to give up — except myself.

———

Those are factors about which therapists have told me, or about which they have written, that affect outcomes of personal crises.

What use can one expect to make of those factors, listed in Table 1.1, when one tries to understand the outcomes of national crises?

On the one hand, of course it's clear at the outset that nations aren't individuals. We'll see that national crises raise numerous issues — issues of leadership, group decision-making, national institutions, and others — that don't arise for individual crises.

On the other hand, of course it's also clear that an individual's coping mechanisms don't exist in isolation from the culture of the nation and of the subnational groups in which the individual has grown up and now lives. That broader culture has big influences on individual traits, such as an individual's behavior, goals, perceptions of reality, and handling of problems. Hence we expect *some* relationships between how individuals cope with individual problems, and how nations composed of many individuals cope with national problems. Among those relationships are the roles (both for individuals and for nations) of accepting responsibility for doing something oneself, rather than viewing oneself as a passive helpless victim; delineating the crisis; seeking help; and learning from models. Obvious as these simple rules are, both individuals and nations ignore or deny them depressingly often.

To set a context for the ways in which nations do or don't resemble individuals in how they cope, consider the following thought experiment. If one compares individuals drawn at random from around the world, one finds that they differ for multiple reasons that may be broadly categorized as individual, cultural, geographic, and genetic. For instance, compare on an afternoon in the month of January the upper-body garments of five men: a traditional Inuit north of the Arctic Circle, two ordinary Americans outdoors on a street of my city of Los Angeles, one American bank president indoors in his office in New York, and one traditional New Guinean in New Guinea's lowland tropical rainforest. For geographic reasons, the Inuit will be wearing a warm hooded parka, the three Americans will be wearing shirts but no parkas, and the New Guinean won't have any upper-body garment at all. For cultural reasons, the bank president will probably be wearing a tie, but the two men on a Los Angeles street will be tie-less. For individual reasons, the two randomly selected Los Angeles men may be wearing shirts of different colors. If the question concerned their hair color rather than their upper-body garment, genetic reasons would also contribute.

Now, for those same five men, consider their differences in core values. While there may be some individual differences between the three American men, they are much more likely to share core values with one another than with the Inuit or the New Guinean man. Such sharings of core values are just one example of cultural features broadly shared among members of the same society, learned as one is growing up. But individual traits differ on the average between individuals of different societies for reasons explicable only partly or not at all in terms of geographic differences. If one of the two Los Angeles men happened to be the president of the United States, his culturally derived core values — e.g., his values about individual rights and responsibilities — would have a strong effect on U.S. national policy.

The point of this thought experiment is that we do expect some relation between individual characteristics and national characteristics, because individuals share a national culture, and because national decisions depend ultimately on the views of the nation's individuals, especially on the views of the nation's leaders who partake of the national culture. For the countries discussed in this book, the views of leaders proved to be especially important for Chile, Indonesia, and Germany.

Table 1.2 lists the dozen factors that this book will discuss in relation to the outcomes of national crises. Comparison with Table

1.1, which listed the factors recognized by therapists as related to outcomes of individual crises, shows that most factors on one list have recognizable analogues on the other list.

Table 1.2. Factors related to the outcomes of national crises

1. National consensus that one's nation is in crisis
2. Acceptance of national responsibility to do something
3. Building a fence, to delineate the national problems needing to be solved
4. Getting material and financial help from other nations
5. Using other nations as models of how to solve the problems
6. National identity
7. Honest national self-appraisal
8. Historical experience of previous national crises
9. Dealing with national failure
10. Situation-specific national flexibility
11. National core values
12. Freedom from geopolitical constraints

For about seven of the dozen factors, the parallels are straightforward:

Factor #1. Nations, as individuals, acknowledge or deny being in crisis. But acknowledgment by a nation requires some degree of national consensus, while an individual acknowledges or denies by himself.

Factor #2. Nations and individuals accept national and individual responsibility to take action to solve the problem, or else deny responsibility by self-pity, blaming others, and assuming the role of victim.

Factor #3. Nations make selective changes in their institutions and policies by "building a fence," to delineate institutions/ policies requiring change from those to be preserved unchanged. Individuals similarly "build a fence" to undertake selective change in some individual traits, but not in other traits.

Factor #4. Nations and individuals may receive material and financial help from other nations and individuals. Individuals but not nations may also receive emotional help.

Factor #5. Nations may model their institutions and policies on those of other nations, just as individuals may model their coping methods on those of other individuals.

Factor #7. Nations, just as individuals, do or don't undertake honest self-appraisal. That requires reaching some degree of national consensus for a nation, but an individual does or doesn't undertake self-appraisal by himself.

Factor #8. Nations have historical experience, while individuals have personal memories, of previous national or individual crises.

In two other cases the correspondence between factors is more general and less specific.

Factor #9. Nations differ in how they deal with failure, and in their willingness to explore other solutions to a problem if the first attempted solutions fail. Think, for example, of the drastically different responses to military defeat on the parts of Germany after World War One, of Germany after World War Two, of

Japan after World War Two, and of the U.S. after the Vietnam War. Individuals also differ in their tolerance for failure or for initial failure, and we often refer to that individual characteristic as "patience."

Factor #12. Nations experience varying limitations on their freedom of choice, for reasons especially of geography, wealth, and military/political power. Individuals also experience varying limitations on their freedom of choice, but for entirely different reasons, such as child-care responsibilities, job requirements, and individual income.

Finally, for the remaining three factors, the individual factor serves just as a metaphor suggesting a factor describing nations:

Factor #6. Psychologists have defined and written at length about the characteristic of individuals termed "ego strength." That characteristic applies only to individuals; one can't talk of national ego strength. But nations do have a national characteristic called national identity, which we shall have frequent occasion to discuss, and which plays a role for nations reminiscent of the role that ego strength plays for individuals. National identity means the features of language, culture, and history that make a nation unique among the world's nations, that contribute to national pride, and that a nation's citizens view themselves as sharing.

Factor #10. Another characteristic of individuals that psychologists have defined and written about at length is individual flexibility, and its opposite, individual rigidity. This is a characteristic that permeates an individual's character; it is not situation-specific. For instance, if a man has a firm practice of never loaning money to friends but is otherwise flexible in his behavior, he would not be branded as having a rigid personality. A rigid personality instead expresses itself in having firm rules of behavior for most situations. It is unclear whether any nation has analogous rigidity permeating most situations. For instance, if one were initially inclined to brand Japan or Germany as "rigid," the fact is that both countries have been extraordinarily flexible at some periods about many important matters, as we shall discuss in Chapters 3 and 6, respectively. Instead, national flexibility may be situation-specific, unlike individual flexibility. We shall return to this question in the Epilogue.

Factor #11. Finally, individuals have individual core values, such as honesty, ambition, religion, and family ties. Nations have what may be termed national core values, some of which overlap with individual core values (e.g., honesty and religion). National core values are related to but not identical to national identities. For instance, the language of Shakespeare and Tennyson is part of Britain's national identity, but Tennyson wasn't the reason why Britain refused to negotiate with Hitler even in the darkest hours of May 1940. Instead, Britain's refusal to negotiate was because of a core value: "We shall never surrender."

As I mentioned in the Prologue, national crises raise additional questions that arise not at all, or else only as distant analogues, for individual crises. Those include:

- the crucial national role of political and economic institutions;
- questions about the role of a nation's leader or leaders in resolving a crisis;
- questions more generally about group decision-making;
- the question of whether a national crisis leads to selective changes through peaceful resolution or through violent revolution;

- the question of whether different types of national changes are introduced simultaneously as part of a unified program, or else separately and at different times;

- the issue of whether a national crisis was triggered by internal developments within the nation, or else by an external shock from another country; and

- the problem of achieving reconciliation (especially after a crisis involving a war or mass killings) between parties that were in conflict — reconciliation either between groups within a country, or else between a country and its neighbors.

To begin to address these questions, the next chapter will present the first of my two examples of national crises that were triggered abruptly by an attack or a threatened attack by another country. We shall see that Finland, the delights of whose language played such a big role in my personal crisis of 1959, will illustrate many of our factors related to outcomes of national crises.

PART 2

NATIONS: CRISES THAT UNFOLDED

FIG. 2 *Map of Finland*

CHAPTER 2

FINLAND'S WAR WITH THE SOVIET UNION

Visiting Finland — Language — Finland until
1939 — The Winter War — The Winter War's end —
The Continuation War — After 1945 — Walking a
tightrope — Finlandization — Crisis framework

F inland is the Scandinavian (Nordic) country of only 6 million
people that borders Sweden to the west and Russia to the east. In
the century before World War One it was just an autonomous part of
Russia, not an independent nation. It was poor and received little
attention within Europe, and almost no attention outside Europe. At
the outset of World War Two, Finland was independent but still
poor, with an economy still focused on agriculture and forest products. Today, Finland is known around the world for its technology
and its industry and has become one of the world's richest countries,
with an average per-capita income comparable to that of Germany
and Sweden. Its security rests on a glaring paradox: it is a liberal
social democracy that for many decades maintained an excellent and
trusting relationship with the communist former Soviet Union, and
now with current autocratic Russia. That combination of features
constitutes a remarkable example of selective change.

If you are visiting Finland for the first time, and you want to understand the Finnish people and their history, a good place to begin is by visiting Hietaniemi Cemetery, the largest cemetery in Finland's capital city of Helsinki. Unlike the United States, which buries its soldiers in Arlington National Cemetery outside Washington and in other separate veterans' cemeteries around the country, Finland does not have separate military cemeteries. Instead, Finland's fallen soldiers are brought home to be buried in the civilian cemeteries of their town or parish. A large section of Hietaniemi Cemetery is devoted to dead soldiers from Helsinki. They hold a place of honor there, just uphill from the graves of Finland's presidents and other political leaders, and around the monument to Finland's Field Marshal Carl Gustaf Mannerheim (1867–1951).

As you approach Hietaniemi Cemetery, the first thing that you'll notice is that you can't understand the street signs and the billboards at all (Plate 2.1). In almost every other European country, even if you don't know the language, you'll be able to recognize some words, because most European languages belong to the Indo-European language family that includes English, and all Indo-European languages share many word roots. Even in Lithuania and Poland and Iceland you'll be able to recognize some words on street signs and billboards. But Finnish words will mostly be unrecognizable to you, because Finnish is one of the few languages in Europe that is totally unrelated to the Indo-European language family.

The next thing that will strike you at Hietaniemi Cemetery is the simplicity and beauty of its design. Finland is world-famous for its architects and decorators, who know how to produce beautiful effects in simple ways. On my first visit to Finland, I remember being invited into the living room of one of my host's homes, and immediately thinking to myself, "This is the most beautiful room that I've ever seen!" On reflection, I then wondered why I found it so beautiful, because the room was a nearly-empty cubicle with just a few pieces of simple furniture. But the materials and form of the room, and those few pieces of furniture, were typically Finnish in their simplicity and beauty.

You may then be shocked by the number of dead Finnish soldiers buried or remembered at Hietaniemi. I counted more than 3,000 named tombstones of soldiers whose bodies had been recovered, arranged in curving row upon row. Setting off that cemetery section with named tombstones was a wall about four feet high and several hundred feet long, divided into 55 panels filled with the names of more soldiers — I counted 715 — who were listed as "missing," because their bodies could not be recovered and brought back. Still another collective monument with no names on it recalls all the uncounted Finnish soldiers who died in enemy prisons. But all of those dead soldiers at Hietaniemi were just from Helsinki; similar sections are devoted to dead soldiers in every town and parish cemetery in Finland. You'll be starting to realize that lots of Finns must have been killed in war.

As you walk among Hietaniemi's gravestones, you'll be struck by the writing on them. Again, you won't be able to understand much of the writing, because it is in Finnish. But most gravestones anywhere, in any language, record the name of the dead person, the person's birthdate and birthplace, and the date and place of death. That format is easy to recognize on the gravestones even in that Finnish cemetery. You'll notice that all of the dates of death are between 1939 and 1944, during World War Two. The majority of the dates of birth are in the 1920's and 1910's, which means that most of those soldiers died while in their 20's, as you'd expect. But you'll be surprised to see that there also were many soldiers killed in their 50's, or while still young teenagers. For instance, Johan Viktor Pahlsten's gravestone records that he was born on August 4, 1885 and was killed on August 15, 1941, 11 days after his 56th birthday. Klara Lappalainen was born on July 30, 1888; she was killed on October 19, 1943 at the age of 55. At the other extreme, the schoolboy Lauri Martti Hämäläinen was born on July 22, 1929, volunteered to fight, and was killed on June 15, 1943 at the age of 13, five weeks short of his 14th birthday. Why was Finland calling up as soldiers not just the usual 20-year-olds, but also men and women in their 50's plus young teenagers (Plate 2.2)?

As you read the dates and places of death recorded on the grave-stones, you'll notice that deaths were concentrated in a few time periods and locations. The largest number of deaths occurred from late February to early March of 1940, then in August 1941, and then again in June and August of 1944. Many of the places of death are recorded as Viipuri, or at several sites that a Finnish friend can identify for you as being near Viipuri, such as Syväri, Kannas, and Ihantola. That will make you wonder: what was the big deal about Viipuri, and why did so many Finns get killed there within such short time spans?

The explanation is that Viipuri used to be the second-largest city of Finland until it was ceded to the Soviet Union, along with one-tenth of the total area of Finland, after a ferocious war in the winter of 1939–1940, plus a second war from 1941 to 1944. In October 1939 the Soviet Union made territorial demands on four Baltic countries: Finland, Estonia, Latvia, and Lithuania. Finland was the only country that refused those demands, despite the Soviet Union having an enormous army and a population almost 50 times larger than that of Finland. The Finns nevertheless put up such a fierce resistance that they succeeded in preserving their independence, even though their nation's survival remained in grave doubt through a series of crises lasting a decade. The heaviest casualties were incurred during the three peak periods evidenced by the tombstones, as the Soviet army closed in on Viipuri in February–March 1940, then as the Finns recaptured Viipuri in August 1941, and finally as the Soviet army advanced again upon Viipuri in the summer of 1944 (Plates 2.3, 2.4).

Finland's death toll in its war against the Soviet Union was nearly 100,000, mostly men. To modern Americans and Japanese and non-Finnish Europeans, who remember the nearly instantaneous death tolls of 100,000 each in the bombings of single cities (Hiroshima and Hamburg and Tokyo), and the total war deaths of around 20 million each suffered by the Soviet Union and China during World War Two, Finland's death toll of just 100,000 over the course of five years may seem modest. But it represented 2½% of Finland's then-total population of 3,700,000, and 5% of its males. That proportion is the same as if 9,000,000 Americans were to be killed in a war today: almost 10 times the total number of American deaths in all the wars of our 240-year history. My most recent visit to Hietaniemi Cemetery was on Sunday, May 14, 2017. Even though the last death commemorated in Hietaniemi's military section had occurred more than 70 years previously (in 1944), I saw fresh flowers on many graves, and families walking among the graves. I stopped to chat with a family of four, of whom the oldest was a man who appeared to be in his 40's. That meant that the fallen soldier whose grave that family was visiting couldn't have been their parent, but must have been their grandparent or great-grandparent. When I commented to the man on the continued visits, remembrance, and fresh flowers, he explained, "Every Finnish family lost family members then."

My first visit to Finland was in the summer of 1959. That was only 15 years after the end of Finland's war with the Soviet Union, and only four years after the Soviet Union had evacuated its military base on Finnish soil on the outskirts of Helsinki. My Finnish hosts were veterans, widows, and children of the war against the Soviet Union, plus Finnish soldiers on active duty. They recounted to me their own life stories and their country's recent history. I learned enough of the wonderful Finnish language to make my way around as a tourist, to appreciate how the language contributes to Finland's sense of uniqueness, and to precipitate my own life crisis that I described in the previous chapter. For those of you readers who haven't had the good fortune to visit Finland, some features of my book's framework of crisis and change to keep in mind as you read the following account include: the strength and origins of Finnish national identity; Finns' ultra-realistic assessment of their country's geopolitical situation; the resulting paradoxical combination of selective changes that I mentioned in my opening paragraph; and Finland's *lack* of freedom of choice, *lack* of help received from allies at crucial moments, and *lack* of available successful models.

———

Finland identifies with Scandinavia and is considered part of Scandinavia. Many Finns are blue-eyed blonds, like Swedes and Norwegians. Genetically, Finns are in effect 75% Scandinavian like Swedes and Norwegians, and only 25% invaders from the east. But geography, language, and culture make Finns different from other Scandinavians, and they are proud of those differences. As for geography, descriptions of Finland by Finns reiterate two themes: "We are a small country," and "Our geography will never change." By the latter phrase, Finns mean that Finland's land border with Russia (or with Russia's previous incarnation as the Soviet Union) is longer than that of any other European country. Finland is in effect a buffer zone between Russia and the rest of Scandinavia.

Out of the nearly 100 native languages of Europe, all are related members of the Indo-European language family except for the isolated Basque language and four others. Those four are Finnish, the closely related Estonian language, and the distantly related

Hungarian and Lapp (Saami) languages, all of which belong to the Finno-Ugric language family. Finnish is a beautiful language, and the focus of Finland's national pride and identity. Finland's national epic poem, the *Kalevala*, holds an even bigger place in Finland's national consciousness than do the plays of Shakespeare for English-speakers. To outsiders, Finnish is not only a beautiful language with a singing quality, but also a very difficult one to learn. One thing that makes it difficult is its vocabulary, because its words don't have familiar Indo-European roots. Instead, most Finnish words have to be memorized one by one.

The other things that make Finnish difficult are its sounds and its grammar. The letter *k* is very common in Finnish: of the 200 pages of my Finnish-to-English dictionary, 31 pages are for words beginning with *k*. (Try savoring these lines from the *Kalevala*: "Kullervo, Kalervon poika, sinisukka äijön lapsi, hivus keltainen, korea, kengän kauto kaunokainen.") I have nothing against *k*'s — but, alas, Finnish, unlike English, has double consonants (like *kk*) pronounced differently from single consonants (like *k*). That was the feature of Finnish pronunciation that made it hardest for my tolerant Finnish hosts to understand me on the few occasions when I gave short speeches in Finnish. The consequences of failing to pronounce single and double consonants distinctly can be serious. For instance, the Finnish verb meaning "to meet" is "tapaa" with a single *p*, while the verb "to kill" is "tappaa" with a double *p*. Hence if you ask a Finn to meet you but you mistakenly double the *p*, you may end up dead.

Finnish also has what are called short vowels and long vowels. For instance, the word for border is "raja" with a short first *a*, but the word for leg or arm is "raaja" with a long first *a*, and that caused me to be misunderstood when I was near the border of a Finnish national park and mistakenly lengthened the first *a* in my attempt to talk about the border. Three Finnish vowels, *a* and *o* and *u*, exist in two forms, pronounced either in the back or in the front of the mouth, and written, respectively, as *a* and *ä*, *o* and *ö*, and *u* and *y*. Within a single word, all three of those vowels must either be back vowels or else front vowels; that's termed vowel harmony. For example, the Finnish word for "night," which I had frequent occasion to use in saying "good night," has only front vowels ("yötä"), while the word for "riverbed" has only back vowels ("uoma").

If you find yourself confused by the four cases of the German language or the six cases of the Latin language, you'll be horrified to know that the Finnish language has 15 cases, many of which replace prepositions in English. One of the most delightful hours of my first visit to Finland came when a Finnish soldier, who spoke no English and could communicate with me only in Finnish, taught me the six Finnish locative cases (replacing the English prepositions on, off, onto, in, out of, into) by pointing to a table ("pöytä") on which ("pöydällä": vowel harmony!) was a cup and in which ("pöydässä") was a nail, and by moving the cup onto ("pöydälle") and off of ("pöydältä") the table, and driving the nail into ("pöytään") and out of ("pöydästä") the table.

Among the other cases, the two that foreigners find most confusing are the accusative and the partitive cases. In Latin and German, which lack a partitive case, all direct objects are expressed with the accusative case: "I hit the ball" in English is "ich schlage den Ball" in German. But in Finnish, whenever you use a direct object, you have to decide whether your verb is doing something to the whole object (requiring the accusative case) or to only a part of the object (requiring the partitive case). It may be easy to decide whether you are hitting the whole ball or hitting only a part of the ball. But it's harder to decide whether to use the accusative case or the partitive case in Finnish when you have an abstract noun. For example, if you have an idea, the Finnish language requires you to decide whether you are having the whole idea or only part of the idea, because that determines whether it is correct to use the accusative case or the partitive case. One of my Finnish hosts in 1959 was a Swedish Finn whose home language was Swedish but who was fluent in Finnish. Nevertheless, he couldn't get a job from any government agency in Finland, because all Finnish government jobs require passing exams in both the Finnish and the Swedish languages. My friend told me that if, in the 1950's, you made only a single mistake in choosing between the accusative case and the partitive case, you flunked the exam and couldn't get a government job.

All of those features contribute to making the Finnish language distinctive, beautiful, a source of national pride, and spoken by almost no one other than Finns themselves. The Finnish language formed the core of the Finnish national identity for which so many Finns were willing to die in their war against the Soviet Union.

Other central pieces of Finland's national identity are its music composers, its architects and designers, and its long-distance runners. The Finnish musician Jean Sibelius is considered one of the greatest composers of the 20th century. Finnish architects and interior designers are renowned worldwide. (American readers will think of the St. Louis Arch, Dulles Airport outside Washington, and the TWA terminal at New York's Kennedy Airport, all of them designed by the Finnish-born architect Eero Saarinen.) After World War One, when many new countries (including Finland) were created by the victorious Allies, Finland stood out because of Sibelius and Finland's most famous record-setting long-distance runner, Paavo Nurmi, nicknamed the Flying Finn. In the 1924 Olympic Games he won and set an Olympic record in the 1,500-meter race, then again in the 5,000-meter race an hour later; then he won the 10,000-meter cross-country race two days later; then he won the 3,000-meter race on the next day. He held the world record in the mile for eight years. That gave rise to the saying that Nurmi and other Finnish runners "ran Finland onto the world map." All of those achievements also contributed to Finns' awareness of their distinctiveness, their national identity, and their willingness to fight the Soviets against overwhelming odds.

———

Speakers of a proto-Finnish language arrived in Finland in prehistorical times, several thousand years ago. In historical times, i.e., after the first detailed written accounts of Finland began to be recorded around AD 1100, possession of Finland was contested between Sweden and Russia. Finland remained mostly under Swedish control until it was annexed by Russia in 1809. For most of the 19th century, Russia's tsars let Finland have much autonomy, its own parliament, its own administration, and its own currency, and they didn't impose the Russian language. But after Nicholas II became tsar in 1894 and appointed as governor a nasty man called Bobrikov (assassinated by a Finn in 1904), Russian rule became oppressive. Hence towards the end of World War One, when the Bolshevik Revolution broke out in Russia in late 1917, Finland declared its independence.

The result was a bitter Finnish Civil War, in which conservative Finns called Whites, consisting of Finnish troops trained in Germany and assisted by German troops who landed in Finland, fought against communist Finns called Reds, as well as against Russian troops still stationed in Finland. When the Whites consolidated their victory in May 1918, they shot about 8,000 Reds, and a further 20,000 Reds died of starvation and disease while rounded up in concentration camps. As measured by percentage of a national population killed per month, the Finnish Civil War remained the world's most deadly civil conflict until the Rwandan genocide of 1994. That could have poisoned and divided the new country — except that there was quick reconciliation, the surviving leftists received back their full political rights, and by 1926 a leftist had become Finland's prime minister. But the memories of the civil war did stoke Finland's fear of Russia and of communism — with consequences for Finland's subsequent attitude towards the Soviet Union.

During the 1920's and 1930's Finland continued to be fearful of Russia, now reconstituted as the Soviet Union. Ideologically, the two countries were opposites: Finland a liberal capitalist democracy, the Soviet Union a repressive communist dictatorship. Finns remembered oppression by Russia under the last tsar. They were afraid that the Soviet Union would seek to re-acquire Finland, for example by supporting Finnish communists to subvert the Finnish government. They watched with concern Stalin's reign of terror and paranoid purges of the 1930's. Of most direct concern to Finland, the Soviets were constructing airfields and railroad lines in sparsely populated areas of the Soviet Union east of the Finnish border. Those railroad lines included ones running towards Finland, ending in the middle of forest short of the border, and serving no conceivable purpose except to facilitate an invasion of Finland.

In the 1930's Finland began to strengthen its army and its defenses under its General Mannerheim, who had led the victorious White troops during the civil war. Many Finns volunteered to spend the summer of 1939 at work strengthening Finland's main defense line, called the Mannerheim Line, across the Karelian Isthmus, which separated southeastern Finland from Leningrad, the nearest and second-largest Soviet city. As Germany re-armed under Hitler and became increasingly antagonistic to the Soviet Union, Finland tried to maintain a foreign policy based on neutrality, to ignore the Soviet Union, and to hope that no threat would materialize from that direction. The Soviet Union in turn remained suspicious of its bourgeois neighbor that had defeated the communist side during the Finnish Civil War with the aid of German troops.

Just as Finland had strong geographic and historical reasons for being concerned about the Soviet Union, the Soviet Union also had strong geographic and historical reasons for being concerned about Finland. The pre–World War Two border between Finland and the Soviet Union lay only 30 miles north of Leningrad (see map on p. 56). German troops had already fought in Finland against communists in 1918; British and French troops had already entered the Gulf of Finland to blockade or attack Leningrad (formerly and now again known as St. Petersburg) during the Crimean War of the 1850's; and France had built a big fortress in Helsinki harbor in the 1700's to prepare for an attack on St. Petersburg. In the late 1930's Stalin's fear of Germany under Hitler was growing, for good reason. Communists and Nazis exchanged virulent propaganda. Hitler had written in his autobiography, *Mein Kampf*, of his vision of Germany expanding to the east, i.e. into the Soviet Union. Stalin had watched Hitler's Germany absorb Austria in March 1938, take over Czechoslovakia in March 1939, and begin to threaten Poland. France, Britain, and Poland rejected Stalin's proposals to cooperate in the defense of Poland against the growing German threat.

In August 1939 Finland and the rest of the world were stunned to learn that Hitler and Stalin had abruptly called off their propaganda war and signed the German-Soviet Non-aggression Pact, also termed the Molotov-Ribbentrop Pact. The Finns suspected, correctly, that the pact included secret agreements dividing up spheres of influence, with Germany acknowledging that Finland belonged to the Soviet sphere. The signing of the pact was quickly followed by Germany's blitzkrieg invasion of Poland, followed within a few weeks by the Soviet Union's invasion of eastern Poland. Stalin understandably wanted to push the Soviet Union's

border as far westwards as possible, in order to anticipate the growing German threat.

In October 1939 the Soviet Union, still fearful of an eventual
German attack, was eager to push even more of its western border
back as far westwards as possible. With the temporary security
offered by the Molotov-Ribbentrop Pact, the Soviet Union issued
ultimata to its four Baltic neighbors: the so-called Baltic Republics
of Lithuania, Latvia, and Estonia, plus Finland. From the Baltic
Republics the Soviet Union demanded Soviet military bases on
their soil, plus right of transit of Soviet troops to those bases.
Although the stationing of Soviet troops obviously left the republics defenseless, the republics were so small that they saw resistance
as hopeless, accepted the Soviet demands, and were unable to avoid
annexation by the Soviet Union in June of 1940. Encouraged by that
success, in early October 1939 the Soviet Union made two demands
upon Finland. One demand was that the Soviet/Finnish border on
the Karelian Isthmus be moved back farther from Leningrad, so
that Leningrad could not be bombarded or quickly captured (e.g.,
by German troops stationed again in Finland as they already had
been in 1918). While there was no risk of Finland itself attacking
the Soviet Union, it was realistic to fear some major European
power attacking the Soviet Union through Finland. The second
Soviet demand was that Finland let the Soviet Union establish a
naval base on Finland's south coast near the capital of Helsinki,
and cede some small islands in the Gulf of Finland.

Secret negotiations between Finland and the Soviet Union continued through the months of October and November of 1939. The
Finns were willing to make some concessions, but not nearly as
many as the Soviets wanted, even though Finland's General Mannerheim urged the Finnish government to make more concessions
because he knew the weakness of the Finnish army and (as a former
lieutenant general in tsarist Russia's army) understood the

geographic reasons for the Soviet demands from the Soviet point of view. But Finns from all parts of the Finnish political spectrum — leftists and rightists, Reds and Whites in the civil war — were unanimous in refusing to compromise further. All Finnish political parties agreed with that refusal by their government, whereas in Britain in July 1940 there were leading British politicians in favor of compromising with Hitler in order to buy peace.

One reason for Finns' unanimity was their fear that Stalin's real goal was to take over all of Finland. They were afraid that giving in to supposedly modest Soviet demands today would make it impossible for Finland to resist bigger Soviet demands in the future. Finland's giving up its land defenses on the Karelian Isthmus would make it easy for the Soviet Union to invade Finland overland, while a Soviet naval base near Helsinki would allow the Soviet Union to bombard Finland's capital by land and by sea. The Finns had drawn a lesson from the fate of Czechoslovakia, which had been pressured in 1938 into ceding to Germany its Sudeten borderland with its strongest defense line, leaving Czechoslovakia defenseless against total occupation by Germany in March 1939.

Finns' second reason for not compromising was their miscalculation that Stalin was only bluffing and would settle for less than what he was demanding. Correspondingly, Stalin also miscalculated and thought that the Finns, too, were only bluffing. Stalin could not imagine that a tiny country would be so crazy as to fight against a country with a population almost 50 times larger. Soviet war plans expected to capture Helsinki within less than two weeks. A third reason for Finns' refusal to make further concessions was their miscalculation that countries traditionally friendly to Finland would help defend Finland. Finally, some Finnish political leaders calculated that Finland's army could resist a Soviet invasion for at least six months, even though General Mannerheim warned them that that was impossible.

On November 30, 1939 the Soviet Union attacked Finland, claiming that Finnish artillery shells had landed in the Soviet Union and killed some Soviet soldiers. (Khrushchev later admitted that those shells had actually been fired by Soviet guns from inside the Soviet Union, under orders from a Soviet general who wanted to provoke war.) The war that followed is known as the Winter War. Soviet armies attacked along the whole length of the Finnish/Soviet border, and Soviet planes bombed Helsinki and other Finnish cities. The Finnish civilian casualties in that first night of bombing accounted for 10% of Finland's total civilian war casualties during the entire five years of World War Two. When Soviet troops crossed the Finnish border and captured the nearest Finnish village, Stalin immediately recognized a Finnish communist leader named Kuusinen as head of a so-called "democratic" Finnish government, in order to give the Soviet Union the excuse that it was not invading Finland but just coming to the defense of "the" Finnish government. The establishment of that puppet government helped convince any still-doubting Finns that Stalin really did want to take over their country.

———

At the time that war broke out on November 30, 1939, the details of this absurd military mismatch were as follows. The Soviet Union had a population of 170 million, compared to Finland's population of 3,700,000. The Soviet Union attacked Finland with "only" four of its armies, totaling 500,000 men, and keeping many other armies in reserve or for other military purposes. Finland defended itself with its entire army, consisting of nine divisions totaling only 120,000 men. The Soviet Union supported its attacking infantry with thousands of tanks, modern war planes, and modern artillery; Finland was almost without tanks, modern war planes, modern artillery, anti-tank guns, and anti-aircraft defenses. Worst of all, though the Finnish army did have good rifles and machine guns, it had very limited stocks of ammunition; soldiers were told to save ammunition by holding fire until Soviet attackers were close.

All of those disparities made Finland's chances of defeating the Soviet Union zero, if Stalin were determined to win. The world had already seen how quickly Poland, with a population 10 times that of Finland and far more modern military equipment, had been defeated within a few weeks by German armies half the size of the Soviet Union's armies. Hence Finns were not so insane as to imagine that they could achieve a military victory. Instead, as a Finnish friend expressed it to me, "Our aim was instead to make Russia's victory as slow, as painful, and as costly for the Russians as possible." Specifically, Finland's goal was to resist for long enough that the Finnish government would have time to recruit military help from friendly countries, and that Stalin would tire of the military costs to the Soviet Union.

To the great surprise of the Soviet Union and of the rest of the world, Finland's defenses held. The Soviets' military plan of attacking Finland along the entire length of their shared border included attacks on the Mannerheim Line across the Karelian Isthmus, plus attempts to "cut Finland at the waist" by driving all the way across the middle of Finland at the country's narrowest point. Against Soviet tanks attacking the Mannerheim Line, the Finns compensated for their deficiencies in anti-tank guns by inventing so-called "Molotov cocktails," which were bottles filled with an explosive mixture of gasoline and other chemicals, sufficient to cripple a Soviet tank. Other Finnish soldiers waited in a foxhole for a tank to come by, then jammed a log into the tank's tracks to bring it to a stop. Daredevil individual Finnish soldiers then ran up to the crippled tanks, pointed their rifles into the cannon barrels and observation slits, and shot Soviet soldiers inside the tanks. Naturally, the casualty rate among Finland's anti-tank crews was up to 70%.

What most won the admiration of world observers for the Finnish defenders was their success in destroying the two Soviet divisions that attacked Finland at its waist. The Soviets advanced with motor vehicles and tanks along the few roads leading from the Soviet Union into Finland. Small groups of Finnish soldiers mounted on skis, wearing white uniforms for camouflage against the snow, moved through the roadless forest, cut the Soviet columns into segments, and then annihilated one segment after another (Plate 2.5). A Finnish veteran described to me in 1959 the tactics that he and his fellow soldiers had used in those winter battles. At night, Soviet soldiers who had parked their vehicles in a long column along a narrow one-lane forest road gathered around big bonfires to keep themselves warm. (Finnish soldiers instead stayed warm at night with small heaters inside their tents, invisible from the outside.) My friend and his platoon skied through the forest, invisible in their white camouflage uniforms, to within firing range of a Soviet column (Plate 2.6). They then climbed nearby trees while carrying their rifles, waited until they could identify the Soviet officers in the light of the bonfire, shot and killed the officers, and then skied off, leaving the Soviets frightened, demoralized, and leaderless.

———

Why did the Finnish army prevail for so long in defending itself against the Soviet army's overwhelming advantages of numbers and of equipment? One reason was motivation: Finnish soldiers understood that they were fighting for their families, their country, and their independence, and they were willing to die for those goals. For example, when Soviet forces were advancing across the frozen Gulf of Finland, which was defended only by small groups of Finnish soldiers on islands in the gulf, the Finnish defenders were told that there would be no means of rescuing them: they should stay on those islands and kill as many Soviets as possible before they themselves were killed; and they did. Second, Finnish soldiers were accustomed to living and skiing in Finnish forests in the winter, and they were familiar with the terrain on which they were fighting. Third, Finnish soldiers were equipped with clothing, boots, tents, and guns suitable for Finnish winters, but Soviet soldiers were not. Finally, the Finnish army, like the Israeli army today, was effective far out of proportion to its numbers, because of its informality that emphasized soldiers' taking initiative and making their own decisions rather than blindly obeying orders.

But the tenacity and temporary successes of the Finnish army were just buying time. With the expected melting of the winter ice and snow in the spring, the Soviet Union could finally put its numerical and equipment superiority to use in advancing across the Karelian Isthmus and across the Gulf of Finland. Finland's hopes depended upon receiving assistance of volunteers, equipment, and army units from other countries. What was happening on that diplomatic front?

Widespread sympathy for little Finland bravely fighting the big Soviet aggressor inspired 12,000 foreign volunteers, mostly from Sweden, to come to Finland to fight. But most of those volunteers had not yet completed their military training by the time that the war ended. Some countries sent military equipment, of varying degrees of usefulness. For example, one Finnish veteran told me of old artillery pieces, dating from World War One, that were sent from Italy. When one shoots a projectile from an artillery piece, the gun recoils backwards, so it must be secured on a strong mounting. Each artillery piece requires not only a gunner at the gun itself, but also someone called a spotter stationed some distance in front of the gun, in order to spot where the shell lands and thereby to correct the range setting for the next shot. But, according to my veteran friend, those old Italian artillery pieces were so poorly designed for absorbing recoil that each gun required two spotters: one, the usual spotter in front of the gun, to watch where the shell landed; plus another spotter behind the gun, to see where the gun landed!

Realistically, the only countries from which Finland had any hopes of receiving many troops and/or supplies were Sweden, Germany, Britain, France, and the U.S. Neighboring Sweden, although closely connected to Finland through long shared history and shared culture, refused to send troops out of fear of becoming embroiled in war with the Soviet Union. While Germany had sent troops to support Finnish independence and had long-standing ties of culture and friendship with Finland, Hitler was unwilling to violate the Molotov-Ribbentrop Pact by helping Finland. The U.S. was far away, and President Roosevelt's hands were tied by U.S. neutrality rules resulting from decades of American isolationist policies.

That left only Britain and France as realistic sources of help. Britain and France did eventually offer to send troops. But both were already at war with Germany, and that war was the overwhelming preoccupation of the British and French governments, which could not permit anything else to interfere with that goal. Germany was importing much of its iron ore from neutral Sweden. Much of that ore was being exported from Sweden across Norway by railroad to the ice-free Norwegian port of Narvik, and then by ship to Germany. What Britain and France really wanted was to gain control of the Swedish iron fields, and to interrupt the ship traffic from Narvik. Their offer to send troops across neutral Norway and Sweden to help Finland was just a pretext for achieving those true aims.

Hence while the British and French governments offered help to Finland in the form of tens of thousands of troops, it turned out that most of those troops would be stationed at Narvik and along the Narvik railroad and in the Swedish iron fields. Only a tiny fraction of those troops would actually reach Finland. Even those stationings of troops would of course require the permission of the Norwegian and Swedish governments, which were remaining neutral and refused permission.

———

In January 1940 the Soviet Union finally began to digest the lessons of its horrifying troop losses and military defeats in December. Stalin disowned the puppet Finnish government that he had set up under the Finnish communist leader Kuusinen. That meant that Stalin was no longer refusing to acknowledge the real Finnish government, which sent out peace feelers. The Soviets stopped wasting effort on their attempts to cut Finland at the waist, and instead assembled huge concentrations of troops and artillery and tanks on the Karelian Isthmus, where the open terrain favored the Soviets. Finnish soldiers had been fighting continually at the fronts for two months and were exhausted, while the Soviet Union could throw in unlimited fresh reserves. Early in February, Soviet attacks finally broke through the Mannerheim Line, forcing the Finns to retreat to their next and much weaker defense line. Although the other Finnish generals under Mannerheim begged him to retreat even further to a better defensive position, Mannerheim had iron nerves: despite the heavy casualties now being inflicted on the Finnish army, he refused to pull back further, because he knew that it was essential for Finland still to be occupying as much of its territory as possible at the time of the inevitable peace negotiations.

In late February 1940, when the exhausted Finns were finally ready for peace, the British and French still urged the Finns to hold out. The French prime minister, Daladier, urgently wired Finland that he would send 50,000 troops by the end of March, that he had

100 bomber planes that were ready to take off, and that he guaranteed to "arrange" the passage of those troops by land across Norway and Sweden. That offer induced the Finns to keep fighting for another week, during which several thousand more Finns were killed.

But the British then admitted that Daladier's offer was a deceitful bluff, that those troops and planes were not ready, that Norway and Sweden were still refusing passage to the offered troops, and that the French offer was being made merely to advance the Allies' own aims and to save face for Daladier. Hence Finland's prime minister led a Finnish delegation to Moscow for peace negotiations. At the same time, the Soviet Union maintained its military pressure on Finland by advancing upon Finland's second-largest city of Viipuri, capital of the Finnish province of Karelia. That fighting accounts for all those gravestones labeled "Viipuri, February or March 1940" that you'll see in Hietaniemi Cemetery.

The conditions that the Soviet Union imposed in March 1940 were much harsher than the conditions that the Finns had rejected in October of 1939. The Soviets now demanded the entire province of Karelia, other territory farther north along the Finland/Soviet border, and use of the Finnish port of Hanko near Helsinki as a Soviet naval base. Rather than remain in their homes under Soviet occupation, the entire population of Karelia, amounting to 10% of Finland's population, chose to evacuate Karelia and withdrew into the rest of Finland. There, they were squeezed into rooms in apartments and houses of other Finns, until almost all of them could be provided with their own homes by 1945. Uniquely among the many European countries with large internally displaced populations, Finland never housed its displaced citizens in refugee camps. Nineteen years later, my Finnish hosts during my visit still remembered the huge strain of finding housing and support for all those Karelians.

Why, in March 1940, did Stalin not order the Soviet army to keep advancing and to occupy all of Finland? One reason was that the fierce Finnish resistance had made clear that a further advance would continue to be slow and painful and costly to the Soviet Union, which now had much bigger problems to deal with — namely, the problems of reorganizing its army and re-arming to prepare for a German attack. The poor performance of the huge Soviet army against the tiny Finnish army had been a big embarrassment to the Soviet Union: about eight Soviet soldiers killed for every Finn killed. The longer a war with Finland went on, the higher was the risk of British and French intervention, which would drag the Soviet Union into war with those countries and invite a British/French attack on Soviet oil fields in the Caucasus. Some authors concluded that the harsh March 1940 peace terms demonstrate that the Finns should indeed have accepted the milder terms demanded by Stalin in October 1939. But Russian archives opened in the 1990's confirmed Finns' wartime suspicion: the Soviet Union would have taken advantage of those milder territorial gains and the resulting breaching of the Finnish defense line in October 1939 in order to achieve its intent of taking over all of Finland, just as it did to the three Baltic Republics in 1940. It took the Finns' fierce resistance and willingness to die, and the slowness and cost of the war against Finland, to convince the Soviet Union not to try to conquer all of Finland in March 1940.

———

After the March 1940 armistice, the Soviet Union reorganized its army and annexed the three Baltic Republics. Germany occupied Norway and Denmark in April 1940 and then defeated France in June 1940, so that Finland was now cut off from any possible outside help — except from Germany. Finland rebuilt its own army, especially with German equipment.

Hitler decided to attack the Soviet Union in the following year (1941). At some point, German military planners began discussions with Finnish military planners about "hypothetical" joint operations against the Soviet Union. While Finland had no sympathy with Hitler and Nazism, the Finns understood the cruel reality that it would be impossible for them to avoid choosing sides and to preserve their neutrality in a war between Germany and the Soviet Union: otherwise, one or both of those countries would seek to occupy Finland. Finland's bitter experience of having to fight the Soviet Union alone in the Winter War made the prospect of repeating that experience worse than the alternative of an alliance of expedience with Nazi Germany — "the least awful of several very bad options," to quote from Steven Zaloga's biography of Mannerheim. The poor performance of the Soviet army in the Winter War had convinced all observers — not only in Finland but also in Germany, Britain, and the U.S. — that a war between Germany and the Soviet Union would end with a German victory. Naturally, too, the Finns wanted to regain their lost province of Karelia. On June 21, 1941 Germany did attack the Soviet Union. Finland declared that it would remain neutral, but on June 25 Soviet planes bombed Finnish cities, giving the Finnish government the excuse that night to declare that Finland was once again at war with the Soviet Union.

This second war against the Soviet Union, following the first Winter War, is called the Continuation War. This time, Finland mobilized one-sixth of its entire population to serve in or work directly for the army: the largest percentage of any country during World War Two. That's as if the U.S. today were to reinstitute the draft and to build up an army of over 50 million. Serving directly in the armed forces were males from age 16 to their early 50's, plus some women near the front lines. All Finns of both sexes not actually in the armed forces, ages 15 to 64, had to work in a war industry, agriculture, forestry, or other sector necessary for defense. Teen-age children worked in the fields, sawmills, and anti-aircraft.

With the Soviet army preoccupied in defending itself against the German attack, the Finns quickly reoccupied Finnish Karelia, and (more controversially) also advanced beyond their former border into Soviet Karelia. But Finland's war aims remained strictly limited, and the Finns described themselves not as "allies" but just as "co-belligerents" with Nazi Germany. In particular, Finland adamantly refused German pleas to do two things: to round up Finland's Jews (although Finland did turn over a small group of non-Finnish Jews to the Gestapo); and to attack Leningrad from the north while Germans were attacking it from the south. That latter refusal of the Finns saved Leningrad, enabled it to survive the long German siege, and contributed to Stalin's later decision that it was unnecessary to invade Finland beyond Karelia (see below).

Nevertheless, the fact remained that Finland was fighting alongside Nazi Germany. The distinction between "ally" and "co-belligerent" was lost on outsiders who did not understand Finland's situation. When I was growing up in the U.S. during World War Two, I just thought of Finland as the fourth Axis power, along with Germany and Italy and Japan. Under pressure from Stalin, Britain declared war on Finland. But the only action that Britain took was to send one bombing raid against the Finnish city of Turku, where the British pilots intentionally dropped their bombs offshore into the ocean rather than hit Turku itself.

After early December 1941, the Finnish army ceased its advance, and nothing further happened in the Continuation War between the Soviet Union and Finland for almost three years. On the one hand, Finland had no other goals after occupying Karelia. On the other hand, the Soviet army was too busy fighting the German army to be able to spare troops against Finland. Finally, after the Soviet Union had made sufficient progress in pushing German troops out of the Soviet Union that it felt able to divert attention to Finland, in June 1944 it launched a big offensive against the Karelian Isthmus. Soviet troops quickly broke through the Mannerheim Line, but (just as in February 1941) the Finns succeeded in stabilizing the front. The Soviet advance then petered out, partly because Stalin set a higher priority on using his army to reach Berlin from the east ahead of American and British armies advancing from the west; and partly because of the dilemmas already faced during the Winter War: the expected high costs of overcoming further Finnish resistance, of guerrilla warfare in Finland's forests, and of figuring out what to do with Finland if and when the Soviet Union did succeed in conquering it. Thus, in 1944 as in 1941, Finnish resistance achieved the realistic goal expressed by my Finnish friend: not of defeating the Soviet Union, but of making further Soviet victories prohibitively costly, slow, and painful. As a result, Finland became the sole continental European country fighting in World War Two to avoid enemy occupation.

Once the battlefront re-stabilized in July 1944, Finland's leaders again flew to Moscow to sue for peace and signed a new treaty. This time, Soviet territorial demands were almost the same as they had been in 1941. The Soviet Union took back Finnish Karelia and a naval base on the south coast of Finland. The Soviet Union's only additional territorial acquisition was to annex Finland's port and nickel mines on the Arctic Ocean. Finland did have to agree to drive out the 200,000 German troops stationed in northern Finland, in order to avoid having to admit Soviet troops into Finland to do that. It took Finland many months, in the course of which the retreating Germans destroyed virtually everything of value in the whole Finnish province of Lapland. When I visited Finland in 1959, my Finnish hosts were still bitter that their former German allies had turned on Finland and laid waste to Lapland.

Finland's total losses against the Soviets and the Germans in the two wars, the Winter War and the Continuation War, were about 100,000 men killed. In proportion to Finland's population then, that's as if 9 million Americans were killed in a war today. Another 94,000 Finns were crippled, 30,000 Finnish women were widowed, 55,000 Finnish children were orphaned, and 615,000 Finns lost their homes. That's as if a war resulted in 8 million Americans being crippled, 2½ million American women being widowed, half-a-million American children being orphaned, and 50 million Americans losing their homes. In addition, in one of the largest child evacuations in history, 80,000 Finnish children were evacuated (mainly to Sweden), with long-lasting traumatic consequences extending to the next generation (Plate 2.7). Today, daughters of those Finnish mothers evacuated as children are twice as likely to be hospitalized for a psychiatric illness as are their female cousins born to non-evacuated mothers. The Soviet Union's much heavier combat losses against Finland were estimated at about half-a-million dead and a quarter-of-a-million wounded. That Soviet death toll includes the 5,000 Soviet soldiers taken prisoner by the Finns and repatriated after the armistice to the Soviet Union, where they were immediately shot for having surrendered.

The armistice treaty required Finland "to collaborate with the Allied powers in the apprehension of persons accused of war crimes." The Allied interpretation of "Finnish war criminal" was: the leaders of Finland's government during Finland's wars against the Soviet Union. If Finland hadn't prosecuted its own government leaders, the Soviets would have done so and imposed harsh sentences, probably death sentences. Hence Finland felt compelled to do something that in any other circumstance would have been considered disgraceful: it passed a retroactive law, declaring it illegal for its government leaders to have defended Finland by adopting policies that were legal and widely supported under Finnish law at the time that those policies were adopted. Finnish courts sentenced to prison Finland's wartime President Ryti, its wartime Prime Ministers Rangell and Linkomies, its wartime foreign minister, and four other ministers plus its ambassador to Berlin. After those leaders had served out their sentences in comfortable special Finnish prisons, most of them were voted or appointed back into high public positions.

The peace treaty required Finland to pay heavy reparations to the Soviet Union: $300,000,000, to be paid within six years. Even after the Soviet Union extended the term to eight years and reduced the amount to $226,000,000, that was still a huge burden for the small and un-industrialized Finnish economy. Paradoxically, though, those reparations proved to be an economic stimulus, by forcing Finland to develop heavy industries such as building ships and factories-for-export. (The reparations thereby exemplify the etymology of the Chinese word "wei-ji," meaning "crisis," which consists of the two characters "wei," meaning "danger," and "ji," meaning "opportunity.") That industrialization contributed to the economic growth of Finland after the war, to the point where Finland became a modern industrial country (and now a high-tech country) rather than (as formerly) a poor agricultural country.

In addition to paying those reparations, Finland had to agree to carry out much trade with the Soviet Union, amounting to 20% of total Finnish trade. From the Soviet Union, Finland imported especially oil. That proved to be a big advantage for Finland, because it didn't share the dependence of the rest of the West on Middle Eastern oil supplies. But, as part of its trade agreement, Finland also had to import inferior Soviet manufactured goods, such as locomotives, nuclear power plants, and automobiles, which could otherwise have been obtained more cheaply and with much higher quality from the West. Finns coped with their frustration through black humor, just as they had in dealing with the antiquated Italian artillery that I mentioned earlier. For instance, at the time of my

1959 visit, many Finns had Soviet cars of the Moskvich model, which frequently broke down. Many European and American car models then had sun roofs: sliding panels that one could use to open the roof and let in the sun during beautiful weather. According to a widespread Finnish joke, new models of Moskviches were going to have not just a sun roof, but also a sun floor: another sliding panel, this one in the floor. Question: what's the advantage of having a sun floor, which can't let in the sun? Answer: whenever your Moskvich breaks down, which will happen often, you can put your feet through the opening in the sun floor, stand up on the ground inside your Moskvich, and push it forwards!

Finns refer to the years 1945–1948 as "the years of danger." In retrospect, we know that Finland survived, but during those years that happy outcome seemed uncertain. The foremost danger was that of a communist take-over, through domestic communist subversion supported by the Soviet Union. Paradoxically for a democratic country that had been fighting for its survival against the communist Soviet Union, Finland's Communist Party and its allies won a quarter of the seats in the March 1945 free elections for Finland's parliament, and they tried to take over the police force. The Soviet Union had already occupied East Germany, was in the process of engineering communist take-overs of four Eastern European countries (Poland, Hungary, Bulgaria, and Romania), engineered a successful coup in Czechoslovakia, and supported an unsuccessful guerrilla war in Greece. Would Finland be next? The cost of reparations to the Soviet Union represented a heavy burden on the still largely agricultural, not-yet-industrialized Finnish economy. War had destroyed Finland's infrastructure: farms had been neglected, manufacturing facilities had fallen into disrepair, two-thirds of Finland's shipping fleet had been destroyed, and trucks were worn out, without spare parts, and reduced to burning wood instead of gasoline. Hundreds of thousands of displaced Karelians, crippled Finns, orphans, and widows required housing, money, and emotional support from those Finnish families that remained intact and healthy. Tens of thousands of Finnish children who had been evacuated to Sweden were returning, having been traumatized, forgotten their Finnish language, and nearly forgotten their parents during their years in exile.

In those years of danger, Finland devised a new post-war policy for averting a Soviet take-over. That policy became known as the Paasikivi-Kekkonen line, after Finland's two presidents who formulated, symbolized, and rigorously implemented it for 35 years (Juho Paasikivi, 1946–1956; Urho Kekkonen, 1956–1981). The Paasikivi-Kekkonen line reversed Finland's disastrous 1930's policy of ignoring Russia. Paasikivi and Kekkonen learned from those mistakes. To them, the essential painful realities were that Finland was a small and weak country; it could expect no help from Western allies; it had to understand and constantly keep in mind the Soviet Union's point of view; it had to talk frequently with Russian government officials at every level, from the top down; and it had to win and maintain the Soviet Union's trust, by proving to the Soviet Union that Finland would keep its word and fulfill its agreements. Maintaining the Soviet Union's trust would require bending over backwards by sacrificing some of the economic independence, and some of the freedom to speak out, that strong unthreatened democracies consider inalienable national rights.

Both Paasikivi and Kekkonen knew the Soviet Union and its people very well — Paasikivi, from conducting the October 1939 and March 1940 and September 1944 negotiations with the Soviet Union, and from serving as ambassador to Moscow. Paasikivi concluded that Stalin's driving motivation in his relationship with Finland was not ideological but strategic and geopolitical: i.e., the

Soviet Union's military problem of defending its second-largest city (Leningrad / St. Petersburg) against further possible attacks via Finland or via the Gulf of Finland, as had already happened in the past. If the Soviet Union felt secure on that front, Finland would be secure. But Finland could never be secure as long as the Soviet Union felt insecure. More generally, conflict anywhere in the world could make the Soviet Union uneasy and prone to place demands on Finland, so Finland had to become active in world peace-keeping. Paasikivi, and then Kekkonen, were so successful in developing a trusting relationship with Stalin, and then with Khrushchev and with Brezhnev, that, when Stalin was once asked why he had not tried to maneuver the Communist Party into power in Finland as he had in every other Eastern European country, he answered, "When I have Paasikivi, why would I need the Finnish Communist Party?"

Here is President Kekkonen's explanation of his own and Paasikivi's policy, from his political autobiography: "The basic task of Finnish foreign policy is to reconcile the existence of our nation with the interests which dominate Finland's geopolitical environment.... [Finnish foreign policy is] preventive diplomacy. The task of this diplomacy is to sense approaching danger before it is too close and take measures which help to avoid this danger — preferably in such a way that as few as possible notice that it has been done.... Particularly for a small state which harbors no illusions that the stances it takes can swing the scales one way or another, it is vitally important to be able in good time to form a correct conception of the strength of those factors on which future development in the military and political sector will depend.... A nation should rely only on itself. The war years taught us an expensive lesson in this respect.... Experience also taught us that a small country purely and simply cannot afford to mix emotions — be they feelings of sympathy or antipathy — into its foreign policy solutions. A realistic foreign policy should be based on awareness of the essential factors in international politics, namely national interests and the power of relationships between states."

The concrete pay-offs from Finland's adherence to the Paasikivi-Kekkonen line have consisted of what the Soviet Union (and, today, Russia) has and hasn't done to Finland during the past 70 years. It hasn't invaded Finland. It didn't engineer a take-over of Finland by the Finnish Communist Party when that party existed. It did reduce the amount and extend the period of the war reparations that Finland owed and paid off to the Soviet Union. In 1955 it did evacuate its naval base and did withdraw its artillery on the Finnish coast at Porkkala, just 10 miles from Helsinki. It did tolerate Finland's increasing its trade with the West and decreasing its trade with the Soviet Union, Finland's association with the EEC (European Economic Community), and Finland's joining EFTA (the European Free Trade Association). It was fully within the Soviet Union's power to do, not to do, or to forbid most of those things. The Soviet Union would never have behaved as it did if it had not trusted and felt secure with Finland and with Finland's leaders.

———

In its foreign relations Finland constantly walked a tightrope between developing its relations with the West and retaining Soviet trust. To establish that trust immediately after the Continuation War in 1944, Finland fulfilled on time all the conditions of its armistice and subsequent peace treaty with the Soviet Union. That meant driving German troops out of Finland, conducting war crimes trials against Finland's own wartime leaders, legalizing the Finnish Communist Party and bringing it into the government while preventing it from taking over Finland, and punctually paying its war reparations to the Soviet Union, even though that involved individual Finns contributing their jewelry and gold wedding rings.

In expanding its Western involvement, Finland made efforts to reduce chronic Soviet suspicion that Finland might become economically integrated into the West. For instance, Finland found it prudent to refuse the U.S.'s offer of badly needed Marshall Plan aid. While reaching agreements with or joining the Western European associations EEC and EFTA, Finland simultaneously made agreements with Eastern European communist countries, guaranteed most-favored-nation status to the Soviet Union, and promised the Soviet Union the same trade concessions that Finland was making to its EEC partners.

At the same time as Western countries were Finland's major trade partners, Finland became the Soviet Union's second-leading Western trade partner (after West Germany). Container shipments through Finland were a major route for Western goods to be imported into the Soviet Union. Finland's own exports to the Soviet Union included ships, ice-breakers, consumer goods, and materials to build entire hospitals, hotels, and industrial towns. For the Soviet Union, Finland was its major source of Western technology and its major window onto the West. The result was that the Soviets no longer had any motivation to take over Finland, because Finland was so much more valuable to the Soviet Union independent and allied with the West than it would have been if conquered or reduced to a communist satellite.

Because Soviet leaders trusted Presidents Paasikivi and Kekkonen, Finland chose not to turn over its presidents as in a normal democracy but maintained those two in office for a total of 35 years. Paasikivi served as president for 10 years until just before his death at age 86, while his successor Kekkonen served for 25 years until failing health compelled him to resign at age 81. When

Kekkonen visited Brezhnev in 1973 at the time of Finland's negotiations with the EEC, Kekkonen defused Brezhnev's concerns by giving Brezhnev his personal word that Finland's EEC relationship wouldn't affect Finland's relationship with Russia. Finland's parliament then enabled Kekkonen to fulfill that promise, by adopting an emergency law to extend his term for another four years, thereby postponing the presidential election scheduled for 1974.

Finland's government and press avoided criticizing the Soviet Union and practiced voluntary self-censorship not normally associated with democracies. For example, when other countries condemned the Soviet invasions of Hungary and Czechoslovakia and the Soviet war against Afghanistan, the Finnish government and press remained silent. A Finnish publishing house cancelled its plans to publish Solzhenitsyn's novel *Gulag Archipelago* for fear of offending Soviet sensitivities. When a Finnish newspaper in 1971 did offend the Soviet Union by stating (truthfully) that the Baltic Republics were occupied by the Soviet Union in 1939, a Soviet newspaper denounced that statement as a bourgeois attempt to disrupt neighborly relations between Finland and the Soviet Union, and the Soviet foreign minister warned Finland that the Soviet Union expected the Finnish government to prevent such incidents in the future. The Finnish government obliged by calling on the Finnish press to exercise more "responsibility," i.e., to self-censor such potentially offensive statements.

Finland's tightrope act served to combine independence from the Soviet Union with economic growth. In this respect, too, Finland as a small country has had to face realities: today's 6 million Finns will never develop the economic advantages of scale enjoyed by 90 million Germans or 330 million Americans. Finland will never succeed in economic spheres dependent on a low standard of living and the resulting ability to pay workers the low wages still widespread outside Europe and North America. By world standards, Finland will always have few workers, who will always expect high wages. Hence Finland has had to make full use of its available workforce, and to develop industries earning high profits.

In order to make productive use of its entire population, Finland's school system aims to educate everybody well, unlike the U.S. school system, which now educates some people well but more people poorly. Finland has egalitarian, high-quality public schools with few private schools. Astonishingly to rich Americans, even those few Finnish private schools receive the same level of funding from the government as do public schools, and are not permitted to increase their funding by charging tuition, collecting fees, or raising endowments! While U.S. schoolteachers have low social status and are drawn predominantly from the lower-performing ranks of college students, Finnish schoolteachers go through a very competitive selection process, are drawn from the brightest high school and university students, enjoy high status (even more than university teachers!), are well paid, all have advanced degrees, and have lots of autonomy in how they teach. As a result, Finnish students score at or near the top of world national rankings in literacy, math, and problem-solving abilities. Finland gets the best out of its women as well as out of its men: it was the second country in the world (after New Zealand) to extend the vote to women, and its president happened to be a woman at the time of one of my visits. Finland even gets the best out of its police: again astonishingly to Americans, Finnish police have to have a university bachelor's degree, are trusted by 96% of Finns, and almost never use their guns. Last year, Finnish police on duty fired only six shots, five of them just warning shots: that's fewer than an average week of police gunshots in my city of Los Angeles.

That strong focus on education yields a productive workforce. Finland has the world's highest percentage of engineers in its population. It is a world leader in technology. Its exports account for nearly half of its GDP (gross domestic product), and its main exports are now high-tech — heavy machinery and manufactured goods — instead of timber and other conventional forest products as was the case before World War Two. Finland has become a world leader in the development of new high-tech products from its forests, such as electricity generation, fertilizers, textile fibers to replace wool and copper, and even guitars. Finland's combined private and government investment in research and development equals 3.5% of its GDP, almost double the level of other European Union countries, and (along with the percentage of its GDP spent on education) close to the highest in the world. The result of that excellent educational system and those high investments in research and development is that, within just half-a-century, Finland went from being a poor country to being one of the richest in the world. Its average per-capita income is now equal to that of France, Germany, and the United Kingdom, all of which have populations 10 times that of Finland and have been rich for a long time.

———

When I visited Finland in 1959, knowing almost nothing about the history of Finland's two wars with the Soviet Union, I asked my Finnish hosts why Finland deferred to the Soviet Union in so many ways, imported those inferior Moskvich cars, and was so afraid about the possibility of a Soviet attack on Finland. I told my Finnish hosts that the United States would surely defend Finland if the Soviet Union attacked. In retrospect, there was nothing more cruel, ignorant, and tactless that I could have said to a Finn. Finland had bitter memories that, when it actually was attacked by the Soviet Union in 1939, it had not been helped by the U.S., Sweden, Germany, Britain, or France. Finland had to learn from its history that its survival and independence depended on itself, and that Finland would be safe only if the Soviet Union felt safe and trusting towards Finland.

My ignorant attitude has been shared by many non-Finns who should have known better, but who instead labeled Finnish policy by the derogatory term "Finlandization." As a definition of Finlandization, here is one from the *New York Times* in 1979: "A deplorable state of affairs in which a small and weak neighbor, awed by the might and political ruthlessness of a totalitarian superpower, makes shameless and embarrassing concessions of its sovereign liberties." Those who decry Finlandization consider Finland's policy to be cowardly.

Many Finnish actions do indeed horrify Western European and American observers. It could never happen in the U.S. or Germany that a presidential election would be postponed, a presidential candidate would withdraw his or her candidacy, a publisher would cancel a book, or the press would censor itself, just to avoid inflaming Soviet sensitivities. Such actions seem to violate a democracy's right to freedom of action.

But the sensitivities of other countries are a problem for every country. To quote President Kekkonen again, "A country's independence is not usually absolute ... there was not a single state in existence that did not have to bow to historical inevitabilities." There are obvious reasons why Finland has to bow much more to historical inevitabilities than does the U.S. or Germany: Finland is small and borders on Russia, while the U.S. and Germany do not. What do the critics who decry Finlandization think that Finland should instead have been doing? — risk still another Soviet invasion, by not considering Soviet reactions?

Part of the fear behind non-Finnish critics' objections to Finlandization stemmed from their concern that the communist Soviet Union might lull their own countries into deference to the Soviet Union. But other Western European countries and the U.S.

exist in an entirely different geopolitical situation and don't have to deal with Finland's geopolitical problems. Kekkonen's defense of Finland's policy was summarized in the phrase "Finlandization is not for export."

In fact, Finland's foreign policy towards the Soviet Union has of necessity been Byzantinely complex. The end result is that, in the 70 years since the end of World War Two, Finland has come no closer to becoming a Soviet or (now) a Russian satellite. Instead, it has succeeded in steadily increasing its ties with the West while still maintaining good ties with Russia. At the same time, Finns know that life is uncertain, and so military service is still compulsory for Finnish men and voluntary for Finnish women. Training lasts up to a year and is rigorous, because Finland expects that its soldiers must really be able to fight. After that year of training, Finns are called up for reserve duty every few years until age 30–35 or older. The reserve army constitutes 15% of Finland's population — as if the U.S. maintained a reserve army of 50 million.

———

Let's now evaluate, in the light of Finland's recent history, the dozen factors postulated as associated with resolution of national crises (Table 1.2), by analogy to the factors relevant to personal crises (Table 1.1). Among those factors, seven of them favored, one of them initially hindered and subsequently favored, and the lack of three of them hindered Finland's resolution of its fundamental problem: the threat from its powerful neighbor.

The seven factors associated with crisis solution that Finland conspicuously displayed were acceptance of responsibility (factor #2), building a fence (#3), strong national identity (#6), honest self-appraisal (#7), dealing with national failure (#9), flexibility (#10), and national core values (#11). First, among the nations discussed

93

in this book, Finland is the outstanding example of acceptance of responsibility and honest ultra-realistic self-appraisal. Its reappraisal was especially painful because Soviet armies had killed, widowed, orphaned, or made homeless a large fraction of Finland's population. Finns had to avoid falling into the trap of letting self-pity and resentment paralyze their relations with the Soviet Union. But they finally recognized realities: that Finland is small; that it shares a long border with the Soviet Union; that it could not count on its allies for effective support; that the responsibility for its survival lay entirely with itself; and that it was strong enough to resist the Soviet Union for a while, and to make a Soviet invasion slow and costly and painful for the Soviets, but that it could not resist the Soviets forever. Finns learned from the mistakes of their pre-war foreign policy. They finally faced the fact that the only way that they could retain their political independence was by earning Soviet trust, and by sacrificing some economic independence and freedom to speak out.

Finland illustrates well our theme of selective change and building a fence (factor #3). In its eventual response (after September 1944) to the Soviet attack, Finland reversed its long-standing previous policy of trying to ignore and not deal with the Soviet Union. It adopted a new policy of economic involvement and frequent political discussions with the Soviet Union. But those changes were highly selective, because Finland remained unoccupied, politically self-governing, and a socially liberal democracy. That coexistence of two seemingly contrasting identities, one changed and the other unchanged, has puzzled and angered many non-Finns, who coined the scornful term "Finlandization" and implied that Finland could and should have done something different.

Finland exhibits outstandingly strong national identity (factor #6) — much more than someone unfamiliar with Finland would have expected of such a small country that otherwise seems typically Scandinavian. Finland's national identity and belief in Finland's uniqueness have arisen especially from its beautiful but unique and difficult language, which few outsiders even attempt to learn; from the oral epic poetry associated with that language (the *Kalevala*); and from Finland's century-long history of autonomy under Russian tsarist rule, when Finland already had its own administration, currency, and parliament. Further contributing to Finland's national identity has been the worldwide recognition of its musicians, athletes, architects, and designers. Today, Finland's national identity also rests heavily on pride in its military achievements during the Winter War. Finns view World War Two with pride, more than do the citizens of any other country except Britain. Finland's 2017 centenary celebrations of its independence focused on its World War Two achievements at least as much as on its 1917 achievement of independence: that's as if American celebrations of our Independence Day (July 4) were to focus on our victory in World War Two rather than on our Declaration of Independence in 1776.

Finland illustrates willingness to tolerate initial failure, and to persist in experimenting with solutions to a crisis until it finds a solution that worked (factor #9). When the Soviet Union issued its demands to Finland in October 1939, Finland did not respond by offering the economic and political involvement that it eventually adopted. Even if Finland had made such an offer then, Stalin would probably have refused the offer; it required Finland's ferocious resistance in the Winter War to convince Stalin to leave Finland independent. Instead, from 1944 onwards, when Finland recognized the failure of its pre-war policy of ignoring the Soviet Union and of its wartime policy of seeking a military solution, Finland went through a long and almost uninterrupted period of experimentation in order to discover how much economic and political independence it could retain, and what it had to do to satisfy the Soviet Union in return.

Finland illustrates flexibility born of necessity (factor #10). In response to Soviet fears and sensitivities, Finland did things unthinkable in any other democracy: it put on trial and imprisoned its own wartime leaders according to a retroactive law; its parliament adopted an emergency decree to postpone a scheduled presidential election; a leading presidential candidate was induced to withdraw his candidacy; and its press self-censored statements likely to offend the Soviet Union. Other democracies would consider those actions as disgraceful. In Finland those actions instead reflected flexibility: sacrificing sacred democratic principles to the extent required to retain political independence, the principle held most sacred. Quoting again from Zaloga's biography of Mannerheim, Finns have excelled at negotiating "the least awful of several very bad options."

Finland's history illustrates belief in a non-negotiable core value (factor #11): independence, and not being occupied by another power. Finns were prepared to fight for that core value, even though they thereby risked mass death. Fortunately for Finns, they survived and also retained their independence. There is no universal correct answer to that agonizing dilemma. Poles in 1939, Yugoslavs in 1941, and Hungarians in 1956 also refused, respectively, German, German, and Soviet demands and fought for their independence, but without Finland's fortunate outcome: all three countries lost, became or remained occupied, and suffered cruelly under occupation. Conversely, Czechoslovakia in 1938, Estonia and Latvia and Lithuania in 1939, and Japan in August 1945 accepted, respectively, a German or Soviet or American ultimatum, because they judged their situation to be militarily hopeless. In retrospect, the situations of Czechoslovakia and Estonia may not have been hopeless: but we shall never know.

The factor that initially hindered and subsequently favored Finland's crisis resolution was lack of national consensus about the crisis, and then the achievement of consensus (factor #1). Throughout the 1930's Finland largely ignored the impending crisis with the Soviet Union, and then in 1939 miscalculated that Stalin's demands were partly a bluff. From 1944 onwards there was instead a consensus, formulated as the Paasikivi-Kekkonen line, that the Finnish government had to talk frequently with Soviet political leaders and learn to see things from the Soviet point of view.

The three factors favorable to crisis solution that Finland conspicuously lacked, and for whose lack Finland had to compensate in other ways, were support from allies (factor #4), available models (factor #5), and freedom from geopolitical constraints (factor #12). Of the nations discussed in this book, none received less support from allies than did Finland: all of Finland's traditional and potential friends refused to provide the substantive help for which Finland had been hoping during the Winter War. (Sweden did provide small non-governmental help in the form of about 8,000 volunteers and accepting refugee Finnish children, while Germany did provide essential military and economic help during the Continuation War.) Finland could not look to any model of a weak country that had succeeded in resisting Soviet or Nazi demands: almost all other European countries either acceded to such demands and lost their independence (like the Baltic Republics), or resisted and were brutally conquered (like Poland and Yugoslavia), or resisted successfully through their own military power, far exceeding Finland's (only Britain), or preserved their independence through concessions far milder than those that the Soviet Union demanded of Finland (Switzerland's and Sweden's accommodations to Nazi Germany). Conversely, no other nation could use Finland's successful tightrope act with the Soviet Union as a model ("Finlandization is not for export"). Finland's freedom of choice was severely limited by the geopolitical constraint of its long border with its powerful Soviet neighbor; only post–World War Two Germany approached Finland in the degree to which more powerful countries limited its freedom to act.

Among our questions specific to national crises and not arising for personal crises, two warrant discussion for Finland: the role of leadership, and reconciliation after conflict. Finland did benefit from skilled military and political leadership during and after World War Two. As military leader, General Mannerheim was a master of allocating scarce resources, judging the relative dangers posed by Soviet threats on different war fronts, keeping cool and thinking clearly in excruciatingly painful situations, and retaining the confidence of his troops and officers. Finland's prime minister and later president Juho Paasikivi and his successor Urho Kekkonen, besides both speaking fluent Russian, proved skillful in negotiating with Stalin from a position of weakness, winning and keeping Stalin's trust despite his paranoia, and convincing Stalin that maintaining Finland's independence would be good policy for the Soviet Union. (Imagine yourself in Paasikivi's shoes in September 1944, when he flew to Moscow to meet Stalin for the peace negotiations to end the Continuation War, after he had already flown to Moscow for the peace negotiations of March 1940 to end the Winter War, and after Finland had broken that March 1940 agreement by siding with Germany and reconquering Karelia in the summer of 1941. What would *you* have said to Stalin in 1944? — "Believe me, you can trust me this time"?) But Mannerheim's, Paasikivi's, and Kekkonen's impacts as leaders should not be exaggerated, because their aims and strategies were similar to those of other leading Finnish generals and politicians, although their skills were exceptional.

The other question specific to national crises concerns reconciliation after cruel internal conflict or civil war. Reconciliation in

Finland after its civil war of 1918 was much speedier and more complete than reconciliation in Chile after the Pinochet military dictatorship (Chapter 4), while Indonesians have still done little to reach closure after the army-instigated genocide of 1965 (Chapter 5). A partial explanation involves national differences in the extent to which the army remained powerful and continued to threaten its former adversaries. The army stayed in power in Indonesia after 1965, and remained visible and threatening in Chile even after Pinochet had stepped down as president, whereas Finland's army became less visible after the civil war. Another part of the explanation is Finns' sense of the distinctiveness shared by all Finns: that both the winners and the losers of the Finnish Civil War shared the same egalitarian tradition, and were unique among the world's people in speaking the Finnish language, reciting the *Kalevala*, and being the countrymen of Jean Sibelius and Paavo Nurmi.

Finland is thus the first of our two examples of countries experiencing a crisis due to a sudden external shock. In the next chapter, on Meiji-Era Japan, we shall discuss another country with strong national identity and a distinctive language, much more distinctive culturally than Finland, with even more drastic selective change, and with outstanding realism like Finland's but with a different geopolitical situation that permitted Japan to pursue a long-term strategy more independent than Finland's.

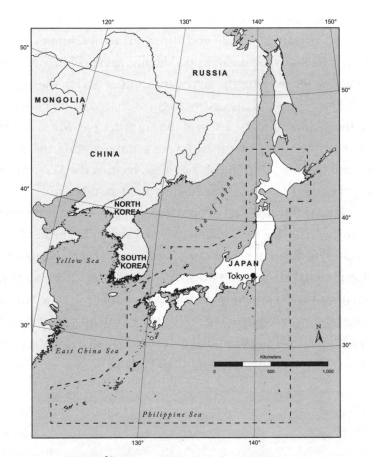

FIG. 3 *Map of Japan*

CHAPTER 3

THE ORIGINS OF MODERN JAPAN

My Japanese connections — Japan before 1853 —
Perry — 1853 to 1868 — The Meiji Era — Meiji
reforms — "Westernization" — Overseas
expansion — Crisis framework — Questions

U nlike the other countries discussed in this book, for Japan I
don't speak the language, haven't lived there for prolonged periods, and visited it for the first time only two decades ago. However,
I have had much opportunity to learn second-hand about Japan's
selective changes and its mixture of European with traditional Japanese features. When I moved to California from Boston on the
U.S.'s East Coast, where I was born and grew up, I found myself in a
part of the U.S. with a much larger Asian population, many of them
Japanese or Japanese-Americans. Asians now form the largest proportion of the student body of my university (the University of California at Los Angeles), outnumbering students of European
descent. I have many Japanese friends and colleagues, including a
wonderful Japanese research assistant, who know the U.S. and
Europe very well from having lived there for a long time, and who
in some cases have intermarried. Conversely, I have many

American friends and colleagues who know Japan very well from having lived there for a long time, and again in some cases from having intermarried. I myself acquired Japanese cousins and nieces when I married into a family with two Japanese branches.

As a result, I hear constantly about the differences between Japan and the U.S. or Europe, from Japanese, Americans, and Europeans with long experience of living both in Japan and in the U.S. and/or Europe. All of my Japanese relatives, students, friends, and colleagues talk about the big differences coexisting with the big similarities between Japanese and American/European societies. In alphabetical order without trying to rank them in importance, some of the differences that they identify involve: apologizing (or not apologizing), the difficulty of learning to read and write, enduring hardships silently, extensive socializing with prospective business clients, extreme politeness, feelings towards foreigners, openly misogynous behavior, patient/doctor communication, pride in beautiful penmanship, reduced individualism, relations with parents-in-law, standing out as different from other people, the status of women, talking directly about feelings, unselfishness, ways of disagreeing with other people — and many other features.

All of those differences are legacies of traditional Japan, coexisting with Western influences on modern Japan. That mixing began with a crisis exploding on July 8, 1853, and accelerated with the Meiji Restoration of 1868 (of which more below), when Japan embarked on a program of selective change that extended over half-a-century. Meiji-Era Japan is perhaps the modern world's outstanding example of selective national change, and of using other nations as models. Like Finland's crisis, which we discussed in the previous chapter, Japan's began abruptly with a foreign threat (but not with an actual attack). Like Finland, Japan exhibited outstanding honest self-appraisal, and patience at experimenting with different solutions until it found ones that worked. Unlike Finland, Japan adopted much more comprehensive selective changes and enjoyed greater freedom of action. Hence Japan in the Meiji Era offers a good case study to pair with our discussion of Finland.

———

Japan was the first modern non-European country to match European societies and overseas neo-European societies (the U.S., Canada, Australia, and New Zealand) in standard of living, industrialization, and technology. Japan today resembles Europe and neo-Europes not only economically and technologically but also in many political and social respects, such as in being a parliamentary democracy, having high literacy, adopting Western dress, and adopting Western music along with traditional Japanese music. But in other respects, especially social and cultural ones, Japan is still more different from all European societies than any European society is from other European societies. There is nothing surprising about those non-European aspects of Japanese society. They are entirely to be expected, because Japan lies 8,000 miles from Western Europe and has been heavily influenced by nearby countries of the Asian mainland (especially China and Korea), with which Japan shares a long history.

Before 1542, no European influence had reached Japan. There was then a period of influence associated with Europe's overseas expansion (but limited by the great intervening distance) from 1542 to 1639, followed by a period of reduced influence until 1853. Most of the European aspects of contemporary Japanese society have arrived since 1853. Of course, they haven't replaced everything about traditional Japan, of which much remains. That is, Japan, like Cocoanut Grove's survivors after the fire, and like Britain after World War Two, is a mosaic of its old self and its new self — more so than any of the other six societies discussed in this book.

Until the Meiji Restoration, Japan's actual ruler was a hereditary military dictator called the shogun, while the emperor was a figurehead without real power. Between 1639 and 1853, the shoguns limited Japanese contact with foreigners, thereby continuing a long Japanese history of lesser isolation arising from the effects of their island geography. That history may at first surprise us when we glance at a world map and compare Japan's geography with that of the British Isles.

Superficially, these two archipelagoes appear to be geographic equivalents of each other off Eurasia's east and west coasts, respectively. (Just look at a map to convince yourself.) Japan and Britain look roughly similar in area, and both lie near the Eurasian continent, so one would expect similar histories of involvement with the continent. In fact, since the time of Christ, Britain has been successfully invaded from the continent four times, Japan never. Conversely, Britain has had armies fighting on the continent in every century since the Norman Conquest of AD 1066, but until the late 19th century there were no Japanese armies on the continent except during two brief periods. Already during the Bronze Age over 3,000 years ago, there was vigorous trade between Britain and mainland Europe; British mines in Cornwall were the main source of tin for making European bronze. A century or two ago, Britain was the world's leading trading nation, while Japanese overseas trade still remained small. Why do these huge differences apparently contradict straightforward geographic expectations?

The explanation for that contradiction involves important details of geography. While Japan and Britain look at a glance similar in area and isolation, Japan is actually five times farther from the continent (110 versus 22 miles), and 50% larger in area and much more fertile. Hence Japan's population today is more than double Britain's, and its production of land-grown food and timber and in-shore seafood is higher. Until modern industry required importation of oil and metals, Japan was largely self-sufficient in essential resources and had little need for foreign trade — unlike Britain. That's the geographic background to the isolation that characterized most of Japanese history, and that merely increased after 1639.

Europeans first reached China and Japan by sea in AD 1514 and 1542, respectively. Japan, which had already been doing some trade with China and Korea, then began trading with four groups of Europeans: Portuguese, Spanish, Dutch, and British. That did not consist of direct trade between Japan and Europe, but instead of trade at settlements on the Chinese coast and elsewhere in Southeast Asia. Those European contacts affected spheres of Japanese society ranging from weapons to religion. When the first Portuguese adventurers reaching Japan in 1542 shot ducks with their primitive guns, Japanese observers were so impressed that they avidly developed their own firearms, with the result that by 1600 Japan had more and better guns than any other country in the world. The first Christian missionaries arrived in 1549, and by 1600 Japan had 300,000 Christians.

But the shoguns had reasons to be concerned about European influence in general, and about Christianity in particular. Europeans were accused of meddling in Japanese politics, and of supplying weapons to Japanese rebels against the Japanese government. Catholics preached intolerance of other religions, disobeyed Japanese government orders not to preach, and were perceived as loyal to a foreign ruler (the Pope). Hence after crucifying thousands of Japanese Christians, between 1636 and 1639 the shogun cut most ties between Japan and Europe. Christianity was banned. Most Japanese were forbidden to travel or live overseas. Japanese fishermen who drifted to sea, got picked up by European or American ships, and managed to return to Japan were often kept under house arrest or forbidden to talk about their experiences overseas. Visits by foreigners to Japan were banned except for Chinese traders confined to one area of the port city of Nagasaki, and Dutch traders confined to Deshima Island in Nagasaki harbor. (Because those Dutch were Protestants, they were considered non-Christian by Japan.) Once every four years, those Dutch traders were ordered to bring tribute to the Japanese capital, traveling by a prescribed route under watchful eyes, like dangerous microbes kept inside a sealed container. Some Japanese domains did succeed in continuing to trade with Korea, China, and the Ryukyu Islands, the archipelago several hundred miles south of Japan that includes Okinawa. Intermittent Korean trade visits to Japan were disguised to Japanese audiences as visits tolerated to receive Korean "tribute." But all of those contacts remained limited in scale.

The small trade between the Netherlands and Japan was economically negligible. Instead, its significance to Japan was that those Dutch traders became an important source of information about Europe. Among the courses of instruction offered by Japanese private academies were so-called "Dutch studies." Those classes taught information acquired from the Netherlands about practical and scientific subjects: especially Western medicine, astronomy, maps, surveying, guns, and explosives. Within the Japanese government's Bureau of Astronomy was an office devoted to translating Dutch books on those subjects into Japanese. Much information about the outside world (including Europe) also came to Japan via China, Chinese books, and European books translated into Chinese.

In short, until 1853 Japan's contact with foreigners was limited, and was controlled by the Japanese government.

———

Japan in 1853 was very unlike Japan today, and even unlike Japan in 1900, in important ways. Somewhat like medieval Europe, Japan in 1853 was still a feudal hierarchical society divided into domains, each controlled by a lord called a daimyo, whose power exceeded that of a medieval European lord. At the apex of power stood the shogun (Plate 3.1), of the Tokugawa line of shoguns that had ruled Japan since 1603, and that controlled one-quarter of Japan's rice-growing land. Daimyo required the shogun's permission to marry, move, or erect or repair a castle. They were also required, in alternate years, to bring their retainers and take up residence at the shogun's capital, at great expense to themselves. Besides the resulting tension between the shogun and the daimyo, other problems in Tokugawa Japan arose from the growing gap between the shogun's expenses and his income, increasingly frequent rebellions, urbanization, and the rising merchant class. But the Tokugawa shoguns had coped with problems and had remained in power for 250 years, and were at no imminent risk of being overthrown. Instead, the shock that led to their overthrow was the arrival of the West.

The background to Western pressure on Japan was Western pressure on China, which produced far more goods desired by the West than did Japan. European consumers especially wanted Chinese tea and silk, but the West produced little that China wanted in return, so Europeans had to make up that trade deficit by shipping silver to China. In order to reduce the hemorrhaging of their silver stocks, British traders got the bright idea of shipping cheap opium from India to sell to China at prices below those of existing Chinese sources. (No, that British opium policy is not an invented anti-Western slander: it really was true, and needs to be remembered when one wants to understand modern Chinese

attitudes towards the West.) The Chinese government understandably responded by denouncing opium as a health hazard,
banning its importation, and demanding that European smug-
glers surrender all the opium stored on their ships anchored off
China's coast. Britain objected to that Chinese response as an
illegal restraint of trade.

The result was the Opium War of 1839–1842 between Britain
and China, the first serious test of military strength between China
and the West. Although China was far larger and more populous
than Britain, it turned out that Britain's navy and army were far
better equipped and trained than China's. Hence China was
defeated and forced into humiliating concessions, paying a large
indemnity, and signing a treaty that opened five Chinese ports to
British trade. France and the U.S. then extracted the same concessions from China.

When the Japanese government learned of these developments in China, it feared that it would be only a matter of time
until some Western power demanded a similar treaty port system in Japan. It did happen, in 1853, and the Western power
responsible was the U.S. The reason why, among Western powers,
the U.S. was the one that became motivated to act first against
Japan was the U.S.'s conquest of California from Mexico in 1848,
accompanied by the discovery there of gold, which caused an
explosion of American ship traffic to the Pacific coast. Sailings of
American whaling and trading ships around the Pacific also
increased. Inevitably, some of those American ships got wrecked,
some of those wrecks occurred in ocean waters near Japan, and
some of their sailors ended up in Japan, where they were killed or
arrested according to Tokugawa Japan's isolationist policy. But
the U.S. wanted those sailors instead to receive protection and
help, and it wanted American ships to be able to buy coal in
Japan.

THE ORIGINS OF MODERN JAPAN

Hence U.S. President Millard Fillmore sent Commodore Matthew Perry to Japan with a fleet of four ships, including two gun-bearing steam-powered warships infinitely superior to any Japanese ships at that time. (Japan had neither steamships nor even steam engines.) On July 8, 1853 Perry sailed his fleet uninvited into Edo Bay (now called Tokyo Bay), refused Japanese orders to leave, delivered President Fillmore's letter of demands, and announced that he expected an answer when he returned the following year.

For Japan, Perry's arrival, and his open threat of overwhelming force, conformed to our definition of "crisis": a serious challenge that cannot be solved by existing methods of coping. After Perry's departure, the shogun circulated Fillmore's letter to the daimyo to ask their opinion about how best to respond; that was already unusual. Among their varied proposed responses, common themes were a strong desire to maintain Japan's isolation, but recognition of the practical impossibility of Japan defending itself against Perry's warships, hence the suggestion of compromising to buy time during which Japan could acquire Western guns and technology to defend itself. It was the latter view that prevailed.

When Perry returned on February 13, 1854, this time with a fleet of nine warships, the shogun responded by signing Japan's first treaty with a Western country. Although Japan succeeded in putting off Perry's demand for a trade agreement, it did make other concessions that ended its 215-year policy of isolation. It opened two Japanese ports as harbors of refuge for American ships, accepted an American consul to reside at one of those ports, and agreed to treat shipwrecked American sailors humanely. After the signing of that agreement between Japan and the U.S., the British and Russian and Dutch naval commanders in the Far East quickly reached similar agreements with Japan.

———

The 14-year period that began in 1854, when the shogun's government (called the bakufu) signed Perry's treaty ending Japan's centuries of isolation, was a tumultuous period of Japanese history. The bakufu struggled to solve the problems resulting from Japan's forced opening. Ultimately, the shogun failed, because the opening triggered unstoppable changes in Japanese society and government. Those changes in turn led to the shogun's overthrow by his Japanese rivals, and then to much more far-reaching changes under the new government that was led by those rivals.

Perry's treaty and its British, Russian, and Dutch equivalents didn't satisfy the Western goal of opening Japan to trade. Hence in 1858 the new American consul in Japan negotiated a broader treaty that did address trade, and that was again soon followed by similar treaties with Britain, France, Russia, and the Netherlands. Those treaties became regarded in Japan as humiliating and were termed the "unequal treaties," because they embodied the Western view that Japan did not deserve to be treated in the way that Western powers treated one another. For instance, the treaties provided for extraterritoriality of Western citizens in Japan, i.e., that they were not subject to Japanese laws. A major goal of Japanese policy for the next half-century became the undoing of the unequal treaties.

Japan's military weakness in 1858 relegated that goal to the distant future. Instead, the bakufu's more modest immediate goal in 1858 was to minimize the intrusion of Westerners, and of their ideas and influence. That was achieved by Japan's keeping up the fiction of obeying the treaties, while actually frustrating them by delaying, unilaterally changing agreements, taking advantage of Western unfamiliarity with ambiguous Japanese place names, and playing off different Western countries against one another.

Through the 1858 treaties, Japan succeeded in limiting trade to just two Japanese ports, termed "treaty ports," and in restricting foreigners to specified districts within those ports beyond which foreigners were forbidden to travel.

The bakufu's basic strategy from 1854 onwards was one of buying time. That meant satisfying Western powers (with as few concessions as possible), but in the meantime acquiring Western knowledge, equipment, technology, and strength, both military and non-military, so as to be able to resist the West as soon as possible. The bakufu, and also the powerful domains of Satsuma and Choshu[4] that were nominally subject to the bakufu but enjoyed much autonomy, purchased Western ships and guns, modernized their militaries, and sent students to Europe and the U.S. Those students studied not just practical matters such as Western navigation, ships, industry, engineering, science, and technology, but also Western laws, languages, constitutions, economics, political science, and alphabets. The bakufu developed an Institute for the Study of Barbarian (i.e., foreign) Books, translated Western books, and sponsored the production of English-language grammars and an English pocket dictionary.

But while the bakufu and the big domains were thus trying to build up strength, problems resulting from Western contact were developing in Japan. The bakufu and domains became heavily indebted to foreign creditors as a result of expenses such as

---

4 Those two powerful rival domains — Satsuma at the south tip of the southernmost Japanese island of Kyushu, Choshu at the southwest tip of the main Japanese island of Honshu — played a major role at many stages of recent Japanese history. Both were defeated by Tokugawa armies in 1600. In the early 1860's both took the lead in attacking Westerners and Western ships, and hence received the brunt of Western retaliation. Both buried their rivalry in order to overthrow the last shogun in 1868, but then staged the biggest revolts against the Meiji government in the 1870's.

weapons purchases and sending students overseas. Consumer prices and the cost of living rose. Many samurai (the warrior class) and merchants objected to the bakufu's efforts to monopolize foreign trade. Now that the shogun had asked the daimyo for advice after Perry's first visit, some daimyo wanted to become further involved in policy and planning, rather than leaving it all to the shogun as before. It was the shogun who had negotiated and signed treaties with Western powers, but the shogun couldn't control outlying daimyo who violated those treaties.

The result was several sets of intersecting conflicts. Western powers were in conflict with Japan about whether to open Japan more (the Western goal) or less (the prevalent Japanese goal) to the West. Domains such as Satsuma and Choshu, which had already traditionally been in conflict against the bakufu, were now in sharper conflict, each side trying to use Western equipment and knowledge and allies against the other. Conflicts increased between domains. There was even conflict between the bakufu and the figurehead emperor at the imperial court, on whose behalf the bakufu supposedly acted. For instance, the imperial court refused to approve the 1858 treaty that the bakufu had negotiated with the U.S., but the bakufu proceeded to sign it anyway.

The sharpest conflict within Japan arose over Japan's basic strategy dilemma: whether to try to resist and expel the foreigners now, or instead to wait until Japan could become stronger. The signing of the unequal treaties by the bakufu created a backlash in Japan: anger at the foreigners who had dishonored Japan, and anger at the shogun and other lords who had permitted Japan to be dishonored. Already around 1859, resentful, hotheaded, naïve young sword-wielding samurai began to pursue a goal of expelling foreigners by a campaign of assassination. They became known as "shishi," meaning "men of high purpose." Appealing to what they believed were traditional Japanese values, they considered themselves morally superior to older politicians.

The following statement of shishi principles, issued in 1861, conveys the flavor of their anger: "It is a source of deepest grief to our Emperor that our magnificent and divine country has been humiliated by the barbarians, and that the Spirit of Japan, which was transmitted from antiquity, is on the point of being extinguished.... It is said that, when one's lord is humiliated, his retainers must choose death. Must we not set even greater emphasis on the present situation, in which the Imperial Country is about to know disgrace?... We swear by our deities that, if the Imperial Flag is once raised, we will go through fire and water to ease the Emperor's mind, to carry out the will of our former lord, and to purge this evil from our people. Should any, in this cause, seek to put forward personal considerations, he shall incur the punishment of the angered gods, and be summoned before his fellows to commit hara-kiri."

Shishi terrorism was directed against foreigners, and even more often against Japanese working for or compromising with foreigners. In 1860 a group of shishi succeeded in beheading the regent Ii Naosuke, who had advocated signing treaties with the West. Japanese attacks against foreigners climaxed in two incidents in 1862 and 1863 involving the domains of Satsuma and Choshu. On September 14, 1862 a 28-year-old English merchant, Charles Richardson, was attacked by Satsuma swordsmen on a road and left to bleed to death, because he was considered to have failed to show proper respect for a procession that included the father of Satsuma's daimyo. Britain demanded indemnities, apologies, and execution of the perpetrators not only from Satsuma but also from the bakufu. After nearly a year of unsuccessful British negotiations with Satsuma, a fleet of British warships bombarded and destroyed most of Satsuma's capital of Kagoshima and killed an estimated 1,500 Satsuma soldiers. The other incident occurred in late June 1863, when Choshu coastal guns fired on Western ships and closed the crucial Shimonoseki Strait between the main Japanese islands of Honshu and Kyushu. A year later, a fleet of 17 British, French, American, and Dutch warships bombarded and destroyed those coastal guns and carried off Choshu's remaining cannon.

Those two Western retaliations convinced even Satsuma and Choshu hotheads of the power of Western guns, and of the futility of Japan's attempting to expel the foreigners while in its current weak condition. The hotheads would have to wait until Japan had achieved military equality with the West. Ironically, that was the policy that the bakufu had already been following, and for which the hotheads had been excoriating the bakufu.

But some domains, especially Satsuma and Choshu, were now convinced that the shogun was incapable of strengthening Japan to the point where it could resist the West. The daimyo concluded that, while they shared the bakufu's goal of acquiring Western technology, achieving that goal required reorganizing Japan's government and society. Hence they sought gradually to outmaneuver the shogun. Satsuma and Choshu had formerly been rivals, had been suspicious of each other, and had fought against each other. Recognizing that the shogun's efforts to build up military strength threatened both domains, they now formed an alliance.

After the former shogun's death in 1866, the new shogun launched a crash program of modernization and reform, including importing military equipment and military advisors from France. That increased the perceived threat to Satsuma and Choshu. When the former emperor also died in 1867, his 15-year-old son succeeded to the imperial throne (Plate 3.2). Satsuma and Choshu leaders conspired with the new emperor's grandfather and thereby enlisted the support of the imperial court. On January 3, 1868 the conspirators seized the gates of the Imperial Palace in the city of Kyoto, convened a council stripping the shogun of his lands and of his position on the council, and ended the shogunate. The council proclaimed the fiction of "restoring" the responsibility for governing Japan to the emperor, although that responsibility had previously actually been the shogun's. That event is known as the Meiji Restoration, and it marks the beginning of what is termed the Meiji Era: the period of rule of the new emperor.

———

After that coup gave them control of Kyoto, the immediate problem facing the Meiji leaders was to establish control over all of Japan. While the shogun himself accepted defeat, many others did not. The result was a civil war between armies supporting and armies opposing the new imperial government. Only when the last opposition forces on Japan's northern main island of Hokkaido had been defeated in June 1869 did foreign powers recognize the imperial government as the government of Japan. And only then could Meiji leaders proceed with their efforts to reform their country.

At the beginning of the Meiji Era, much about Japan was up for grabs. Some leaders wanted an autocratic emperor; others wanted a figurehead emperor with actual power in the hands of a council of "advisors" (that was the solution that eventually prevailed); and still another proposal was for Japan to become a republic without an emperor. Some Japanese who had come to appreciate Western alphabets proposed that alphabets replace Japan's beautiful but complex writing system, consisting of Chinese-derived characters combined with two Japanese syllabaries. Some Japanese wanted to launch a war against Korea without delay; others argued for waiting. The samurai wanted their private militias to be retained and used; others wanted to disarm and abolish the samurai.

Out of this turmoil of conflicting proposals, the Meiji leaders decided soon in favor of three basic principles. First, although some of the leaders had been among the hotheads who wanted immediately to expel Westerners, realism quickly prevailed. It became as clear to Meiji leaders as it had been to the shogun that Japan was presently incapable of expelling Westerners. Before that could be done, Japan had to become strong by adopting Western sources of strength, meaning not just guns themselves but also far-reaching political and social reforms that provided the underpinnings of Western strength.

Second, an ultimate goal of Meiji leaders was to revise the unequal treaties that had been imposed upon Japan by the West. But that required Japan to be strong *and* to be seen by the West as a legitimate Western-style state, with a Western-style constitution and laws. For example, Britain's foreign secretary, Lord Granville, bluntly told Japanese negotiators that Britain would recognize Japanese "jurisdiction over British subjects [resident in Japan] in precise proportion to their [Japanese] advancement in enlightenment and civilization," as judged by Britain according to British standards of advancement. It ended up taking 26 years from the Meiji coup until the time when Japan could get the West to revise the unequal treaties.

The third basic principle of Meiji leaders was to identify, adopt, and modify, in each sphere of life, the foreign model that was best matched to Japanese conditions and values. Meiji Japan variously borrowed especially from British, German, French, and American models. Different foreign countries ended up as models in different spheres: for instance, the new Japanese navy and army became modeled on the British navy and the German army, respectively. Conversely, within a given sphere, Japan often tried a succession of different foreign models: for example, in creating a Japanese civil law code, the Justice Ministry relied on a French scholar to produce a first draft, and then turned instead to a German model for the next draft.

Meiji Japan's borrowing from the West was massive, conscious, and planned. Some of the borrowing involved bringing Westerners to Japan: for instance, importing Western schoolteachers to teach or to advise on education, and bringing two German scholars to help write a Japanese constitution drawing heavily on Germany's constitution. But more of the borrowing involved Japanese traveling as observers to Europe and the U.S. A crucial step, undertaken just two years after the Meiji government had consolidated its power, was the Iwakura Mission of 1871–1873 (Plate 3.3). Consisting of 50 government representatives, it toured the U.S. and a dozen European countries, visited factories and government offices, met U.S. President Grant and European government leaders, and published a five-volume report providing Japan with detailed accounts of a wide range of Western practices. The mission announced its purpose as being "to select from the various institutions prevailing among enlightened nations such as are best suited to our present condition." When war broke out between France and Prussia in 1870, Japan even sent two observers with a much narrower purpose: to watch first-hand how Europeans fought.

A by-product of these foreign travels was that Japanese with overseas experience tended to become Meiji Japan's leaders, both in government and in private spheres. For example, of the two most important younger men who rose to power in the Meiji government in the 1880's, Ito Hirobumi (who led the design of Japan's new constitution) had made several long visits to Europe, while Yamagata Aritomo (who became prime minister) had studied military science in Germany. Godai Tomoatsu used his European experience to become president of Osaka's chamber of commerce and a Japanese railroad and mining entrepreneur, while Shibusawa Eiichi (financial comptroller of an 1867 Japanese mission in Paris) went on to develop Japanese banking and textile industries.

In order to make this massive borrowing from the West palatable to Japanese traditionalists, innovations and borrowings in Meiji Japan were often claimed to be not new at all, but just returns to Japan's traditional ways. For example, when the emperor himself in 1889 promulgated Japan's first constitution, based heavily on the German constitution, in his speech he invoked his ascent "to the Throne of a lineal succession unbroken for ages eternal," and "the right of sovereignty of the State [that] we have inherited from Our Ancestors." Similarly, new rituals invented for the imperial court during the Meiji Era were claimed to be timeless old court rituals.

This reframing of innovations as supposedly retained traditions — the phenomenon of "invented traditions" often invoked by innovators in other countries besides Japan — contributed to the success of Meiji leaders in carrying out drastic changes. The cruel fact was that the leaders faced a dangerous situation when they assumed power in January 1868. Japan was at risk of attacks by foreign powers, at risk from the civil war between the bakufu's opponents and its supporters, at risk of wars between domains, and at risk of revolts by groups threatened with losing their former rank and power. Abolition of the samurai's privileges did provoke several samurai rebellions, the most serious of them the Satsuma revolt of 1877. Armed peasant uprisings did break out periodically in the 1870's. But opposition to Meiji reforms turned out to be less violent than might have been anticipated. Meiji leaders proved skilled at buying off, co-opting, or reconciling their actual or potential opponents. For instance, Enomoto Takeaki, the admiral of the fleet that held out on Hokkaido against Meiji forces until 1869, ended up being absorbed into Meiji ranks as a cabinet minister and envoy.

———

Let's now consider what selective changes actually became adopted in Meiji Japan. The changes affected most spheres of Japanese life: the arts, clothing, domestic politics, the economy, education, the emperor's role, feudalism, foreign policy, government, hairstyles, ideology, law, the military, society, and technology. The most urgent changes, effected or launched within the first few years of the Meiji Era, were to create a modern national army, to abolish feudalism, to found a national system of education, and to secure income for the government by tax reform. Attention then shifted to reforming the law codes, designing a constitution, expanding overseas, and undoing the unequal treaties. In parallel with this attention to pressing practical matters, Meiji leaders also began to address the challenge of creating an explicit ideology to enlist the support of Japan's citizens.

Military reform began with purchasing modern Western equipment, enlisting French and German officers to train the army, and (later) experimenting with French and British models to develop a modern Japanese navy. The result illustrates Meiji skill at selecting the best foreign model: instead of selecting just one foreign country's armed forces as the model for all branches of the Japanese military, Japan ended up modeling its army on Germany's army but modeling its navy on Britain's navy (because in late 19th-century Europe Germany had the strongest army but Britain had the strongest navy!). As one example, when Japan wanted to learn how to build the fast battleships called battle-cruisers invented in Britain, Japan commissioned a British shipyard to design and build the first Japanese battle-cruiser, then used it as the model for building three more battle-cruisers in three different Japanese shipyards.

A national conscription law, adopted in 1873 and based on European models, provided for a national army of men armed with guns and serving for three years. Formerly, each feudal domain had had its own private militia of samurai swordsmen, useless in modern war but still a threat to the Japanese national government (Plate 3.4). Hence the samurai were first forbidden to carry swords or to administer private punishment, then hereditary occupations (including that of being a samurai) were abolished, then the ex-samurai were paid off in government stipends, and finally those stipends were converted to interest-bearing government bonds.

Another urgent order of business was to end feudalism. To make Japan strong required building a centralized Western-style state. That posed a delicate problem, because as of January 1868 the only real powers of the new imperial government were those just surrendered by the shogun; other powers remained with the daimyo (the feudal lords). Hence in March 1868 four daimyo, including those of Satsuma and Choshu who had instigated the Meiji Restoration, were persuaded to offer their lands and people to the emperor by an ambiguously worded document. When the emperor accepted that offer in July, the other daimyo were commanded to make the same offer, and as a sop they were then appointed as "governors" of their former feudal domains. Finally, in August 1871 the daimyo were told that their domains (and governorships) would now be swept away and replaced with centrally administered prefectures. But the daimyo were allowed to keep 10% of their former domains' assessed incomes, while being relieved of the burden of all the expenses that they had formerly borne. Thus, within three-and-a-half years, centuries of Japanese feudalism were dismantled.

The emperor remained the emperor: that didn't change.

However, he was no longer cloistered in Kyoto's Imperial Palace: he was transferred to the effective capital of Edo, renamed Tokyo. In his 45 years of rule, the emperor made 102 trips outside of Tokyo and around Japan, compared with a total of just three trips by all emperors combined during the 265 years of the Tokugawa Era (1603–1868).

Education was subject to big reforms, with big consequences. For the first time in its history, Japan acquired a national system of education. Compulsory elementary schools were established in 1872, followed by the founding of Japan's first university in 1877, middle schools in 1881, and high schools in 1886. The school system at first followed the highly centralized French model, shifting in 1879 to the American school model of local control, and then in 1886 to a German model. The end result of that educational reform is that Japan today ties for having the world's highest percentage of literate citizens (99%), despite also having the world's most complicated and hard-to-learn writing system. While the new national system of education was thus inspired by the West, its proclaimed purposes were thoroughly Japanese: to make Japanese people loyal and patriotic citizens revering their emperor and imbued with a sense of national unity.

A more mundane but equally important purpose of educational reform was to train recruits for jobs in government, and to develop Japan's human capital so that Japan could rise in the world and prosper. In the 1880's, recruitment for the central government bureaucracy became based on an exam testing Western knowledge, rather than testing knowledge of Confucian philosophy. National education, along with the government's official abolition of hereditary occupations, undermined Japan's traditional class divisions, because now higher education rather than birth became the stepping-stone to high government office. Partly as a result, among the world's 14 large rich democracies today, Japan is the one with the most equal division of wealth, and the one with proportionately the fewest billionaires in its population; the U.S. lies far at the opposite extreme in both respects.

The Meiji government's remaining top priority was to devise an income stream to finance its government operations. Japan had never had Western-style national taxes. Instead, each daimyo had separately taxed his own lands to fund his own operating costs, while the shogun had similarly taxed just his own lands but also demanded additional money for specific purposes from all the daimyo. Yet the Meiji government had just relieved the ex-daimyo of their responsibilities as "governors," had converted their ex-domains into prefectures, and had decreed that those prefectures would now be administered by the central government, leaving the ex-daimyo with no need (so said Meiji leaders) for revenues to finance administrative operations of their own. Hence the Meiji Finance Ministry reasoned that it now needed at least as much annual revenue as the shogun and all the daimyo combined had previously extracted. It achieved that aim in a Western manner, by imposing a national 3% land tax. Japanese farmers periodically complained and rioted, because they had to pay cash every year regardless of the size of the harvest. But they might have considered themselves lucky if they could have foreseen modern Western tax rates. For example, here in my state of California we pay a state 1% property tax, *plus* a state income tax of up to 12%, *plus* a national income tax of currently up to 44%.

Less urgent matters included substituting a Western-style legal system for Japan's traditional system of justice. Law courts with appointed judges were introduced in 1871, followed by a Supreme Court in 1875. Criminal, commercial, and civil law reforms followed different paths of Westernization by experimenting with different foreign models. The criminal law code was initially reformed on a French model, then changed to a German model; the commercial law code used a German model; and the civil law code used French, British, and indigenous Japanese concepts before ending up as German-inspired. In each case, challenges influencing the choices included finding solutions compatible with Japanese views, plus adopting Western institutions in order to achieve international respectability necessary for revising the unequal treaties. For instance, that required abolishing traditional Japanese torture and broad use of the death penalty, which the West no longer considered respectable.

Modernization of Japan's infrastructure began early in the Meiji Era. The year 1872 saw the founding of a national post system, and the building of Japan's first railroad and its first telegraph line, followed by establishment of a national bank in 1873. Gas street lighting was installed in Tokyo. The government also got involved in Japan's industrialization by setting up factories to produce bricks, cement, glass, machinery, and silk with Western machinery and methods. After Japan's successful war of 1894–1895 against China, government industrial spending came to concentrate on war-related industries such as coal, electricity, gun factories, iron, steel, railroads, and shipyards.

Government reform was especially important if Japan was to achieve international respectability — and especially challenging. Cabinet government was introduced in 1885. Already in 1881, it had been announced that a constitution would be forthcoming, partly in response to public pressure. It then took eight years to devise a Western-style constitution in harmony with Japanese circumstances. The solution to that challenge depended on taking as a model not the U.S. constitution but the German constitution, because German emphasis on a strong emperor corresponded to Japanese conditions. Japan's constitution invoked Japanese belief that its emperor was descended from the gods through an unbroken line of previous emperors extending back millennia in time. In a ceremony taking place in the imperial palace's audience chamber, on a date (February 11) that was the 2,549th anniversary of the day traditionally associated with the empire's founding, the emperor himself invoked his ancestors and presented the scroll of the new constitution to the prime minister, as the emperor's gift to Japan. Present at the ceremony were representatives of the foreign diplomatic corps and foreign community, to make sure that they did not miss the point. Japan was now a civilized nation with a constitutional government, equal to the world's other constitutional governments (and — hint hint — no longer to be singled out by unequal treaties).

Like other spheres of Japanese life, Japanese culture became a mosaic of new Western elements and traditional Japanese elements. Western clothing and hairstyles are overwhelmingly prevalent in Japan today and were adopted quickly — by Japanese men (Plates 3.5, 3.6). For instance, a group photograph taken of five members of the Iwakura Mission in 1872, only four years after the Meiji Restoration and only 19 years after Commodore Perry's arrival, shows four of the members with Western suits, ties, top-hats, and hairstyle, and only one (Iwakura himself) still in Japanese robes and with his hair in a traditional Japanese top-knot (Plate 3.3). In the arts, traditional Japanese music, painting, woodblock prints, kabuki theater, and Noh plays survived alongside Western ballroom dancing, military bands, orchestras, operas, theater, painting, and novels.

Any nation risks falling apart if its citizens do not feel joined by some unifying national ideology. Each nation has its own familiar ideals and phrases responding to that task of creating a unifying ideology. For example, American ideals have included democracy, equality, freedom, liberty, and opportunity, as captured in phrases such as "rags to riches," "melting pot," "land of liberty," "land of equal opportunity," and "land of unlimited possibilities." Particularly in newly independent countries such as Indonesia (Chapter 5), or in countries undergoing rapid change such as Meiji Japan, governments consciously formulate and promote unifying national ideologies. How did Meiji Japan do it?

The need for a unifying Meiji ideology was expressed in a widely circulated 1891 commentary on the emperor's 1890 Rescript on Education: "Japan...is a small country. Since there are now those that swallow countries with impunity, we must consider the whole world our enemy...thus any true Japanese must have a sense of public duty, by which he values his life lightly as dust, advances spiritedly, and is ready to sacrifice himself for the sake of the nation.... The purpose of the Rescript is to strengthen the basis of the nation by cultivating the virtues of filiality and fraternal love, loyalty and sincerity, and to prepare for any emergency by nurturing the spirit of collective patriotism.... If we do not unite the people, fortifications and warships will not suffice. If we do unite them, then even a million formidable foes will be unable to harm us."

In the last two decades of the Meiji Era, having dealt with mundane but urgent issues such as tax reform and law codes, the Meiji government was able to devote more attention to that task of imbuing Japanese with a sense of public duty. That was achieved partly by government support for traditional religion, and even more by government attention to education. Traditional Japanese religion served to unify Japanese people by teaching shared beliefs in the emperor's divine descent, patriotism, civic duty, filial piety, respect for the gods, and love of country. Hence the government promoted the traditional Shinto religion and Confucian philosophy, subsidized the leading national Shinto shrines, and appointed their priests. Those values, associated with worship of the emperor as a living god, were featured prominently in the uniform national textbooks prescribed at every level of Japanese education.

———

Now that we've summarized the main components of selective change in Meiji Japan — other than changes in policies of overseas expansion, to be examined in the following pages — let's reflect on Meiji changes and dispel some possible misunderstandings.

The goal of Meiji leaders was emphatically not to "Westernize" Japan, in the sense of converting it into a European society far from Europe — unlike Australia's British colonists, whose goal was indeed to convert Australia into a British society far from Britain (Chapter 7). Instead, the Meiji goal was to adopt many Western features, but to modify them to suit Japanese circumstances, and to retain much of traditional Japan. Those adopted and modified Western features were grafted onto a Japanese core retained from Japanese history. For example, Japan didn't need Europe as a model of literacy and urbanization: Tokugawa Japan already had high literacy, and the bakufu capital city Edo (renamed as Tokyo) was already the world's largest city a century and a half before Commodore Perry's arrival. Nor did Meiji Westernization consist of blindly imitating specific pieces of Western institutions: Meiji leaders operated from a remarkably clear overall understanding of Western society that underlay the Western military, educational, and other institutions adopted in Japan with modifications.

Meiji Japan was able to draw on many models. Those included multiple Western models: variously Britain, Germany, France, and the U.S. in different spheres. There were also many indigenous Japanese models on which to draw: late Tokugawa Japan consisted of 240 separate domains, differing in their tax policies and in other institutions. In addition to those positive models, Meiji Japan profited from an important negative model: China, whose fate of domination by the West made clear what Japan wanted to avoid.

Meiji reforms were directed at two different "audiences": a

domestic Japanese audience, and an overseas Western audience. On the one hand, the reforms were aimed at Japan itself: in order to strengthen the nation militarily and economically, and to imbue Japanese people with a unifying ideology. On the other hand, the reforms also aimed to make Western countries respect Japan as an equal, because Japan had now adopted Western institutions that the West respected. Those institutions included ones of basic governance such as a Western-style constitution and law codes; and ones of outward appearance, such as men's Western clothing and hairstyles, and the emperor's celebrating a Western-style wedding with a Western-style single wife, the empress. (Previous Japanese emperors had openly had many concubines.)

While Meiji leaders were in agreement on their overall goal of strengthening Japan so that it could resist the West, they did not start off with an encompassing blueprint. Instead, Meiji reforms were devised and adopted piecemeal in stages: first, creating a national army, an income stream, and a national system of education, and abolishing feudalism; then, a constitution, and civil and criminal law codes; and even later, overseas expansion by wars (to be discussed in the next pages). Nor were all of these reforms adopted smoothly and unanimously: there was internal conflict in Meiji Japan, such as the already mentioned samurai rebellions and peasant uprisings.

———

The remaining major line of selective change in the Meiji Era that we have not already considered was Japan's transformation from being a target to being an agent of overseas expansion and military aggression. We saw that Tokugawa Japan isolated itself and had no aspirations of overseas conquests. In 1853 Japan appeared to be at imminent risk from militarily much stronger foreign powers.

By the beginning of the Meiji Era in 1868, however, Japan's

military reforms and industrial build-up had removed that imminent risk and permitted instead a stepwise expansion. The first step was Japan's formal annexation, in 1869, of the northern island of Hokkaido, originally inhabited by a people (the Ainu) quite different from the Japanese, but already partly controlled by the bakufu. In 1874 a punitive military expedition was sent to the island of Taiwan, whose aborigines had killed dozens of Ryukyu fishermen. At the end of the expedition, however, Japan pulled back its forces and refrained from annexing Taiwan. In 1879 the Ryukyu Islands themselves (the archipelago several hundred miles south of Japan) were annexed. From 1894 to 1895 Meiji Japan fought and won its first overseas war, against China, and did annex Taiwan.

Japan's 1904–1905 war against Russia enabled Meiji Japan for the first time to test itself against a Western power; both Japan's navy and its army defeated the Russians (Plates 3.7, 3.8). That was a milestone in world history: the defeat of a major European power by an Asian power in an all-out war. By the resulting peace treaty, Japan annexed the southern half of Sakhalin Island and gained control of the South Manchurian Railroad. Japan established a protectorate over Korea in 1905 and annexed it in 1910. In 1914 Japan conquered Germany's Chinese sphere of influence and Micronesian island colonies in the Pacific Ocean (Plate 3.9). Finally, in 1915 Japan presented China with the so-called Twenty-One Demands that would have converted China virtually into a vassal state; China gave in to some but not all of the demands.

Japan had already considered attacking China and Korea before 1894 but drew back, because it recognized that it wasn't strong enough and that it risked giving European powers an excuse to intervene. The only occasion on which Meiji Japan overestimated its strength was in 1895, at the end of its war against China. The concessions that Japan had extracted from China then included China's ceding to Japan the Liaotung Peninsula, which controls the sea and land routes between China and Korea. But France, Russia, and Germany reacted by joining together to force Japan to abandon the peninsula, which Russia proceeded to lease from China three years later. That humiliating setback made Japan aware of its weakness, standing alone, vis-à-vis European powers. Hence in 1902 Japan made an alliance with Britain, for protection and insurance, before attacking Russia in 1904. Even with the security offered by that British alliance, Japan waited to issue its demands against China, until the armed forces of European powers were tied up in World War One and unable to threaten intervention, as they had done in 1895.

In short, Japan's military expansion in the Meiji Era was consistently successful, because it was guided at every step by honest, realistic, cautious, informed self-appraisal of the relative strengths of Japan and its targets, and by a correct assessment of what was realistically possible for Japan. Now, compare that successful Meiji Era expansion with Japan's situation as of August 14, 1945. On that date Japan was at war simultaneously with China, the U.S., Britain, Russia, Australia, and New Zealand (as well as with many other countries that had declared war against Japan but were not actively fighting). That was a hopeless combination of enemies against which to fight. Much of the Japanese army had been pinned down for years in China. American bombers had gutted most major Japanese cities. The two atomic bombs had obliterated Hiroshima and Nagasaki. A British/American fleet was bombarding the Japanese coast. Russian armies were advancing against weak Japanese resistance in Manchuria and Sakhalin. Australian and New Zealand troops were mopping up Japanese garrisons on some Pacific islands. Almost all of Japan's larger warships and merchant fleet had been sunk or knocked out of service. More than 3 million Japanese people had been killed.

It would have been bad enough if blunders of Japanese foreign policy had been responsible for Japan being attacked by all those countries. Instead, Japan's blunders were worse: Japan itself had been the one to attack those countries. In 1937 Japan launched a full-scale war against China. It fought two brief but bloody border wars with Russia in 1938 and 1939. In 1941 Japan simultaneously and suddenly attacked the U.S. and Britain and the Netherlands, even while Japan was still susceptible to resumption of fighting with Russia. Japan's attack on Britain automatically resulted in declarations of war by Britain's Pacific dominions Australia and New Zealand; Japan proceeded to bomb Australia. In 1945 Russia did attack Japan. On August 15, 1945 Japan finally bowed to the long-delayed but inevitable outcome, and surrendered. Why did Japan from 1937 onwards blunder stepwise into such an unrealistic and ultimately unsuccessful military expansion, when Meiji Japan from 1868 onwards had carried out stepwise such a realistic and successful military expansion?

There are numerous reasons: the successful war against Russia, disillusionment with the Treaty of Versailles, the collapse of Japan's export-led economic growth in 1929, and others. But one additional reason is especially relevant to this book: a difference between Meiji-Era Japan and the Japan of the 1930's and 1940's, in knowledge and capacity for honest self-appraisal on the part of Japanese leaders. In the Meiji Era many Japanese, including leaders of Japan's armed forces, had made visits abroad. They thereby obtained detailed first-hand knowledge of China, the U.S., Germany, and Russia and their armies and navies. They could make an honest appraisal of Japan's strength compared to the strengths of those other countries. Then, Japan attacked only when it could be confident of success. In contrast, in the 1930's the Japanese army on the Asian mainland was commanded by young hothead officers who didn't have experience abroad (unless in Nazi Germany), and who didn't obey orders from experienced Japanese leaders in Tokyo.

Those young hotheads didn't know first-hand the industrial and military strength of the U.S. and of Japan's other prospective opponents. They didn't understand American psychology, and they considered the U.S. a nation of shopkeepers who wouldn't fight.

Quite a few older leaders of the Japanese government and armed forces (especially of the navy) in the 1930's did know the strength of the U.S. and Europe first-hand. The most poignant moment of my first visit to Japan, in 1998, came when my dinner table partner one evening turned out to be a retired Japanese steel executive, at that time in his 90's, who recalled for me his visits to American steel factories in the 1930's. He told me that he had been stunned to discover that the U.S.'s manufacturing capacity for high-quality steel was 50 times Japan's, and that that fact alone had convinced him that it would be insane for Japan to go to war with the U.S.

But Japan's older leaders with overseas experience in the 1930's were intimidated and dominated, and several were assassinated, by young hotheads lacking overseas experience — much as shishi hotheads in the late 1850's and 1860's had assassinated and intimidated Japan's leaders then. Of course, the shishi had no more overseas experience of the strength of foreign countries than did Japan's young officers of the 1930's. The difference was that shishi attacks against Westerners provoked the bombardments of Kagoshima and Shimonoseki Strait by powerful Western warships, which demonstrated convincingly even to the shishi that their strategy had been unrealistic. In the 1930's there were no such foreign bombardments of Japan to force realism upon the young officers who had not been overseas.

In addition, the historical experience of the generation of Japanese leaders who came of age in Meiji Japan was virtually the opposite of the experience of Japan's leaders of the 1930's. Meiji leaders had spent their formative years in a weak Japan at risk of attack by strong potential enemies. But to Japan's leaders of the 1930's, war instead meant the intoxicating success of the Russo-Japanese War, the destruction of Russia's Pacific fleet in Port Arthur harbor by a surprise attack that served as the model for Japan's surprise attack against the American fleet at Pearl Harbor (Plate 3.7), and the spectacular destruction of Russia's Baltic fleet by the Japanese navy in the Battle of Tsushima Strait (Plate 3.8). When we discuss Germany in Chapter 6, we shall encounter another example of successive generations within the same country holding drastically different political views as the result of different historical experiences.

Thus, part — not all, but part — of the reason for Japan initiating World War Two against such hopeless odds was that young army leaders of the 1930's lacked the knowledge base and historical experience necessary for honest, realistic, cautious self-appraisal. The result was disastrous for Japan.

———

Meiji Japan strikingly illustrates parallels to most of the dozen factors identified in Chapter 1 as affecting outcomes of individual crises. For one factor (factor #5 of Table 1.2) Japan provides *the* outstanding illustration among our seven countries; for another factor (#7), it provides one of the two outstanding illustrations; seven other factors (#1, 3, 4, 6, 9, 10, and 11) are also important; and one factor (#12) operated both positively and negatively.

More than any other nation discussed in this book, Meiji Japan illustrates change by borrowing from foreign models (factor #5), after careful comparison of different models in order to identify which one best suited Japanese circumstances in a particular sphere. The result was that Japan's constitution and army came to be based on German models, its fleet on the British model, its initial draft civil law code on the French model, and its 1879 educational reforms on the American model. Even the U.S. Declaration of Independence appears to have served as a model for a government reform proposal drafted in 1870 by Itagaki Taisuke and Fukuoka Kotei, who began their proposal with a preamble stating that all men were by rights equal, from which they went on to draw many conclusions. (Think of the second sentence of our Declaration of Independence: "We hold these truths to be self-evident, that all men are created equal...," leading to many conclusions.) Itagaki's and Fukuoka's proposed American model of government was not adopted, but many other foreign models did get adopted.

We discussed in the preceding section the role of realistic self-appraisal (factor #7) in Meiji Japan, rivaled only by its role in Finland. Our discussion made clear that successful national self-appraisal requires two elements. One is a willingness to confront painful truths: in Japan's case, the truth that the hated barbarians were stronger than Japan, and that Japan could gain strength only by learning from those barbarians. The other prerequisite is knowledge. It wasn't enough that Meiji leaders, and the shishi of the decade preceding the Meiji Restoration, possessed the willingness to confront the painful truth of Western military strength: they required knowledge of that strength from first-hand observation or experience. But Japan's young army officers of the 1930's lacked first-hand knowledge of Western military strength. Meiji realistic self-appraisal was linked to another of our outcome predictor factors: widespread Japanese consensus about the crisis with which Commodore Perry's visit confronted Japan (factor #1).

Meiji Japan illustrates well the necessity of building a fence, and of adopting change selectively (factor #3). Massive change was adopted in many spheres of Meiji society, including the economic, legal, military, political, social, and technological spheres. But other features of traditional Japan were retained in the Meiji Era, including Confucian morality, emperor worship, ethnic homogeneity, filial piety, Shintoism, and Japan's writing system. Initially, changes were proposed for some of those features, too, such as proposals to make Japan a republic, and to adopt a Western alphabet. But Japan quickly built a fence separating traditional features to be retained from those considered in need of change. While the desire for change was strong, the desire to remain traditional was also so strong that some of the changes had to be portrayed as fictitious retentions of "invented traditions" in order to make them palatable. This coexistence of drastic change with conservative retention also illustrates the factor of situation-specific national flexibility (factor #10).

Along with the value of foreign models, Meiji Japan illustrates the value of foreign help (factor #4). Innumerable examples include the Nagasaki-based British trader Thomas Glover, who sent a group of 19 Satsuma men to study in England already in 1864; the many Westerners in Europe and the United States who hosted Japanese visitors; the German advisors Albert Mosse and Hermann Roesler, who came to Japan in 1886 to help Ito Hirobumi devise a constitution for Japan; and the British shipyard Vickers's construction of Japan's first battle-cruiser *Kongo*, which then served as the model for the battle-cruisers *Haruna*, *Hiei*, and *Kirishima* to be built in Japan.

Meiji Japan, and Japan today, illustrate strong national identity (factor #6). Japanese people and their leaders considered Japan unique, superior, and set apart from the rest of the world. That shared belief enabled Japanese to endure the stresses of the Meiji Era, sometimes differing about how best to secure Japan's future, but never doubting their country's value.

Meiji Japan exemplifies patience, the willingness to tolerate initial failure, and persistence until a workable solution is found (factor #9). Japan's initial response to the foreign threats of the 1850's and 1860's was to try to keep the foreigners out, then (once foreigners had been admitted at specific Japanese treaty ports) to try to expel them again. But it gradually became clear, and accepted by the bakufu and the shishi and Meiji leaders, that that approach didn't work, and that a different approach was necessary: opening Japan to the West, learning from the West, and thereby strengthening Japan. Similarly, Meiji efforts to devise law codes, a national system of education, and a constitution took years of drafts, experimentation, and changes. In each of those three spheres the Meiji government initially tried one or more foreign models, discarded them as inappropriate to Japanese circumstances, and finally settled on a different foreign model: e.g., the civil law code, which began with French-inspired and British-inspired drafts and ended up German-inspired.

Non-negotiable core values (factor #11) united the Japanese in their willingness to make sacrifices. High among those values was loyalty to the emperor. That was dramatically illustrated at the end of World War Two, when the U.S. demanded unconditional surrender. Even after the two atomic bombs, and in a hopeless military situation, Japan still insisted on one condition: "that the said [surrender] declaration does not include any demand which prejudices the prerogatives of His Majesty as a sovereign ruler." Without acceptance of that condition, Japan was prepared to resist the threatened U.S. invasion of the Japanese mainland. The strength of Japanese core values was also illustrated in World War Two by the willingness of large numbers of Japanese soldiers to commit suicide, far beyond the willingness of the soldiers of any other modern nation. Best-known were the kamikaze pilots of conventional aircraft and the baka pilots of rocket-powered gliders, who crashed their bomb-carrying machines into enemy warships; and the kaiten sailors who rode and piloted torpedoes launched from Japanese ships into enemy warships. The high-tech kamikaze, baka, and kaiten suicide weapons introduced only towards the end of World

War Two were preceded by several years of low-tech suicides, when Japanese soldiers feigning surrender detonated hidden hand grenades to kill their captors as well as themselves. All of those forms of suicide served immediate military purposes by killing enemy troops. In addition, defeated Japanese soldiers and officers also routinely killed themselves without killing any enemy, in deference to the inculcated value of "no surrender." For instance, of the 2,571 elite Japanese troops defending Tarawa atoll in November 1943 against invading American troops, 2,563 died, many of the last ones by suicide, leaving only eight to be taken prisoner.

Japan, as an island archipelago without land borders, is in a relatively favorable situation with regard to geopolitical constraints (factor #12), compared to nations such as Finland and Germany, which do share land borders with other countries. We saw in the last chapter that Finland's long border with Russia constitutes Finland's fundamental problem. We'll see in Chapter 6 that land borders with powerful neighbors have also been a main theme of German history. Nevertheless, powerful other nations did constitute the fundamental problem for Tokugawa and Meiji Japan, even though those other nations lay half-way around the world from Japan, separated by the world's oceans. Already in the 19th century, and even more so in today's modern world, technology modifies geopolitical constraints — but does not eliminate them completely.

———

Let's conclude our discussion of Meiji Japan by asking where it falls with respect to four questions arising for national crises and not for individual crises: revolution versus evolution, leadership, group conflict and reconciliation, and presence or absence of a unified vision.

National crises may take the form of violent revolution (Chile in

1973, Indonesia in 1965) or of peaceful evolution (post-war Australia). Meiji Japan is intermediate, but closer to the latter end of the continuum. The shogunate was ended on January 3, 1868 by a nearly bloodless coup. Some supporters of the shogun, but not the shogun himself, then resisted and were eventually defeated in a civil war lasting a year-and-a-half. But that civil war caused proportionally many fewer casualties than did the Indonesian coup and counter-coup of 1965, the Chilean coup of 1973 and its aftermath, or the Finnish Civil War of 1918.

There was no leader who dominated the Meiji Restoration to the degree that Hitler, Pinochet, and Suharto put their personal stamps on Nazi Germany, post-1973 Chile, and post-1965 Indonesia, respectively. Instead, at any one time there were multiple Meiji leaders, and there was a gradual leadership transition in the 1880's. The various leaders all shared the qualification of first-hand experience of the West, and they shared commitment to a basic strategy of strengthening Japan by selectively using foreign models. Japan's emperor remained a symbolic figurehead rather than an actual leader.

As for group conflict and reconciliation, from 1853 to 1868 there were disagreements about basic strategy within Japan. From around 1868 onwards, when the basic strategy became established, there were the normal disagreements arising in any country about policies to effect that strategy. Until 1877, some of those disagreements were resolved by violence: especially between the bakufu and the Satsuma-Choshu alliance until 1869, between shishi and Japanese moderates in the 1860's, and between the Meiji government and dissident samurai in the samurai revolts. The level of violence was again modest compared to that in Chile and Indonesia. Subsequent reconciliation between the opposing parties of those Japanese disagreements was much more complete than in Chile and far more so than in Indonesia: in part because many fewer people had been killed; and in part because Meiji government leaders went to more effort and displayed more skill in reconciling with their opponents than did Chile's and Indonesia's military leaders. Among the other countries discussed in this book, Finland after its 1918 civil war offers the closest parallel to Meiji Japan in dispelling the legacies of violent conflicts.

Resolutions of most national crises require numerous policy changes, which may either be adopted piecemeal or else may all be part of one unified vision. Meiji Japan is our case study that comes closest to the latter extreme of the unified vision. That isn't to say that Meiji leaders launched all of their policy changes simultaneously: they knew that some problems were more urgent than other problems. They began by creating an imperial army, implementing tax reform, and solving a few other pressing matters in the early 1870's, but did not unleash their first full-fledged overseas war until 1894. However, all of these policies stemmed from a principle on which agreement had been reached at the beginning of the Meiji Era: the need to strengthen Japan in many different spheres, by learning selectively from the West.

Meiji Japan has thus offered us a good second case for exploring the issues involved in resolving national crises through selective change. Finland (our first case) and Meiji Japan were similar in facing crises that exploded on one day, when an external military threat that had been developing for years suddenly materialized. Both Finns and Japanese have strong national identities and core values that they defended by sacrificing their lives against overwhelming odds; the Japanese were put to that test in World War Two rather than in the Meiji Era. Both Finns and Meiji Japanese were brutally honest and realistic. In some other respects, though, Finns and Meiji Japanese found themselves at opposite extremes. Meiji Japan received help from many nations, the very ones that threatened it; Finns received virtually no help during the Winter

War. Japan solved its problems by drawing on abundant models; Finland could draw on none. Japan's large population, economic strength, and distance from its enemies gave Japan the time and space necessary to achieve military equality with the nations threatening it; the proximity and relative sizes of Finland and Russia eliminated that option for Finland. In the next two chapters we shall turn to nations whose crises climaxed as suddenly as did those of Finland and Meiji Japan, but whose explosions were internal.

FIG. 4 *Map of Chile*

CHAPTER 4

A CHILE FOR ALL CHILEANS

Visiting Chile — Chile until 1970 — Allende — The
coup and Pinochet — Economics until "No!" —
After Pinochet — Pinochet's shadow — Crisis
framework — Returning to Chile

I n 1967 I spent a sabbatical in Chile, at a time when everything
there seemed peaceful. My Chilean hosts emphasized to me that
Chile was very different from other Latin American countries.
Chile had a long history of democratic government, they explained,
punctuated by only a few relatively bloodless military coups. Chile
didn't have frequent military governments, as did Peru and Argentina and other South and Central American countries. It rated as
the most politically stable country in all of Latin America.

Chileans identify with Europe and with the U.S., rather than
with Latin America. For instance, my visit to Chile was under a
University of Chile / University of California exchange program.
That program had been founded not just to recognize the geographic fact that Chile and California occupy similar positions in
the Mediterranean zones on the west coasts of their respective
continents — but also to acknowledge that Chile and California are

similar in their social atmosphere and political stability. My Chilean friends summed it up by the sentence "We Chileans know how to govern ourselves."

But just six years after my visit, in 1973, Chile was taken over by a military dictatorship that smashed previous world records for government-perpetrated sadistic torture. In the course of a military coup on September 11, Chile's democratically elected president committed suicide in the presidential palace. Not only did the Chilean junta kill Chileans in large numbers, torture them in larger numbers, devise vile new techniques of psychological and physical torture, and drive still more Chileans into exile. It also directed terrorist political killings outside Chile, including what was, until the World Trade Towers attack of September 11 of 2001 (coincidentally on the anniversary of Chile's coup), the only terrorist political killing of an American citizen on American soil (in Washington, DC, in 1976). That military government remained in power for almost 17 years.

Today, 29 years after the military government stepped down, Chile is struggling with that government's legacy. Some torturers and military leaders have been sent to prison, but the top military leaders were not imprisoned. Many Chileans, while deploring the torture, still view the military coup as necessary and unavoidable.

As you read about recent Chilean history in the following pages, you'll find many questions to keep in mind. How can one explain such an abrupt reversal of direction in a country with strong democratic traditions? How can Chile and other countries deal with a hideous recent past? How do this book's themes of national crisis and change play out in Chile? You'll recognize big selective changes in government economic policy and in political compromise. You'll also recognize some recurrent themes: honest self-appraisal and the lack thereof, freedom of action and the lack thereof, support or opposition from allies, and the role of a model or a presumed model. Two of Chile's leaders pose the recurrent historical question of whether leaders with distinctive personalities really change the course of history.

Most of all for my fellow Americans, Chile raises a frightening question to keep in mind as you read this chapter. The U.S. shares with Chile a strong democratic tradition. The yielding of that tradition to a dictatorship seemed utterly inconceivable to Chileans in 1967, just as it seems inconceivable to many Americans today. But it did happen in Chile, and the warning signs there were visible in retrospect. Could it also happen to the U.S.?

———

Let's begin with Chile's geography, history, and people. When you look at a map (page 140) you'll be struck by the fact that Chile is the longest and thinnest country in the world. While averaging only slightly more than 100 miles wide from west to east, it's nearly 3,000 miles long from north to south: almost as long as the U.S. is wide. Geographically, Chile is isolated from other countries by the high chain of the Andes in the east separating it from Argentina, and by the world's most barren desert in the north separating it from Bolivia and Peru. As a result, the only foreign wars that Chile has fought since achieving independence were two with its northern neighbors Bolivia and Peru in the years 1836–1839 and 1879–1883.

Despite that enormous length, Chile's productive farmland, agriculture, and population are concentrated in just a fraction of the country's area, within the Central Valley surrounding the capital city of Santiago. Only 60 miles from Santiago is Chile's main port of Valparaíso, the largest port on the west coast of South America. That geographic concentration, plus Chile's ethnic homogeneity mentioned below, has contributed to the unity of Chile, which has never had to deal with the geographic secessionist movements that have plagued most other countries of Chile's territorial extent.

Unlike South America's other countries, which are tropical, Chile shares with Argentina and Uruguay the two big advantages resulting from being located in the temperate zone at the southern end of South America. Those advantages are the higher average agricultural productivity and the lower average disease burden of temperate-zone areas compared to the tropics. As a consequence, Chile, Argentina, and Uruguay are the South American countries with the highest average per-capita incomes, even despite the chronically misguided economic policies of Argentine governments. Chile's relative prosperity arises from its agriculture, fisheries, minerals (more about that below), and manufacturing industries. Chile was already a big exporter of wheat to both California and Australia at the time of the Californian and Australian gold rushes of the 1840's, and has remained an agricultural exporter ever since. In recent decades Chile became the leading exporter of fish products in South America, and among the leading ones in the world. Chile eventually developed more manufacturing than did most other Latin American countries.

As for Chile's history and people, before European arrival the area that is now Chile supported only a sparse Native American population, lacking the cultural and political achievements of the rich, populous, powerful Inca Empire to the north in what is now Bolivia, Peru, and Ecuador. As in most of the rest of South and Central America, the Europeans who conquered and settled Chile were Spaniards, beginning in the 1540's. They imported few African slaves and intermarried with the Native Americans. Thus, unlike most other South American countries, Chile today is ethnically rather homogeneous and doesn't have large unmixed Native American or African minorities. Instead, Chileans are overwhelmingly Spanish and mestizo (meaning the mixed offspring of Spaniards and Native Americans), almost all of them Catholic, and almost all of them Spanish-speaking (unlike the large minorities speaking Native American languages in other Latin American countries). The largest minority group, the Mapuche Native Americans, constitutes only 1% of the population. Relatively few people are of other than Spanish and Native American ancestry.

Thus, Chile's geography, history, and people have all contributed to its unity. That's been a positive force in Chilean history, tending to make it less tumultuous than the histories of other Latin American countries. But a big negative force is one that Chile does share with many other Latin American countries: Spanish colonists established large land-holdings unlike the small farms established by European settlers of North America. Hence whereas the U.S. and Canada developed broad-based democratic governments from the very beginnings of their settlement by Europeans, in Chile a small oligarchy controlled most of the land, wealth, and politics. That concentration of political power has constituted a basic problem of Chilean history.

The underlying conflict between the intransigent oligarchy's traditional power and the rising power of other classes of society could either have been resolved through political compromise or have remained unsolved due to political stalemate. The latter outcome became increasingly frequent after Chile adopted in 1925 a new constitution that staggered the elections of the president, Senate, and lower house of Congress among different years. That well-intentioned idea, adopted in the name of the virtuous principle of balance of power, unfortunately resulted in the presidency, control of the Senate, and control of the lower house usually belonging to different political parties, depending on which party happened to be strongest in a particular election year. Two further subsequent changes in voting procedures increased the left-wing vote at the expense of the oligarchy's previous dominance. One change was that Chilean women finally obtained the right to vote in municipal elections in 1934, and in presidential elections in 1949. The other change was that voting in Chile had traditionally been open and in public, making it easy for land-owners to observe and influence how peasants voted. Hence adoption of voting by secret ballot in 1958 produced a leftwards shift.

Chilean political parties came to constitute three blocks — left, center, and right — that were similar in strength. Hence the government was variously either left-controlled or right-controlled, depending on which way the center chose to lean. Each of those blocks themselves contained more extreme and less extreme elements in conflict with each other. For example, within the left block, there were moderates (including most orthodox communists) who wanted to achieve change by constitutional means, competing with a radical left that was impatient and wanted revolutionary change. The army stayed out of modern Chilean political struggles — until 1973.

Chile's most recent presidential election before I lived there in 1967 had taken place in 1964. Exceptionally for Chile, where the leading presidential candidate had usually obtained just a plurality rather than a majority of votes, the 1964 election produced a big majority for the center's candidate, Eduardo Frei. He was regarded as well-intentioned and honest. Fear of the Marxist program and rising strength of the left-wing coalition led many right-wing voters to support Frei, and his party also won control of Congress's lower house in the 1965 elections. That raised hopes that Frei could adopt major change and end Chile's political gridlock.

Frei acted quickly to enable the Chilean government to buy 51% control of Chile's U.S.-owned copper-mining companies. He poured government investment into the Chilean economy, expanded access to educational opportunities for poor Chileans, succeeded in making Chile the biggest per-capita recipient of U.S.

economic aid in Latin America, and initiated a program of agrarian reform to break up large land-holdings. But Frei's ability to change Chilean society was restricted by Chile's long-standing political stalemate. On the one hand, Frei's program was too radical for the Chilean right. On the other hand, Frei wasn't radical enough for Chilean left-wingers, who wanted even more Chilean control of the copper-mining companies, even more government investment, and even more land redistribution. Under Frei, the Chilean economy continued to suffer from strikes, inflation, and shortages. For instance, during my months in Chile there were chronic meat shortages: even whale meat and tough beef were available in butchers' shops only occasionally, although sheep eyes were available every day of the week. Friends of mine fell victim to street violence. By 1969, all three Chilean political blocks — right, left, and center — were feeling frustrated by Chilean politics.

———

Developments in Chile from 1970 onwards were guided by two consecutive leaders who represented opposite extremes in politics and personality: Salvador Allende and Augusto Pinochet. They were similar only in sharing the fact that, to this day, it remains unclear why each of them acted as he did.

My understanding of Allende is based on public information about him, and on the recollections of a Chilean friend of mine who knew him and his family well. Allende was a quintessential Chilean professional, from an upper-middle-class family, rich, intelligent, idealistic, a good speaker, and endowed with an appealing personality (Plate 4.1). Already in his student days he became a declared Marxist, and a founder of Chile's Socialist Party, which was more extreme left-wing than Chile's Communist Party. But Allende rated as moderate by Chilean socialist standards, because his aim was to bring Marxist government to Chile by democratic means, not by armed revolution. He graduated medical school, and at the age of just 31 became Chile's minister of health, a job that he carried out with acknowledged success. He ran for president of Chile in 1952, 1958, and 1964 and was defeated all three times, twice by large margins. Hence by the time that Allende once again ran for president in 1970 at the head of a Popular Unity coalition of socialists, communists, radicals, and centrists, his reputation was that of an unthreatening perennial loser.

In the 1970 elections Allende received the largest share of the popular vote (36%), but only barely, because the much larger percentage (64%) of the electorate opposed to him was split between a right-wing coalition (35%, only 1.4% lower than Allende's share!) and a center coalition (28%). Since Allende had obtained only a plurality rather than a majority of votes, his election required confirmation by Congress, which did confirm him in return for a series of constitutional amendments guaranteeing freedom of the press and other freedoms. Despite the unthreatening personality and history of behavior of Allende himself, his election immediately provoked an unsuccessful attempt by the U.S. government to muster Chilean congressional support for rejecting his confirmation, and also provoked the emigration of the family of one of my Chilean friends who didn't care to wait and see what policies Allende would implement. Why was the election of that gentle moderate as president greeted with such a strong negative reaction?

The reason was Allende's and his party coalition's declared goal of bringing Marxist government to Chile: a prospect that horrified the Chilean right-wing and centrists, the Chilean armed forces, and the U.S. government. Today, decades after the collapse of the Soviet Union and the end of the Cold War, my younger readers who were not alive during the 1940's, 1950's, and 1960's cannot imagine why those powerful constituencies were so adamant that a Marxist government in Chile had to be forestalled by any means. The explanation begins with the fact that, after World War Two, the Soviet Union embarked on a policy of world domination and developed its own atomic bombs, hydrogen bombs, and intercontinental ballistic missiles. It attempted to strangle democratic West Berlin in 1948 by closing all road access. It carried out brutal communist take-overs and bloody crushings of revolts in Czechoslovakia, East Germany, Hungary, and Poland. It established dictatorships propped up by Soviet troops in those and other Eastern European countries.

Most dangerous of all, after Fidel Castro had installed a Marxist government in Cuba, Castro and Khrushchev began to station ballistic missiles to be armed with nuclear warheads in Cuba only 90 miles from the coast of the U.S. For one terrifying week in October 1962, seared unforgettably into the memories of all of us who were alive then and old enough to remember it, the world was closer to the brink of nuclear war than at any other time in history, before or since (Plate 4.2). Subsequent to the crisis, the gradual release of formerly classified information by both the U.S. and the Soviet Union made clear that we had been even closer to destruction than had been appreciated at the time. Unbeknownst to America's military leaders then, who knew that at least 162 missiles had already been stationed in Cuba but who thought that the missiles' nuclear warheads had not yet arrived, many of the warheads had actually already reached Cuba.

After the Cuban Missile Crisis, the Soviet Union responded by accelerating its programs to develop more powerful nuclear weapons and intercontinental ballistic missiles. The U.S. responded with the determination that never again would it tolerate the installation of a communist government in the Western Hemisphere. Any American president who failed to prevent such an installation would have been immediately impeached and removed from office for gross neglect of American interests, just as President

Kennedy was warned that he would be impeached if he failed to get Soviet missiles out of Cuba. Beginning in the 1960's, the U.S. also became preoccupied with communist threats in Vietnam and other Southeast Asian countries. The Chilean right, center, and armed forces were equally adamant that there would be no Marxist government in Chile, because they had seen what had happened to Cuba and to anti-Marxist Cubans after Castro had come to power. They wouldn't tolerate that history repeating itself in Chile.

The other U.S. motive for concern about Chile was that Chile's copper-mining companies, which are the biggest sector of the Chilean economy, were U.S.-owned and developed by U.S.-invested capital, because Chile in the 19th century lacked the capital and the technology to develop copper mines by itself. Under President Frei, Chile had already expropriated (and paid for) a 51% interest in the companies; the U.S. feared (correctly, as it turned out) that Allende might expropriate the remaining 49% without paying. Hence, from the 1960's onwards, through a program called the Alliance for Progress, the U.S. government supported Latin American (including Chilean) centrist reform parties and poured foreign aid money into Latin American countries governed by such parties, in order to pre-empt support for leftist revolutions. Under President Frei, Chile became the leading recipient of U.S. development money in Latin America.

Given those realities, what policies did Allende adopt upon becoming president? Even though he knew that his candidacy had been supported by only 36% of Chilean voters and had been opposed by the Chilean armed forces and the U.S. government, he rejected moderation, caution, and compromise, and instead pursued policies guaranteed to be anathema to those opposing forces. His first measure, with the unanimous support of Chile's Congress, was to nationalize the U.S.-owned copper companies without paying compensation; that's a recipe for making powerful

PLATE 0.1. Boston's Cocoanut Grove fire of November 28, 1942 killed 492 people in a crowded nightclub, and thereby led to the foundation of crisis therapy.

> Alueella pysäköinti sallittu
> vain alueen yritysten
> asiakkaille ja työntekijöille.
> **PITKÄAIKAIKAISPYSÄKÖINTI**
> **(yli 24h)**
> sallittu vain tontinhaltijan
> erityisluvalla
>
> Ajokone Oy, Herkkuravintola Takkatupa, Savarin Katsastus Oy

PLATE 2.1. A sign in the Finnish language, incomprehensible to non-Finns, but a focus of Finland's national identity.

PLATE 2.2. Finland in the Winter War called up as soldiers not just 20-year-olds, but also young teen-agers as well as older men and women.

PLATE 2.3. Viipuri, at that time Finland's second-largest city, under Russian bombardment in February 1940.

PLATE 2.4. The same scene as Plate 2.3, but decades later: former Finnish Viipuri, now a Russian city.

PLATE 2.5. Finnish soldiers mounted on skis, wearing white uniforms for camouflage, advancing through the forests against Soviet columns tied to roads.

PLATE 2.6. A Soviet motorized unit, ambushed and destroyed by Finnish ski troops.

PLATE 2.7. Finnish children evacuated to Sweden, in history's largest wartime evacuation of children.

PLATE 3.1. The shogun, actual ruler of Japan until his overthrow launched the Meiji Restoration.

PLATE 3.2. Japan's emperor who succeeded to the throne in 1867 and presided over the Meiji Era of selective change.

PLATE 3.3. Japan's Iwakura Mission to the U.S. and Europe in 1871–1873 to learn about Western practices. Already, all except one wore Western clothes.

PLATE 3.4. Samurai swordsmen, the traditional private militia of Japan until the Meiji Restoration.

PLATE 3.5. A Japanese sports team of the Meiji Era, already in Western garb.

PLATE 3.6. Japanese visitors to the U.S. in the Meiji Era, already in Western garb.

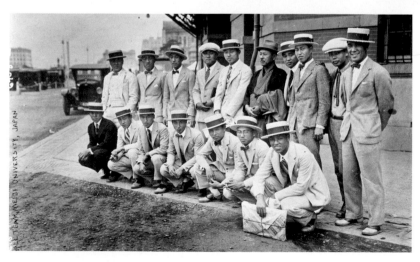

PLATE 3.7. A Russian battleship sunk in harbor by Japanese torpedoes in 1904 at the outset of the Russo-Japanese War.

PLATE 3.8. The 1905 Battle of Tsushima Strait, in which the Japanese navy annihilated a Russian fleet.

PLATE 3.9. German colonial soldiers captured by Japanese troops in 1914.

PLATE 4.1. Salvador Allende, Chile's democratically elected president who died during the coup of 1973.

PLATE 4.2. A Soviet nuclear missile base under construction in Cuba in 1962: a main reason why the U.S. and the Chilean right, center, and armed forces were adamantly determined to thwart President Allende's announced goal of installing a Marxist government in Chile.

PLATE 4.3. Chilean soldiers and tanks carrying out the September 11, 1973 coup in Chile's capital city of Santiago.

PLATE 4.4. General Augusto Pinochet (seated and wearing sunglasses), Chile's military dictator after the 1973 coup.

PLATE 4.5. The famous leftist Chilean folk singer Victor Jara, whom the military junta killed after the 1973 coup by chopping off all of his fingers and shooting him 44 times.

PLATE 4.6. A poster of the successful 1988 "No!" campaign opposed to the re-election of General Pinochet as Chile's president.

PLATE 4.7. General Pinochet returning to Chile in 2000, standing up from the wheelchair to which he was supposedly confined for medical reasons, and greeting Chilean generals present to congratulate him.

PLATE 5.1. Sukarno, Indonesia's founding president.

PLATE 5.3. Suharto, Indonesia's military dictator and eventually seven-term president after the failed 1965 coup.

PLATE 5.2. Sukarno (center) sitting with the leaders of China and Egypt, pursuing Third World anti-colonial politics.

PLATE 5.4. Indonesian soldiers rounding up presumed communists after the failed 1965 coup.

PLATE 5.5. Indonesia's huge Pancasila Monument, commemorating the seven generals killed during the failed 1965 coup.

PLATE 5.6. The skyscrapers of modern Jakarta, Indonesia's capital.

PLATE 5.7. The slums of modern Jakarta, Indonesia's capital.

international enemies. (Allende's pretext for not paying compensation was to label company profits already earned above a certain rate of return as "excess profits," to be counted against compensation and cancelling out the compensation owed.) He nationalized other big international businesses. He horrified the Chilean armed forces by bringing large numbers of Cubans into Chile, by carrying a personal machine gun given to him by Fidel Castro, and by inviting Castro to Chile for a visit that stretched out to five weeks. He froze prices (even of small consumer items like shoe-laces), replaced free-market elements of Chile's economy with socialist-style state planning, granted big wage increases, greatly increased government spending, and printed paper money to cover the resulting government deficits. He extended President Frei's agrarian reform by expropriating large estates and turning them over to peasant cooperatives. While that agrarian reform and others of Allende's goals were well-intentioned, they were carried out incompetently. For instance, one Chilean friend of mine, at that time still a 19-year-old not-yet-graduated student economist, was given major responsibility for setting Chilean prices of consumer goods. Another Chilean friend described Allende's policies as follows: "Allende had good ideas, but he executed them poorly. Although he correctly recognized Chile's problems, he adopted wrong solutions to those problems."

The result of Allende's policies was the spread of economic chaos, violence, and opposition to him. Government deficits covered by just printing money caused hyperinflation, such that real wages (i.e., wages adjusted for inflation) dropped below 1970 levels, even though wages not corrected for inflation nominally increased. Foreign and domestic investment, and foreign aid, dried up. Chile's trade deficit grew. Consumer goods, including even toilet paper, became scarce in markets, which were increasingly characterized by empty shelves and long queues. Rationing of food and even of water became severe. Workers, who had been Allende's natural supporters, joined the opposition and mounted nation-wide strikes; especially damaging to Chile's economy were strikes by copper miners and truckers. Street violence and predictions of a coup grew. On the left, Allende's radical supporters armed themselves; on the right, street posters went up proclaiming "Yakarta viene." Literally, that means "Jakarta is coming," a reference to Indonesian right-wing massacres of communists in 1965, to be discussed in the next chapter. That was an open threat by the Chilean right-wing to do the same to Chilean leftists, as it turned out that they actually did. Even Chile's powerful Catholic Church turned against Allende when he proposed mandatory educational curriculum reforms at private Catholic schools as well as at government schools, aimed at creating a generation of cooperative and unselfish Chilean "New Men" by sending students into the fields as manual laborers.

The outcome of all those developments was the 1973 coup that many of my Chilean friends characterize as inevitable, even though the form that the coup took was not inevitable. An economist friend summed up for me Allende's fall as follows: "Allende fell because his economic policies depended on populist measures that had failed again and again in other countries. They produced short-term benefits, at the cost of mortgaging Chile's future and creating runaway inflation." Many Chileans admired Allende and viewed him almost as a saint. But saintly virtues don't necessarily translate themselves into political success.

I introduced my account of Allende by saying that it remains unclear why he acted as he did. I keep asking myself: why on earth did Allende, an experienced politician and a moderate, pursue extremist policies that he knew were unacceptable to most Chileans, as well as to Chile's armed forces? My Chilean friends have suggested a couple of possible answers, but no one can be sure which answer, if any, truly explains Allende's reasoning. One possibility is that Allende's previous political successes misled him into thinking that he could defuse the opposition. He had already been successful as minister of health; he had initially assuaged congressional doubts over his election by constitutional amendments that didn't tie his hands about economic policies; and Congress had unanimously approved his expropriation of the copper companies without compensation. He now hoped to placate the armed forces by bringing all three of their commanders into his cabinet. The other possibility is that Allende was pushed to extreme measures, against his better judgment, by his most radical supporters, the Movement of the Revolutionary Left (Spanish acronym MIR), who wanted a quick revolution to overthrow Chile's capitalist state. They were accumulating weapons, adopted the slogan "Arm the people," complained about Allende being too weak, and refused to listen to his entreaties, "Just wait patiently for a few more years."

Even if either or both of these possible explanations constituted Allende's motives, I find them unsatisfying. It seems to me that, even at the time, and not just with the wisdom of hindsight, Allende's policies were based on unrealistic appraisals.

———

The long-expected coup took place on September 11, 1973, after all three branches of the Chilean armed forces — army, navy, and air force — had agreed on a plan 10 days previously. Although the CIA had been constantly supporting opposition to Allende and seeking to undermine him, even Americans who exposed CIA meddling in Chilean affairs agree that the coup was executed by Chileans themselves, not by the CIA. The Chilean air force bombed the president's palace in Santiago, while Chilean army tanks shelled it (Plate 4.3). Recognizing his situation to be hopeless, Allende killed himself with the machine gun presented to him by Fidel Castro. I confess that I had been skeptical about that claim, and had suspected that Allende had actually been killed by coup soldiers. But an investigative commission set up by Chile's restored democratic government after the end of military government concluded that Allende really did die alone, by suicide. That conclusion was confirmed for me by a Chilean friend who knew a fireman of the fire brigade that went to the burning palace and met Allende's surviving final companions, including the last person to see Allende alive.

The coup was welcomed with relief and broad support from centrist and rightist Chileans, much of the middle class, and of course the oligarchs. By then, Chile's economic chaos, foolish governmental economic policies, and street violence under Allende had become intolerable. Coup supporters regarded the junta merely as an unavoidable transition stage towards restoring the previous status quo of middle- and upper-class civilian political domination that had prevailed before 1970. One Chilean friend recounted to me the story of a dinner party of 18 people that he had attended in December 1973, just three months after the coup. When the subject of conversation turned to the question how long the guests present expected the junta to remain in power, 17 of the 18 guests predicted just two years. The 18th guest's prediction of seven years was considered absurd by the other guests; they said that that couldn't happen in Chile, where all previous military governments had quickly returned power to a civilian government. No one at that dinner party foresaw that the junta would remain in power for almost 17 years. It suspended all political activity, closed Congress, banned left-wing political parties and even the centrist Christian Democrats (to the great surprise of those centrists), took over Chile's universities, and appointed military commanders as university rectors.

The junta member who became its leader, essentially by accident, had joined it at the last minute and had not led the coup planning: General Augusto Pinochet (Plate 4.4). Just a couple of weeks before the coup, the Chilean army had pressured its previous chief of staff into resigning, because he was opposed to a military intervention. By default, the new army chief of staff became Pinochet, who had commanded the army units in the Santiago area. Even at that time, Pinochet was considered relatively old (58 years). Chile's other army generals and armed forces commanders thought that they understood their colleague, as did the CIA, which had gathered extensive information about him. The CIA's appraisal of Pinochet was: quiet, mild-mannered, honest, harmless, friendly, hard-working, businesslike, religious, modest in lifestyle, a devoted tolerant husband and father, with no known interests outside the military and the Catholic Church and his family — in short, not a person likely to lead a coup. The junta expected itself to be a committee of equals, with rotating leadership. They chose Pinochet as their initial leader mainly because he was its oldest member, because he was chief of staff of the largest branch of the Chilean armed forces (the army itself), and perhaps because they shared the CIA's view of Pinochet as unthreatening. When the junta took power, Pinochet himself announced that its leadership would rotate.

But when it came time for Pinochet to rotate off and to step down as leader, he didn't do so. Instead, he succeeded in intimidating his fellow junta members by a secret service that he set up. Hundreds of incidents unfolded that involved dissent within the junta, but Pinochet usually succeeded in getting his way. Neither his fellow junta members, nor the CIA, nor anyone else anticipated Pinochet's ruthlessness, his strong leadership, and his ability to cling to power — at the same time as he continued to project an image of himself as a benign old man and devout Catholic, depicted by the state-controlled media with his children and going to church.

The barbaric deeds that happened in Chile after September 11, 1973 cannot be understood without recognizing the role of

Pinochet. Like Hitler in the Germany of the 1930's and 1940's, Pinochet, while part of a broader context, was a leader who imposed his stamp on the course of history. He was even more of an enigma than was Allende. Whereas I mentioned two interpretations that have been offered for Allende's actions, I haven't heard any plausible explanation for the sadism managed by Pinochet. As one Chilean friend expressed it to me, "I didn't understand Pinochet's psychology."

As soon as the junta took power, it rounded up leaders of Allende's Popular Unity Party and other perceived leftists (such as university students and the famous Chilean folk singer Victor Jara; Plate 4.5), with the goal of literally exterminating the Chilean left-wing. Within the first 10 days, thousands of Chilean leftists were taken to two sports stadiums in Santiago, interrogated, tortured, and killed. (For instance, Jara's body was found in a dirty canal with 44 bullet holes, all of his fingers chopped off, and his face disfigured.) Five weeks after the coup, Pinochet personally ordered a general to go around Chilean cities in what became known as the "Caravan of Death," killing political prisoners and Popular Unity politicians whom the army had been too slow at killing. The junta banned all political activities, closed Congress, and took over universities.

Two months after the coup, Pinochet founded an organization that evolved into DINA, a national intelligence organization and secret police force. Its chief reported directly to Pinochet, and it became Chile's main agent of repression. It was notorious for its brutality, even judged by the standards of brutality of the other intelligence units of the Chilean armed forces. It set up networks of secret detention camps, devised new methods of torture, and made Chileans "disappear" (i.e., murdered them without a trace). One center called La Venda Sexy specialized in sexual abuse to extract information — for example, by rounding up a prisoner's family members and sexually abusing them in front of the prisoner, by methods too revolting to describe in print and utilizing rodents and trained dogs. If you visit Santiago, have a strong stomach, and aren't susceptible to nightmares, you can tour one such detention center at Villa Grimaldi, now transformed into a museum.

In 1974 DINA began to operate outside Chile. It started in Argentina by planting a car bomb that killed Chile's former army commander-in-chief General Carlos Prats and his wife Sofia, because Prats had refused to join the coup and was feared by Pinochet as a potential threat. DINA then launched an international campaign of government terrorism, called Operation Condor, by convening a meeting of the heads of the secret police of Chile, Argentina, Uruguay, Paraguay, Bolivia, and eventually Brazil, in order to cooperate on cross-border manhunts of exiles, leftists, and political figures. Hundreds of Chileans were tracked down and killed in other South American countries, Europe, and even one in the U.S. The U.S. case occurred in 1976, in Washington, DC, only 14 blocks from the White House, when a car bomb killed the former Chilean diplomat Orlando Letelier (minister of defense under Allende), plus an American colleague. As I mentioned previously, that was the only known case of a foreign terrorist killing an American citizen on American soil — until the World Trade Towers attack of 2001.

By 1976, Pinochet's government had arrested 130,000 Chileans, or 1% of Chile's population. While the majority of them were eventually released, DINA and other junta agents killed or "disappeared" thousands of Chileans (most of them under the age of 35), plus four American citizens and various citizens of other countries. The killings were often preceded by torture, aimed at least partly at extracting information. It isn't clear, though, to what extent the torture was also motivated by pure sadism; Chilean students with whom I have discussed the matter have suggested both motives to me. About 100,000 Chileans fled into exile, many of them never to return.

One has to wonder how a previously democratic country could descend to such depths of behavior, which far exceeded the previous military interventions of Chilean history in duration, number of killings, and sadism. Partly, the answer involves Chile's increasing polarization, violence, and breakdown of political compromise, culminating under Allende in the arming of the Chilean far left and in the "Yakarta viene" warnings of impending massacres by the far right. Allende's Marxist designs and Cuban connections, much more than previous Chilean leftist programs, had made the armed forces fearful and prepared to take preventive actions. The other part of the answer, according to Chileans with whom I've talked, involves Pinochet himself, who was an unusual person, even though he seemed so ordinary and sought to project an image of himself as a benign, devoutly Catholic old man. Few documents link Pinochet directly to atrocities; perhaps the closest thing to a smoking gun was his order to the general whom he sent to carry out the Caravan of Death. Many Chilean rightists believe to this day that Pinochet didn't order the tortures and killings himself, and that the carnage was instead ordered by other generals and leaders. But I find it impossible to believe that Pinochet could meet every week or every day with the head of his secret service (DINA), or that many other Chilean military officials could routinely perform torture, without Pinochet's explicit orders.

Pinochet, like Hitler, thus seems to be an example of an evil leader who did make a difference to the course of history. Yet Chilean military crimes can't be blamed on Pinochet alone, because no one has ever suggested that he personally shot or tortured anyone. At its peak, DINA had over 4,000 employees, whose job it was to interrogate, torture, and kill. I don't interpret that to mean that most Chileans are uniquely evil: every country has thousands of

sociopaths who would commit evil if ordered or even just permitted to do it. For example, any of you who has been imprisoned
even in generally non-evil countries like Britain and the U.S., and
who has had the misfortune to experience there the sadism of
jailers and law enforcement officers who have not been specifically
ordered to be sadistic, can imagine how those jailers and officers
would have behaved if they had indeed received explicit orders to
be sadistic.

———

The other main effort of Pinochet's dictatorship, besides exterminating the Chilean left, was to reconstruct the Chilean economy on
a free-market basis, reversing Chile's prior norm of extensive government intervention. That reversal did not happen during Pinochet's first year-and-a-half in power, when the economy continued
to contract, inflation persisted, and unemployment rose. But from
1975 onwards, Pinochet turned over economic management to a
group of neo-liberal economic advisors who became known as the
Chicago Boys, because many of them had trained at the University
of Chicago in association with the economist Milton Friedman.
Their policies emphasized free enterprise, free trade, market orientation, balanced budget, low inflation, modernization of Chilean
businesses, and reduced government intervention.

South American military governments usually prefer an economy that they control themselves for their own benefit, rather than
a free-market economy that they don't control. Hence the junta's
adoption of the Chicago Boys' policies was unexpected, and it
remains uncertain why it happened. It might not have happened at
all without Pinochet, because the policies were opposed by some
senior Chilean military officers, including one junta member (Air
Force General Gustavo Leigh) whom Pinochet finally forced to
resign in 1978. The adoption is sometimes attributed to the 1975

Chilean visit of Milton Friedman himself, who met with Pinochet for 45 minutes and followed up the meeting by sending Pinochet a long letter full of recommendations. But Friedman came away from the meeting with a low opinion of Pinochet, who asked Friedman only one question during their conversation. In fact, the Chicago Boys' program differed significantly from Friedman's recommendations and drew on detailed plans that Chilean economists had already laid out in a document nicknamed "the brick" (because it was so lengthy and heavy).

A possible explanation is that Pinochet recognized that he knew nothing about economics, portrayed himself as (or was) a simple man, and found appealing the Chicago Boys simple, consistent, persuasive proposals. Another factor may be that Pinochet identified the Chicago Boys and their policies with the U.S., which strongly supported Pinochet, shared his hatred of communists, and resumed its loans to Chile immediately after Pinochet's coup. As true of some other actions of Pinochet (and of Allende), the motives in this case as well are not clear.

Whatever the motives, the resulting free-market policies included the re-privatization of hundreds of state-owned businesses nationalized under Allende (but not of the copper companies); the slashing of the government deficit by across-the-board cuts of every government department's budget by 15% to 25%; the slashing of average import duties from 120% to 10%; and the opening of Chile's economy to international competition. That caused the Chicago Boys' program to be opposed by Chile's oligarchy of industrialists and traditional powerful families, whose inefficient businesses had previously been shielded from international competition by high duties and were now forced to compete and innovate. But the results were that the rate of inflation declined from its level of 600% per year under Allende to just 9% per year, the Chilean economy grew at almost 10% per year, foreign investments soared,

Chilean consumer spending rose, and Chilean exports eventually diversified and increased.

These positive results were not without setbacks and painful consequences. An unfortunate decision to tie the value of the Chilean peso to the U.S. dollar produced a big trade deficit and an economic crisis in 1982. The economic benefits for Chileans were unequally distributed: middle-class and upper-class Chileans prospered, but many other Chileans suffered and found themselves living below the poverty level. In a democracy it would have been difficult to inflict such widespread suffering on poor Chileans, as well as to impose government policies opposed by rich business oligarchs. That was possible only under a repressive dictatorship. Still, one Chilean friend not otherwise sympathetic to Pinochet explained to me, "Yes, but so many Chileans had already been suffering from Chile's previous economic problems under Allende, without hope of an eventual improvement." When it became clear that the junta wasn't just a temporary transitional phase but intended to remain in power, many middle-class and upper-class Chileans nevertheless continued to support Pinochet because of that (unequally distributed) economic improvement, and despite governmental repression. Optimism, and a sigh of relief about the end of the economic chaos that had prevailed under Allende, arose among those Chileans outside the sectors of Chilean society that were being tortured or killed.

Like many Chileans, the U.S. government supported Pinochet for more than half of the duration of his military dictatorship — in the U.S.'s case, because of his strong anti-communist stance. U.S. government policy was to extend economic and military aid to Chile, and publicly to deny Pinochet's human rights abuses, even when those being tortured and killed were American citizens. As American Secretary of State Henry Kissinger expressed it, "...however unpleasantly they [the junta] act, this government [i.e., Pinochet's] is better for us than Allende was." That American government support of Pinochet, and that blind eye to his abuses, continued through the presidencies of Richard Nixon, Gerald Ford, Jimmy Carter, and initially Ronald Reagan.

But from the mid-1980's onwards, two things turned the U.S. government against Pinochet. One was the accumulated evidence of abuses, including abuses against American citizens — evidence that became increasingly hard to ignore. A turning point was the horrifying killing in Santiago of Rodrigo Rojas, a Chilean teen-ager who was a U.S. legal resident, and who died after being doused with gasoline and set on fire by Chilean soldiers. The other factor turning the Reagan government against Pinochet was Chile's economic downturn of 1982–1984, which turned more of the Chilean public against Pinochet. Because the economic recovery from 1984 onwards failed to improve the lot of many Chileans, the Chilean left gained strength, Chile's Catholic Church became an open focus of opposition (despite Pinochet's being a devout Catholic), and even the Chilean military was becoming dissatisfied with him. In short, Pinochet was not just evil: worse yet from the perspective of the U.S. government, he had become a liability for American political interests.

In 1980 the junta proposed a new constitution that would entrench right-wing and military interests, and asked voters to legitimize Pinochet by voting to extend his term as president for eight years (from 1981 to 1989). After an election campaign tightly controlled by the junta, a big majority of Chilean voters approved the new constitution and Pinochet's extended term. As that extended term approached its end in 1989, the junta announced another plebiscite in 1988 that would extend Pinochet's presidency for yet another eight years until 1997, when he would be 82 years old.

This time, though, Pinochet miscalculated and was

outmaneuvered by his opponents. International attention forced the campaign to be conducted openly, and the balloting to be conducted honestly. The U.S. threw its resources behind the opposition, which organized a massive effort to register 92% of potential voters and mounted a brilliantly designed campaign around the simple slogan "No!" (Plate 4.6). To Pinochet's surprise, the "No!" campaign prevailed, with 58% of votes cast. Although Pinochet's initial response on the night of the election was to try to deny the vote's outcome, the other junta members forced him to accept it. But — 42% of Chileans had still voted for Pinochet, in that free election of 1988.

———

With that "No!" victory, Pinochet's opponents at last gained the opportunity to return to power in the presidential elections scheduled for 1990. But the "No!" campaigners had consisted of 17 different groups, with 17 different visions for Chile after Pinochet. Hence Chile risked going down the path trodden by the Allied democracies that had defeated Germany and Japan in World War Two, and of whom Winston Churchill had written as the theme of the last volume of his six-volume history of World War Two, *Triumph and Tragedy*, "How the great democracies triumphed, and so were able to resume the follies which had so nearly cost them their life." A similar question was pending for Chile: would Chileans resume their follies of intransigence and of the no-compromise posture that had cost many of them their lives, and that had cost their country its democratic government?

Of Pinochet's leftist opponents who were not killed by Pinochet, 100,000 fled into exile, beginning around 1973. They remained in exile for a long time, about 16 years (until 1989). They thus had ample time to reflect on their former intransigence. Many of them went to Western or Eastern Europe, where they spent years watching how socialists, communists, and other leftists of European countries operated, and how those leftists fared. Those Chilean exiles who went to Eastern Europe tended to become depressed upon discovering that intransigent leftist idealists in power didn't create national happiness. Those exiles who fled to Western Europe instead observed moderate social democracies in action, the resulting high standard of living, and a calmer political atmosphere than the atmosphere that had prevailed in Chile. They discovered that leftists don't have to be radical and intransigent, but that they could achieve many of their goals by negotiating and compromising with people who hold different political views. The exiles experienced the collapse of the Soviet Union and of Eastern Europe's communist governments, and China's bloody suppression of demonstrations in 1989. All of those observations served to temper extremism and communist sympathies of Chile's leftists.

Already during the "No!" campaign of 1989, "No!" backers of disparate views realized that they couldn't win unless they learned to cooperate with each other. They also realized that Pinochet still enjoyed wide support among Chile's business community and upper class, and that they couldn't win, or (if they did win) that they would never be permitted to assume power, unless Pinochet supporters could be assured of their personal safety in a post-Pinochet era. Painful as the prospect was, leftists in power would have to practice tolerance towards former enemies whose views they loathed, and whose behavior towards them had been horrible. They had to declare their willingness to build "a Chile for all Chileans": the goal that Patricio Aylwin, Chile's first democratically elected president after Pinochet, proclaimed in his inaugural speech of March 12, 1990.

Once the alliance of the 17 "No!" groups had thus won the referendum, the alliance's leftists faced the necessity of convincing the alliance's centrists of the Christian Democratic Party that a new leftist government wasn't to be feared and wouldn't be as radical as Allende's leftist government had been. Hence leftist and centrist parties joined in an electoral alliance termed Concertación. Leftists agreed that, if the alliance could win the 1990 election (which it did), they would let the presidency alternate between a leftist and a centrist, and would let the Christian Democrats fill the presidency first. Leftists agreed to those conditions because they realized that that was the only way that they could eventually return to power.

In fact, Concertación proceeded to win the first four post-Pinochet elections, in 1990, 1993, 2000, and 2006. The first two presidents were the Christian Democrats Patricio Aylwin and Eduardo Frei, Jr. (son of former president Eduardo Frei). The next two presidents were the socialists Ricardo Lagos and Michelle Bachelet; the latter was Chile's first woman president, and also was the daughter of a general who had been tortured and imprisoned by Pinochet's junta. In 2010 Concertación was defeated by a right-wing president (Sebastián Piñera), in 2014 socialist Bachelet returned to power, and in 2018 right-winger Piñera again. Thus, Chile after Pinochet reverted to being a functioning democracy still anomalous for Latin America, but with a huge selective change: a willingness to tolerate, compromise, and share and alternate power.

Besides abandoning political intransigence, the other major change of direction by Chile's new democratic Concertación governments compared to the democratic governments of the pre-Pinochet era was with respect to economic policy. The new governments continued most of Pinochet's free-market economic policies, because those policies were seen to have been largely beneficial in the long run. In fact, Concertación governments carried those policies even further, by reducing import tariffs so that they

NATIONS: CRISES THAT UNFOLDED

came to average only 3% by 2007, the lowest in the world. Free trade agreements were signed with the U.S. and with the European Union. The main change introduced by Concertación into the military government's economic policies was to increase government spending on social programs and to reform labor laws.

The result has been that, since the 1990 change of government, the Chilean economy has grown at an impressive rate, and that Chile leads the rest of Latin America economically. Average incomes in Chile were only 19% of U.S. averages in 1975; that proportion had risen to 44% by the year 2000, while average incomes in the rest of Latin America were dropping over that same time. Inflation rates in Chile are low, the rule of law is strong, private property rights are well protected, and the pervasive corruption with which I had to deal during my 1967 visit has decreased. A consequence (and also a partial cause) of this improved economic climate was a doubling of foreign investment that took place quickly in Chile during the first seven years of the return of democracy.

Today, Santiago looks completely different from the city that I knew in 1967. It is bristling with skyscrapers (including the tallest one in South America) and has a new subway and new airport. However, Chile's economic performance is far from a uniformly distributed success. Economic inequality remains high, socioeconomic mobility is low, and Chile continues as before to be a land of contrasting wealth and poverty, although Chile's rich people today tend to be new business leaders rather than the families of former large land-owners. But the overall big improvement of the Chilean economy means that, while the *relative* gap between rich and poor persists, the *absolute* economic status of the poor in Chile has become much better. The percentage of Chileans living below the poverty line dropped from its level of 24% during Pinochet's last year in power to only 5% by 2003.

166

The "No!" electoral victory of 1989 did not mean that Chile was free of Pinochet and the armed forces. Far from it: before stepping down as president, Pinochet obtained legislation naming him senator-for-life, permitting him to appoint several new Supreme Court justices, and retaining him as commander-in-chief of the armed forces until he finally retired in 1998 at the age of 83. That meant that Pinochet, and his implicit threat of another military coup, were constantly on the minds of Chile's democratic leaders. As one Chilean friend explained it to me, "It's as if, upon Nazi Germany's surrender on 9 May 1945, Hitler hadn't committed suicide but remained senator-for-life and the German army's commander-in-chief!" Further strengthening the Chilean military's position, Pinochet's constitution included a provision (still in effect today) specifying that 10% of Chile's national copper *sales* revenue (yes: sales, not just profits!) must be spent each year on the military budget. That gives Chile's armed forces a financial basis far in excess of the money needed to defend Chile against any credible foreign threat — especially considering that Chile's last (and only its second) war ended over a century ago in 1883, that Chile's borders are protected by ocean and desert and high mountains, and that Chile's neighbors (Argentina, Bolivia, Peru) are not dangerous. Instead, the only likely use of Chile's armed forces is against the Chilean people themselves.

The Chilean constitution approved under Pinochet contained three provisions favoring the right wing. One provision specified that, of the Senate's 35 members, 10 were not elected by the public but were instead designated by the president from a list of officials likely to consist only of right-wingers (e.g., former chiefs of the army and navy). Former presidents became appointed senators-for-life. A second provision (not overturned until 2015) specified that each Chilean congressional district elected two representatives, the first of whom required just a plurality of voters, but the other of whom required an 80% majority; that made it very difficult for any district to elect two leftists. The last provision requires a 5/7ths voter majority to change the constitution — but it's difficult in a democracy (especially one as fractured as Chile) to get 5/7ths of the electorate to agree to anything. As a result, although decades have passed since Pinochet was voted out of the presidency, Chile still operates under a modified version of his constitution that most Chileans consider illegitimate.

It is painful for any country to acknowledge and atone for evil deeds that its officials committed against its own citizens or against citizens of other countries. It's painful because nothing can undo the past, and often many of the perpetrators are still alive, unrepentant, powerful, and widely supported. Acknowledgment and atonement have been especially difficult for Chile, because Pinochet was supported by such a large minority of Chilean voters even in the 1989 uncoerced plebiscite, because Pinochet remained commander-in-chief of the armed forces, and because the democratic government had good reason to fear another military coup if it proceeded against military perpetrators. On two occasions — when Pinochet's son was being investigated, and when a human rights commission was beginning its work of investigating the atrocities — soldiers did appear on the streets in full military garb. Their appearance was supposedly just on a "routine exercise" — but the implicit threat was obvious to everyone.

Patricio Aylwin, the first post-Pinochet president, proceeded cautiously. When he promised justice "insofar as it is possible," Chileans hopeful for a reckoning felt disillusioned and feared that his phrase was just a euphemism for "no justice." But Aylwin did establish a Truth and Reconciliation Commission, which in 1991 published the names of 3,200 Chileans who had been killed or "disappeared," and a second commission in 2003 reported on torture. Speaking on television, Aylwin was nearly in tears as he begged the families of victims for forgiveness, on behalf of the Chilean government. Such heartfelt apologies by government leaders for government cruelties have been vanishingly rare in modern history; the closest parallel is German chancellor Willy Brandt's equally heartfelt apology at the Warsaw Ghetto to the victims of Germany's former Nazi government (see Chapter 6 for details).

A turning point in the reckoning with Pinochet was the British arrest warrant issued against him in 1998 while he was visiting a London clinic for medical treatment. The warrant was issued at the request of a Spanish judge seeking extradition of Pinochet to Spain to answer for crimes against humanity, and for the killings of Spanish citizens in particular. Pinochet's lawyers initially argued that Pinochet should be immune from prosecution because torture and killings are legitimate functions of government. When the British House of Lords eventually rejected that defense, Pinochet's lawyers then claimed that he was old and infirm and should be released on humanitarian grounds. The lawyers allowed him to be photographed only while he was in a wheelchair. After 503 days under house arrest, Britain's home secretary denied Spain's extradition request, supposedly because Pinochet lacked the strength to testify at a trial, but possibly because of the help that Pinochet's government had given to Britain during Britain's Falkland Islands War of 1982 against Argentina. Pinochet then immediately flew to Chile. Upon his plane's arrival he was unloaded in a wheelchair, and then stood up and walked across the tarmac to shake hands with the Chilean generals present to greet and congratulate him (Plate 4.7).

But even Chilean rightists were shocked by a U.S. Senate subcommittee's revelation that Pinochet had stashed $30 million in 125 secret U.S. bank accounts. While rightists had been prepared to tolerate torturing and killing, they were disillusioned to learn that Pinochet, whom they had considered different from and better than other dishonest Latin American dictators, stole and hid money. Chile's Supreme Court stripped Pinochet of the immunity from prosecution that he had enjoyed as senator-for-life. Chile's tax authority (the equivalent of the U.S.'s Internal Revenue Service) issued a complaint against Pinochet for filing false tax returns. (Perhaps the authorities were inspired by the example of the notorious American gangster Al Capone, who successfully avoided conviction for committing and ordering murders, bootlegging, and running gambling and prostitution rings, but who was finally sent to jail for federal income tax evasion.) Pinochet was then indicted for other financial crimes and murders, and was placed under house arrest, and his wife and four children were also arrested. But in 2002 he was declared unfit to stand trial because of dementia. He died of a heart attack in 2006, at the age of 91.

Eventually, hundreds of Chilean torturers and killers were indicted, and dozens of them were sent to prison — including General Manuel Contreras, director of Pinochet's secret intelligence agency DINA, sentenced to 526 years in prison, and unrepentant to his death. Many older Chileans continue to regard the sentences as too harsh, and continue to regard Pinochet as a wonderful man who was unjustly persecuted. Many other Chileans regard the sentences as too mild, too few, too late, aimed mainly at low-ranking rather than high-ranking criminals, and resulting in their being sent to special comfortable resort-like prisons. For instance, not until 2015 did Chilean judges charge 10 military officers with killing the famous singer Victor Jara in 1973, and seven others with killing Rodrigo Rojas in 1986: 42 and 29 years, respectively, after those deeds. In 2010 Chile's President Michelle Bachelet opened a Villa Grimaldi Museum in Santiago that documents in horrifying detail the tortures and killings under the military government.

That would have been utterly unthinkable as long as Pinochet remained army commander-in-chief.

Chileans are still wrestling with the moral dilemma of how to weigh the positive and the negative sides of their country's former military government: especially, the dilemma of how to balance its economic benefits against its crimes. The dilemma is insoluble. A simple answer would be: Why even try to weigh the benefits against the crimes? Why not just acknowledge that the military government did both beneficial things and horrible things? But Chileans did have to weigh them in the 1989 plebiscite, when they were offered only the choice between voting "yes" or "no" to keeping Pinochet as president for eight more years, and when they couldn't vote "yes but..." or "no but..." Faced with that choice, 42% of Chileans voted "yes," despite the sickening deeds that eventually went on display at the Villa Grimaldi Museum. While most younger Chileans now scorn Pinochet, the division of views among Chileans old enough to remember the Allende and Pinochet years was exemplified for me by two Chilean husband-and-wife couples whom I interviewed. In each case the husband and the wife asked me to interview them separately, because their views of such painful matters differed. In each case the husband then said to me, in effect, "Pinochet's policies benefitted Chile economically, but his torturings and killings were inexcusable." The wives said to me, in effect, "Pinochet's torturings and killings were evil, but you have to understand that his policies benefitted Chile economically."

——

From the perspective of our book's framework about factors facilitating or impeding crisis outcome, Chile illustrates many of them.

First, the changes in Chile were indeed selective and big (factor #3 of Table 1.2). Initially, Chile broke its long-standing tradition of minimal military intervention, and it resolved its long-standing tension between government economic intervention and a government hands-off economic approach by adopting a drastic shift to a hands-off approach. Eventually, when the shift to military intervention was reversed, that reversal itself was made selectively: yes, democratic government was restored, but the shift to a free-market economy that the military had introduced was retained. That became one of Chile's two lasting selective changes, which also illustrates remarkable flexibility (factor #10): the socialists who eventually returned to power abandoned their commitment to socialism and continued the economic policies of the hated military government. Chile's other lasting selective change was an end (at least for the last several decades) to the intransigent rejection of political compromise that had characterized national politics for most of Chile's recent history.

Chile achieved those selective changes through two rounds of uncertainty and failure (factor #9). The first round was Allende's failed attempt to resolve Chile's chronic economic and social problems by rejecting compromise and ushering in a Marxist government. The second round was Pinochet's failed attempt also to reject compromise, and to create a lasting military government and an extended presidency for himself, which was averted by his miscalculation of the outcome of the 1988 referendum.

How did Chile emerge from almost 17 years of military repression and record-smashing government cruelty without even deeper trauma than it did suffer? While Chile today is still struggling with the aftermath of the Pinochet years, I'm pleasantly surprised that Chileans are not more tormented. For that outcome, Chileans' national identity and pride get much of the credit (factor #6). Chileans still embrace the words of my Chilean friends to me in 1967: "Chile is very different from other Latin American countries; we Chileans know how to govern ourselves." Chileans have made a big effort to remain different from those other Latin American countries, and to govern themselves effectively. They have been willing to adhere to their motto of "building a Chile for all Chileans," despite the powerful motives of so many Chileans not to accept other kinds of Chileans as belonging to that same fatherland. Without that national identity, Chile could not have escaped political paralysis, and could not have returned to being the most democratic and the richest country in Latin America.

Chile illustrates both an honest realistic appraisal of strength at one stage, and a lack of such realism at another stage (factor #7). Pinochet and his fellow military leaders proved correct in 1973 that they could prevail over their adversaries inside Chile and abroad; Allende proved wrong in his belief that he could succeed in democratically bringing Marxist government to Chile. This difference further illustrates a sad truth: that success is not guaranteed to well-intentioned decent people, nor necessarily denied to evil people.

Chile illustrates the role both of support and of lack of support from others (factor #4), and of models from which to learn (factor #5). The opposition of the U.S. played a role in Allende's downfall, and the prompt restoration of U.S. economic aid following the 1973 coup played a role in the military government's long survival. Pinochet's perception (not entirely true to reality) of the U.S. economy as a model of a free-market economy played a role in his embracing the economic policies of the Chicago Boys.

Similarly, Chile illustrates both the advantages of freedom of action, and the disadvantages of lack of freedom of action (factor #12). Chile's geographic isolation by mountains and deserts from its Latin American neighbors greatly reduced the need for Allende or Pinochet to be concerned that their policies might provoke interventions by neighboring Argentina, Peru, and Bolivia. In contrast, dictatorial governments in Uganda, Rwanda, East Pakistan, Cambodia, and many other countries were toppled by interventions by neighboring countries. But Allende's freedom of action was constrained by the distant U.S., while the freedom of action of all Chilean governments has been constrained by the exposure of Chile's copper industry (the biggest pillar of the Chilean economy) to world market conditions beyond Chile's control.

Those are features of Chile's crisis viewed from the perspective of individual crises. Now, let's consider features unique to national crises (i.e., not shared with individual crises), and let's compare events in Chile with those in the other nations that we are discussing.

First, Chile's crisis in 1973, like Indonesia's of 1965 to be discussed in the next chapter, was an internal one, unlike the external shocks to Japan in 1853 and to Finland in 1939. (This is not to deny the role of external pressure from the U.S. in Chile's crisis.) Both Chile's and Indonesia's internal crises arose from political polarization, disagreement about deeply held core values, and a willingness to kill and to risk being killed rather than to compromise.

Second, Chile's history illustrates the theme of peaceful evolution versus violent revolution. In Germany in 1848 and again in the radical violence that began there in 1968, violent revolution failed, but subsequent peaceful evolution succeeded in achieving many of the same goals. Australia's changes from 1945 onwards were achieved entirely by peaceful evolution, without even any attempts at violent revolution. In contrast, crises both in Chile and in Indonesia, in 1973 and 1965, respectively, culminated in violent revolutions that brought long-lasting military governments into power. But both of those military governments were removed from power by peaceful protests. While the success of those protests was not assured at the time that they began, the other option of trying to remove Pinochet and Indonesia's Suharto from power by a violent revolt would surely have provoked and been crushed by the armed forces. But neither the Chilean nor the Indonesian armed forces could bring themselves to shoot at huge crowds of peaceful protestors on the streets.

Third, Chile, again like Indonesia in 1965 and Germany in 1933 but unlike Meiji Japan or post–World War Two Australia, illustrates the role of one exceptional leader: in the case of Pinochet, a leader who was exceptionally evil (in my view). Chilean friends tell me that Chile's growing polarization in the late 1960's and early 1970's made it likely that the resolution of that polarization would be violent. Even before the coup of September 11, 1973, violence had been increasing for six years. What surprised Chileans, such as my friends at the December 1973 dinner party who expected the military government to remain in power for less than two years, was the duration of the violence. It wasn't just a quick spasm of killings for a few days or weeks after the coup; Chileans continued to be tortured and killed for many years, and Pinochet continued to hold on to power for almost 17 years. That outcome was unexpected not only to ordinary Chileans, but also to the two groups of people whom one would expect to be best able to predict Pinochet's behavior: his Chilean partners in the junta, who had followed and shared his professional career for several decades; and the CIA, part of whose job it is to understand what may happen in other countries. Pinochet's junta partners were as surprised as was the CIA by his ruthlessness and determination to cling to power, so contrary to the traditions of all previous coup leaders in Chile's history. His individual psychology continues to baffle historians.

The remaining theme illustrated by modern Chilean history involves constraints that pose obstacles to coming to grips with evil deeds of the past. In May 1945 Nazi Germany was militarily completely defeated, many of its Nazi leaders committed suicide, and the whole country was occupied by its enemies. After World War Two, there were still plenty of ex-Nazis in German government, but they could not openly defend Nazi crimes. Thus, Germany did eventually deal publicly with Nazi crimes. At the opposite extreme, when the Indonesian army killed or arranged the killings of over half-a-million Indonesians in 1965, the Indonesian government behind those mass killings remained in power, and it is still in power today. Not surprisingly, even today, more than 50 years after the mass killings, Indonesians hesitate to talk about them.

Chile is an intermediate case. The Chilean military government that ordered killings yielded peacefully to a democratic government. But the military leaders remained alive and retained much power. Chile's new democratic government initially didn't dare proceed against military criminals. Today, it is still proceeding cautiously. Why is it cautious? Because the army might come back. Because there are still lots of Chileans who defend Pinochet. Because "a Chile for all Chileans" means, unfortunately, a Chile that includes former war criminals.

Finally, many of my American readers, concerned about growing political polarization in the U.S. today, will find this account of recent Chilean history frightening. Despite Chile's strong democratic traditions, Chile's political polarization and breakdown of compromise culminated in violence and a dictatorship that few Chileans had foreseen. Could that happen in the U.S.?

One might immediately object, "No, of course not! The U.S. is different from Chile. The U.S. army would never revolt and usher in a dictatorship."

Yes, the U.S. is indeed different from Chile. Some of those differences reduce, and some of them increase, the risk of an end of democracy in the U.S. If democracy does end in the U.S., it won't be through an uprising led by the heads of the armed forces; there are other ways to end democracy. I'll defer further discussion of these questions about the U.S. to Chapter 9.

———

When I returned to Chile in 2003, for the first time since I left that country in 1967, I visited Allende's presidential palace, now open as a tourist attraction. I had been told that the public is free to enter. At the front door was a grim-looking policeman (carabinero), holding a rifle and standing on a box one-and-a-half feet high, so that he towered over me. He looked down at me, glared without smiling, and asked what I wanted. I replied that I was a tourist, and he let me pass. But I found myself wondering what he might do, and whether I was unknowingly violating some regulation. I reflected: "It was a policeman or soldier like that who doused Rodrigo Rojas with gasoline and set him on fire!" I felt frightened and left after only a minute, with a better understanding of why Chile's democratic government has proceeded cautiously in indicting Pinochet's torturers and killers.

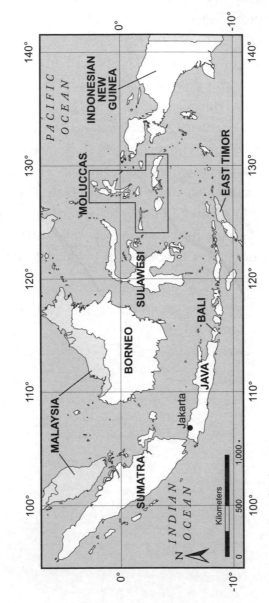

FIG. 5 *Map of Indonesia*

CHAPTER 5

INDONESIA, THE RISE OF A NEW COUNTRY

In a hotel — Indonesia's background — The colonial
era — Independence — Sukarno — Coup — Mass
murder — Suharto — Suharto's legacies — Crisis
framework — Returning to Indonesia

Indonesia is the world's fourth most populous country, with about
260 million inhabitants, exceeded only by China, India, and the
United States. It's also the world's most populous country with a
predominantly Muslim population, home to more inhabitants than
even Pakistan, Bangladesh, or Iran. Those facts could lead one to
expect Indonesia to get lots of attention from American and European newspapers.

In fact, the word "Muslim" makes Westerners think instead of
other countries that figure much more in Western consciousness
than does Indonesia. Nowadays, American and European newspapers mention the country only infrequently. The few occasions in
the last 15 years when I can recall front-page articles about it were
when two big earthquakes and a plane crash killed many people in
2018, when several drug-runners who included foreign citizens
were executed in 2015 in spite of foreign protests, when 200,000

179

people were killed by a tsunami in 2004, and when a bombing in Bali in 2002 claimed many victims. That general lack of attention is because Indonesia today isn't characterized by things that are the stuff of international headlines, like civil wars, sending terrorists or waves of immigrants overseas, being either rich or else desperately poor, or making lots of noise in international politics. Insofar as we Americans think of Indonesia at all, our image is of a developing country with pleasant tourist attractions, especially the scenery and beaches and Hindu temples of Bali, the world's richest coral reefs and best scuba diving and snorkeling, and beautiful batik textiles.

My first trip to Indonesia was in 1979, when I began my visit by staying in a hotel whose lobby walls were decorated with paintings telling the story of Indonesian history. In the United States a similar exhibit might display paintings of the American Revolution, the Civil War, the California gold rush, the transcontinental railroads, and other such subjects from 150 to 250 years ago. But in that Indonesian hotel lobby, all of the paintings showed events of just the previous 35 years. The event that was the subject of most paintings was termed the 1965 Communist Revolt. Paintings, and explanatory text below them, vividly depicted how communists tortured and killed seven generals; and how one of the generals that the communists tried to kill managed to escape from his house over a wall, but his five-year-old daughter was shot by accident and died a few days later. The exhibit left the impression that the torture and killing of those generals and the young girl were the most horrible act that had ever happened in Indonesian history.

The exhibit made no mention of what followed the deaths of the generals: the murder of about half-a-million other Indonesians at the instigation of the Indonesian armed forces. Not mentioning those killings in an exhibit on Indonesian history is quite an omission, because, among mass killings around the world since World War Two, only a few others have exceeded that Indonesian death toll. In the two decades since that first visit of mine, during many return visits and lengthy stays in Indonesia, not once did I hear those killings mentioned by my Indonesian friends — until a change of government in 1998. It's as if General Pinochet's government in Chile had killed 100 times more Chileans than it actually did, but as if those killings were never mentioned by surviving Chileans, nor by Chilean accounts of Chilean history.

Among the issues of crisis and change to keep in mind as you read the following pages, one is of course the comparison between Indonesia and Chile. Both countries experienced a breakdown of political compromise, a leftist effort to gain control of the government, and a military coup that ended that effort and installed a long-lasting dictatorship. Both countries illustrate the role of not one but two successive leaders, with distinctive but contrasting personalities. In achieving national reconciliation after the massacre of one political group by its opponents, Indonesia proves to lie at the opposite extreme from Finland, with Chile in the middle. More than any other country discussed in this book, you'll see that Indonesia, our youngest country, illustrates the process of successfully building a national identity.

———

To understand what happened in Indonesia's crisis of 1965 and its aftermath, let's begin with some background. Indonesia is a new country that didn't become independent until 1945, and that didn't even become unified as a colony until around 1910. It's tropical, lies on the equator between New Guinea and Australia on the east and Asia on the west, and has high mountains, including many active volcanoes. One of them, Krakatoa, is famous for the most catastrophic eruption in recent history (1883), an eruption that blew out almost the whole island and injected enough ash into the atmosphere to change the world's climate for the following year. Of Indonesia's islands, the best known are Java, Bali, Sumatra, and Sulawesi, plus the islands of Borneo and New Guinea that Indonesia shares with other countries (page 178).

Geographically, Indonesia is the most splintered country in the world, with thousands of inhabited islands scattered over an expanse of 3,400 miles from west to east. For most of the last 2,000 years, there were indigenous states on some Indonesian islands. But none of them came to control most of the Indonesian archipelago, nor was there a name or a concept for what we know today as Indonesia. Linguistically, Indonesia is one of the world's most diverse countries, with more than 700 different languages. It is also religiously diverse: while most Indonesians are Muslims, there are also large Christian and Hindu minorities, as well as Buddhists, Confucians, and followers of local traditional religions. Although there have been religious violence and rioting, they have been on a much smaller scale than in South Asia and the Middle East. Many Indonesians of different religions are relatively tolerant of one another. I have been in parts of Indonesia where Christian and Muslim villages were next to each other, and I didn't even recognize what was the religion of some particular village that I happened to be in, until I noticed a mosque or church.

———

Beginning after 1510, the Portuguese, then (from 1595 onwards) the Dutch, and then the British attempted to establish colonies in the island chain that is now Indonesia. British control eventually became confined to parts of Borneo, and the only Portuguese colony that survived was in the eastern half of the island of Timor. The most successful colonists were the Dutch, concentrated on the island of Java, which had by far the largest native population (more than half of the population of modern Indonesia). In the 1800's, in order to make their colonial efforts pay for themselves and then produce a profit, the Dutch developed export plantations on Java and Sumatra. But it was only around 1910, more than three centuries after their arrival in the Indonesian archipelago, that the Dutch gained control of the whole far-flung island chain. As an example of how long much of the archipelago remained unexplored by the Dutch, it wasn't until that year of 1910 that a Dutch governor discovered that the eastern Indonesian island of Flores and the nearby small island of Komodo are home to the world's largest lizard, the so-called Komodo dragon. Although it's up to 10 feet long and weighs up to several hundred pounds, it had remained unknown to Europeans for four centuries.

It should be emphasized that the word "Indonesia" didn't even exist until it was coined by a European around 1850. The Dutch called their colony the "Indies," the "Netherlands Indies," or the "Dutch East Indies." The archipelago's inhabitants themselves did not share a national identity, nor a national language, nor a sense of unity in opposition to the Dutch. For example, Javanese troops joined Dutch troops to conquer the leading state on the island of Sumatra, a traditional rival of Javanese states.

In the early 1900's the Dutch colonial government began efforts to switch from a purely exploitative policy for their colony to what they termed an "ethical policy" — i.e., finally trying to do some good for Indonesians. For example, the Dutch opened schools, built railroads and irrigation projects on Java, set up local government councils in the main towns, and attempted to relieve Java's overpopulation by supporting emigration to less densely populated outer islands (against the wishes of those islands' native populations). But those efforts of Dutch ethical policy produced limited results — partly because the Netherlands itself was too small to put much money into Indonesia; and partly because the efforts of the Dutch, as well as of subsequent independent Indonesia, to improve people's lives were frustrated by rapid population growth, creating more mouths to feed. Indonesians today consider the negative effects of Dutch colonialism far to have outweighed the positive effects.

By around 1910, increasing numbers of inhabitants of the Dutch East Indies were developing the beginnings of a "national consciousness." That is, they began to feel that they were not just inhabitants of their particular Dutch-governed sultanate in some part of Java or Sumatra, but that they belonged to a larger entity called "Indonesia." Indonesians with those beginnings of a wider identity formed many distinct but often overlapping groups: a Javanese group that felt culturally superior, an Islamic movement seeking an Islamic identity for Indonesia, labor unions, a communist party, Indonesian students sent to the Netherlands for education, and others. That is, the Indonesian independence movement was fragmented along ideological and geographic and religious lines, presaging problems that continued to plague Indonesia after independence.

The result was not only strikes, plots, and agitation against the Dutch, but also conflict between those Indonesian groups, making for a confused situation. Their actions against the Dutch nevertheless reached the point that in the 1920's the Dutch adopted a policy of repression and sent many of the leaders to what was in effect a concentration camp, in a remote disease-plagued area of Dutch New Guinea.

An important contribution to eventual Indonesian unity was the evolution and transformation of the Malay language, a trade language with a long history, into Bahasa Indonesia, the shared national language of all Indonesians today. Even the largest of

Indonesia's hundreds of local languages, the Javanese language of Central Java, is the native language of less than one-third of Indonesia's population. If that largest local language had become the national language, it would have symbolized Java's domination of Indonesia and thereby exacerbated a problem that has persisted in modern Indonesia, namely, fear of Javanese domination on the part of Indonesians of other islands. The Javanese language has the additional disadvantage of being hierarchy-conscious, with different words used in speaking to people of higher or lower status. Today, I share with Indonesians their appreciation for the advantages of the wonderful Bahasa Indonesia as their national language. It's easy to learn. Only 18 years after Indonesia took over Dutch New Guinea and introduced Bahasa there, I found it being spoken even by uneducated New Guineans in remote villages. Bahasa's grammar is simple but supple at adding prefixes and suffixes to many word roots, in order to create new words with immediately predictable meanings. For example, the adjective meaning "clean" is "bersih," the verb "to clean" is "membersihkan," the noun "cleanliness" is "kebersihan," and the noun "cleaning up" is "pembersihan."

——

After Japan declared war on the United States in December 1941 and began its expansion throughout the Pacific Islands and Southeast Asia, it rapidly conquered the Dutch East Indies. The oil fields of Dutch Borneo, along with Malayan rubber and tin, were in fact a major motive behind Japan's declaring war, perhaps the biggest single motive, because Japan itself lacked oil and had depended on American oil exports, which the American president Roosevelt had cut off in retaliation for Japan's war against China and occupation of French Indo-China. The Borneo oil fields were the nearest alternative source of oil for Japan.

At first, Japanese military leaders occupying the Dutch East Indies claimed that Indonesians and Japanese were Asian brothers in a shared struggle for a new anti-colonial order. Indonesian nationalists initially supported the Japanese and helped to round up the Dutch. But the Japanese mainly sought to extract raw materials (especially oil and rubber) from the Dutch East Indies for the Japanese war machine, and they became even more repressive than had been the Dutch. As the war turned against the Japanese, in September 1944 they promised independence to Indonesians, though without setting a date. When Japan did surrender on August 15, 1945, only two days later Indonesians declared independence, ratified a constitution on the next day, and founded local militias. But they quickly discovered that the defeat of the Dutch by the Japanese, then the promise of independence by the Japanese, and finally the defeat of the Japanese by the U.S. and its allies did not ensure independence for Indonesia. Instead, in September 1945 British and Australian troops arrived to take over from the Japanese, and then Dutch troops arrived with the aim of restoring Dutch control. Fighting broke out that pitted British and Dutch troops against Indonesian troops.

The Dutch, invoking the ethnic diversity and huge territorial extent of the Indonesian archipelago, and probably driven by their own motive of "divide and rule" to retain control, promoted the idea of a federation for Indonesia. They set up separate federal states within areas that they reconquered. In contrast, many Indonesian revolutionaries sought a single unified republican government for all of the former Dutch East Indies. By a preliminary agreement reached in November 1946, the Dutch recognized the Indonesian Republic's authority — but only in Java and Sumatra. However, by July 1947 the Dutch became exasperated and launched what they termed a "police action," with the goal of destroying the

Republic. After a cease-fire, then another Dutch "police action," and United Nations and U.S. pressure, the Dutch gave way and agreed to transfer authority to the Republic. The final transfer took place in December 1949 — but with two big limitations that infuriated Indonesians and that took them 12 years to overturn. One limitation was that the Dutch did not yield the Dutch half (the western half) of the island of New Guinea. Instead, they retained it under Dutch administration, on the grounds that New Guinea was much less developed politically than was the rest of the Dutch East Indies, that it was not even remotely ready for independence, and that most New Guineans are ethnically as different from most Indonesians as either group is from Europeans. The other limitation was that Dutch companies such as Shell Oil maintained ownership over Indonesian natural resources.

Dutch efforts to re-establish control over Indonesia between 1945 and 1949 were carried out with brutal methods that my Indonesian colleagues still recounted to me with bitterness 30 years later, and that were vividly depicted in the paintings of Indonesian history in my Indonesian hotel lobby in 1979. (For instance, one of those paintings showed two Dutch soldiers raping an Indonesian woman.) Simultaneously, other brutal methods were employed by Indonesians against other Indonesians, because within Indonesia itself there was much resistance to the Indonesian Republic, viewed by many eastern Indonesians and Sumatrans as Javanese-dominated. Again, I still heard much resentment and longing for political separation from Indonesia on the part of my non-Javanese Indonesian friends in the 1980's. There was also opposition to the Republican leadership from Indonesian communists, culminating in a 1948 revolt crushed by the Republican Army that killed at least 8,000 Indonesian communists — a foretaste of what was to happen on a much larger scale after the failed coup of 1965.

———

The new nation faced crippling problems that had been carried over from the pre-independence era, and some of which now became further exacerbated. As an ex-colony long governed by the Netherlands for the Netherlands' benefit, independent Indonesia began its existence greatly underdeveloped economically. Population growth (at nearly 3% per year during the 1960's) continued to place a heavy burden on the economy after independence, as it had in Dutch times. Many Indonesians still lacked a sense of national identity and continued to identify themselves as Javanese, Moluccans, Sumatrans, or members of some other regional population, rather than as Indonesians. The Indonesian language that would eventually contribute to Indonesian unity was not yet widely established; instead, the 700 local languages were used. Those who did consider themselves Indonesian differed in their visions for Indonesia. Some Indonesian Muslim leaders wanted Indonesia to become an Islamic state. The Indonesian Communist Party wanted Indonesia to become a communist state. Some non-Javanese Indonesians wanted either much regional autonomy or else outright regional independence, and staged regional revolts, which the Republic's military eventually defeated.

The military itself was a focus of schisms, and of debates about its role. Should the military be controlled, as in other democracies, by civilian politicians, of whom Indonesian military officers were becoming increasingly suspicious? Or should the military instead be more autonomous and pursue its own policies for Indonesia? The military saw itself as the savior of the revolution, the bulwark of national identity, and demanded a guaranteed voting block in parliament. The civilian government, on the other hand, sought to save money by eliminating military units, reducing the size of the officer corps, and pushing soldiers out of the military and off the government payroll. There were also internal disagreements between branches of the armed forces, especially disagreements pitting the air force against the other branches. There were disagreements between army commanders themselves, especially between revolutionary regional commanders and conservative central commanders. Military leaders extorted money from other Indonesians and from businesses for army purposes, raised money by smuggling and by taxing radio ownership and electricity, and increasingly took over regional economies, thereby institutionalizing the corruption that remains today one of Indonesia's biggest problems.

Indonesia's founding president, Sukarno (1901–1970), had begun his political career already in Dutch times as a nationalist leader against the Dutch colonial government (Plate 5.1). (Like many Indonesians, Sukarno had only a single name, not a first name and a family name.) The Dutch sent him into exile, from which the Japanese brought him back. It was Sukarno who issued Indonesia's Proclamation of Independence on August 17, 1945. Well aware of Indonesia's weak national identity, he formulated a set of five principles termed Pancasila, which to this day serves as an umbrella ideology to unify Indonesia and was enshrined in the 1945 constitution. The principles are broad ones: belief in one god, Indonesian national unity, humanitarianism, democracy, and social justice for all Indonesians.

As president, Sukarno blamed Indonesia's poverty on Dutch imperialism and capitalism, abrogated Indonesia's inherited debts, nationalized Dutch properties, and turned over the management of most of them to the army. He developed a state-centered economy that the army, the civil bureaucracy, and Sukarno himself could milk for their benefit. Not surprisingly, Indonesian private enterprise and foreign aid both declined. Both the U.S. and the British governments became alarmed and sought to destabilize Sukarno's position, just as the U.S. had tried to destabilize Allende in Chile. Sukarno responded by telling the U.S. to "go to hell with your aid"; then in 1965 he expelled the American Peace Corps and withdrew from the United Nations, World Bank, and International Monetary Fund. Inflation soared, and Indonesia's currency (the rupiah) lost 90% of its value during 1965.

At the time that Indonesia became independent, it had had no history of democratic self-government. Its experience of government was instead that of Dutch rule, which in the final decades approximated a police state, as did Japanese rule after 1942. Fundamental to any functioning democracy are widespread literacy, recognition of the right to oppose government policies, tolerance of different points of view, acceptance of being outvoted, and government protection of those without political power. For understandable reasons, all of those prerequisites were weak in Indonesia. Hence during the 1950's, prime ministers and cabinets rose and fell in quick succession. In the September 1955 elections an astonishingly high 92% of registered voters went to the polls, but the outcome was a stalemate, because the four leading parties each obtained between 15% and 22% of votes and parliamentary seats. They could not compromise and fell into political gridlock. That breakdown of compromise among several parties equally matched in strength is already familiar to us from Chile and its Pinochet coup (Chapter 4) — with the difference that Chile at least had an educated literate population and a long history of democratic government, whereas Indonesia had neither.

Beginning in 1957, President Sukarno ended the gridlock by proclaiming martial law, then replaced Indonesian democracy with what he termed "guided democracy," which he considered more suitable to Indonesia's national character. Under "guided democracy," the Indonesian parliament was supposed to practice "mutual cooperation" or "consensus through deliberation," instead of the usual democratic concept of the legislature as a setting in which parties compete. In order to ensure that parliament would mutually cooperate with his (Sukarno's) goals, more than half of the seats in parliament were no longer elected offices but were instead appointed by Sukarno himself and assigned to so-called "functional groups" rather than political parties, the army being one such "functional group."

Sukarno became convinced that he was uniquely capable of divining and interpreting the wishes (including the unconscious wishes) of the Indonesian people, and of serving as their prophet. After the 1955 Bandung conference of Asian and African states, Sukarno extended his goals to the world stage and began to view it as his personal responsibility to have Indonesia play a leading role in Third World anti-colonial politics at a time when Indonesia's own internal problems were so pressing (Plate 5.2). In 1963 he let himself be declared president-for-life.

Sukarno launched two campaigns to translate his anti-colonial stance into deeds, by trying to annex two territories on the verge of independence. The first campaign was directed at Dutch New Guinea, which because of its ethnic distinctness the Dutch had refused to cede to Indonesia after the revolution. The Dutch launched a crash program to prepare New Guineans for independence, and New Guinea leaders adopted a national flag and a national anthem. But Sukarno claimed Dutch New Guinea for Indonesia, increased diplomatic pressure on the Dutch, and in 1961 ordered all three branches of the Indonesian armed forces to take Dutch New Guinea by force.

The result was a political success for Sukarno, but a tragedy for many of the Indonesian troops involved, and for those Dutch New Guineans looking forward to independence. While one of the paintings displayed in my Indonesian hotel lobby in 1979 depicted what was described as an Indonesian "battleship" sailing against the Dutch, it was in fact just a small patrol boat sunk by a Dutch warship, causing the deaths of many Indonesian sailors. Indonesian paratroops were dropped by Indonesian air force planes into Dutch New Guinea, with results described to me by a friend who served then in the Dutch defense forces. Presumably out of fear of Dutch anti-aircraft capabilities during daylight hours, the paratroops were dropped blindly at night over forested terrain, in an incredible act of cruelty. The unfortunate paratroops floated down into a hot, mosquito-infested sago swamp, where those who survived impact on sago trees found themselves hanging from the trees by their parachutes. The even smaller fraction who managed to free themselves from their parachutes dropped or clambered down into standing swamp water. My friend and his Dutch unit surrounded the swamp, waited a week, and then paddled into the swamp with boats to retrieve the few paratroops still alive.

Despite those Dutch military successes, the U.S. government wanted to appear to support the Third World anti-colonial movement, and it was able to force the Dutch to cede Dutch New Guinea. As a face-saving gesture, the Dutch ceded it not directly to Indonesia but instead to the United Nations, which seven months later transferred administrative control (but not ownership) to Indonesia, subject to a future plebiscite. The Indonesian government then initiated a program of massive transmigration from other Indonesian provinces, in part to ensure a majority of Indonesian non–New Guineans in Indonesian New Guinea. Seven years later, a hand-picked assembly of New Guinean leaders voted under pressure for incorporation of Dutch New Guinea into Indonesia. New Guineans who had been on the verge of independence from the Netherlands launched a guerrilla campaign for independence from Indonesia that is continuing today, over half-a-century later.

Sukarno's other campaign to translate his anti-colonial stance into deeds was directed at parts of Malaysia, a group of former British colonies. Malaysia consists of states on the Malay Peninsula of the Asian mainland that achieved independence in 1957, plus two ex–British colonies (Sabah and Sarawak) on the island of Borneo, which is shared with Indonesia and with Brunei. Sabah and Sarawak joined independent Malaysia in 1963. Whereas Sukarno claimed an Indonesian right of inheritance to Dutch New Guinea as a former part of the Dutch East Indies, he could make no such claim to Malaysian Borneo. Nevertheless, encouraged by his success in Dutch New Guinea, Sukarno began what he termed a "confrontation" with Malaysia in 1962, followed by military attacks on Malaysian Borneo in the next year. But the population of Malaysian Borneo showed no sign of wanting to join Indonesia, while British and Commonwealth troops provided effective military defense, and the Indonesian army itself lost its appetite for confrontation.

———

During the 1960's a complex and confusing three-way power struggle unfolded among the strongest forces in Indonesia. One force was Sukarno, the charismatic leader and skilled politician who enjoyed widespread support among Indonesians as the father of their country's independence, and as the first and (until then) only president. The second force was the armed forces, which monopolized military power. The third force was the Indonesian Communist Party (PKI = Partai Komunis Indonesia), which lacked military power but had become by far the strongest and best-organized political party.

But each of these three forces was divided and pulled in different directions. While Sukarno's "guided democracy" rested on an alliance between himself and the armed forces, Sukarno also aligned himself increasingly with the PKI as a counter-weight against the armed forces. Chinese Indonesians had become so alarmed by anti-Chinese sentiment in Indonesia that many had returned to China. Yet Indonesia simultaneously increased its diplomatic alliance with China and announced that it would soon imitate China by building its own atomic bomb — to the horror of the U.S. and Britain. The armed forces became divided among Sukarno's supporters, PKI supporters, and officers who wanted the armed forces to destroy the PKI. Army officers infiltrated the PKI, which in turn infiltrated the army. To remedy its military weakness, in 1965 the PKI with Sukarno's support proposed arming peasants and workers, ostensibly to serve as a fifth national armed forces branch along with the army, navy, air force, and police. In frightened response, anti-communist army officers reportedly set up a Council of Generals to prepare measures against the perceived growing communist threat.

This three-way struggle came to a climax around 3:15 A.M. during the night of September 30–October 1, 1965, when two army units with leftist commanders and 2,000 troops revolted and sent squads to capture seven leading generals (including the army's commander and the minister of defense) in their homes, evidently to bring them alive to President Sukarno and to persuade him to repress the Council of Generals. At 7:15 A.M. on October 1 the coup leaders, having also seized the telecom building on one side of the central square in the Indonesian capital city of Jakarta, broadcast an announcement on Indonesia radio declaring themselves to be the 30 September Movement, and stating that their aim was to protect President Sukarno by pre-empting a coup plotted by corrupt generals who were said to be tools of the CIA and the British. By 2:00 P.M. the leaders made three more radio broadcasts, after which they fell silent. Note: despite the account of a communist coup described vividly in the lobby display of my 1979 Indonesian hotel, the revolt was by Indonesian army units, not by a communist mob.

But the coup was badly bungled. The seven squads assigned to kidnap the generals were untrained, jittery, and assembled at the last minute. They hadn't rehearsed the kidnappings. The two most important squads, assigned to kidnap (*not* to kill) Indonesia's two highest-ranking generals, were led by inexperienced low-ranking officers. The squads ended up killing three of the generals in their houses, two by shooting and one by bayonet. A fourth general succeeded in escaping over the back wall of his house compound. The squad accidentally shot his five-year-old daughter as depicted in one of the paintings in my Indonesian hotel, and also killed his staff lieutenant, whom they mistook for the general himself. (For brevity, I'll still refer to "seven generals.") The squads succeeded in capturing alive only the remaining three of the generals, whom they nevertheless proceeded to murder instead of carrying out their instructions to bring the generals alive to Sukarno.

Despite the fact that the coup leaders included a commander of President Sukarno's bodyguard, whose job it was to know where Sukarno was at all times, the leaders could not find Sukarno, who happened to be spending the night at the home of one of his four wives. A crucial error was that the coup leaders made no attempt to capture the headquarters of the Indonesian Army Strategic Reserve (called Kostrad), located on one side of the central square, although coup troops did capture the other three sides of the square. The coup leaders had neither tanks nor walkie-talkies. Because they closed down the Jakarta telephone system at the time that they occupied the telecom building, coup leaders trying to communicate with one another between different parts of Jakarta were reduced to sending messengers through the streets. Incredibly, the coup leaders failed to provide food and water for their troops stationed on the central square, with the result that a battalion of hungry and thirsty soldiers wandered off. Another battalion went to Jakarta's Halim air force base, where they found the gates closed and spent the night loitering on the streets outside. The PKI leader who apparently was one of the coup organizers failed to alert and coordinate actions with the rest of the PKI, hence there was no mass communist uprising.

The commander of the Army Strategic Reserve was, after Sukarno, Indonesia's second political leader with unusual qualities that influenced the course of history. He resembled Sukarno in having the confusingly similar name of Suharto, and in being Javanese and politically skilled (Plate 5.3). Suharto differed from Sukarno in being 20 years younger (1921–2008), not having played a significant role in the struggle against the Dutch colonial government, and being little known outside Indonesian army circles until the morning of October 1, 1965. When Suharto learned of the uprising early on that morning, he adopted a series of counter-measures while playing for time and trying to figure out a fast-moving and confusing series of developments. He summoned the commanders of the two army battalions on the central square to come meet him inside Kostrad headquarters, where he told them that they were in revolt and commanded them to take orders from him; they dutifully obeyed. The coup leaders, plus Sukarno, to whom the fast-moving situation may have been as confusing as it was to Suharto, now gathered at Halim air force base, because the air force was the branch of the Indonesian Armed Forces most sympathetic to the communists. Suharto responded by sending reliable troops to capture first the telecom building, then Halim air force base, which the troops succeeded in doing with minimal fighting. At 9:00 P.M. on that evening of October 1, Suharto announced in a broadcast over the radio that he now controlled the Indonesian army, would crush the 30 September Movement, and would protect President Sukarno. The coup leaders fled from Halim base and from Jakarta, proceeded separately by train and plane to other cities in Central Java, and organized other uprisings in which other generals were killed. But those uprisings were suppressed by loyalist army troops within a day or two, just as had been the uprising in Jakarta.

———

To this day, many questions about the failed coup remain unanswered. What seems clear is that the coup was a joint effort by two sets of leaders: some junior military officers with communist sympathies, and one or more PKI leaders. But why did professional military officers stage such an amateurishly bungled coup, with such lack of military planning? Why didn't they hold a press conference to enlist public support? Was the involvement of the PKI in the coup confined to just a few of its leaders? Was Communist China involved in planning and supporting the coup? Why didn't the coup leaders include Suharto on their list of generals to be kidnapped? Why didn't the coup forces capture the Kostrad headquarters on one side of the central square? Did President Sukarno know of the coup in advance? Did General Suharto know of the coup in advance? Did anti-communist generals know of the coup in advance but nevertheless allow it to unfold, in order to provide them with a pretext for previously laid plans to suppress the PKI?

The last possibility is strongly suggested by the speed of the military's reaction. Within three days, military commanders began a propaganda campaign to justify round-ups and killings of Indonesian communists and their sympathizers on a vast scale (Plate 5.4). The coup itself initially killed only 12 people in Jakarta on October 1, plus a few other people in other cities of Java on October

2. But those few killings gave Suharto and the Indonesian military a pretext for mass murder. That response to the coup was so quick, efficient, and massive that it could hardly have been improvised spontaneously within a few days in response to unexpected developments. Instead, it must have involved previous planning that awaited only an excuse, which the bungled coup attempt of October 1 and 2 provided.

The military's motives for that mass murder arose from Indonesia's breakdown of political compromise and democratic government in the 1950's and early 1960's, culminating in the three-way power struggle in 1965 among the PKI, the armed forces, and President Sukarno. It appeared that the armed forces were starting to lose that struggle. As Indonesia's largest and best-organized political party, the PKI threatened the army's political power and the money that the army extracted from state-owned businesses, smuggling, and corruption. The PKI's proposal to arm workers and peasants as a separate armed force threatened the army's monopoly of military power. As subsequent events would show, President Sukarno alone could not resist the army. But Sukarno was looking to the PKI as a potential ally to serve as a counter-weight to the army. In addition, the military itself was divided and included communist sympathizers, who were the organizers of the coup (along with one or more PKI leaders). Hence the coup gave anti-communist army officers an opportunity to purge their political opponents within the army itself. Not surprisingly, army commanders alarmed by the PKI's rising power prepared their own contingency plan, for which the coup offered a trigger. It remains unknown whether Suharto himself was already involved in drawing up that contingency plan, or whether (like Chile's General Pinochet) he became at the last minute the leader of a military take-over prepared by others.

On October 4 Suharto arrived at an area called Lubang Buaya

("Crocodile Hole" in the Indonesian language), where the coup squads had thrown the bodies of the kidnapped generals down a well. In front of photographers and television cameras, the decomposing bodies were pulled out of the well. On the next day, October 5, the generals' coffins were driven through Jakarta's streets, lined by thousands of people. The military's anti-communist leadership quickly blamed the PKI for the murders, even though the murders had actually been carried out by units of the military itself. A propaganda campaign that could only have been planned in advance was immediately launched to create a hysterical atmosphere, warning non-communist Indonesians that they were in mortal danger from the communists, who were said to be making lists of people to kill, and to be practicing techniques for gouging out eyes. Members of the PKI's women's auxiliary were claimed to have carried out sadistic sexual torture and mutilation of the kidnapped generals. President Sukarno tried to minimize the significance of the October 1 coup attempt and objected to the scale of the military's counter-measures, but the military had now wrested control of the situation from Sukarno. From October 5 onwards, the military began a round-up aimed at eliminating every member of the PKI and of every PKI-affiliated organization, and all of the families of those members.

The PKI reaction was not what one would expect of an organization that had been planning a coup. Throughout October and November, when PKI members were summoned to come to army bases and police stations, many came willingly, because they expected just to be questioned and released. The PKI could have supported the coup and thwarted military counter-measures by mobilizing railroad workers to sabotage trains, mechanics to sabotage army vehicles, and peasants to block roads; but it did none of those things.

Because the Indonesian killings were not carried out with the meticulous organization and documentation of the Nazi killings in World War Two concentration camps, there is much uncertainty about the number of Indonesian victims. The highest estimates are about 2 million; the most widely cited figure is the contemporary estimate of half-a-million arrived at by a member of President Sukarno's own fact-finding commission. Indonesian killing technology was much simpler than that of the Nazis: victims were killed one by one, with machetes and other hand weapons and by strangling, rather than by killing hundreds of people at once in a gas chamber. Indonesian disposal of bodies was also haphazard, rather than carried out by utilizing specially built large ovens. Nevertheless, what happened in Indonesia in 1965 and 1966 still ranks as one of the world's biggest episodes of mass murder since World War Two.

A common misconception is that the killings were only or mainly of Chinese Indonesians. No, most of the victims were non-Chinese Indonesians; the targets were Indonesian suspected communists and their affiliates, not specifically Chinese. Another misconception is that the killings were a spontaneous explosion by a population of irrational, emotionally unstable, and immature people prone to "run amok," a Malay expression that refers to individuals who go crazy and become murderers. No, I'm unaware of any evidence that Indonesians are intrinsically unstable and murderous. Instead, the Indonesian military planned and orchestrated the killings in order to protect its own interests, and the military's propaganda campaign convinced many Indonesian civilians to carry out the killings in order to protect in turn their own interests. The military's killing campaign was evil but not irrational: it aimed to destroy the military's strongest opponents, and it succeeded in that aim.

The situation as of the end of October 1965 was thus that Suharto commanded the loyalty of some but not all military leaders. Sukarno was still president-for-life, was still revered by much of the public as Indonesia's founding father, was still popular among military officers and soldiers, and was politically skilled. Suharto couldn't just push Sukarno aside, any more than some ambitious American general could have pushed George Washington aside half-way through our beloved founding father's second term as president.

Suharto had previously been considered just as an efficient general, and nothing more. But he now proceeded to display political skills exceeding even Sukarno's. He gradually won the support of other military leaders, replaced military and civil service officers sympathetic to the PKI with officers loyal to him, and over the next two-and-a-half years proceeded slowly and cautiously to displace Sukarno while pretending to act on Sukarno's behalf. In March 1966 Sukarno was pressured into signing a letter ceding authority to Suharto; in March 1967 Suharto became acting president, and in March 1968 he replaced Sukarno as president. He remained in power for another 30 years.

———

In contrast to Sukarno, Suharto did not pursue Third World anticolonial politics and had no territorial ambitions outside the Indonesian archipelago. He concentrated instead on Indonesian domestic problems. In particular, Suharto ended Sukarno's armed "confrontation" with Malaysia over Borneo, rejoined the United Nations, abandoned Sukarno's ideologically motivated alignment with Communist China, and aligned Indonesia instead with the West for economic and strategic reasons.

Suharto himself lacked a university education and had no understanding of economic theory. Instead, he placed Indonesia's "official" economy (in contrast to the unofficial economy described below) in the hands of highly qualified Indonesian economists, many of whom had obtained degrees at the University of California at Berkeley. That resulted in the nickname of "the Berkeley mafia." Under Sukarno, the Indonesian economy had become saddled with deficit spending resulting in heavy debt and massive inflation. Like General Pinochet's Chicago Boys in Chile, Suharto's Berkeley mafia instituted economic reforms by balancing the budget, cutting subsidies, adopting a market orientation, and reducing Indonesia's national debt and inflation. Taking advantage of Suharto's abandonment of Sukarno's left-leaning policy, the Berkeley mafia encouraged foreign investment and attracted American and European aid for developing Indonesia's natural resources, especially its oil and minerals.

Indonesia's other body of economic planning was the military. Suharto declared, "The armed forces have a great interest in the process of modernizing the state and society, and wish to play a vital role in its process.... If the army stands neutral in the face of problems in consolidating the New Order, it disavows its role as well as the call of history.... The military has two functions, that is, as an armed tool of the state and as a functional group to achieve the goals of the revolution." Just imagine an American general becoming president, and saying that about the U.S. army! In effect, the Indonesian military developed a parallel government with a parallel budget approximately equal to the official government budget. Under Suharto, military officers constituted more than half of Indonesia's mayors, local administrators, and provincial governors. Local military officers had the authority to arrest and hold indefinitely anyone suspected of actions "prejudicial to security."

Military officers founded businesses and practiced corruption and extortion on a huge scale, in order to fund the military and to line their private pockets. While Suharto himself did not conduct an ostentatiously lavish lifestyle, his wife and children were reputed to practice enormous corruption. Without even investing their own funds, his children launched businesses that made them rich. When his family was then accused of corruption, Suharto became angry and insisted that their new wealth was just due to their skills as business people. Indonesians gave to Suharto's wife (Ibu Tien = Madam Tien) a nickname meaning "Madam Ten Percent," because she was said to extract 10% of the value of government contracts. By the end of Suharto's reign, Indonesia was ranked among the most corrupt countries in the world.

Corruption pervaded all aspects of Indonesian life. For instance, while I was working in Indonesia for the international environmental organization World Wildlife Fund (WWF), an Indonesian friend also working for WWF pointed out to me an Indonesian WWF office director and whispered that his nickname was "Mr. Corruption" — because he was not just normally corrupt, but exceptionally corrupt; a boat that overseas WWF donors had bought for that particular WWF office had ended up as a private boat of Mr. Corruption. As another example of non-governmental corruption, my work in Indonesia routinely required me to fly with heavy luggage that incurred excess baggage charges. I became accustomed to the fact that, whenever I checked in at the counter of an Indonesian domestic airport, the airline check-in employees came out to me from behind the counter and demanded the excess baggage charges in cash for their own pockets, not for the airline.

Suharto replaced Sukarno's governing principle of "guided democracy" with what came to be known as the "New Order," which supposedly meant going back to the pure concepts of Indonesia's 1945 constitution and to the five principles of Pancasila. Suharto claimed to be stripping away the bad changes subsequently introduced by Indonesia's political parties, for which he had no use. He considered Indonesian people to be undisciplined, ignorant, susceptible to dangerous ideas, and unready for democracy. In his autobiography he wrote, "In Pancasila democracy there is no place for a Western-style opposition. In the realm of Pancasila democracy, we recognize musyawarah [deliberation] to reach the mufakat [consensus] of the people ... we do not recognize opposition as in the West. Here we do not recognize opposition based on conflict, opposition which is just trying to be different.... Democracy must know discipline and responsibility, because without both those things democracy means only confusion."

These Suharto leitmotivs — that there is only one way, and that there should be no disputes — applied to many spheres of Indonesian life. There was only one acceptable ideology, Pancasila, which civil servants and members of the armed forces had to study under a bureaucratic indoctrination program. Of course, labor strikes were forbidden: they were contrary to Pancasila. The only acceptable ethnic identity was uniformly Indonesian, so Chinese Indonesians were forbidden to use Chinese writing or to keep their Chinese names. National political unity admitted no local autonomy for Aceh, East Timor, Indonesian New Guinea, or other distinct regions. Ideally, Suharto would have preferred just one political party, but parliamentary elections contested by multiple parties were necessary for an Indonesian government to appear legitimate on the international scene. However, a single government "functional group" named Golkar always won elections with up to 70% of the vote, while all other political parties were merged into two other functional groups, one of them Islamic and the other non-Islamic, which always lost elections. Thus, Indonesia under Suharto came to be a military state, much as it was in the last decade of Dutch colonial government — with the difference that the state was now run by Indonesians, rather than by foreigners.

The historical display that I saw in the Indonesian hotel lobby in 1979 reflected Suharto's emphasis on the aborted 1965 coup as a Communist Party plot, portrayed as *the* defining moment in modern Indonesian history. At the huge Pancasila Monument erected in 1969 to commemorate the killings of the seven generals (Plate 5.5), considered "seven heroes of the revolution," a solemn ceremony of remembrance and of re-dedication to Pancasila was (and still is) held each year. A bas-relief on the monument and an adjacent Museum of PKI Treason depict the history of post-colonial Indonesia as a sequence of treasonous communist acts culminating in the 1965 coup attempt. On September 30 every year, all Indonesian TV stations were required to broadcast, and all Indonesian schoolchildren were required to watch, a grim four-hour-long government-commissioned film about the seven kidnappings and killings. There was of course no mention of the half-a-million Indonesians killed in retaliation. Not until a dozen years later, in the year (1979) when I began to work in Indonesia, were most political prisoners finally released.

Indonesia's parliament reelected Suharto as president for one five-year term after another. After nearly 33 years, just after parliament had acclaimed him as president for a seventh five-year term, his regime collapsed quickly and unexpectedly in May 1998. It had been undermined by a combination of many factors. One was an Asian financial crisis that reduced the value of Indonesia's currency by 80% and provoked rioting. Another was that Suharto himself, at age 77, had grown out of touch with reality, lost his political skills, and was shaken by the death in 1996 of his wife, who had been his closest partner and anchor. There was widespread public anger at corruption and at the wealth accumulated by his family. Suharto's own successes had created a modern industrialized Indonesian society, whose citizens no longer tolerated his insistence that they were unfit to govern themselves. The Indonesian military evidently concluded, as had the Chilean military after the "No!" vote of 1998, that it couldn't stop the wave of protests, and that Suharto (like Pinochet) should resign before the situation got out of control.

In 1999, the year after Suharto's fall, Indonesia carried out its first relatively free elections in more than 40 years. Since then, Indonesia has had a series of elections with voter turnouts far higher than voter turnouts in the U.S.: turnouts of 70%–90%, whereas voter turnouts in the U.S. barely reach 60% even for presidential elections. In 2014 Indonesia's latest presidential election was won by an anti-establishment civilian, the former mayor of Jakarta, Joko Widodo, whose defeated opponent was an army general. Corruption has decreased, and sometimes it gets punished.

———

Let's summarize the Suharto regime, and the legacies of the crisis provoked by the 1965 failed coup attempt and the successful counter-coup. The bad legacies are obvious. Worst are the mass murder of half-a-million Indonesians, and the imprisonment of a hundred thousand for more than a decade. Massive corruption reduced Indonesia's rate of economic growth below the level that it would have enjoyed if so much money had not been diverted into the pockets of the military, running its own parallel government with a parallel budget. That example of corruption was widely imitated through Indonesian society (even by airline clerks). Suharto's belief that his subjects were incapable of governing themselves postponed for several decades the opportunity for Indonesians to learn how to govern themselves democratically.

From the events of 1965, the Indonesian armed forces drew the lesson that success would be achieved by using force and killing people, rather than by solving problems that make people dissatisfied. That policy of murderous army repression has cost Indonesia dearly in Indonesian New Guinea, in Sumatra, and especially on the eastern Indonesian island of Timor, which had been divided politically between a Portuguese colony in the east and Indonesian territory in the west. When Portugal was shedding its last colonies in 1974, all geographic logic argued for East Timor becoming another province of Indonesia, which already accommodated so many provinces with different cultures, languages, and histories. Of course one can object that national boundaries aren't shaped just by geographic logic: Canada isn't part of the U.S., and Denmark isn't part of Germany. But East Timor isn't comparable to Canada or Denmark: it's just the eastern half of one small island in a long chain of many islands, all the rest of which are wholly Indonesian. Had the Indonesian government and army displayed even a minimum of tact, they might have negotiated an arrangement to incorporate East Timor with some autonomy into Indonesia. Instead, the Indonesian army invaded, massacred, and annexed East Timor. Under international pressure, and to the horror of the Indonesian army, Indonesia's President Habibie, who succeeded Suharto, permitted a referendum on independence for East Timor in August 1999. By then, the population of course voted overwhelmingly for independence. Thereupon, the Indonesian army organized pro-Indonesia militias to massacre yet again, forcibly evacuated much of the population to Indonesian West Timor, and burned most of the new country's buildings — to no avail, as international troops restored order and East Timor eventually took control of itself as the nation of Timor-Leste. The costs to the East Timorese were that about one-quarter of the population died, and that the survivors now constitute Asia's poorest mini-nation, whose per-capita income is six times lower than that of Indonesia. The costs to Indonesians were that they now have in their midst a separate nation with sovereignty over a potentially oil-rich seabed whose revenues will not flow to Indonesia.

Now that we've dwelt on those appalling legacies of the Suharto regime, it may seem that there is nothing further to be said about it. But history rarely presents us with either pure evil or pure good, and history should be reviewed honestly. Hideous as it was in other respects, the Suharto regime did have positive legacies. It created and maintained economic growth, even though that growth was reduced by corruption (Plates 5.6, 5.7). It attracted foreign investment. It concentrated its energy on Indonesia's domestic problems, rather than dissipating it on world anti-colonial politics or on the effort to dismantle neighboring Malaysia. It promoted family planning, and thereby addressed one of the biggest fundamental problems that have bedeviled independent Indonesia as well as the previous Dutch colonial regime. (Even in the most remote villages of Indonesian New Guinea, I saw government posters describing family planning.) It presided over a green revolution that, by providing fertilizer and improved seeds, greatly increased the yields of rice and other crops, thereby massively raising agricultural productivity and Indonesians' nutrition. Indonesia *was* under great strain before 1965; today, Indonesia shows no imminent risk of falling apart, although its fragmentation into islands, territorial extent of thousands of miles, hundreds of indigenous languages, and coexistence of religions were all recipes for disaster. Eighty years ago, most Indonesians didn't think of themselves as Indonesians; now, Indonesians take their national identity for granted.

But many people, Indonesians and non-Indonesians, give the Suharto regime zero credit rather than some credit. They object: Indonesia might have made those same advances under a regime other than Suharto's. That's a historical "what if?" question, but such questions can't be answered with confidence. One can only compare what actually did happen in Indonesia after 1965 with what might have happened under the only two available alternatives: continuation of the Sukarno regime that was in power until 1965, or its replacement by a communist regime under the PKI that was seeking to take power. On the one hand, the Sukarno regime had brought Indonesia to political chaos and economic standstill as of 1965. The tortures, killings, grinding poverty, and insane policies associated with communist dictatorships in Cambodia, North Korea, and other countries warn us that a communist alternative to Suharto could have been worse for Indonesia than was Suharto. On the other hand, there are people who argue that Sukarno's regime was leading to something wonderful, or that an Indonesian communist regime under the PKI would have proved different from communist regimes elsewhere in the world. We'll never know.

———

How does Indonesia's crisis fit into our framework that contrasts national crises with individual crises?

Indonesia does illustrate selective change, and the drawing of a fence (factor #3, Table 1.2). Within the fence were major areas considered ripe for change. Those areas included Suharto's replacement of civilian government by a military dictatorship, the reverse change by his successors, Suharto's embracing of Western-trained economists to replace economic regression with economic growth, and Suharto's abandonment of Sukarno's aspirations to Third World political leadership. On the other hand, outside the fence lay major features of Indonesia that were preserved intact after 1965, including national territorial integrity, considerable religious tolerance, and a non-communist government. Those continuities were considered non-negotiable core values by Sukarno *and* by Suharto *and* by Suharto's successors, except for Sukarno's willingness to align himself with communists.

Some factors in Indonesia made it difficult for the country to solve its problems. As a newly independent ex-colony, Indonesia began with only limited national identity (factor #6) — unlike Finland, which had already enjoyed considerable autonomous self-government for a century before it achieved independence. As a new country, Indonesia could not draw confidence from a previous history of successful change, except for its independence struggles of 1945–1949 (factor #8). Honest realistic self-appraisal (factor #7) was deficient in President Sukarno, who believed himself endowed with a unique ability to interpret the unconscious wishes of the Indonesian people. The core values of many or most officers of the Indonesian military were ones that they were willing to kill for, but not to die for (factor #11). Indonesia's freedom of action was limited by the internal constraints of poverty and of population growth (factor #12).

On the other hand, Indonesia also enjoyed advantages in solving its problems. As an island archipelago, it enjoys freedom from external constraints, like Chile and unlike Finland: there has been no nation that threatens Indonesia since the departure of the Dutch (factor #12 again). Berkeley's mafia of economists was able to draw on models well tested in other countries in order to reform the Indonesian economy and achieve economic growth (factor #5). After Suharto abandoned his predecessor's pro–Communist China foreign policy and adopted a pro-West policy, Indonesia received a great deal of investment and foreign aid from Western countries in rebuilding its economy (factor #4).

Suharto did often illustrate honest, realistic, Machiavellian self-appraisal (factor #7). In gradually pushing aside Indonesia's popular founding father and first president Sukarno, Suharto proceeded cautiously, figured out at each step what he could get away with and what he couldn't get away with, and eventually succeeded in replacing Sukarno, even though it took time. Suharto was also realistic in abandoning Sukarno's foreign policy ambitions beyond Indonesia's means, including guerrilla warfare against Malaysia and the attempt to lead a world anti-colonial movement.

Indonesia also illustrates three issues about national crises that do not arise for individual crises. Like Chile but unlike Finland, Indonesia illustrates the breakdown of political compromise that produced the log jam and secessionist movements of the early 1950's, leading to Sukarno's installation of "guided democracy," then to the Indonesian Communist Party calling for arming the workers and peasants, which led in turn to the army responding by committing mass murder. Also like Chile but unlike Finland, Indonesia illustrates the role played by unusual leaders. In the case of Indonesia, those were Sukarno, blessed by charisma and cursed by overconfidence in that charisma; and Suharto, blessed by patience, caution, and political skills, and cursed by his policy of murderous cruelty, by his blindness to the corruption of his own family, and by his lack of faith in his own countrymen. Finally, as for reconciliation after killings provoked by the breakdown of political compromise, Indonesia stands at the opposite extreme from Finland, with Chile intermediate: rapid reconciliation in Finland after the Finnish Civil War; much open discussion and trials of perpetrators in Chile, but incomplete reconciliation; and very limited discussion or reconciliation, and no trials, in Indonesia. Factors responsible for Indonesia's lack of trials include the country's weak democratic traditions; the fact that post-Pinochet Chile's motto "a fatherland for all Chileans" found less echo in post-Suharto Indonesia; and, most of all, that Indonesia remained a military dictatorship for 33 years after the mass killings, and that the armed forces remain much more powerful in Indonesia today than in Chile.

———

I can add my personal experience of the selective changes in Indonesia. I worked there for 17 years during the Suharto era, from 1979 to 1996. I then didn't go back until 2012 (14 years after Suharto's fall) and have continued to visit Indonesia ever since. Many surprises awaited me upon my return.

The first surprise involved air travel. In the 1980's and 1990's the operations of Indonesian commercial airlines were often care-less and dangerous. In addition to being shaken down for bribes and diverted excess baggage charges, I experienced one flight on which large fuel drums were placed unsecured in the passenger cabin, the steward remained standing during take-off, and seat-belts and vomit bags for passengers (including one who was vom-iting) were lacking. During another flight on a large passenger jet into the provincial capital of Jayapura, the pilot and co-pilot were so absorbed in chatting with the stewardesses through the open cabin door that they failed to notice that they were approaching the runway at too high an altitude, tried to make up for their neglect by going into a steep dive, had to brake hard on landing, and succeeded in stopping the plane only 20 feet short of the run-way perimeter ditch. But by 2012 Indonesia's leading airline, Garuda, was rated as one of the best regional carriers in the world. Every time since 2012 that I have checked in with overweight bag-gage, I have been sent to Garuda's excess baggage office to pay the charges by credit card to Garuda itself in return for a receipt. I was regularly asked for bribes until 1996; I have never been asked for a bribe since 2012.

While at sea in Indonesian coastal waters in 2012, I spotted a military-looking vessel nearby, asked what it was, and learned to my surprise that it was a government patrol boat looking for illegal fishing boats. Until 1996, I would have regarded the phrase "Indo-nesian government patrol boat" as a self-contradicting oxymoron like "jumbo shrimp." I had become accustomed to the Indonesian military's activities as creating a need for patrolling, rather than as carrying out patrolling.

When I landed on the coast of Indonesian New Guinea in 2014, I was astonished to encounter big or colorful birds, which had for-merly been the prime target of illegal hunting, now calling and dis-playing near and even in coastal villages: imperial pigeons, hornbills, Palm Cockatoos, and birds of paradise. Previously, those species were shot out or trapped near villages, and encountered only far from habitation.

Upon my return to Indonesian New Guinea, Indonesian friends related to me what at first sounded like the same old stories that used to happen in the 1980's and 1990's. In this New Guinea village, an Indonesian policeman had recently shot four New Guineans; in that district, the district administrator had been very corrupt. Ho-hum, of course, so what else is new? The difference, this time, was that both the policeman and the administrator were put on trial and sent to jail; that wouldn't have happened before.

While these are signs of progress, they shouldn't be exaggerated. Many of Indonesia's old problems persist, to varying degrees. Bribery is reportedly still widespread, though I no longer encounter it myself. My own Indonesian friends still don't talk about the mass killings of 1965: my younger friends today weren't alive then, and my older friends who were alive in 1965 have remained silent about it to me, although American colleagues tell me that they do encounter many Indonesians interested in the killings. There is still fear of Indonesian military interference in Indonesian democracy: when a civilian politician defeated a general in the 2014 presidential elections, anxious months passed before it became clear that the general wouldn't succeed in his efforts to annul the election. In 2013 a rifle shot from the ground broke the windshield of my chartered helicopter in the air over Indonesian New Guinea; it remained uncertain whether the shot had been fired by New Guinean guerrillas still fighting for independence, or by Indonesian troops themselves feigning guerrilla activity in order to justify a crackdown.

My remaining personal observation requires more explanation. Among the nations discussed in this book, Indonesia is the one with the shortest national history and the greatest linguistic diversity by far, and initially was the only nation at serious risk of its territory falling apart. The former Dutch colony of the Dutch East Indies might have dissolved into several separate nation-states, just as the former French colony of Indo-China did dissolve into Vietnam, Cambodia, and Laos. That dissolution was evidently the intention of the Dutch when they tried to establish separate federal states within their colony in the late 1940's, in order to undermine the nascent unified Republic of Indonesia.

But Indonesia didn't fall apart. It built from scratch, surprisingly quickly, a sense of national identity. That sense grew partly spontaneously, and partly was reinforced by conscious government efforts. One basis of that sense is pride in the revolution of 1945–1949, and in the throwing-off of Dutch rule. The government reinforces that spontaneous sense of pride by retelling the story of 1945–1949, with considerable justification, as a heroic struggle for national independence — just as American schools retell the story of our own revolution to all American schoolchildren. Indonesians are proud of their wide territorial extent, expressed in an Indonesian national song "Dari Sabang sampai Merauke" ("From Sabang to Merauke," Indonesia's western and eastern extremities, respectively, 3,400 miles apart). Another basis of national identity is Indonesians' rapid adoption of their easily learned and wonderfully supple Bahasa Indonesia as *the* national language, coexisting with the 700 local languages.

In addition to those underlying roots of national identity, the Indonesian government continues to try to reinforce identity by emphasizing the five-point framework of Pancasila, and by annual ceremonies remembering the seven murdered generals at Jakarta's Pancasila Monument. But, despite having stayed in many Indonesian hotels since my return to Indonesia in 2012, I haven't seen another hotel lobby display like the account of the "communist coup" that greeted me in the lobby of the first Indonesian hotel where I stayed in 1979. Indonesians now feel sufficiently secure in their national identity that they don't need misleading accounts of a "communist coup" to reinforce it. To me as a visitor to Indonesia, that deepening sense of national identity is among the biggest changes that I've experienced.

FIG. 6 *Map of Germany*

CHAPTER 6

REBUILDING GERMANY

Germany in 1945 — 1945 to 1961 — Germans
holding judgment — 1968 — 1968's aftermath —
Brandt and re-unification — Geographic
constraints — Self-pity? — Leaders and realism —
Crisis framework

Germany's surrender on May 7 and 8, 1945 marked the end of World War Two in Europe. The situation in Germany as of that date was as follows.

The Nazi leaders Hitler, Goebbels, Himmler, and Bormann had committed or were about to commit suicide. Germany's armies, after conquering most of Europe, had been driven back and defeated. About 7 million Germans had been killed, either as soldiers, as civilians killed by bombs, or as civilian refugees killed while fleeing, particularly from the advancing Soviet armies in the east taking revenge for the horrible things that the German military had done to Soviet civilians.

Tens of millions of Germans who survived had been traumatized by severe bombing (Plate 6.1). Virtually all of Germany's major cities had been reduced to rubble, from bombing and fighting (Plate 6.2). Between one-quarter and one-half of the housing in German cities had been destroyed.

One-quarter of Germany's former territory was lost to Poland and to the Soviet Union. What remained of Germany was divided into four occupation zones that would eventually become two separate countries.

About 10 million Germans were homeless refugees. Millions of Germans were searching for missing family members, of whom some miraculously turned up alive years later. But most never turned up, and for many of them the time and place and circumstances of their deaths remain forever unknown. My first German teacher, living in exile in 1954, happened to mention having a son. When I naïvely asked him about his son, my teacher burst out in pain, "They took him away, and we never heard anything about him again!" By the time that I met my teacher, he and his wife had been living with that uncertainty for 10 years. Two of my later German friends were "luckier": one learned of her father's probable death "only" a year after the last news from him, and another learned of his brother's death after three years.

As of 1945, the German economy had collapsed. The German currency was rapidly losing its value through inflation. The German people had undergone 12 years of Nazi programming. Virtually all German government officials and judges had been convinced or complicit Nazis, because they had had to swear a personal oath of allegiance to Hitler in order to hold a government job. German society was authoritarian.

Today, Germany is a liberal democracy. Its economy is the fourth largest in the world, and is one of the world's leading export economies. Germany is the most powerful country in Europe west of Russia. It established its own stable currency (the Deutsche Mark); then it played a leading role in establishing a common European currency (the euro), and in establishing the European Union that now joins it peacefully with the countries that it had so recently attacked. Germany has largely dealt with its Nazi past. German society is much less authoritarian than it once was.

What happened between May 1945 and today to produce those changes? I first visited Germany in 1959, lived there for much of 1961, and have frequently returned for visits ever since. I'll now discuss five of the changes that I witnessed in post-war Germany. Two of them (partition and West German economic recovery) were nearly complete by the time of my residence in Germany; two others (Germans facing the legacies of Naziism, and social changes) were already underway then but accelerated afterwards; and one (re-unification) happened only decades later and seemed utterly inconceivable to me and to my German friends in 1961. From the perspective of this book's framework of crisis and change, Germany represents an extreme case in many respects, including in its geopolitical constraints and in the role of distinctive leaders for bad and for good. Most of all, Germany represents an extreme in the magnitude of the crisis that it faced. Meiji Japan was merely threatened by attack; Finland and Australia were attacked but remained unoccupied; but Germany and Japan in 1945 had been attacked, conquered, occupied, and far more devastated than any other nation discussed in this book.

———

World War Two's victorious Allies carved Germany into four occupation zones: American in the south, French in the southwest, British in the northwest, and Soviet in the east. While the capital city of Berlin lay in the middle of the Soviet zone, it too was divided into occupation sectors of all four powers, like an island of non-Soviet occupation within the Soviet zone. In 1948 the Soviets imposed a blockade on American, British, and French overland access to their enclaves within Berlin, in order to compel the three Western Allies to abandon their enclaves. The Allies responded with the Berlin airlift and supplied Berlin by air for nearly a year, until the Soviets gave up and abandoned their blockade in 1949.

In that same year of 1949, the Allies joined their zones into one entity, called the Federal Republic of Germany, also known as West Germany, or Bundesrepublik Deutschland. The Soviet zone became a separate entity called the German Democratic Republic, also known as East Germany or its German-language acronym DDR. Today, East Germany is routinely dismissed as a failed communist dictatorship that eventually collapsed and became in effect absorbed by West Germany. The term "German Democratic Republic" is remembered as a big lie, like the name "Democratic People's Republic of Korea" that North Korea adopts for itself today. It's easy now to forget that not just Soviet brute force but also German communist idealism contributed to East Germany's founding, and that numerous German intellectuals *chose* to move to East Germany from West Germany or from exile overseas.

But the standard of living and freedom in East Germany eventually fell far behind that of West Germany. While American economic aid was pouring into West Germany, the Soviets imposed economic reparations on their zone, dismantled and carted away whole factories to Russia, and reorganized East German agriculture as collective farms. Increasingly, over the next two generations until re-unification in 1990, East Germans grew up unable to learn the motivation, acquired by people in Western democracies, to work hard to better their lives.

As a result, East Germans began fleeing to the West. Hence in 1952 East Germany sealed its borders to the West, but East Germans could still escape by passing from East Berlin into West Berlin, then flying from West Berlin to West Germany. The pre-war public transport system in Berlin (U-Bahn and S-Bahn) included lines that connected West and East Berlin, so that anyone in East

Berlin could get into West Berlin just by hopping on a train. When I first visited Berlin in 1960, like other Western tourists I took the U-Bahn to visit East Berlin and to return to West Berlin.

In 1953 dissatisfaction in East Germany blew up in a strike that turned into a rebellion, crushed by Soviet troops. Dissatisfied East Germans continued to escape to the West by way of the Berlin public transport system. Finally, on the night of August 13, 1961, while I was living in Germany, the East German regime suddenly closed the East Berlin U-Bahn stations and erected a wall between East and West Berlin, patrolled by border guards who shot and killed people trying to cross the wall (Plate 6.3). I recall the disbelief, shock, and rage of my West German friends the morning after the wall's erection. The East Germans justified the wall by claiming that it was built to protect East Germany from West German infiltrators and criminals, rather than admitting that it was aimed at preventing dissatisfied East Germans from fleeing to the West. The Western Allies didn't dare to breach the wall, because they knew that they were powerless to do anything for a West Berlin surrounded by East German and Russian troops.

From then on, East Germany remained a separate state from which there was no possibility of fleeing to West Germany without high probability of being killed at the border. (Over a thousand Germans died in the attempt.) There was no realistic hope for the re-unification of Germany, given the polarization between the Soviet Union and the communist East European block on the one hand, and the U.S. and Western Europe on the other hand. It was as if the United States became divided at the Mississippi River between a communist eastern U.S. and a democratic western U.S., with no prospect of re-unification for the foreseeable future.

As for West Germany just after World War Two, one policy considered by the victorious Western Allies was to prevent it from ever rebuilding its industries, to force its economy to revert just to agriculture under the so-called Morgenthau Plan, and to extract war reparations as the Allies had done after World War One and as the Soviets were now doing in East Germany. That strategy stemmed from the widespread Allied view that Germany had been responsible not only for instigating World War Two under Hitler (as is widely agreed) but also for instigating World War One under Kaiser Wilhelm II (a much-debated historical question), and that permitting Germany to re-industrialize could lead to yet another world war.

What caused that Allied view to change was the development of the Cold War, and the resulting realization that the real risk of another world war came not from Germany but from the Soviet Union. As I explained in Chapter 4 in connection with U.S. policy towards Chile, that fear was the dominating motive underlying American foreign policy in the decades following World War Two. The communist take-overs of all Eastern European countries already occupied by Soviet troops, Soviet acquisition of atomic bombs and then of hydrogen bombs, the Soviet attempt in 1948–1949 to blockade and strangle the Western enclave in Berlin, and the strength of communist parties even in some Western European democracies (especially Italy) made Western Europe seem the most likely site for the Cold War to explode into another world war. As late as 1961, when I was about to go live in Germany, my (American) father advised me in all seriousness to be ready to flee to a safe refuge in Switzerland at the first signs of danger in Europe.

From that perspective, West Germany, lying in the center of Europe, and bordering on communist East Germany and Czechoslovakia, was crucial to the freedom of Western Europe. The Western Allies needed West Germany to become strong again, as a bulwark against communism. Their other motives for wanting Germany to become strong were to reduce the risk that a weak and frustrated Germany might descend again into political extremism (as had happened after World War One), and to reduce the economic costs to the Allies of having to continue to feed and support an economically weak West Germany.

After 1945, it took several years, during which the West German economy continued to deteriorate, for that change of view to mature among the Western Allies. Finally, in 1948 the U.S. began to extend to West Germany the Marshall Plan economic aid that the U.S. had already begun to provide to other Western European countries in 1947. Simultaneously, West Germany replaced its weak and inflated currency with a new currency, the Deutsche Mark. When the Western Allies merged their occupation zones into a single West Germany, they retained veto power over its legislation. However, West Germany's first chancellor, Konrad Adenauer, proved skilled at exploiting American fears of a communist assault, in order to obtain Allied acquiescence to delegate more and more authority to West Germany and less and less to the Allies. Adenauer's economics minister, Ludwig Erhard, instituted modified free-market policies and utilized Marshall Plan aid to fuel a spectacularly successful economic recovery that became known as the "Wirtschaftswunder," or "economic miracle." Rationing became abolished, industrial output and living standards soared, and the dream of being able to buy a car and a home became reality for West Germans.

By the time that I moved from Britain to West Germany, West Germany felt more prosperous and contented than was Britain. Note the irony, often noted bitterly by my British friends: *Germany* had lost World War Two and *Britain* had won it, but it was West Germany rather than Britain that then created the economic miracle. Politically, by 1955 West Germany had regained sovereignty, and Allied military occupation ended. After the Allies had fought two world wars in order to defeat and disarm Germany, West Germany began to rearm and to rebuild an army — not at its own initiative, but (incredibly!!) at Western urging and against a vote of the West German parliament itself, so that West Germany would have to share with the Allies the burden of defending Western Europe. From a 1945 perspective, that represented the most astonishing change in American, British, and French policy towards Germany.

The West German economy has been characterized by relatively good labor relations, infrequent strikes, and flexible conditions of employment. Employees and employers tacitly agree that employees won't strike, so that businesses can prosper, and that employers will share the resulting business prosperity with their workers. German industry developed an apprentice system that it still has today, in which young people become apprenticed to companies that pay them while they are learning their trade. At the end of the apprenticeship they then have jobs with that company. Today, Germany has Europe's largest economy.

———

At the end of World War Two, the Allies prosecuted the 24 top surviving Nazi leaders at Nuremberg for war crimes. Ten were condemned to death, of whom the highest ranking were the foreign minister Joachim von Ribbentrop and the Luftwaffe chief Hermann Göring. (The latter succeeded in committing suicide by poison during the night before his scheduled execution.) Seven others were sentenced to long or lifelong prison terms. The Nuremberg court also tried and sentenced numerous lower-level Nazis to shorter prison terms. The Allies subjected much larger numbers of Germans to "denazification" proceedings, consisting of examining their Nazi past and re-educating them.

But the Nuremberg trials and denazification proceedings didn't solve the legacies of Naziism for Germans. Millions of lower-level Germans who had either been convinced Nazis or had followed

Nazi orders were not prosecuted. Because the trials were conducted by the Allies rather than by Germans themselves, the prosecutions did not involve Germans taking responsibility for German actions. In Germany the trials became dismissed as "Siegerjustiz": mere revenge taken by the victors upon the vanquished. West Germany's own court system also carried out its own prosecutions, but their scope was initially limited.

A practical problem for both the Allies and the Germans themselves in developing a functioning post-war government in Germany was that any government requires officials with experience. But as of 1945, the vast majority of Germans who had acquired experience in government acquired it under the Nazi government, which meant that all potential post-war German government officers (including judges) had either been convinced Nazis or at the very least had cooperated with the Nazis. The sole exceptions were Germans who had either gone into exile or had been sent by the Nazis to concentration camps, where they couldn't acquire experience in governing. For example, West Germany's first chancellor after the war was Konrad Adenauer, a non-Nazi whom the Nazis had driven out of his office as mayor of Cologne. Adenauer's policy upon becoming chancellor was described as "amnesty and integration," which was a euphemism for not asking individual Germans about what they had been doing during the Nazi era. Instead, the government's focus was overwhelmingly on the urgent tasks of feeding and housing tens of millions of underfed and homeless Germans, rebuilding Germany's bombed cities and ruined economy, and re-establishing democratic government after 12 years of Nazi rule.

As a result, most Germans came to adopt the view that Nazi crimes were the fault of just a tiny clique of evil individual leaders, that the vast majority of Germans were innocent, that ordinary German soldiers who had fought heroically against the Soviets were guiltless, and that (by around the mid-1950's) there were no further important investigations of Nazi crimes left to be carried out. Further contributing to that failure of the West German government to prosecute Nazis was the widespread presence of former Nazis among post-war government prosecutors themselves: for instance, it turned out that 33 out of 47 officials in the West German federal criminal bureau (Bundeskriminalamt), and many members of the West German intelligence service, had been leaders of the Nazi fanatical SS organization. During my 1961 stay in Germany I occasionally heard defenses of the Nazi era by older Germans who had been in their 30's or 40's during that time, whom I had gotten to know well, and who were talking to me in private. For example, the husband of a woman musician with whom I played cello-and-piano sonatas eventually explained to me that the purported extermination of millions of Jews was mathematically impossible and the biggest lie ever told. Another older German friend eventually played for me a recorded speech by Hitler, to which she listened with a mixture of pleasure and amusement.

In 1958 the justice ministers of all West German states finally set up a central office to pool their efforts to prosecute Nazi crimes committed anywhere inside and even outside West German territory. The leading figure in those prosecutions was a German Jewish lawyer named Fritz Bauer, who had been a member of the anti-Nazi Social Democratic Party and had been compelled to flee Germany to Denmark in 1935. He began prosecuting cases as soon as he returned to Germany in the year 1949. From 1956 until his death in 1969 he served as chief prosecutor for the German state of Hessen. The central principle of Fritz Bauer's career was that Germans should hold judgment upon themselves. That meant prosecuting ordinary Germans, not just the leaders whom the Allies had prosecuted.

Bauer first became famous for what were known in Germany as the Auschwitz trials, in which he prosecuted low-level Germans who had been active at Auschwitz, the largest of the Nazi

extermination camps. The Auschwitz personnel whom he prosecuted consisted of very minor officials, such as clothes room man-
agers, pharmacists, and doctors. He then went on to prosecute
low-level Nazi police; German judges who had ruled against Jews or
against German resistance leaders or had issued death sentences;
Nazis who had persecuted Jewish business people; those involved
in Nazi euthanasia, including doctors, judges, and euthanasia personnel; officials in the German foreign office; and, what was most
disturbing to German people, German soldiers guilty of atrocities
particularly on the eastern front — disturbing because of the widespread German belief that atrocities had been committed by fanatical groups such as the SS but not by ordinary German soldiers.

In addition to those prosecutions, Bauer tried to track down the
most important and most evil Nazis who had disappeared after the
war: Hitler's assistant Martin Bormann; the Auschwitz concentration camp doctor Josef Mengele, who had carried out medical
experiments on prisoners; and Adolf Eichmann, who had organized the round-up of Jews. Bauer did not succeed in tracking
down Mengele, who eventually died in Brazil in 1979, or Bormann,
who it later turned out had committed suicide in 1945 around the
same time as did Hitler.

But Bauer did receive information about the location of Eichmann, who had fled to Argentina. Bauer concluded that he couldn't
safely pass that information to the German Secret Service for them
to capture and punish Eichmann, because he feared that they
would just tip off Eichmann and allow him to escape. Instead, he
relayed the news of Eichmann's whereabouts to the Israeli Secret
Service, which eventually succeeded in kidnapping Eichmann in
Argentina, secretly flying him to Israel in an El Al jet, putting him
on public trial, and eventually hanging him after a trial that drew
worldwide attention not just to Eichmann but to the whole subject
of individual responsibility for Nazi crimes.

Bauer's prosecutions attracted wide attention within Germany. More than anything else, they revealed to Germans of the 1960's what Germans of the 1930's and 1940's had been doing during the Nazi era. The Nazi defendants being prosecuted by Bauer all tended to offer the same set of excuses: I was merely following orders; I was conforming to the standards and laws of my society at the time; I was not the person who had responsibility for those people getting killed; I merely organized railroad transport of Jews being transported to extermination camps; I was just a pharmacist or a guard at Auschwitz; I didn't personally kill anyone myself; I was blinded by belief in authority and ideology proclaimed by the Nazi government, and that made me incapable of recognizing that what I was doing was wrong.

Bauer's response, which he formulated again and again at the trials and in public, was as follows. Those Germans whom he was prosecuting were committing crimes against humanity. The laws of the Nazi state were illegitimate. One cannot defend one's actions by saying that one was obeying those laws. There is no law that can justify a crime against humanity. Everybody must have his own sense of right and wrong and must obey it, independently of what a state government says. Anyone who takes part in what Bauer called a murder machine, such as the Auschwitz extermination apparatus, thereby becomes guilty of a crime. In addition, it became clear that many of the defendants whom he put on trial, and who gave as an excuse that they did what they did because they were forced to do it, were acting not out of compulsion but out of their own convictions.

In reality, many, perhaps most, of Bauer's prosecutions failed: the defendants were often acquitted by German courts even in the 1960's. Bauer himself was frequently the target of verbal attacks and even of death threats. Instead, the significance of Bauer's work was that he, a German, in German courts, demonstrated to the

German public again and again, in excruciating detail, the beliefs and deeds of Germans during the Nazi era. Nazi misdeeds were not just the work of a few bad leaders. Instead, masses of ordinary German soldiers and officials, including many who were now high-ranking officials of the West German government, had carried out Nazi orders, and had therefore been guilty of crimes against humanity. Bauer's efforts thereby formed an essential background to the German student revolts of 1968, to be discussed below.

The change in German views of the Nazi era after I lived in Germany was made brutally clear to me by an experience 21 years later, in 1982. In that year my wife Marie and I spent a vacation in Germany. As we were driving along the autobahn and approaching Munich, an autobahn exit sign pointed to a suburb called Dachau, site of a former Nazi concentration camp (German acronym, KZ) that Germans had converted into a museum. Neither of us had previously visited a KZ site. But we didn't anticipate that a "mere" museum exhibit would affect us, after all that we already knew of KZs through the stories of Marie's parents (KZ survivors) and the newsreels of my childhood. Least of all did we expect to be affected by how Germans themselves explained (or explained away) their own camps.

In fact, our visit to Dachau was a shattering experience — at least as powerful as was our subsequent visit to the much larger and more notorious Auschwitz, which is also an exhibit but not a German exhibit, because it lies within Poland. Photographs, and texts in German, vividly depicted and explained Dachau KZ and its background: the Nazi rise to power in 1933, the Nazi persecution of Jews and of non-Nazi Germans during the 1930's, Hitler's steps towards war, the operation of Dachau KZ itself, and the operation of the rest of the Nazi camp system. Far from shirking German responsibility, the exhibit exemplified Fritz Bauer's motto "Germans holding judgment upon themselves."

What my wife and I saw then at Dachau is part of what all German children have seen from the 1970's onwards. They are taught at length in school about Nazi atrocities, and many of them are taken on school outings to former KZs that, like Dachau, have been turned into exhibits. Such national facing-up to past crimes isn't to be taken for granted. In fact, I know of no country that takes that responsibility remotely as seriously as does Germany. Indonesian schoolchildren still are taught nothing about the mass killings of 1965 (Chapter 5); young Japanese whom I have known tell me that they were taught nothing about Japan's war crimes (Chapter 8); and it is not national policy in the U.S. for American schoolchildren to be taught in grim detail about American crimes in Vietnam, and against Native Americans, and against African slaves. In 1961 I had seen much less of that German acknowledgment of their nation's dark past. Insofar as one can consider a single year to be the symbolic watershed for Germany in that respect, it was — as we shall now see — 1968.

———

Revolts and protests, especially by students, spread through much of the free world in the 1960's. They began in the U.S. with the Civil Rights Movement, protests against the Vietnam War, the Free Speech Movement at the University of California at Berkeley, and the movement called Students for a Democratic Society. Student protests were also widespread in France, Britain, Japan, Italy, and Germany. In all of those other countries as in the U.S., the protests partly represented a revolt of the younger generation against the older generation. But that confrontation of generations achieved a particularly violent form in Germany for two reasons. First, the Nazi involvement of the older generation of Germans meant that the gulf between the younger and the older generation was far deeper there than it was in the U.S. Second, the authoritarian attitudes of traditional German society made older and younger generations there especially scornful of each other. While protests leading to liberalization were growing in Germany throughout the 1960's, the lid blew off of those protests in 1968 (Plate 6.4). Why 1968?

Not just in Germany but also in the U.S., different generations have different experiences and acquire different names. In the U.S. we talk about broadly defined generations: baby boomers, Gen X, millennials, and so on. But changes from year to year have been more rapid and profound in Germany than in the U.S. When you are getting to know a new American friend, and you and your new friend are relating to each other your life histories, you probably do not begin by saying, "I was born in 1945, and just knowing that fact will help you figure out a lot about my life and my attitudes without my having to tell you." But Germans do begin to explain themselves to one another by saying, for example, "Ich bin Jahrgang 1945," meaning "My year of birth was 1945." That's because all Germans know that their fellow citizens went through very different life experiences, depending on when they were born and were growing up.

Examples are the experiences of my German friends of my own age, born around the year 1937. None of them grew up with what we Americans or younger modern Germans would recognize as normal lives. All of them had bad things happen to them as children, due to the war. For example, among my six closest German friends born around 1937, one was orphaned when her soldier father was killed; one watched from a distance the district where his father lived being bombed, although his father survived; one was separated from her father from the time that she was one year old until she was 11 years old, because he was a prisoner of war; one lost his two older brothers in the war; one spent the nights of his childhood years sleeping out of doors under a bridge, because his town was bombed every night and it was unsafe to sleep in a house; and one was sent by his mother every day to steal coal from a railroad yard, so that they could stay warm. Thus, my German friends of Jahrgang 1937 were old enough to have been traumatized by memories of the war, and by the chaos and poverty that followed it, and by the closure of their schools. But they weren't old enough to have had Nazi views instilled into them by the Nazi youth organization called the Hitler Jugend. Most of them were too young to be drafted into the new West German army established in 1955; Jahrgang 1937 was the last Jahrgang not called up for that draft.

Those facts about the different experiences of Germans born in different years help explain why Germany experienced a violent student revolt in the year 1968. On the average, the German protestors of 1968 had been born around 1945, just at the end of the war. They were too young to have been raised as Nazis, or to have experienced the war, or to remember the years of chaos and poverty after the war. They grew up mostly after Germany's economic recovery, in economically comfortable times. They weren't struggling to survive; they enjoyed enough leisure and security to devote themselves to protest. In 1968 they were in their early 20's. They were teenagers during the 1950's and early 1960's, when Fritz Bauer was revealing the Nazi crimes of ordinary Germans of their parents' generation. The parents of protestors born in 1945 would themselves have mostly been born between 1905 and 1925. That meant that the parents of Germany's 1945 generation were viewed by their children as the Germans who had voted for Hitler, had obeyed Hitler, had fought for Hitler, or had been indoctrinated in Nazi beliefs by Hitler Jugend school organizations.

All teenagers tend to criticize and challenge their parents. As Fritz Bauer in the 1960's was publicizing his findings, most of the parents of young Germans born in 1945 didn't talk then about Nazi times but instead retreated into their world of work and the post-war economic miracle. If a child did ask, "Mommy and Daddy, what were *you* doing during Nazi times?," those parents answered their children with responses similar to those that older Germans willing to talk gave me in 1961: "You young person, you have no idea what it's like to live under a totalitarian state; one can't just act on one's beliefs." Of course that excuse didn't satisfy young people.

The result was that Germans of Jahrgang around 1945 discredited their parents and their parents' generation as Nazis. That helps explain why student protests also took a violent form in Italy and Japan, the other two aggressor countries of World War Two. In contrast, in the United States the parents of Americans born in 1945 were not viewed as war criminals for fighting in World War Two, but instead as war heroes. That doesn't mean that American teenagers of the 1960's, any more than teenagers elsewhere, refrained from criticizing their parents; it just means that they couldn't dismiss their parents as war criminals.

Widely remembered as a symbolic moment of 1968 in Germany was an act by a young German non-Jewish woman named Beate Klarsfeld (several years older than Jahrgang 1945), married to a Jewish man whose father had been gassed at Auschwitz. On November 7, 1968 she shrieked "Nazi!" at West Germany's chancellor Kurt Kiesinger and slapped him in the face, because he had been a Nazi party member. But while their parents' complicity in Nazi crimes made Germans born around 1945 particularly prone to despise their parents, the Nazi past itself was not the only cause of the German protests of 1968. German students were protesting even more against things similar to what American students and "hippies" of 1968 were protesting: the Vietnam War, authority, bourgeois life, capitalism, imperialism, and traditional morality. German 1968-ers equated contemporary capitalist German society with fascism, while conservative older Germans in turn regarded the violent young leftist rebels as "Hitler's children," a reincarnation of the violent fanatical Nazi SA and SS organizations. Many of the rebels were extreme leftists; some actually moved to East Germany, which in turn funneled money and documents to sympathizers in West Germany. Older West Germans responded by telling the rebels, "All right, go to East Germany if you don't like it here!"

German student radicals in 1968 turned to violence far more than did contemporary American student radicals. Some of them went to Palestine for training as terrorists. The best known of those German terrorist groups called themselves the Rote Armee Fraktion = Red Army Faction (acronym RAF), also known as the Baader-Meinhof gang after two of its leaders (Ulrike Meinhof and Andreas Baader) who became especially notorious. The terrorists began by carrying out arson attacks on stores, then proceeded to kidnappings, bombings, and killings. Over the years the victims whom they kidnapped or killed included leaders of the German "establishment," such as the president of the West Berlin Supreme Court, a candidate for mayor of West Berlin, Germany's federal prosecutor, the chief of Deutsche Bank, and the head of West Germany's Employers' Association. As a result, even most German leftists themselves felt increasingly endangered by the violence of the radical left, and withdrew their support. West German terrorism peaked during the years 1971 to 1977, reaching a climax in 1977 when Andreas Baader and two other RAF leaders committed suicide in prison after the failure of a terrorist attempt to free imprisoned terrorists by hijacking a Lufthansa airplane. Two further waves of terrorism followed, until the RAF announced in 1998 that it had dissolved.

———

The German student revolt of 1968 is sometimes described as "a successful failure." That is, while the student extremists failed in their goals of replacing capitalism with a different economic

234

system, and of overthrowing West Germany's democratic government, they did achieve some of their goals indirectly, because parts of their agenda became co-opted by the West German government, and many of their ideas were adopted by mainstream German society. In turn, some of the 1968 radicals later rose to leading political positions in West Germany's Green Party — such as Joschka Fischer, who after being active as a stone-throwing radical developed a taste for fine suits and wines and became West Germany's foreign minister and vice-chancellor.

Traditional German society had been politically and socially authoritarian. Those qualities, already present long before Hitler, were made explicit in Nazi society by its emphasis on the "Führerprinzip," literally "the leader principle." Not only was Hitler himself officially known as the "Führer" to whom all Germans swore unquestioning political obedience; social as well as political obedience to leaders was expected in other spheres and at other levels of German life under the Nazis.

Although Germany's crushing defeat in World War Two discredited the authoritarian German state, the old elites and their thinking remained alive after World War Two. Here are some non-political examples that I encountered during my stay in Germany in 1961. Spanking of children was widespread then, not merely permitted but often considered obligatory for parents. I worked in a German scientific research institute whose director completely by himself made the decisions controlling the careers of his institute's 120 scientists. For instance, to obtain a university teaching job in Germany required a degree beyond the PhD, called "Habilitation." But my director permitted only one of his 120 scientists to be "habilitated" each year, and chose that person himself. Wherever one went — on the street, on lawns, in schools, in private and public buildings — there were signs saying what was forbidden (verboten), and instructing how one should and shouldn't behave. One morning, one of my German colleagues arrived at work livid, because the previous evening he had come home to find the grass lawn outside his apartment building, which served as his children's play area, surrounded by barbed wire (indelibly associated in Germany with concentration camps). When my friend confronted the apartment manager, the latter was unapologetic: "It's forbidden to walk on the grass (Betreten des Rasens verboten), but those spoiled children (verwöhnte Kinder) were nevertheless walking on the grass, so I felt entitled (ich fühlte mich berechtigt) to prevent them from doing so by putting up barbed wire (Stacheldraht)."

In retrospect, authoritarian behaviors and attitudes in Germany were already starting to change by and just after the time of my 1961 visit. A famous example was the Spiegel Affair of 1962. When the weekly magazine *Der Spiegel*, which was often critical of the national government, published an article questioning the strength of the German army (Bundeswehr), Chancellor Adenauer's defense minister Franz Josef Strauss reacted with authoritarian arrogance by arresting *Der Spiegel*'s editors and seizing their files on suspicion of treason. The resulting enormous public outcry forced the government to abandon its crackdown and compelled Strauss to resign. But Strauss nevertheless remained powerful, served as premier of the German state of Bavaria from 1978 to 1988, and ran for chancellor of Germany in 1980. (He was defeated.)

After 1968, the liberalizing trends that had already been underway became stronger. In 1969 they resulted in the defeat of the conservative party that had ruled Germany uninterruptedly in coalitions for 20 years. Today, Germany is socially much more liberal than it was in 1961. There is no spanking of children; in fact, it's now forbidden by law! Dress is more informal, women's roles are less unequal (cf. the long-serving woman chancellor Angela Merkel), and there is more use of the informal pronoun "Du" and less use of the formal pronoun "Sie" to mean "you."

But I'm still struck today by all of those "verboten" signs whenever I visit Germany. My German friends with experience of the U.S. variously either rate Germany today as much less authoritarian than the U.S., or else tell me horror stories of current German hierarchical behavior. Conversely, when I ask American visitors to Germany whether they perceive the country as authoritarian, I get either of two answers, depending on my respondent's age. Younger American visitors, born in or after the 1970's, who didn't experience the Germany of the 1950's, instinctively compare Germany today with the U.S. today and say that German society is still authoritarian. Older American visitors like me, who did experience Germany in the (late) 1950's, instead compare Germany today with Germany of the 1950's and say that Germany today is much less authoritarian than it used to be. I think that both of those comparisons are accurate.

———

Peaceful government's achievement of many of the goals of 1968 student violence accelerated under West Germany's chancellor Willy Brandt. He had been born in 1913, was forced to flee from the Nazis because of his political views, and spent the war years in Norway and Sweden. In 1969 he became West Germany's first left-wing chancellor as head of the SPD Party, after 20 uninterrupted years of conservative German chancellors belonging to Konrad Adenauer's CDU Party. Under Brandt, Germany began social reforms in which the government pursued student goals such as making Germany less authoritarian and promoting women's rights.

But Brandt's biggest achievements were in foreign relations. Under West Germany's previous conservative leadership, the West German government had refused even to recognize legally the existence of the East German government, and had insisted that West Germany was the only legitimate representative of the

German people. It had had no diplomatic relations with any Eastern European communist country other than the Soviet Union. It had refused to recognize the de-facto loss of all German territories east of the Oder and Neisse Rivers: East Prussia to the Soviet Union, and the rest to Poland.

Brandt adopted a new foreign policy that reversed all of those refusals. He signed a treaty with East Germany and established diplomatic relations with Poland and other Eastern Bloc countries. He acknowledged the Oder-Neisse Line as the Polish/German border, and he thereby accepted the irrevocable loss of all German territories east of that line, including areas that had long been German and central to German identity: Silesia and parts of Prussia and Pomerania. That renunciation was an enormous step and constituted an unacceptably bitter pill for Germany's conservative CDU Party, which announced that it would reject the treaties if it were returned to power in the elections of 1972. In fact, German voters endorsed Brandt's swallowing of the bitter pill, and Brandt's party won the 1972 elections with an increased majority.

The most dramatic moment of Brandt's career happened during his visit to Poland's capital, Warsaw, in 1970. Poland had been the country that had had the highest percentage of its population killed during World War Two. It had been the site of the biggest Nazi extermination camps. Poles had good reason to loathe Germans as unrepentant Nazis. On his visit to Warsaw on December 7, 1970, Brandt visited the Warsaw Ghetto, the site of an unsuccessful Jewish revolt against Nazi occupation in April and May 1943. In front of the Polish crowds, Brandt spontaneously fell down on his knees, acknowledged the millions of victims of the Nazis, and asked for forgiveness for Hitler's dictatorship and World War Two (Plate 6.5). Even Poles who continued to distrust Germans recognized Brandt's behavior as unplanned, sincere, and deeply meant. In today's world of carefully scripted, unemotional diplomatic statements, Brandt's kneeling at the Warsaw Ghetto stands out as a unique heartfelt apology by the leader of one country to the people of another country who had suffered greatly. By contrast, think of the many other leaders who did not kneel and apologize: American presidents to Vietnamese, Japanese prime ministers to Koreans and Chinese, Stalin to Poles and Ukrainians, de Gaulle to Algerians, and others.

The political pay-off for West Germany from Brandt's behavior did not come until 20 years after his Warsaw Ghetto visit, and long after Brandt himself had resigned as chancellor in 1974. In the 1970's and 1980's there was still nothing that a West German chancellor could do directly to bring about the re-unification of West and East Germany. The two chancellors who followed Brandt, Helmut Schmidt of the SPD and then Helmut Kohl of the CDU, both continued Brandt's policies of trading with East Germany, seeking reconciliation with Eastern European countries, and cultivating good personal relationships with leaders of the major countries on both sides of the Iron Curtain. The U.S. and Western Europe reached the conclusion that West Germany was now to be trusted as a democracy and a dependable ally. The Soviet Union and its Eastern Bloc partners reached the conclusion that West Germany was now to be valued as a major trade partner, and was no longer to be feared as a military or territorial threat.

Brandt's treaty, and Schmidt's and Kohl's subsequent agreements, between the two Germany's enabled hundreds of thousands of West Germans to visit East Germany, and a small number of East Germans to visit West Germany. Trade between the two Germany's grew. Increasingly, East Germans succeeded in watching West German television. That enabled them to compare for themselves the high and rising living standards in West Germany, and the low and declining living standards in East Germany. Economic and political difficulties were also growing in the Soviet Union itself, which was becoming less able to impose its will on other

Eastern Bloc countries. Against that background, the beginning of the end for East Germany was a step completely beyond the control of either West or East Germany: on May 2 of 1989, Hungary, an Eastern Bloc country separated from East Germany to the north by another Eastern Bloc country (Czechoslovakia), decided to remove the fence separating it on the west from Austria, a Western democracy bordering on West Germany. When Hungary then officially opened that border four months later, thousands of East Germans seized the opportunity to flee by way of Czechoslovakia and Hungary to the West. (That official border opening date was September 11, coincidentally also the date of Pinochet's 1973 coup in Chile and of the 2001 World Trade Towers attack in the U.S.) Soon, hundreds of thousands of East Germans protesting against their government took to the streets in Leipzig, then in other East German cities. The East German government intended to respond by announcing that it would issue permits for direct travel to West Germany. However, the official making the announcement on television bungled it and said instead that the government would permit travel to West Germany "immediately." That night (November 9, 1989), tens of thousands of East Germans seized the opportunity to cross immediately into West Berlin, unmolested by the border guards.

While West Germany's chancellor at the time, Helmut Kohl, did not create this opening, he did know how to exploit it cautiously. In May 1990 he concluded a treaty of economic and social welfare unification (but not yet political unification) between East and West Germany. He worked hard and tactfully to defuse Western and Soviet reluctance to permit German re-unification. For example, in his crucial July 1990 meeting with Soviet President Gorbachev, he offered the Soviet Union a big package of financial aid, and persuaded Gorbachev not only to tolerate German re-unification but also to tolerate the re-unified Germany remaining within NATO. On October 3, 1990 East Germany was dissolved, and its districts joined (West) Germany's as new states (Bundesländer).

——

Can we profitably discuss post-war German history, as we have now summarized it in this chapter, in the light of the same framework that we used to discuss the four nations of Chapters 2–5? Post-war German history was seemingly very different. The histories of all four nations of Chapters 2–5 were marked by a single crisis abruptly exploding on one day: Commodore Perry's arrival in a Japanese harbor on July 8, 1853, the Soviet attack on Finland of November 30, 1939, Pinochet's coup in Chile on September 11, 1973, and Indonesia's coup attempt of October 1, 1965. In contrast, there was no single, overwhelmingly dominant explosion in post-war Germany, which seems instead to have experienced several overlapping and gradually unfolding challenges from 1945 to 1990. We shall see in the next chapter (Chapter 7) that post-war events in Australia as well followed the gradual German pattern and differed from the explosive pattern that we saw in Chapters 2–5. Is it misleading to extend the term "crisis" from the explosive cases to the gradual cases?

In fact, there is no sharp dividing line between the two sets of cases: the differences between them are just ones of degree. Germany did experience abrupt blows, in fact three of them rather than just a single blow. First, Germany's devastated condition at the time of its surrender of May 7 and 8, 1945 posed the worst crisis faced by any nation discussed in this book. The erection of the Berlin Wall on August 13, 1961, and the student revolts peaking over several months of 1968, then represented two further crises. Conversely, Perry's arrival in Japan and Pinochet's coup in Chile actually weren't unexpected isolated events of a single day. They were instead the culminations of developments that had extended over many previous decades, and whose (partial) resolution would take many subsequent decades: both of those statements also apply to post-war German history. In the following pages we shall see that the factors emerging for the so-called "acute national crises" of Chapters 2–5 are similar to those emerging for the so-called "gradual national crises" of this chapter and the next one.

Hence I have found it useful to consider both sets of histories within the same framework. In particular, post-war German history not only illustrates most of our framework's factors; it illustrates four of them to an extreme degree. Let's begin by discussing those four features, then several other less extreme but still significant features.

The first respect in which Germany is extreme consists of the geographic constraints (factor #12, Table 1.2) on its ability to undertake successful independent initiatives; hence the necessity, instead, to await favorable opportunities arising from actions of other countries. Among the six countries discussed in Chapters 2–7, only Finland rivals Germany in the limitations on its ability to act independently. This idea may initially seem absurd to non-Germans, accustomed to thinking of 20th-century Germany as doing the opposite of holding back from independent action, and instead (under Emperor Wilhelm II and Hitler) taking bold military initiatives leading to both world wars. In fact, the two world wars support my generalization: both ended disastrously for Germany, because Wilhelm and Hitler didn't wait for favorable opportunities but instead did take initiatives, with dreadful consequences.

To understand the geographic constraints on German initiatives, just look at the current map on page 216 and also recent historical maps of Europe. Today, Germany shares land borders with nine countries (Netherlands, Belgium, Luxembourg, France, Switzerland, Austria, Czech Republic, Poland, and Denmark), while its North Sea and Baltic coasts are exposed over water to eight other countries (Britain, Norway, Sweden, Finland, Russia, Estonia, Latvia, and Lithuania). In addition, Germany acquired three other land neighbors when it annexed Austria in 1938 (Italy, Yugoslavia, and Hungary), and one more land neighbor (Lithuania) between 1918 and 1939. Some of those countries formed part of two large land neighbors (Russia and the Habsburg Empire) until 1918. That makes a total of 20 recent historical neighbors of Germany (if one counts each historical entity only once, rather than double-counting land and overwater neighbors or else former and modern successor states). Of those 20, 19 — all except Switzerland — have either invaded, attacked by sea, had German troops stationed or (Sweden) in transit, or been invaded by Germany between 1866 and 1945. Five of those 20 neighbors are or were powerful (France, Russia, the Habsburg Empire, Britain, and formerly Sweden).

It's not just that Germany has neighbors. Most other countries also have neighbors, but borders between neighboring countries often coincide with protective geographic barriers. However, northern Germany is part of the flat North European Plain (Plate 6.6), which is not dissected by any natural defense barriers: no mountain chains (unlike the Pyrenees that divide Spain from France, or the Alps that ring Italy), and only narrow rivers easily crossed by armies throughout history. (Not even the Rhine has been a serious barrier to armies.) For example, when my Polish-American wife Marie and I flew from Berlin to Warsaw, Marie, with the black humor that has permitted Poles to retain their sanity throughout their history, looked down from our airplane on the flat plain in which Germany and Poland invisibly merge into each other, and commented: "Excellent terrain for tank warfare!" She was thinking of Hitler's tanks rolling into Poland in 1939. But a historically minded German would instead have been thinking of all the armies that rolled into northern Germany from the east and from the west, including the Soviet and Allied armies in World

War Two, Napoleon's armies two centuries ago, and other armies before that.

Germany's central geographic location surrounded by neighbors seems to me to have been the most important factor in German history. Of course, that location has not been without advantages: it has made Germany a crossroads for trade, technology, art, music, and culture. A cynic would note that Germany's location also facilitated its invasion of many countries during World War Two.

But the political and military disadvantages of Germany's location have been enormous. The Thirty Years' War, which was the major religious and power struggle between most of the leading nations of 17th-century Western and Central Europe, was fought mainly on German soil, reduced the population there by up to 50%, and inflicted a crushing economic and political setback whose consequences persisted for the next two centuries. Germany was the last large Western European country to be unified (in 1871), and that unification required the leadership of a highly skilled diplomat (Bismarck) with a unique ability to take account of the possible reactions of many other European powers. The military nightmare for the resulting unified Germany was the risk of a two-front war against both its western neighbor (France) and its eastern neighbor (Russia); that nightmare did materialize and led to Germany's defeat in both world wars. After World War Two, three of its neighbors plus the U.S. partitioned Germany. There was nothing that the West German government could do directly to achieve re-unification: it had to await favorable opportunities created by events in other countries.

Differing geographic constraints have meant that bad leadership results in much more painful consequences for Germany than for geographically less constrained countries. For instance, while Germany's Emperor Wilhelm II and his chancellors and ministers were notorious for their blunders and unrealism, Germany has had no monopoly on poor leadership: the U.S. and Britain and other countries have had their share. But the seas protecting the U.S. and Britain meant that inept leaders doing stupid things didn't bring disaster upon their countries, whereas the ineptness of Wilhelm and his chancellors did bring disaster upon Germany in World War One.

The philosophy guiding the foreign policy of successful German politicians was summed up in a metaphor by Bismarck: "One should always try to see where God is striding through world history, and in what direction He is heading. Then, jump in and hold on to His coattails, to get swept along as far as one can go." That was also Chancellor Helmut Kohl's strategy in 1989–1990, when political developments in East Germany and the Soviet Union finally, after Willy Brandt's initiatives of 1969–1974, created the opportunity for German re-unification. An equivalent strategy in the American game of football is "Play for the breaks." That philosophy would have been unthinkable to Britain at the height of its imperial power, and still is unthinkable to the U.S. today (in foreign policy, but not in football). Instead, imperial Britain expected, and the U.S. today expects, to take initiatives and to be able to impose their will.

———

Another respect in which Germany constitutes an extreme among our case studies concerns self-pity and sense of victimization (factor #2). This is an especially illuminating subject for discussion, because Germany actually constitutes not one but two opposite extremes: in its contrasting reactions to World War One and to World War Two.

By October 1918, shortly before the end of World War One, Germany's last military offensives on the western front had failed, Allied armies were advancing and had been strengthened by a million fresh U.S. troops, and Germany's defeat had become just an inevitable matter of time. But German armies were still conducting an orderly retreat, and the Allies had not yet reached Germany's borders. Armistice negotiations were hastened to a conclusion by a mutiny of the German fleet and by outbreaks of armed insurrections in Germany. This permitted post-war German agitators, especially Adolf Hitler, to claim that the German army had not been defeated militarily but had been betrayed by a "stab in the back" from treacherous civilian politicians. The conditions of the Treaty of Versailles imposed upon Germany by the victorious Allies, including a notorious "war guilt clause" branding Germany as the aggressor responsible for the war, provoked further German resentment. As a result, although many post-war German historians themselves analyzed pre-war Germany's political blunders that had plunged Germany into war under unfavorable conditions, the prevalent post-war view of the German public was that Germany was a victim whose leaders had not been responsible for their country's misfortunes.

Now, contrast this German sense of victimization after World War One with Germany's post-war view after World War Two. In May 1945 Germany's armies had been defeated on all fronts, all of Germany had been conquered by Allied troops, and Germany's surrender was unconditional. No German or non-German denied that World War Two in Europe had resulted solely from Hitler's intention. Germans gradually learned of the unprecedented atrocities committed by German government policy in the concentration camps, and by the German military on the eastern front. German civilians themselves also suffered: especially in the bombings of Hamburg and Dresden and other German cities, in the flight of German civilians before the advancing Soviet troops, and in the expulsion of all ethnic German residents of Eastern Europe and former eastern German territory by Poles, Czechs, and other

Eastern European governments just after the war's end. The Soviet advance and the expulsions are estimated to have sent more than 12 million German civilians fleeing as refugees, killed more than 2 million of them, and subjected on the order of a million German women to rape.

Those sufferings of German civilians receive some attention in post-war Germany. But self-pity and sense of victimization have not dominated Germans' view of themselves after World War Two, as they did after World War One. Part of the reason has been German recognition that the horrors inflicted by Russians, Poles, and Czechs on German civilians resulted from the horrors that Germans had so recently inflicted on those countries. But we should not take for granted Germans' rejection of the victim role and assumption of shame after World War Two, because it contrasts with the assumption of the victim role by Germans themselves after World War One and by Japanese after World War Two (Chapter 8). The result of this painful reckoning with the past has been to Germany's advantage today, in the form of much better security and better relations with former enemies than prevailed for Germany after World War One or for Japan today.

———

Two further respects in which Germany is an extreme case for our purposes are linked: the role of leadership, and honest self-appraisal or the lack thereof (factor #7). Because Germany's central European geographic location has chronically exposed it to more difficulties and dangers than face Britain and the U.S., protected by water barriers, the effects of good or bad leadership have been more obvious for Germany than for Britain or the U.S.

Among leaders whose effects were bad, Hitler enjoys pride of first place in recent world history. One can of course debate whether the combination of the Treaty of Versailles, the collapse of

Germany's currency in 1923, and the unemployment and economic depression beginning in 1929 would have spurred Germany to go to war to overturn the treaty even without Hitler. But one can still argue that a World War Two instigated by Germany without Hitler would have been very different. His unusual evil mentality, charisma, boldness in foreign policy, and decision to exterminate all Jews were not shared by other revisionist German leaders of his era. Despite his initial military successes, his unrealistic appraisals led him repeatedly to override his own generals and ultimately to cause Germany's defeat. Those fatally unrealistic decisions included his unprovoked declaration of war against the U.S. in December 1941 at a time when Germany was already at war with Britain and the Soviet Union, and his overriding of his generals' pleas to authorize retreat by the German army trapped at Stalingrad in 1942–1943.

Second to Hitler in bad leadership in recent German history was Kaiser Wilhelm II, whose 30-year rule ended with his abdication and Germany's defeat in World War One. One can again debate whether there would still have been a World War One without Wilhelm. However, such a war as well would probably have taken a different form, because Wilhelm, like Hitler, was unusual, albeit in a different way. While Wilhelm was much less powerful than Hitler, he still appointed and dismissed Germany's chancellors, held the loyalty of most Germans, and commanded Germany's armed forces. Although not evil, he was emotionally labile and unrealistic, had poor judgment, and was spectacularly tactless on numerous occasions that created unnecessary problems for Germany. Among his many policies that resulted in Germany's entering World War One under unfavorable circumstances leading to defeat was his non-renewal of Bismarck's treaty between Germany and Russia, thereby exposing Germany to that already mentioned military nightmare arising from its geographic location: a two-front war simultaneously against Russia and France.

A German counter-example of successful leadership and realistic appraisal is provided by Willy Brandt, whose recognition of East Germany and other Eastern Bloc countries, treaties with Poland and Russia, and acceptance of the loss of German lands beyond the Oder-Neisse Line reversed 20 years of previous West German foreign policies. While West Germany's subsequent chancellors continued Brandt's policies, one can argue that his leadership made a difference. The opposing CDU Party continued to oppose those policies for the next several years; Brandt's acceptance of the Oder-Neisse Line required outstanding realism and political courage lacking in his predecessors; and his successors lacked his charisma that made his visit to the Warsaw Ghetto so convincing and unforgettable. Among other German chancellors since World War Two, Konrad Adenauer, Helmut Schmidt, and Helmut Kohl also stand out as gifted. Overall, as an American I am struck by the uninterrupted good sense of West Germany's chancellors since World War Two, during an era in which the U.S. has been suffering from several failed or undistinguished presidencies.

The remaining German counter-example of successful leadership that made a difference was Otto von Bismarck, the Prussian prime minister and then imperial German chancellor who achieved German unification in 1871. That unification faced overwhelming obstacles — notably, opposition from the smaller German kingdoms other than Prussia, opposition from the neighboring powerful Habsburg Empire and France that could be resolved only by wars, the more distant potential opposition of Russia and Britain, and the vexing question as to which German populations could realistically be incorporated into a unified Germany. Bismarck was an ultra-realist, familiar with the reasons for the failure of Germany's 1848 revolutions, aware of the internal and external opposition to German unification, and accustomed to proceeding stepwise, beginning with small measures and moving on to stronger measures only if smaller measures failed. He recognized that Prussia's ability to initiate major events was limited by geopolitical constraints, and that his policy would have to depend on awaiting favorable opportunities and then acting quickly. No other German politician of his generation approached him in his political skills. Bismarck has often been criticized for failing to groom a suitable successor, and for failing to cure problems in Germany that culminated in World War One, 24 years after his chancellorship had ended. But it seems to me unfair to criticize him for the follies of Wilhelm II and Wilhelm's appointees. Bismarck is also criticized for supposedly being warlike, but Germany could hardly have been unified over the prevailing opposition without Bismarck's three wars, two of them very brief. (The unification of Italy required four wars, but Italy has not been branded as warlike.) Once Germany had been unified in 1871, leaving millions of German-speaking peoples outside its borders, Bismarck was realistic enough to understand that he had achieved the most that was possible, and that other powers would not tolerate further German expansion.

———

Other fits of Germany to our framework can be summarized more briefly. Germany since World War Two does illustrate selective change (factor #3). Of all the countries discussed in this book, Germany is the one that experienced the largest changes in its political borders. It drastically reassessed its Nazi past. It made some large social changes, especially with regard to its former authoritarianism and the status of women. But many other core values of traditional German society have remained little changed, including government support of the arts, government support of everyone's medical care and retirement benefits, and emphasis on community values over untrammeled individual rights. Whenever, as an

American, I return to Germany, I am pleasantly surprised to re-discover that even small German cities have opera houses, that my older German friends can still afford to live comfortably after retir-ing, and that villages preserve local color (because zoning laws specify that your house's roof style has to conform to the local style).

Support from other countries has varied greatly with place and time in recent German history (factor #4). American Marshall Plan aid, and West Germany's wise use of it, made possible West Ger-many's economic miracle after 1948. Conversely, negative eco-nomic aid — i.e., extraction of war reparations — contributed to the undermining of East Germany after World War Two, and of Ger-many's Weimar Republic after World War One.

Germany's strong national identity helped it survive the trau-mas of devastation, occupation, and partition (factor #6). (Some non-Germans would go further, and would argue that Germany has had too strong a national identity.) That national identity and pride are based especially on Germany's world-famous music, art, literature, philosophy, and science; the bond of the German lan-guage as codified by Martin Luther's Bible translation transcend-ing spoken German dialectical variation; and memories of shared history that enabled Germans still to identify themselves as one people despite centuries of political fragmentation.

Germany illustrates patience born of past defeats and initial failures (factor #9), and also illustrates confidence born of past suc-cesses (factor #8). It recovered from defeat in two world wars. Its successes requiring patience included unification against heavy odds culminating in 1871, re-unification also against heavy odds culminating in 1990, and the post-war economic miracle.

Post-war developments in Germany involved both internal trig-gers and external triggers. Internal triggers drove Germany's com-ing to grips with its Nazi past, and the explosion of student revolt in

1968. External triggers — such as Hungary opening its border with Austria in 1989, and the Soviet Union's decline — set in motion the achievement of re-unification.

Among questions arising for national crises without close parallels in individual crises, Germany illustrates to an outstanding degree reconciliation between former opponents. Germany's acknowledgments of its Nazi past, symbolized by Brandt's kneeling at the Warsaw Ghetto, have made possible relatively smooth and honest relations with Germany's neighbors Poland and France — far more so than Japan's relations with Korea and China (Chapter 8). Another question arising specifically for national crises is whether drastic change occurs by revolution or by evolution. Modern Germany has experienced three revolutions or uprisings, two of them failures in their immediate outcomes: the failed 1848 revolutionary attempt at unification and democratization, the 1918 uprisings that did overthrow Germany's kings and emperor, and the 1968 student uprisings that sought violently to change Germany's society, economic system, and form of government. One of those goals was then achieved by evolution: the post-1968 peaceful accomplishment of many of the goals of the student revolutionaries. The drastic change of re-unification in 1989–1990 was also achieved peacefully.

Interestingly, recent German history provides four examples of an interval of 21–23 years between a crushing defeat and an explosive reaction to that defeat. Those four examples are: the 23-year interval between 1848's failed revolutionary unification attempt and 1871's successful unification; the 21-year interval between 1918's crushing defeat in World War One and 1939's outbreak of World War Two that sought and ultimately failed to reverse that defeat; the 23-year interval between 1945's crushing defeat in World War Two and 1968's revolts by the students born around 1945; and the 22-year interval between those 1968 student revolts and 1990's re-unification. Of course, there are big differences between those four sets of events, and external factors played a role in determining those intervals, especially the interval between 1968 and 1990. But I think that there is nevertheless a significance to those parallels: 21–23 years is approximately one human generation. The years 1848, 1918, and 1968 were decisive experiences for Germans who were young adults then, and who two decades later became their country's leaders and finally found themselves in a position to try to complete (1871, 1990) or to reverse (1939) that decisive experience of their youth. For the student revolts of 1968, the leadership and participation required were not of seasoned politicians in their 40's or 50's, but instead of unseasoned radicals in their 20's. As one German friend who experienced 1968 expressed it to me, "Without 1968, there would have been no 1990."

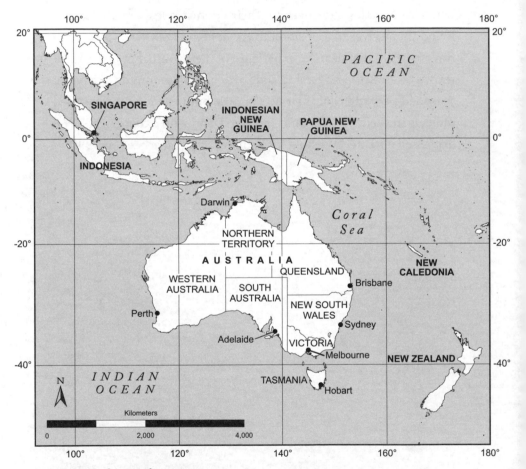

FIG. 7 *Map of Australia*

CHAPTER 7

AUSTRALIA: WHO ARE WE?

Visiting Australia — First Fleet and Aborigines —
Early immigrants — Towards self-government —
Federation — Keeping them out — World War
One — World War Two — Loosening the ties — The
end of White Australia — Crisis framework

first visited Australia in 1964, shortly after I had been living in
Britain for four years. Australia then impressed me as more British than Britain itself — like the Britain of a few decades prior, frozen in time. The streetscape of Sydney, Australia's largest city,
reminded me of England on every corner, with Sydney's own Hyde
Park, King's Cross Station, and Oxford Street just as in London.
Australian people were not just overwhelmingly white in their
ancestry; they were overwhelmingly British white. Australian food
was boring traditional British: the ritual of the Sunday roast, the
preponderance of fish-and-chips shops, and the obligatory break-
fast jar of Vegemite, an Australian imitation of British Marmite.
British-style pubs abounded, with one room for men alone and
another room (the so-called ladies' lounge) for men and women,
and with restricted opening hours similar to those of British pubs
in those years. The alternatives to traditional British food in

Australia were mainly limited to Italian, Greek, and occasionally Chinese restaurants.

Since that first visit to Australia, I've been back dozens of times and watched Australia change. The changes were symbolized for me by an experience in 2008, when I was taking my son Joshua to Australia to spend a college semester abroad at the University of Queensland in Brisbane. As we walked across the university campus, I felt that I was no longer in the Australia that I had known, but instead on the campus of my institution, the University of California at Los Angeles, because so many of the students were Asian. Australia was no longer white-mainly-British.

In 1964 the fundamental fact of Australian society was still the contradiction between Australia's geographic location on the one hand, and its population make-up and emotional and cultural ties on the other hand. Australia's population and national identity were mostly British (Plate 7.1). But Australia is almost half-way around the world from Britain: in the Southern Hemisphere rather than in the Northern Hemisphere, and eight to 10 time zones east of Britain. The Australian landscape of kangaroos, egg-laying mammals, kookaburras, big lizards, eucalyptus trees, and deserts is the most distinctive (and least British) landscape of any continent inhabited by humans (Plate 7.2). Geographically, Australia is much closer to China, Japan, and other East Asian countries than it is to Europe, and 50 times closer to Indonesia than to Britain. Yet as I walked along Australian streets in 1964, there were no signs of that proximity to Asia.

By the time that I brought Joshua to Brisbane 44 years later, Asia's proximity had become obvious, in the large numbers of Asian people (Plate 7.3), and in the Japanese, Thai, and Vietnamese restaurants. The official White Australia policy that had barred Asian immigrants, and the informal policies that had discouraged white Europeans other than British, had disappeared. But Australia's language is still English, the Queen of Britain is still Australia's figurehead of state, and the Australian flag still incorporates the British flag. It's a wonderful country, consistently ranked as one of the world's most desirable places to live, with one of the most contented populations and highest life expectancies. It's one of only two countries to which I seriously considered emigrating. It's British, yet it's not British. What happened to produce those selective changes during the decades that I have been visiting Australia?

As you race through Australian history with me in the following pages, think of where Australia fits among the other five countries whose crises we've been considering. Like Germany as discussed in the previous chapter, and unlike the four countries of Chapters 2–5, Australia underwent a crisis that didn't erupt on one day. (However, three military shocks within the space of 71 days in 1941–1942 stood out in importance.) Instead, Australia's crisis, like Germany's, was partly the unfolding of a response to the years of World War Two. For both Germany and Australia, the war proved that traditional national solutions were no longer working, but the proof was much more cataclysmic and quickly convincing in war-shattered Germany than in Australia. The basic question for Australians, more than for the citizens of any other country discussed in this book, has been the issue of national identity: *who are we?* World War Two started to bring to the surface Australians' recognition that their long-held self-image of being a second Britain halfway around the world was becoming out of date and no longer fitted Australia's changed circumstances. But the war alone wasn't enough to wean most Australians away from that self-image.

It takes time even for just a single person to formulate a new answer to the question *Who am I?* It takes much longer for a nation, composed of millions of individuals divided into groups with competing views of their nation's identity, to figure out: *Who are we?* Hence it should come as no surprise that Australians are still wrestling today with that question. Paradoxically, while crisis resolution in Australia has been slow — so slow that many Australians wouldn't even consider there to have been a crisis at all — Australia is the one among our six nations that experienced the widest unified set of changes announced within the shortest time, 19 days during the month of December 1972. All of these developments, and others, are what I find fascinating in the story of modern Australia that we'll now traverse.

———

Approximately 50,000 years after Australia had been settled by the ancestors of Aboriginal Australians, the first European settlers arrived in January 1788, in a fleet of 11 ships sent out from Britain. The British government had sent that fleet not because it considered Australia a wonderful location attractive to British settlers, but because Britain had a problem with its exploding population of convicts that it wanted to dump somewhere far away. Australia and tropical West Africa had both been suggested as suitably remote locations, but it was becoming clear that West Africa's tropical diseases made it an unhealthy place for Europeans. Australia appeared to offer multiple advantages: it was much more remote than West Africa; it wasn't known to be (and in reality for the most part proved not to be) unhealthy for Europeans; and it offered potential Pacific Ocean bases for British navy ships, merchants, whalers, and timber and flax suppliers. And so the choice fell on Australia — specifically, on the environs of what became the city of Sydney.

The First Fleet consisted of 730 convicts, their guards, administrators, workers, and a British naval officer as governor. More fleets and ships followed, bringing more convicts to Sydney and then to four other locations scattered around the Australian continent. Soon the convicts and their guards were joined by British free settlers. However, 32 years later, in 1820, Australia's European population still consisted of 84% of convicts and former convicts, and convict transport from Britain to Australia did not cease until 1868. To survive and prosper in frontier Australia was difficult, and so modern Australians of convict ancestry regard it as a badge of pride rather than of shame — like the pride felt by modern American descendants of the settlers who arrived on the ship *Mayflower* in 1620.

It was expected (correctly) that it would take a long time for the convicts and settlers to figure out how to grow enough food to feed themselves. Hence the First Fleet carried food shipments, which Britain continued to send out until the 1840's. Several decades passed before Australians could send significant exports back to Britain: at first, just products from hunting whales and seals; then from the 1830's onwards, wool from sheep; gold from a gold rush beginning in 1851; and once refrigerator ships for the long sea journey to Britain became available in the 1880's, meat and butter. Today, one-third of the world's wool is grown by Australia's abundant sheep population, five sheep for every human. But Australia's economy since World War Two has been dominated by mining of the minerals with which the continent is so richly endowed: Australia is a world-leading exporter of aluminum, coal, copper, gold, iron, lead, magnesium, silver, tungsten, titanium, and uranium.

This brief account of the European settlement of Australia from 1788 onwards leaves out what was happening to the Aboriginal population that had settled Australia much earlier. In other British colonies, such as the U.S., Canada, India, Fiji, and West Africa, British colonists dealt with native people either peacefully by negotiating with local chiefs or princes, or else militarily by sending British armies against local armies or sizeable tribal forces. Those methods did not work in Australia, where Aboriginal organization consisted of small bands without armies, chiefs, or princes. Aborigines lived a nomadic lifestyle and did not have fixed villages. To European settlers, that meant that Aborigines did not "own" the land.

Hence European settlers simply took Aboriginal land without

negotiation or payment. There were no battles against Aboriginal armies: just attacks by or against small groups of Aborigines, sometimes provoked by Aborigines killing sheep that they considered no different from the kangaroos and other wild animals that they were accustomed to hunting. In response, European settlers killed Aborigines; the last large massacre (of 32 Aborigines) took place as recently as 1928. When a British governor ordered the trial and hanging of Europeans who had murdered Aborigines, the Australian public strongly supported those murderers, and London's colonial office realized that it could not stop its British subjects in remote Australia from doing what they wanted — such as killing Aborigines.

Because Aborigines were hunter-gatherers rather than settled farmers, white Australians looked down on them as primitive. I continue to be surprised at how widespread that scorn of Aborigines still is even among educated Australians. One Australian senator said, "There is no scientific evidence that he [the Aborigine] is a human being at all." As Aboriginal numbers declined because of diseases and killings and land dispossession, white Australians came to believe that the Aborigines were dying out. An Australian bishop wrote, "The Aborigines are disappearing. In the course of a generation or two, at the most, the last Australian black fellow [i.e., Aborigine] will have turned his face to warm mother earth…missionary work then may only be smoothing the pillow of a dying race."

Aborigines were eventually forbidden to marry non-Aboriginals without government consent. There has been much controversy over a policy, developed in the 1930's, of forcibly removing mixed-race Aboriginal/white children and even Aboriginal children from Aboriginal homes, to be raised (supposedly for their own good) in institutions or foster homes. A movement, beginning in the 1990's, for white Australians to apologize to Aborigines has faced strong opposition. Prime Minister Kevin Rudd did give a formal apology in 2008, but Prime Minister John Howard argued, "Australians of this generation should not be required to accept guilt and blame for past actions and policies over which they had no control."

In short, British Australia's White Australia policy was directed not just at non-white potential immigrants from overseas. It was directed also at the non-white original Australians into whose lands white British settlers were immigrating, whose right to those lands was denied, and who (many white settlers hoped) would die out quickly.

———

Throughout the first decades of the Australian colony, immigrating free settlers as well as convicts came from Britain (including Ireland, at that time still part of Britain). The first substantial group of non-British immigrants began to arrive in 1836 in South Australia. That colony had been founded not as a convict dump but by a land development company that carefully selected prospective settlers from Europe. Among those settlers were German Lutherans seeking religious freedom, a motive for immigration much more conspicuous in the early history of the United States than of Australia. Those German immigrants were skilled and white, developed market gardening and vineyards, adapted quickly to Australia, and aroused minimal opposition. More controversial was the arrival of tens of thousands of Chinese in the 1850's, drawn (along with many Europeans and Americans) by Australia's first gold rush. That influx resulted in the last use of the British army in Australia, to quell riots in which a crowd beat, robbed, and even scalped Chinese.

A third wave of non-British arrivals arose from the development of sugar plantations in Queensland beginning in the 1860's. The plantation workers were Pacific Islanders from New Guinea, other Melanesian islands, and Polynesia. While some of them were voluntary recruits, many were kidnapped from their islands by raids accompanied by frequent murders, in a practice known as black-birding (because the islanders were dark-skinned). When plantations (especially of coconuts) were subsequently developed in German and Australian New Guinea, that same Australian model was adopted for bringing Pacific Island workers to New Guinea plantations. Such labor recruitment practices continued in New Guinea long into the 20th century: an Australian whom I met in Australian-governed New Guinea in 1966 told me that he was a labor recruiter, but he took pains to explain how he recruited only voluntary laborers to whom he paid cash bonuses. He proudly insisted that he was not a kidnapping black-birder (that was the word that he still used), whereas some of the other recruiters with whom he competed still were. In any case, regardless of whether the dark-skinned workers on Australian sugar plantations from the 1860's onwards had arrived voluntarily or involuntarily, they did not make Australia's resident population less white, because they came on fixed-term contracts and were expelled from Australia at the ends of their terms.

Still another group of non-British immigrants was a small number from the British colony of India. Despite all these arrivals of modest numbers of Germans, Chinese, contract Pacific Islanders, and Indians, Australia remained by policy overwhelmingly British and white until after World War Two.

———

Americans familiar with U.S. history are struck by the difference between the courses with which Britain's American colonies and its Australian colonies dissociated themselves from Britain. The American colonies achieved independence, joined in a union, and severed all political ties with Britain against strong resistance from the British army, after a revolutionary war lasting seven years. Each year on July 4, on the anniversary of the American Declaration of Independence, Americans celebrate Independence Day, which is one of our biggest annual holidays. In contrast, Australia doesn't recognize or celebrate an Independence Day, because there wasn't one. The Australian colonies achieved self-government with no objections from Britain, and never severed their ties with Britain completely. Australia is still joined with Britain in a (British) Commonwealth of Nations, and still recognizes Britain's sovereign as Australia's nominal head of state. Why did the relaxation or severing of ties with Britain unfold differently in Australia and in the U.S.?

There were several reasons. One is that Britain learned lessons from its expensive defeat in the American Revolution, changed its policies towards its white colonies, and readily granted self-government to Canada, New Zealand, and its Australian colonies. In fact, Britain granted many features of self-government to Australia of its own initiative, before Australians had made any requests. A second reason was the much greater sailing distance from Britain to Australia than to the U.S. East Coast. The First Fleet required eight months to reach Australia, and thereafter for much of the early 19th century the sailing times varied from half-a-year to a full year. The resulting slowness of communication made it impossible for the British colonial office in London to exercise close control over Australia; decisions and laws had to be delegated at first to governors, and then to Australians themselves. For example, for the entire decade from 1809 to 1819, the British governor of the Australian colony of New South Wales didn't even bother to notify London of new laws that he was adopting.

A third reason for the difference between Australian and American history was that the British colonial government had to station and pay for a large army in its American colonies. That army served to defend the colonies against the French army that was based in Canada and competing for control of North America, and also against less-well-armed but still formidable populous American Indian tribes with centralized government by chiefs. In contrast, no European power competed with Britain to colonize the Australian continent, and Aborigines were few, without guns, and not centrally led. Hence Britain never needed to station a large army in Australia, nor to levy unpopular taxes on Australians to pay for that army; Britain's levying taxes on the American colonies without consulting them was the immediate cause of the American Revolution. The last small contingent of British troops in Australia was withdrawn in 1870, by British initiative rather than under Australian pressure. Still another factor was that Britain's Australian colonies, in contrast to its American colonies, were too unprofitable and unimportant for Britain to care about and pay much attention to. The American but not the Australian colonies were rich and viewed as able to afford paying taxes to Britain. Much more profitable and important to Britain than Australia were its colonies of Canada, India, South Africa, and Singapore. Finally, as I'll explain in the next section, Britain's principal Australian settlements for a long time remained separate colonies with little political coordination.

The course by which the Australian colonies achieved self-government was as follows. In 1828, 40 years after the arrival of the First Fleet, Britain established appointed (not elected) legislative councils in the two oldest of its Australian colonies, New South Wales and Tasmania. Those appointed councils were followed in 1842 by the first partly elected representative Australian colonial government (in New South Wales). In 1850 Britain drew up constitutions for its Australian colonies, but the colonies were subsequently free to amend those constitutions, which meant that they became largely free to design their own governments. The 1850 constitutions and subsequent amended constitutions did "reserve" for Britain the decisions on some Australian matters such as defense, treason, and naturalization, and left Britain with the theoretical power to disallow any colonial law. In practice, though,

Britain rarely exercised those reserved rights. By the late 1800's, the only major right consistently reserved for Britain was the control of Australian foreign affairs.

Along with those reserved rights that Britain retained, throughout the 1800's it continued to deliver to Australia important services that an independent Australia would have had to provide for itself. One of those services was military protection by British warships, as other European countries and Japan and the United States became increasingly assertive in the Pacific Ocean during the later 1800's. Another service involved the governors that Britain sent out to its Australian colonies. Those governors were not resented tyrants forced on protesting Australian colonies by a powerful Britain. Instead, they played an acknowledged essential role in Australian self-government, in which the Australian colonies often reached impasses. The appointed British governors frequently had to resolve disagreements between the upper and lower houses of a colonial legislature, had to broker the formation of parliamentary coalitions, and had to decide when to dissolve parliament and call an election.

———

So far, I have talked about the historical Australian colonies as if they were straightforward precursors to the unified Australia of today. In fact, Australia arose as six separate colonies — New South Wales, Tasmania, Victoria, South Australia, Western Australia, and Queensland — with far less contact among them than the contact among the American colonies that would later become states of the U.S. That limited contact was due to the geography of Australia, a continent with few patches of productive landscape separated by large distances of desert and other types of unproductive landscape. Not until 1917 did all five of the capital cities on the Australian mainland become connected by railroad. (The sixth capital, Hobart on Tasmania, has never been connected because

Tasmania is an island 130 miles from the Australian mainland.)
Each colony adopted a different railroad gauge (track separation),
ranging from 3 feet 6 inches to 5 feet 3 inches, with the result that
trains could not run directly from one colony into another. Like
independent countries, the colonies erected protective tariff barriers against one another and maintained customs houses to collect
import duties at colonial borders. In 1864 New South Wales and
Victoria came close to an armed confrontation at their border. As a
result, the six colonies did not become united into a single nation of
Australia until 1901, 113 years after the First Fleet.

Initially, the colonies showed little interest in uniting. Settlers
thought of themselves first as overseas British, and then as Victorians
or Queenslanders rather than as Australians. The stirrings of interest in federation emerged only in the latter half of the 1800's, as Japan
increased in military power, and as the United States, France, and
Germany expanded over the Pacific Ocean and annexed one Pacific
island group after another, posing a potential threat to Britain's
Pacific colonies. But it was initially unclear what would be the territorial limits of a union of those British colonies. A first federal council of "Austronesia" that met in 1886 included representatives of the
British colonies of New Zealand and Fiji far from Australia, but only
four of the six colonies that now form Australia were represented.

Although a first draft of an Australian federal constitution was
prepared in 1891, the unified Commonwealth of Australia was not
inaugurated until January 1, 1901. The preamble to that constitution
declares agreement "to unite in one indissoluble Federal Commonwealth under the crown of the United Kingdom of Great Britain and
Ireland," with a federal governor-general appointed by Britain, and
with the provision that decisions of Australia's High Court could be
appealed to Britain's Privy Council (equivalent to Britain's highest
court). Imagine those provisions in the U.S. Constitution! That Australian constitution illustrates that Australians still felt allegiance

to the British Crown, meaning "an acceptance of shared values — the rule of law, a free press, the protection of individual liberties, a claim on the protection offered by the then superpower and represented by the Royal Navy, a shared pride in being part of the Empire upon which the sun never set, and even an affection for the person of Queen Victoria" (Frank Welsh, *Australia*, p. 337). The flag that was adopted then, and that remains the Australian national flag today, consists of the British flag (the Union Jack), framed by the Southern Hemisphere star constellation of the Southern Cross (Plate 7.4).

———

Australians debating the federal constitution argued about many matters but were unanimous about excluding all non-white races from Australia. The following quotes illustrate Australian views then about preserving a White Australia. In 1896 the newspaper *Melbourne Age* wrote, "We wish to see Australia the home of a great homogenous Caucasian race, entirely free from the problems which have plunged the United States into civil war...there is no use in protecting our workers from the pauper labor of the Far East if we admit the paupers themselves." One of the first acts of the new Australian Federation in 1901 was the Immigration Restriction Act, passed by agreement of all political parties, aiming to ensure that Australia would remain white. The act barred the immigration of prostitutes, the insane, people suffering from loathsome diseases, and criminals (despite Australia's origin as a dumping ground for criminals). The act also provided that no blacks or Asians would be admitted, and that Australians should be "one people, and remain one people without the admixture of other races." An Australian labor leader argued, "The influx of these aliens would so lower the aggregate standard of the community that in a very short time social legislation will be ineffective. But if we keep the race pure, and

267

build up a national character, we shall become a highly progressive people of whom the British Government would be proud the longer we live and the stronger we grow."

Examples of other contemporary views from around that time of federation were: "Colored aliens are not nice people to be seen in the lonely bush of Australia"; no Chinese could be expected "to attain that level of civilization which Australia had inherited from the centuries"; and "the beautifully dressed ladies who attend... Church must be pleased to think that perhaps a big fat [unprintable] reeking with the germs of all sorts of diseases carried from the necessary Yokohama, has warmed the seat on which she sits." Even Australia's first federal prime minister, Edmund Barton, wrote, "There is no racial equality. These [non-white] races are, in comparison with white races... unequal and inferior. The doctrine of the equality of man was never intended to apply to the equality of the Englishman and the Chinaman.... Nothing we can do by cultivation, by refinement, or by anything else would make some races equal to others." Another prime minister, Alfred Deakin, declared, "Unity of race is an absolute essential to the unity of Australia."

Britain's colonial secretary objected to the Australian Commonwealth mentioning race explicitly, in part because that created difficulties at a time when Britain was trying to negotiate a military alliance with Japan. Hence the Commonwealth achieved that same goal of race-based immigration control without mentioning race, by requiring entering immigrants to take a dictation test — not necessarily in English, but in any European language at the discretion of the presiding immigration official. When a boatload of workers arrived from the British colony but ethnically mixed Mediterranean island of Malta, with the potential for passing a dictation test in English, they were instead administered a dictation test in Dutch (a language unknown in Malta as well as in Australia) in order to justify expelling them. As for the non-whites already admitted to Australia as laborers, the Commonwealth deported Pacific Islanders, Chinese, and Indians but allowed two small groups of specialists (Afghan camel-drivers and Japanese pearl-divers) to remain.

The motive behind these immigration barriers was mainly the racism of the times, but partly also that the Australian Labor Party wanted to protect high wages for Australian workers by preventing the immigration of cheap labor. However, I don't want to malign Australians as being exceptionally racist. Instead, they merely shared racist views widespread around the world, and differed mainly in being able to translate those views into an immigration policy based on racist exclusion while simultaneously encouraging British immigration because of Australia's low population density. Contemporary Britain and continental European countries didn't encourage or accept immigrants at all. When many people of African origins finally did arrive in Britain from Britain's West Indian colonies after World War Two, the eventual result was Britain's Nottingham and Notting Hill race riots of 1958. Japan still doesn't accept significant numbers of immigrants. The United States, having rejected Australia's devotion to British identity, eventually accepted huge numbers of immigrants from continental Europe, Mexico, and East Asia, but over much resistance.

———

Until things began to change after World War Two, Australians' sense of identity centered on their being British subjects. That emerges most clearly from the enthusiasm with which Australian troops fought beside British troops in British wars that had no direct significance for Australian interests. The first case was in 1885, when the colony of New South Wales (long before federation into the Commonwealth of Australia) sent troops to fight with British troops against rebels in the Sudan, a remote part of the world than which no other could have been more irrelevant to Australia. A bigger opportunity arose in the Boer War of 1899, between Britain and the descendants of Dutch colonists in South Africa, again with zero direct relevance to Australian interests. Australian soldiers performed well in the Boer War, winning five Victoria Crosses (Britain's highest medal for battlefield bravery), and thereby gaining glory and a reputation as loyal British subjects at the cost of only about 300 Australian soldiers dead in battle.

When Britain declared war on Germany in August 1914 at the outset of World War One, it did so without bothering to consult either Australia or Canada. Australia's British-appointed governor-general merely passed on the announcement of war to Australia's elected prime minister. Australians unhesitatingly supported the British war efforts on a far larger scale than in the case of the Boer War or the Sudan War. An Australian journalist wrote, "We must protect our [sic!] country. We must keep sacred from the mailed fist [i.e., of Germany] this sacred heritage." In this case, the war did have a slight effect on Australian interests: it gave Australian troops a pretext to occupy the German colonies of northeast New Guinea and the Bismarck Archipelago. But Australia's main contribution to World War One was to contribute a huge volunteer force — 400,000 soldiers, constituting more than half of all Australian men eligible to serve, out of a total Australian population under 5 million — to defend British interests half-way around the world from Australia, in France and the Mideast. More than 300,000 were sent overseas, of whom two-thirds ended up wounded or killed. Almost every small rural Australian town still has a cenotaph in the town center, listing the names of local men killed in the war.

What became the best-known Australian involvement in World War One was the attack of ANZAC troops (the Australia and New Zealand Army Corps) on Turkish troops holding the Gallipoli Peninsula (Plate 7.5). The ANZAC troops landed on April 25, 1915, suffered high casualties because of incompetent leadership by the British general commanding the operation, and were withdrawn in 1916 when Britain concluded that the operation was a failure. Ever since then, ANZAC Day (April 25), the anniversary of the Gallipoli landings, has been Australia's most important and most emotional national holiday.

To a non-Australian, the emphasis on ANZAC Day as *the* Australian national holiday is beyond comprehension. Why should any country *celebrate* the slaughter of its young men, betrayed by British leadership, half-way around the world, on a peninsula that rivals the Sudan in its irrelevance to Australia's national interests? But I have learned to keep my mouth shut, and not to ask such rational questions, when, still today, my Australian friends dissolve in tears as they talk about the Gallipoli landings of a century ago. The explanation is that nothing illustrated better the willingness of Australians to die for their British mother country than did the slaughter of young Australians at Gallipoli. Gallipoli became viewed as the birth of the Australian nation, reflecting the widespread view that any nation's birth requires sacrifice and the spilling of blood. The slaughter at Gallipoli symbolized the national pride of Australians, now fighting for their British motherland as Australians, not as Victorians or Tasmanians or South Australians — and the emotional dedication with which Australians publicly identified themselves as loyal British subjects.

That self-identification was re-emphasized in 1923, when a conference of British Empire member countries agreed that British dominions could henceforth appoint their own ambassadors or diplomatic representatives to foreign countries, instead of being represented by the British ambassador. Canada, South Africa, and Ireland promptly did appoint their own diplomatic representatives. But Australia did not, on the grounds that there was no public enthusiasm in Australia for seeking visible signs of national independence from Britain.

However, Australia's relationship towards Britain not only has been one of the dutiful child seeking approval from its esteemed mother country, but also includes a love/hate component. One personal example is that of a friend of mine who worked in an Australian sheep slaughterhouse, some of whose produce was sold for domestic consumption in Australia, while other produce was exported frozen to Britain. Into boxes of sheep livers destined for export to Britain, my friend and his mates occasionally dropped a sheep gallbladder, whose contents of bile are unforgettably bitter-tasting. More serious examples of the hatred component of Australia's relationship with Britain are the expressed views, which I shall quote later, of Australian prime ministers after World War Two.

———

The significance of World War Two for Australia was very different from that of World War One, because Australia itself was attacked, and because there was heavy fighting on islands near Australia rather than just half-way around the world. The surrender of Britain's big naval base at Singapore to Japanese troops is often regarded as a turning point in the evolution of Australia's self-image.

During the two decades after World War One, Japan built up its army and navy, launched an undeclared war against China, and emerged as a danger to Australia. In its role as defender of Australia, Britain responded by strengthening its base on the tip of the Malay Peninsula at Singapore, although that base was 4,000 miles from Australia. Australia relied for protection on that remote British base and on the even more remote British fleet concentrated in the Atlantic and the Mediterranean. But Britain cannot be blamed alone for the eventual failure of its Singapore strategy, because Australia simultaneously neglected steps for its own defense. Australia abolished the draft in 1930 and built only a small air force and navy. The latter included no aircraft carriers, battleships, or warships larger than light cruisers, hopelessly inadequate to protect Australia and its international sea connections against Japanese attack. At the same time, Britain itself was facing a more serious and immediate threat from Germany and was lagging in its own military preparations against Japan.

Just as at the outset of World War One, when Britain declared war on Germany again on September 3, 1939, Australia's prime minister promptly announced without even consulting parliament, "Great Britain has declared war, and as a result Australia is also at war [with Germany]." As in World War One, Australia initially had no direct interest in the Second World War's European theater half-way around the world, pitting Germany against Poland, Britain, France, and other Western European countries. But again, just as during World War One, Australia sent troops to fight in the European theater, mainly in North Africa and Crete. As the risk of attack from Japan increased, the Australian government requested the return of those troops to defend Australia itself. The British Prime Minister Winston Churchill tried to reassure Australians by promising that Britain and its fleet would use Singapore to protect Australia against Japanese invasion, and against any Japanese fleet that might appear in Australian waters. As events proved, those promises had no basis in reality.

Japan did attack the U.S., Britain, Australia, and the Dutch East Indies beginning on December 7, 1941. On December 10, just the third day after Japan's declaration of war, Japanese bombers sank Britain's only two large warships available in the Far East to defend Australia, the battleship *Prince of Wales* (Plate 7.6) and the battle cruiser *Repulse*. On February 15, 1942, the British general in command at Singapore surrendered to the Japanese army, sending 100,000 British and Empire troops into prisoner-of-war camps — the most severe military defeat that Britain has suffered in its history (Plate 7.7). Sadly, those troops surrendering included 2,000

Australian soldiers who had arrived in Singapore only three weeks earlier, on January 24, in order to serve in the hopeless task of its defense. In the absence of British ships to protect Australia, the same Japanese aircraft carriers that had bombed the American naval base at Pearl Harbor heavily bombed the Australian city of Darwin on February 19, 1942 (Plate 7.8). That was the first of more than 60 Japanese air raids on Australia, in addition to an attempted raid on Sydney Harbor by a Japanese submarine.

To Australians, the fall of Singapore was not just a shock and a frightening military setback: it was regarded as a betrayal of Australia by its British mother country. While the Japanese advance on Singapore was unfolding, Australia's Prime Minister John Curtin cabled Churchill that it would constitute an "inexcusable betrayal" if Britain evacuated Singapore after all the assurances of the base being impregnable. But Singapore fell because Britain was stretched militarily much too thin between the European theater and the Far East, and because the attacking Japanese forces were tactically superior to the numerically superior defending British and Empire forces.

Australia had been guilty of neglecting its own defense. Nevertheless, Australian bitterness against Britain has persisted for a long time. As late as 1992, 50 years after Singapore's surrender, Australia's Prime Minister Paul Keating scathingly denounced Britain and vented his hatred in a speech to the Australian parliament: "At school... I learned about self-respect and self-regard for Australia — not about some cultural cringe to a country which decided not to defend the Malayan Peninsula, not to worry about Singapore, and not to give us our troops back to keep ourselves free from Japanese domination. This was the country that you people [Australian parliament members belonging to the two conservative parties] wedded yourselves to... even as it walked out on you."

The lessons of World War Two for Australia were two-fold.

First and foremost, Britain had been powerless to defend Australia. Instead, the defense of Australia had depended on massive deployment of American troops, ships, and airplanes, commanded by the American General MacArthur, who established his headquarters in Australia. MacArthur directed operations, including those involving Australian troops, largely by himself: there was no suggestion of an equal partnership between the U.S. and Australia. While there was concern about the possibility of Japanese landings in Australia, they did not materialize. But it was clear that any defense of Australia against landings would have been by the U.S., not by Britain. As the war against Japan slowly unfolded over nearly four years, Australian troops fought against Japanese troops on the islands of New Guinea, New Britain, the Solomons, and finally Borneo. Those Australian troops played a vital front-line role in defeating Japan's attempt in 1942 to advance over the Kokoda Trail to capture Australian New Guinea's colonial capital of Port Moresby. Increasingly thereafter, though, MacArthur relegated Australian troops to secondary operations far from the front lines. As a result, although Australia was attacked directly in World War Two but not in World War One, Australia's casualties in World War Two were paradoxically less than half of those in World War One.

Second, World War Two brought home to Australia that, while Australian troops served in both wars in the remote European theater, there were grave immediate risks to Australia nearby, from Asia. With reason, Australia now came to consider Japan as *the* enemy. About 22,000 Australian troops captured by the Japanese during the war were subjected to unspeakably brutal conditions in Japanese prisoner-of-war camps, where 36% of the Australian prisoners died: a far higher percentage than the 1% death toll of American and British soldiers in German prisoner-of-war camps, and of German soldiers in American and British prisoner-of-war camps. Especially shocking to Australians was the Sandakan Death

March, in which 2,700 Australian and British troops captured by the Japanese and imprisoned at Sandakan on the island of Borneo were marched across Borneo, starved, and beaten until most of the few survivors were executed, resulting in the deaths of almost all of those prisoners.

———

After World War Two there unfolded a gradual loosening of Australia's ties to Britain and a shift in Australians' self-identification as "loyal British in Australia," resulting in a dismantling of the White Australia policy. Even for historians with no particular interest in Australia itself, these changes furnish a model study of changing national answers to the question "Who are we?" Such changes can't occur as quickly for nations, composed of groups with different interests, as they can for individuals. In Australia the changes have been strung out over many decades, and they are still going on today.

World War Two had immediate consequences for Australia's immigration policy. Already in 1943, Australia's prime minister concluded that the tiny population of Australians (less than 8 million in 1945) could not hold their huge continent against threats from Japan (population then over 100 million), Indonesia (just 200 miles away) with a population approaching 200 million, and China (population 1 billion). By comparison with high population densities in Japan and Java and China, Australia looked empty and attractive to Asian invasion — so thought the prime minister, but Asians themselves did not think that way. The other argument for more immigration was the mistaken belief that a large population is essential for any country to develop a strong First World economy.

Neither of those arguments made sense. There always have been, and still are, compelling reasons why Australia has a much lower population density than does Japan or Java. All of Japan and Java is wet and fertile, and much of the area of those islands is suitable for highly productive agriculture. But most of Australia's area is barren desert, and only a tiny fraction is productive farmland. As for the necessity of a large population to build a strong First World economy, the economic successes of Denmark, Finland, Israel, and Singapore, each with a population only one-quarter the size of Australia's, illustrate that quality counts more than quantity in economic success. In fact, Australia would be much better off with a smaller population than it presently has, because that would reduce human impact on the fragile Australian landscape and would increase the ratio of natural resources to people.

But Australia's prime ministers in the 1940's were neither ecologists nor economists, and so post-war Australia did embark on a crash program of encouraging immigration. Unfortunately, there were not nearly enough applications from the preferred sources of Britain and Ireland to fill Australia's immigration target, and the White Australia policy limited Australia's other options. Inducing American servicemen who had been stationed in Australia to stay was not an attractive possibility, because too many of them were African-Americans. Instead, initially the "next best" source (after Britain and Ireland) from which post-war Australia encouraged immigration became Northern Europe. The third choice was Southern Europe, accounting for the Italian and Greek restaurants that I patronized in 1964. Australian immigration supporters announced the surprising discovery, "With proper selection, Italians make excellent citizens" (!!). As a first step in that direction, Italian and German prisoners of war who had been brought to Australia were permitted to remain.

Australia's minister for immigration from 1945 to 1949, Arthur Calwell, was an outspoken racist. He even refused to allow Australian men who had been so unpatriotic as to marry Japanese, Chinese, or Indonesian women to bring their war-brides or children into Australia. Calwell wrote, "No Japanese women, or any half-castes either, will be admitted to Australia; they are simply not wanted and are permanently undesirable... a mongrel Australia is impossible." As an additional source besides Britain, Calwell wrote approvingly about the three Baltic Republics (Estonia, Latvia, and Lithuania), whose annexation by Russia had motivated emigration by thousands of well-educated white people with eye color and hair color resembling those of the British. In 1947 Calwell toured refugee camps in post-war Europe, found that they offered "splendid human material," and noted approvingly of the Baltic Republics, "Many of their people were red-headed and blue-eyed. There were also a number of natural platinum blonds of both sexes." The result of that selective encouragement of immigration was that, from 1945 to 1950, Australia received about 700,000 immigrants (a number nearly equal to 10% of its 1945 population), half of them reassuringly British, the rest from other European countries. In 1949 Australia even relented and permitted Japanese war-brides to remain.

The undermining of the White Australia policy that produced the Asian immigrants and Asian restaurants awaiting me in Brisbane in 2008 resulted from five considerations: military protection, political developments in Asia, shifts of Australian trade, the immigrants themselves, and British policy. As for military considerations, World War Two had made clear that Britain was no longer a military power in the Pacific; instead, Australia's military ties had to be with the U.S. That became officially recognized by the 1951 ANZUS security treaty between the U.S., Australia, and New Zealand, without the participation of Britain. The Korean War, the rise of communist threats in Malaya and Vietnam, and Indonesian military interventions in Dutch New Guinea, Malaysian Borneo, and Portuguese Timor warned Australia of proliferating security problems nearby. The 1956 Suez Crisis, in which Britain failed to topple

President Nasser of Egypt and was forced to yield to U.S. economic pressure, laid bare Britain's military and economic weakness. To the shock of Australians, in 1967 Britain announced its intent to withdraw all of its military forces east of the Suez Canal. That marked the official end to Britain's long-standing role as Australia's protector.

As for Asian political developments, former colonies and pro-tectorates and mandates in Asia were becoming independent nations, including Indonesia, East Timor, Papua New Guinea, the Philippines, Malaysia, Vietnam, Laos, Cambodia, and Thailand. Those countries were near Australia: Papua New Guinea only a few miles away, and Indonesia and East Timor only 200 miles away. They devised their own foreign policies, no longer subservient to the foreign policies of their former colonial masters. They were also rising economically.

As for trade, Britain had formerly been by far the largest trade partner of Australia, accounting for 45% of Australia's imports and 30% of its exports even as late as the early 1950's. A rapid rise in Australian trade with Japan began with Australia's overcoming its racist and World-War-Two–driven hostility to Japan to sign a trade agreement with Japan in 1957, and then in 1960 lifting its ban on exporting iron ore to Japan. By the 1980's Australia's leading trade partner was — Japan! — followed by the U.S., with Britain far behind. In 1982 Japan received 28% of Australian exports, the U.S. 11%, and Britain only 4%. But it was an obvious contradiction that, at the same time as Australia was telling Japan and other Asian countries how eager it was for their trade, it was simultaneously telling them that it considered Japanese and other Asian people themselves unfit to settle in Australia.

The next-to-last factor undermining the pro-British White Australia immigration policy was the shift in Australian immi-grants themselves. All of those Italians, Greeks, Estonians,

Latvians, and Lithuanians who immigrated after World War Two were undoubtedly white, but they were not British. They didn't share Australians' traditional image of themselves as loyal subjects of Britain. They also didn't share the strong racist prejudices against Asians that were prevalent in Britain as well as in Australia as late as the 1950's.

Finally, it was not just that Australia was pulling away from Britain; Britain was also pulling away from Australia. For Britain as for Australia, its interests were changing, and its self-image was becoming increasingly out-of-date. The British government recognized those cruel realities before the Australian government did, but the acknowledgment was intensely painful on both sides. The changes in Britain were at their peak while I was living there between 1958 and 1962. Australians had traditionally viewed their identity as being British citizens within the British Empire, based on the twin realities of population ancestry and of British trade and military protection, all of which were changing. At the same time, the British had traditionally viewed their identity as being based on ownership of the largest empire in world history ("the empire on which the sun never sets"), then on leadership of the British Commonwealth. The Empire and then the Commonwealth had been Britain's leading trade partners, and major sources of troops: think of all those Australians, New Zealanders, Indians, and Canadian troops who died alongside British troops in both world wars. But Britain's trade was decreasing with the Commonwealth and shifting towards Europe, just as Australia's trade with Britain was decreasing and shifting towards Asia and the U.S. Britain's African and Asian colonies were becoming independent, developed their own national identities, formulated their own foreign policies even within the Commonwealth, and (over British objections) forced South Africa out of the Commonwealth because of its racist apartheid policies. As Australia was feeling pressured to choose between

Britain and Asia plus the U.S., Britain was feeling pressured to choose between the Commonwealth and Europe.

In 1955 Britain decided to withdraw from negotiations among six Western European countries (France, Germany, Italy, Belgium, Netherlands, and Luxembourg) to form a European Economic Community (EEC, progenitor of today's Common Market). Contrary to British expectations in 1955, the Six (Western European countries) did succeed in bringing the EEC into existence without Britain in 1957. By 1961, Britain's Prime Minister Harold Macmillan recognized the shift in Britain's interests. Europe was becoming more important to Britain than was the Commonwealth, both economically and politically. Hence Britain applied to join the EEC. That application and its sequels constituted a shock to Australia's and Britain's relationship even more fundamental than had been the fall of Singapore, although the latter was more dramatic and symbolic, and lingers today as a bigger cause of festering resentment to Australians.

Britain's application created an unavoidable clash between British and Australian interests. The Six were erecting shared tariff barriers against non-EEC imports, barriers to which Britain would have to subscribe. Those barriers would now apply to Australian food products and refined metals, for which Britain still represented a major export market. Australian food exports to Britain would now be displaced by French, Dutch, Italian, and Danish foods. Prime Minister Macmillan knew this cruel reality as well as did Australia's Prime Minister Robert Menzies. Macmillan promised Australia and other Commonwealth countries that Britain would insist on defending Commonwealth interests in Britain's negotiations with the EEC. But it seemed doubtful then that Macmillan would prevail, and in fact the Six refused to make significant concessions to Australia's interests.

Australians' reactions to Britain's EEC application were

reminiscent of their reactions to Singapore's fall. The application was denounced as immoral, dishonest, a basis for moral grievance — and a betrayal of Gallipoli, of a century of other Australian sacrifices for the British motherland, and of the British heritage underlying Australia's traditional national identity. That is, the shock was profoundly symbolic, as well as material. Worse symbolic shocks were still to come. Britain's Commonwealth Immigration Act of 1962, actually aimed at halting Commonwealth immigration from the West Indies and Pakistan, avoided appearances of racism by ending the automatic right of *all* Commonwealth citizens (including Australians) to enter and reside in Britain. Britain's 1968 Immigration Act barred automatic right of entry into Britain for all *FOREIGN-ERS* (Australians were now declared to be foreigners!) without at least one British-born grandparent, thereby excluding a large fraction of Australians at that time. In 1972 Britain declared Australians to be *ALIENS* (!). What an insult!

In short, it wasn't the case that Australian sons and daughters of the British motherland were declaring their independence. Instead, the motherland was declaring its own independence, loosening its ties with the Commonwealth, and disowning its children.

British/European negotiations unfolded with agonizing slowness, starts, and stops. France's President de Gaulle vetoed the first British application to the EEC in 1963. He also vetoed a second British application in 1967. Following de Gaulle's resignation and death, the third British application in 1971 was approved by the European Six, and by British citizens in a national referendum. By then, Britain accounted for only 8% of Australian exports. Australian politicians had come to recognize that joining Europe was in Britain's vital interests, that Australia shouldn't and couldn't oppose British interests, and that Australia's previous relationship to Britain had become a myth.

———

From an Australian perspective, it may seem that Australian identity changed suddenly and comprehensively in 1972, when Australia's Labour Party under Prime Minister Gough Whitlam came to power for the first time in 23 years. In his first 19 days in office, even before he had appointed a new cabinet, Whitlam and his deputy embarked on a crash program of selective change in Australia, for which there are few parallels in the modern world in its speed and comprehensiveness. The changes introduced in those 19 days included: end of the military draft (national conscription); withdrawal of all Australian troops from Vietnam; recognition of the People's Republic of China; announced independence for Papua New Guinea, which Australia had been administering for over half-a-century under a mandate from the League of Nations and then from the United Nations; banning visits by racially selected overseas athletic teams (a rule aimed especially at all-white South African teams); abolishing the nomination of Australians for Britain's system of honors (knighthoods, OBEs, KCMGs, and so on) and replacing them with a new system of Australian honors; and — officially repudiating the White Australia policy. Once Whitlam's whole cabinet had been approved, it then adopted more steps in the crash program: reduction of the voting age to 18; increase in the minimum wage; giving representation to both the Northern Territory and the Australian Capital Territory in the federal Senate; granting legislative councils to both of those territories; requiring environmental impact statements for industrial developments; increased spending on Aborigines; equal pay for women; no-fault divorce; a comprehensive medical insurance scheme; and big changes in education that included abolishing university fees, boosts in financial aid for schools, and transfer from the states to the Australian Commonwealth of the responsibility for funding tertiary education.

Whitlam correctly described his reforms as a "recognition of what has already happened" rather than as a revolution arising out of nothing. In fact, Australia's British identity had been gradually decreasing. The fall of Singapore in 1942 had been a first big shock, the 1951 ANZUS Security Treaty an early recognition, communist threats in Eastern Europe and Vietnam warning signs. But Australia still looked to and sided with Britain long after the fall of Singapore. Australian troops fought alongside British troops in Malaya against communist insurgents in the late 1940's, and in Malaysian Borneo against Indonesian infiltrators in the early 1960's. Australia allowed Britain to test British atomic bombs in remote Australian deserts in the late 1950's, in an effort to maintain Britain as a world military power independent of the U.S. Australia was among the few nations to support Britain's widely denounced attack on Egypt in the 1956 Suez Crisis. In 1954 the first visit to Australia by a reigning British monarch, Queen Elizabeth, was greeted by an enormous outpouring of pro-British sentiment: over 75% of all Australians turned out on the streets to cheer her (Plate 7.9). But — by the time that Queen Elizabeth visited Australia again in 1963, two years after Britain's first EEC application, Australians were much less interested in her and in Britain.

The dismantling of Australia's White Australia policy had similarly proceeded in stages before Whitlam made it official, with the admission of Japanese war-brides in 1949 being a first stage. Under the Colombo Plan for Asian development, Australia accepted 10,000 Asian student visitors in the 1950's. The despised dictation test for prospective immigrants was dropped in 1958. The Migration Act of that same year allowed "distinguished and highly qualified Asians" to immigrate. Hence when Whitlam announced the end of the White Australia policy in 1972 and repudiated all official forms of racial discrimination, his actions aroused much less protest than one might have expected for the end of a policy that had been espoused so tenaciously for over a century. Between 1978 and 1982 Australia admitted more Indochinese refugees, as a percentage of its population, than any other country in the world. By the late 1980's, nearly half of Australians were either born overseas or had at least one overseas-born parent. By 1991, Asians represented over 50% of immigrants to Australia. By 2010, the percentage of Australians actually born overseas (more than 25%) was second in the world, trailing only Israel's percentage. The influence of those Asian immigrants has been far out of proportion to their numbers: Asian students have come to occupy over 70% of the places in Sydney's top schools, Asian university students appeared to account for a sizeable fraction of the students whom I saw strolling across the University of Queensland campus in 2008, and Asians and other non-Europeans now make up more than half of Australian medical students.

Other changes in Australia have been political and cultural. In 1986 Australia ended the right of final appeal to Britain's Privy Council, thereby abolishing the last real trace of British sovereignty and making Australia fully independent at last. In 1999 Australia's High Court declared Britain to be a "foreign country." On the cultural front, the 1960's dominance of British cooking in Australia, symbolized by meat pies and beer, was greatly broadened by many styles of international cuisine — and not just by the Italian, Greek, and occasional Chinese restaurants of the 1960's. Australian wines now include some of the greatest wines in the world. (Hint: I especially recommend De Bortoli's Noble One as a great but affordable dessert wine, Penfolds Grange as a great and less affordable red wine, and Morris of Rutherglen's Muscat as a great affordable fortified wine.) The Sydney Opera House (Plate 7.10), opened in 1973, and now viewed as a symbol of Australia as well as one of the world's great achievements of modern architecture, was designed by the Danish architect Jørn Utzon.

The debates about *Who are we?* have concerned not just the reality of Australian identity, but seemingly every possible symbol of identity. Should Australia's currency still be called the non-decimal pound sterling as in Britain, or should it have a distinctively Australian name, such as the roo (short for "kangaroo")? (The eventual decision was to discard the pound in favor of a decimal currency with an American or international name, the dollar.) Should Australia's national anthem still be "God Save the Queen"? (In 1984 that British anthem was finally replaced by "Advance Australia Fair.") Should Australia's national flag still be based on Britain's Union Jack? (It still is.) Should the heroic Australian defeat defending British interests against the Turks at Gallipoli in 1915 still provide Australia's biggest national celebration, or should it instead be provided by the heroic Australian victory defending Australian interests against the Japanese on New Guinea's Kokoda Trail in 1942? (It's still ANZAC Day commemorating Gallipoli.) And — should Australia still acknowledge Britain's Queen at all, or should it become a republic? (It still acknowledges the Queen.)

———

How does Australia fit into our framework of crisis and selective change?

For Australia, more than for any other country that we are discussing, the central issue has been an ongoing debate about questions of national identity and core values (factors #6 and 11, Table 1.2): Who are we? Is Australia a white British outpost that happens to be near Asia but takes little notice of its Asian neighbors? Are Australians loyal British subjects who depend for their self-confidence on approval by Britain, who look to Britain for protection, who feel no need for their nation to have its own ambassadors abroad, and who, to demonstrate their loyalty to the British motherland, volunteer to die in large numbers in remote parts of the world strategically important to Britain but not to Australia? Or, is Australia instead an independent nation on the immediate periphery of Asia, with its own national interests and foreign policy and ambassadors, more involved with Asia than with Europe, and with its British cultural heritage declining with time? That debate did not begin seriously until after World War Two, and it is continuing today. Even as Australia was debating its identity as a proud outpost of the British Empire, Britain was debating its own identity as the proud center of that empire (in decline), and struggling to assume a new identity as a non-imperial power heavily involved with continental Europe.

The theme of honest self-appraisal (factor #7) has increasingly characterized Australia since World War Two, as Australians have come to recognize Australia's changed situation in the modern world. Australians have reluctantly recognized that Britain, their former closest trade partner, is now just a minor trade partner, that their former worst enemy of Japan is now their most important trade partner, and that it is no longer a viable strategy for Australia to operate as a white British outpost on the periphery of Asia.

The impetus for change in Australia has been partly external, partly internal. Part of the impetus has been the declining power of Britain, the end of Britain's overseas empire, and the rising power of Japan, China, and other Asian countries. At the same time, part of the impetus has been internal, as Australia's population has through immigration become decreasingly British and increasingly Asian plus European non-British, and that changing population has chosen different policies.

Australia strikingly illustrates selective change and building a fence (factor #3). Major things that have changed include shifts in how Australians view themselves; the development of an independent foreign policy, instead of leaving Australia's foreign policy decisions to Britain; an increasingly multi-ethnic population and culture (much more so in cities than in rural areas); and political and economic orientation towards Asia and the U.S. At the same time, other major things have remained unchanged. The Australian government is still a parliamentary democracy. Australia still maintains important symbolic ties to Britain, such as that the Queen of Britain is still Australia's head of state, the Queen's portrait still appears on Australia's five-dollar bank note and its coins, and the Australian flag still incorporates the British flag. Australia still maintains highly egalitarian social values and strong individualism. Australian society still has an unmistakably Australian flavor, such as a dedication to sports: especially to the Australian sport of Australian-rules football (invented in Australia and played nowhere else), along with swimming, plus the British sports of cricket and rugby. Australia's leaders themselves embrace the national pastimes even when they're dangerous: Prime Minister Harold Holt died in office by drowning in 1967, while swimming in an ocean area with strong offshore currents.

In most countries that make many selective changes, different changes are made independently over many years. But one of the few examples of a unified program consisting of many changes launched simultaneously is the 19-day whirlwind of Australia's Prime Minister Gough Whitlam from December 1 to December 19 of 1972.

The question of freedom from constraints (factor #12) has been important to Australia, and that freedom (or lack thereof) has changed with time. Until World War Two, the oceans protected Australia from any realistic risk of attack, just as they protected the mainland United States after independence until the World Trade Center attack of September 11, 2001. Since the Japanese bombing raid on Darwin on February 19, 1942, Australians have realized that their country is no longer free from external constraints.

Even before 1942, though, Australia's European-dominated

society has depended on help from supportive friends (factor #4): initially Britain, which in the years after the First Fleet even provided food, and later defense; and, from World War Two onwards, the United States. While Australia was never at risk of direct attack before the Darwin raid, Australians did feel concerns about French, German, American, and Japanese military and colonial expansion to Pacific islands, beginning in the latter half of the 19th century. Australia looked to the British fleet for protection against those concerns, so much so that Australia failed to take responsibility (factor #2) for its own defense during the 1930's and allowed its own armed forces to atrophy.

Australia's changes over the last 70 years have not been in response to an acute crisis, but instead have been a gradual process developing over a long time and accelerating since World War Two, as Australia's British identity degenerated from a reality to a myth. While Australians themselves may not apply the word "crisis" to Australia, I find it useful to think of Australia as having undergone a slowly unfolding crisis, because Australia's issues of selective change have been similar to those issues in other nations responding to sudden crises. In that respect, recent changes in Australia resemble changes during the same decades in Germany (Chapter 6), which also unfolded slowly. There were of course some notable moments in Australia's train of slow developments: particularly the sinking of the *Prince of Wales* and the *Repulse*, Singapore's surrender, and the Darwin air raid, all within the span of 71 days. But crisis and change in Australia involved nothing approaching the transforming shock of the arrival of Commodore Perry's warships for Meiji Japan on July 8, 1853, the Russian attack of November 30, 1939 for Finland, Pinochet's coup and Allende's death on September 11, 1973 for Chile, and the failed October 1, 1965 coup and subsequent genocide for Indonesia.

Australia's reappraisal of its core values, and its train of selective changes, are surely not over. In 1999 Australia held a referendum on whether Australia should abandon the Queen of Britain as its head of state and instead become a republic. While the referendum was defeated by a vote of 55% to 45%, decades earlier it would have been utterly unthinkable even to hold such a referendum, let alone to contemplate the possibility of a 45% "no" vote. The percentage of Australians who were born in Britain is rapidly decreasing. It seems only a matter of time before there will be another referendum on whether Australia should become a republic, and the chances of a "yes" vote will be higher. Within a decade or two, it is likely that Asians will constitute over 15% of Australia's population and its legislators, and over 50% of the students in top Australian universities. Sooner or later, Australia will elect an Asian as its prime minister. (At the moment that I write this sentence, a Vietnamese immigrant is already governor of South Australia.) As those changes unfold, won't it appear incongruous for Australia to retain the Queen of Britain as its head of the state, to retain her portrait on its currency, and to retain an Australian flag based on the British flag?

PART 3

NATIONS AND THE WORLD: CRISES UNDERWAY

CHAPTER 8

WHAT LIES AHEAD FOR JAPAN?

Japan today — Economy — Advantages —
Government debt — Women — Babies — Old and
declining — Immigration — China and Korea —
Natural resource management — Crisis framework

We have now discussed past crises in six nations. In our first four nations the crises exploded suddenly at times ranging between 166 years ago (Meiji Japan) and 46 years ago (Chile). In our next two nations the crises emerged more gradually but were at their peak around half-a-century ago. While one couldn't claim that any of those crises reached a complete resolution (or a complete stalemate), enough decades have nevertheless passed in each case that we can usefully discuss the outcomes.

In the remaining four chapters we shall instead discuss crises that now appear to be unfolding, for which only the future will tell us whether they really did constitute a major crisis, and whose outcomes remain uncertain. These chapters concern contemporary Japan, the U.S., and the whole world.

Just as our discussion of past crises included Japan of the Meiji Era, let's begin our discussion of possible current crises with Japan.

(In this chapter I'll consider only problems specific to Japan, but Japan is of course also exposed to the worldwide problems to be discussed in Chapter 11.) My Japanese friends and relatives, and Japanese people in general, acknowledge several national problems that worry them. There are additional problems that worry me about Japan, but that Japanese people themselves tend to dismiss or ignore. But too many discussions of Japan go either to the extreme of Japan-bashing or to the opposite extreme of uncritical admiration. Hence let's preface our discussion of modern Japan's problems with a discussion of its strengths. We'll see that, for Japan as for other countries, some of its strengths are linked to some of its problems. The strengths that I'll discuss involve Japan's economy, human capital, culture, and environment.

———

Japan today has the world's third-largest economy, only recently overtaken by China's. Japan accounts for about 8% of global economic output, almost half that of the world's largest economy (the U.S.'s), and more than double that of the United Kingdom, another famously productive country. In general, national economic outputs are the products of two numbers: the number of people in a country, multiplied by average output per person. Japan's national output is high both because Japan has a large population (second only to that of the United States among rich democracies) and because it has high average individual productivity.

While Japan's large domestic debt attracts much attention (more about that below), nevertheless Japan is the world's leading creditor nation. It has the world's second-highest foreign exchange reserves, and it rivals China as the biggest holder of U.S. debt.

One important factor behind the economy's strength is Japan's high spending on research and development (abbreviated R & D) to drive innovation. Japan makes the world's third-largest absolute annual investment in R & D, behind only China and the U.S. with their far larger populations. In relative terms, Japan's proportion of its gross domestic product (abbreviated GDP) that it devotes to R & D, 3.5%, is nearly double that of the U.S. (only 1.8%), and still considerably higher than that of two other countries known for their R & D investments, Germany (2.9%) and China (2.0%).

Every year, the World Economic Forum reports for the world's nations a number called the Global Competitiveness Index, which integrates a dozen sets of numbers influencing a country's economic productivity. Japan for many years has consistently ranked among the world's top 10 countries with respect to this index; Japan, Singapore, and Hong Kong are the only three economies outside Western Europe and the U.S. to rate in that top 10. The reasons for Japan's high ranking include two obvious to lay visitors: Japan's excellent infrastructure and transport net, such as the world's best railroads; and its healthy, well-educated workforce especially proficient in math and science (more of that in the next section). Other reasons on the long list are less immediately obvious, but still familiar to foreigners doing business with Japan. In alphabetical order without trying to rank them in importance, the reasons include: control of inflation; cooperative labor/employee relations; highly competitive local markets; high-quality research institutions churning out lots of scientists and engineers; large domestic market; low unemployment; more patents filed per year per citizen than any other country; protection of property rights and intellectual property; rapid absorption of technology; sophisticated consumers and business people; and well-trained business staff. I promise not to give you a quiz on this long indigestible list, but the take-away message is clear: there are many reasons why Japanese businesses are competitive in world markets.

Finally, let's not forget a feature of the Japanese economy that brings huge financial benefits today but that could cause trouble in the future. The only two countries whose economies exceed Japan's are the U.S. and China, but they devote a large fraction of their budgets to military expenditures. Japan saves itself those costs, thanks to a clause of the U.S.-imposed 1947 constitution (now endorsed by a large fraction of Japanese people themselves) that reduced Japan's armed forces to a bare minimum.

———

A second set of strengths of Japan, besides those economic ones, is its "human capital," i.e., the strengths of its human population. That population numbers more than 120 million and is healthy and highly educated. Japanese life expectancy is the highest in the world: 80 years for men, 86 for women. The socio-economic inequality that limits opportunities for a large fraction of Americans is greatly reduced in Japan: Japan is the world's third-most egalitarian nation in its distribution of income, behind only Denmark and Sweden. That's partly a result of Japanese government school policies: schools in socio-economically disadvantaged areas have smaller classes (more favorable teacher-to-student ratios) than do schools in richer areas, thereby making it easier for children of poorer citizens to catch up. (In contrast, the American school system tends to perpetuate inequality by packing more students into classrooms in poor areas.) Social status in Japan depends more on education than on heredity and family connection: again, the reverse of U.S. trends. In short, rather than investing disproportionately in just a fraction of its citizens, Japan invests in all of them — at least, in all of its male citizens. (I'll say more about Japanese women below.)

Literacy and attained educational levels in Japan are close to the highest in the world. Enrollment of Japanese children in both kindergarten and secondary school is almost universal, although neither is compulsory. Student testing in nations around the world shows that Japanese students rank fourth highest in math and science functional literacy, ahead of all European countries and the U.S. Japan is second only to Canada in the percentage of its adults — nearly 50% — who go on to higher education beyond high school. Offsetting these strengths of Japanese education is a frequent criticism by the Japanese themselves that it puts too much pressure on students to focus on test scores, and places insufficient emphasis on self-motivation and independent thinking. A result is that, once Japanese students escape the pressure-cooker atmosphere of high school and reach university, their dedication to studying declines.

While there is no easy way to measure cultural strength, national identity, and quality of life, there is much anecdotal evidence about these characteristics in Japan. As foreign visitors to Japan quickly notice, its capital Tokyo rivals Singapore as the cleanest city in Asia, and is one of the cleanest in the world. That's because Japanese children learn to be clean and to clean up, as part of their responsibility to preserve Japan and to hand it on to the next generation. (Interpretative texts at Japanese archaeological sites sometimes proudly point out site evidence for Japanese cleanliness already in ancient times.) Visitors also notice the safety and low crime rates of Japanese cities. Japan's prison population is far smaller than that of the U.S.: about 80,000, versus nearly 2.5 million, respectively. Rioting and looting are rare in Japan. Ethnic tensions are low compared to the U.S. and Europe, because of Japan's ethnic homogeneity and very small ethnic minorities. (As discussed below, that's another example of an advantage that carries disadvantages along with it.)

Finally, Japan's strengths include big environmental advantages. Japanese agricultural productivity is high because of Japan's combination of temperate climate, freedom from tropical agricultural pests, high rainfall concentrated in the summer growing season, and fertile volcanic soils. That contributes to Japan's ability to support one of the highest average human population densities in the industrial world, calculated with respect to the small percentage (12%) of Japan's land area in which the population and the agriculture are concentrated. (Most of Japan's area consists of steep forests and mountains supporting only small human populations and little agriculture.) Nutrient run-off from those fertile soils makes Japanese rivers and coastal waters productive of fish, shellfish, edible seaweeds, and other aquatic foods. Japan is the world's sixth-largest producer of seafood, formerly obtained just in Japanese coastal waters, although now caught all over the world by ocean-going Japanese fishing fleets. As a result of all those environmental advantages, Japan was unusual in the ancient world in that, already at least 10,000 years before the adoption of agriculture, Japanese hunter-gatherers had settled down in villages and made pottery, rather than living as nomads with few material possessions. Until Japan's population explosion within the last century-and-a-half, Japan was self-sufficient in food.

———

Let's now turn from Japan's strengths to its problems. Asked to name Japan's most serious problem, economists are likely to answer, "Its government's huge national debt." The debt is currently about 2.5 times Japan's annual GDP, i.e., the value of everything produced in Japan in one year. That means that, even if the Japanese were to devote all of their income and efforts to paying off their national debt and produced nothing for themselves, it would still take them two-and-a-half years to pay off the debt. Worse yet, the debt has been continuously rising for years. For comparison, while American fiscal conservatives are greatly concerned by the U.S.'s national debt, it's still "only" about 1.0 times our GDP. Greece and Spain are two European countries notorious for their economic problems, but Japan's debt-to-GDP ratio is double that of Greece and four times that of Spain (as of the moment at which I write this sentence). Japan's government debt is comparable to that of the entire eurozone of 17 countries, whose aggregate population is triple that of Japan.

Why didn't the Japanese government collapse or default long ago under this burden? First, most of the debt is not owed to foreign creditors, but to bond-holding Japanese individuals, Japanese businesses and pension funds (many of them owned by the government itself), and the Bank of Japan, none of which play tough with the Japanese government. In contrast, much of Greece's debt is owed to foreign creditors, who do play tough and press Greece to change its fiscal policies. Despite all the debt that the Japanese government owes to Japanese themselves, Japan is a net creditor nation for other countries, which owe money to Japan. Second, interest rates in Japan are kept low (below 1%) by government policy, in order to keep a lid on government interest payments. Finally, Japanese as well as foreign creditors still have so much confidence in the government's ability to pay that they continue to buy government bonds. In fact, that's the main way in which Japanese individuals and companies invest their savings. But nobody knows how much higher the debt can rise before Japan's creditors lose confidence and the government has to default.

Despite those low interest rates, the sizes of the debt and of Japan's aged and retired population mean that debt interest and health and social security costs consume much of the government's tax income. That reduces government funds that would otherwise be available to invest in education, research and development, infrastructure, and other engines of economic growth that could stimulate tax revenues. Exacerbating that problem, Japanese government tax rates and hence government income are relatively low by developed world standards. Ultimately, the debt is held mainly by older Japanese people, who invested their money either directly (by buying government bonds) or indirectly (by receiving pensions from pension funds heavily invested in government bonds) — while those Japanese people ultimately paying the interest on the debt are mainly younger Japanese still working and paying taxes. Hence Japan's debt in effect represents payments by younger Japanese to older Japanese, constituting an inter-generational conflict and a mortgage on Japan's future. That mortgage is growing, because Japan's young population is shrinking while its older population is growing (see below).

The solutions proposed to reduce the debt include raising tax rates, reducing government spending, and reducing pensions of older Japanese. Those and all other proposed solutions prove to be fraught with difficulties. Thus, Japan's government debt is a big problem that is widely acknowledged in Japan, that has been around for a long time, that has been continuing to get worse for many years, and for which no agreement on a solution is in sight.

———

The other fundamental problems most often acknowledged by Japanese people themselves are the four linked issues of women's roles, Japan's low and declining birth rate, its declining population size, and its aging population. Let's start with the role of women.

In theory, Japanese women and men have the same status. The Japanese constitution of 1947, drafted by the U.S. government of occupation and still in force today, contains a clause (drafted by an American woman) proclaiming gender equality. That draft clause was adopted over fierce Japanese government opposition, and some Japanese lawmakers still want to change the clause.

In reality, Japanese women face many societal barriers to equality. Of course, the barriers that I'll now describe also exist in countries other than Japan. But those barriers are stronger — and the gender gap in health, education, and participation in the workforce and in politics is greater — in Japan than in any other rich industrialized nation except South Korea. I speculate that that's because Japan is the rich industrialized nation in which a woman's role was until recently most subordinate and stereotyped. For instance, while walking in public, a traditional Japanese woman was expected to remain three steps behind her husband. For purposes of brevity I'll describe the societal barriers to women as generalizations, but of course they vary within Japan's population depending on location and age: e.g., stronger in rural areas than in Tokyo, and stronger for older than for younger Japanese.

At home, the gender division within Japanese married couples is often referred to as the "marriage package." An inefficient division of labor prevails, whereby a Japanese husband puts in the work hours of two people outside the house and thereby sacrifices time that could be spent with his children, while his wife stays at home and sacrifices the possibility of a fulfilling career. Employers expect employees (mostly men) to stay late in the office and to go out for drinks with one another after work. That makes it difficult for Japanese husbands to share household responsibilities with their wives even if they want to. Japanese husbands do less housework than do husbands in other rich industrialized nations: e.g., only about two-thirds as many hours per week as American husbands. Japanese husbands with working wives perform no more hours of housework than do husbands whose spouses are full-time housewives. Instead, it is predominately the wives who care for their children, their husbands, their own elderly parents, their husbands' elderly parents — and manage the household finances in their remaining spare time. Many Japanese wives today swear that they will be the last generation of Japanese women to be saddled with those responsibilities.

In the workplace, Japanese women have low participation and low pay. Participation declines steeply with increasing level of responsibility. Whereas women account for 49% of Japanese university students and 45% of entry-level job holders, they account for only 14% of university faculty positions (versus 33%–44% in the U.S., United Kingdom, Germany, and France), 11% of middle-level to senior management positions, 2% of positions on boards of directors, 1% of business executive committee members, and less than 1% of CEOs. At those higher levels Japan lags behind all major industrial countries except (again) South Korea. There are few women in Japanese politics, and Japan has never had a woman prime minister. Japan's male/female pay differential for full-time employees is the third highest (exceeded only by South Korea and Estonia) among 35 rich industrial countries. A Japanese woman employee is paid on average only 73% of a man employee at the same level, compared to 85% for the average rich industrial country, ranging up to 94% for New Zealand. Work obstacles for women include the long work hours, the expectation of post-work employee socializing, and the problem of who will take care of the children if a working mother is expected to stay out socializing, and if her husband is also unavailable or unwilling.

Child care is a big problem for working Japanese mothers. On paper, Japanese law guarantees women four weeks of maternity leave before and eight weeks after childbirth; some Japanese men are also entitled to paternity leave; and a 1992 law entitles parents to take one whole year of unpaid leave to raise a child if they so choose. In practice, virtually all Japanese fathers and most Japanese mothers don't take that leave to which they are entitled. Instead, 70% of Japanese working women quit work upon the birth of their first child, and most of them don't return to work for many years, if ever. While it is nominally illegal for a Japanese employer to pressure a mother into quitting work, Japanese mothers actually are pressured. Little child care is available to Japanese working mothers because of the lack of immigrant women to do private child care (see below), and

WHAT LIES AHEAD FOR JAPAN?

because there are so few private or government child-care centers, unlike the situation in the U.S. and in Scandinavia, respectively. The widespread Japanese view is instead that a mother should stay home, care for her small children herself, and not work.

The result is a dilemma for Japanese women in the workplace. On the one hand, many or most Japanese women want to work, and they also want to have children and to spend time with them. On the other hand, Japanese companies invest heavily in training an employee, expect to offer a lifetime job, and expect in return that the employee will work long hours and will remain for life. Companies are reluctant to hire and train women, because they may want to take off time to have children, may not want to work long hours, and may not return to work after giving birth to a child. Hence women tend not to be offered, and tend not to accept if offered, full-time high-level jobs with Japanese companies.

Japan's current prime minister, Shinzo Abe, is a conservative who formerly did not display interest in women's issues. Recently, however, he reversed course and announced that he wanted to find ways of helping mothers return to work — many people suspect, not because of his suddenly developing a concern for women, but because of Japan's shrinking population and hence shrinking workforce (more about that below). Half of Japanese people in general, and of Japanese university graduates in particular, are women. Hence underemployment of Japanese women constitutes for Japan the loss of half of its human capital. Abe proposed that working mothers should be able to take three years of maternity leave with the assurance of returning to their jobs, that the government expand public child-care centers, and that businesses receive financial incentives to hire women. But many Japanese women, including some of my university-educated Japanese women friends with overseas experience, are opposed to Abe's proposal. They suspect that it is just one more government conspiracy to keep Japanese women at home!

———

The next of Japan's set of linked population problems is its low and declining birth rates. The Japanese recognize this problem's seriousness, but they don't know how to solve it.

Low and dropping birth rates prevail throughout the First World. But Japan has nearly the world's lowest birth rate: 7 births per year per 1,000 people, compared to 13 in the U.S., 19 averaged over the whole world, and more than 40 in some African countries. Furthermore, that already low birth rate in Japan is still declining. If in recent years one had linearly extrapolated the decline from year to year, one would have predicted that Japan's birth rate would hit zero in the year 2017, at which point no more Japanese babies would be born! Obviously, things didn't get that bad, but it's true that Japan's already very low birth rate is still declining.

An alternative way of expressing births is by what's called the total fertility rate: i.e., the total number of babies born to an average woman over her lifetime. For the whole world that number averages 2.5 babies; for the First World countries with the biggest economies, it varies between 1.3 and 2.0 babies (e.g., 1.9 for the U.S.). The number for Japan is only 1.27 babies, at the low end of the spectrum; South Korea and Poland are among the few countries with lower values. But the average number of babies that a woman has to bear in order for the population to remain stable — the so-called replacement rate — is slightly more than 2. Japan along with some other First World countries has an average total fertility rate below that replacement rate. For other First World countries, that's not a problem, because immigration keeps the population size constant or even growing despite low fertility. However, Japan's near-absence of immigration means that Japan's population is actually declining, as we'll discuss.

Part of the reason for Japan's falling birth rate is that Japan's age of first marriage has been rising: it's now around 30 for both men and women. That means fewer pre-menopausal years in which a woman can conceive children. A bigger reason for the falling birth rate is that the rate of marriage itself (i.e., the number of marriages per 1,000 people per year) is falling rapidly in Japan. One might object that the marriage rate is also falling in most other developed countries without causing the catastrophic drop in the birth rate that Japan is experiencing, because so many births are to unwed mothers: 40% of all births in the U.S., 50% in France, and 66% in Iceland. But that mitigation doesn't apply to Japan, where unwed mothers account for a negligible proportion of births: only 2%.

Why are Japanese people increasingly avoiding getting married and having children? When surveyed about this question, Japanese give several reasons. One reason is economics: it's cheaper and more comfortable to remain single and live at home with one's parents than to move out, marry, and have to pay for one's own apartment plus the expenses of children. Especially for women, marriage and motherhood can be economically catastrophic by making it difficult for them to obtain or retain a job. Another reason offered is the freedom of being single, a consideration especially for women who don't want to end up shouldering the responsibility of the household, husband, child care, their own elderly parents, and their husband's elderly parents. Still another reason is that many modern Japanese, both men and women in equal proportions, consider marriage "unnecessary" to a fulfilling life.

Despite those counter-arguments, 70% of unmarried Japanese men and women still claim that they want to get married. Why, then, don't they succeed in finding a suitable mate? Traditionally, that didn't require effort on their part, because Japanese marriages were arranged by go-betweens (called nakoudo) who scheduled formal interviews by which young unmarried people could meet potential marriage partners. As recently as 1960, that was still the predominant form of marriage in Japan. Since then, the declining number of nakoudo, and the rise of the Western idea of romantic marriage, have caused such arranged marriages to drop to only 5% of all marriages. But many modern young Japanese are too busy working, too inexperienced at dating, or too awkward to develop a romantic relationship.

In particular, the phasing-out of arranged marriages in Japan in recent decades has coincided with the rise of electronic non-face-to-face communication by e-mail, texting, and cell phones, and with the consequent decline of social skills. One poignant example was related to me by a Japanese friend who, while eating out in a restaurant, was struck by a young, well-dressed couple sitting awkwardly and silently opposite each other at a nearby table. Both were holding their heads bowed and were staring in their laps rather than at each other. My friend noticed that each was holding a cell phone in his or her lap, and that each was tapping his or her cell phone in alternation. Eventually it dawned on my friend: both the boy and the girl felt too awkward to speak directly to each other, and so they were resorting to texting back and forth across the table. Not a good way to develop and finalize the parameters of a romantic relationship! Of course, young Americans are also addicted to electronic communication, but they (unlike their Japanese contemporaries) are heirs to a cultural tradition of dating.

———

Japan's low and still declining birth and marriage rates are directly responsible for two remaining big problems widely recognized in Japan: the declining population, and the aging population.

Because Japan's birth rate has for many years been below the replacement level, it was clear that Japan's population would eventually cease rising and begin to fall. Still, it was a shock when census figures confirmed that that dreaded moment had actually arrived. After the five-year 2010 census had shown a population of 128,057,352, the 2015 census yielded 127,110,000, a decline of nearly 1 million. From the current trends and age distribution of Japan's population, it's predicted that there will be a further drop by about 40 million by the year 2060, to a population of only 80 million.

The consequences of Japan's falling population and its shift from rural to urban are already visible. Japan is closing schools at a rate of about 500 per year. Rural depopulation is causing villages and small towns to be abandoned. It's feared that, without population growth as the supposed driver of economic growth, a less populous Japan will be poorer and less powerful on the world stage. In 1948 Japan was the world's fifth most populous country; by 2007 it had only the 10th-largest population, behind Nigeria and Bangladesh; and current projections are that within a few decades it will fall behind even such non-powerhouses as the Congo and Ethiopia. That's considered humiliating, on the tacit assumption that a country with a smaller population than the Congo will be weaker and less important than the Congo.

Hence in 2015 Prime Minister Abe declared that his administration would aim to maintain Japan's population at least at 100 million, by trying to boost the average total fertility rate from 1.4 to 1.8 children per woman. But boosting the output of babies will depend on the choices of young Japanese people rather than of Abe. I already discussed the reasons why young Japanese, regardless of whether they think that Japan as a nation would be better off with more babies, are choosing not to produce those extra babies themselves.

Is Japan's declining population a "problem" for Japan? There are many countries that have much smaller populations than Japan's, and that are nevertheless rich and important players on the world stage, including Australia, Finland, Israel, the Netherlands, Singapore, Sweden, Switzerland, and Taiwan. Of course those countries aren't world military leaders, but neither is Japan today because of its constitution and widespread Japanese pacifism. To me, it seems that Japan wouldn't be worse off but instead much better off with a smaller population, because that would mean less need for domestic and imported resources. We'll see later that resource pressure has been one of the curses of modern Japanese history, that it remains so today, and that Japanese themselves think of their country as resource-starved. Hence I see Japan's declining population as one of its great advantages, not as a problem.

Even those Japanese concerned about their country's declining population agree that a much bigger problem is that Japan's population is aging. Japan is already the country with the world's highest life expectancy (84, compared to 77 for the U.S. and just 40–45 for many African countries), and with the highest percentage of old people. Already now, 23% of Japan's population is over 65, and 6% is over 80. By the year 2050 those numbers are projected to be nearly 40% and 16%, respectively. (The corresponding numbers for the African country of Mali are only 3% and 0.1%.) At that point, Japanese people over the age of 80 will outnumber kids under 14, and people over 65 will outnumber those kids by more than 3 to 1.

Mind you, I personally have nothing against people over the age of 80. (That would constitute self-hatred, because I'm now 82.) But there can be too much of a good thing, and that's true for older people. A large number of old people creates a burden on the national health-care system, because older people are much more subject to illnesses than are younger people: especially to chronic, incurable, hard-to-cure or expensive-to-treat illnesses such as heart diseases and dementia. As the percentage of the population over age 65 increases, the population's percentage of retirees also increases, and its percentage of workers decreases. That means fewer young workers to serve as the ultimate sources of support for growing numbers of older retirees: either supporting them directly through financial support and personal care within families, or else supporting them indirectly through government pensions and senior health-care systems funded by the taxed earnings of young workers. Japan's ratio of workers to retirees has been falling catastrophically: from 9 workers per retiree in 1965, to 2.4 today, to a projected 1.3 in 2050.

But you may be objecting that Japan isn't the only country with a falling birth rate, aging population, and rising burden on its pension and social security systems. Those same problems also occur throughout the developed world; Japan just has those problems to an extreme degree. We Americans are also concerned about the future underfunding of our social security system. All Western European countries also have birth rates below the replacement value, two of them even lower than Japan's. But the U.S. and Europe aren't as concerned about those problems as is Japan, because they haven't fallen into the bind of a shrinking population and an increasingly top-heavy old population. Why not? How have they escaped those traps?

The answer involves the first of what I see as Japan's remaining three major problems: the ones that aren't widely acknowledged as problems in Japan itself. That first remaining problem is Japan's lack of immigration.

———

Japan is, and prides itself on being, the most ethnically homogenous affluent or populous country in the world. It doesn't welcome immigrants, makes it difficult for anyone who wants to immigrate to do so, and makes it even more difficult for anyone who has succeeded in immigrating to receive Japanese citizenship. As a percentage of a country's total population, immigrants and their children constitute 28% of Australia's population, 21% of Canada's, 16% of Sweden's, and 14% of the U.S.'s, but only 1.9% of Japan's.

Among refugees seeking asylum, Sweden accepts 92%, Germany 70%, Canada 48%, but Japan only 0.2%. (For instance, Japan accepted only six and eleven refugees in the years 2013 and 2014, respectively.) Foreign workers constitute 15% of the workforce in the U.S. and 9% in Germany, but only 1.3% in Japan. Japan does admit temporary foreign workers (so-called guest workers) who receive work visas of one to three years because of their high professional skills (e.g., as ship-builders, or as construction workers for the 2020 Tokyo Olympics). But such foreigners in Japan find it difficult to obtain permanent residency or citizenship.

The only significant immigration to Japan in modern times was of several million Koreans before and during World War Two, when Korea was a Japanese colony. However, many or most of those Koreans were involuntary immigrants imported as slave labor. For instance, it is not widely known that 10% of the victims killed at Hiroshima by the first atomic bomb were Korean laborers working there.

A couple of Japanese cabinet ministers have recently called for more immigration. For instance, Shigeru Ishiba, minister for local regions, said, "At one time, people from Japan migrated to South and North America and managed to fit in with the locals while maintaining their pride as Japanese.... It doesn't make sense to say no to foreigners who come to Japan when our people did the same thing overseas." For instance, Peru has had a Japanese president, while the U.S. has had Japanese senators, Congress members, and university chancellors. But the Japanese government is currently not reconsidering its opposition to immigration.

That government opposition reflects the negative views of immigration expressed by Japanese citizens in many public opinion polls, in which Japanese opinions fall at one extreme of the opinions held in other affluent countries. The percentage of Japanese opposed to increasing the number of foreign residents is 63%; 72% agree that immigrants increase crime rates; and 80% deny that immigrants improve society by introducing new ideas, unlike the 57%–75% of Americans, Canadians, and Australians who do believe that immigrants improve society. Conversely, vanishingly few Japanese (only 0.5%) consider immigration as the most important issue facing the country, whereas up to 15% of Americans, French, Swedes, and British do so.

Let's be clear: I'm not saying that Japanese resistance to immigration is "wrong" and should be changed. In every country, immigration creates difficulties while simultaneously bringing benefits. It's a matter for each country to weigh those benefits against those difficulties, in order to arrive at its own immigration policy. It comes as no surprise that Japan, an ethnically homogenous country with a long history of isolation and no immigration, values highly its ethnic homogeneity, while the U.S., an ethnically heterogeneous country almost all of whose citizens are the descendants of modern immigrants, has no ethnic homogeneity to value. Instead, Japan's dilemma is that it suffers from widely acknowledged problems that other countries mitigate by means of immigration, but that Japan hasn't figured out how to solve without resorting to immigration.

The biggest of those problems is the linked problem set discussed above of declining birth rate, aging population, and resulting economic burden of fewer and fewer tax-paying healthy young workers to fund the pensions and health-care expenses of more and more non-working pensioners with the increasing health problems of old age. Despite the U.S., Canada, Australia, and Western Europe sharing Japan's falling birth rate and aging of their *native* populations, those countries minimize the consequences by admitting large numbers of young immigrant workers. Japan can't offset that declining workforce by employing more of its non-working educated mothers, because the large pool of immigrant women hired as private child-care workers by so many American working mothers scarcely exists in Japan. The large pool of immigrant men and women who furnish most caretakers of senior citizens and most hospital nurses and other hospital staff in the U.S. also doesn't exist in Japan. (I write these lines while recovering from the horrible experience of the death of a terminally ill Japanese relative, whose family was expected to provide her meals and do her personal laundry while she was in the hospital.)

While innovation is vigorous in Japan as judged by the large numbers of patents awarded to Japanese inventors, Japanese are concerned about hosting less breakthrough innovation than one would expect from Japan's large investment in research and development. That's reflected in the relatively modest number of Nobel Prizes awarded to Japanese scientists. Most U.S. Nobel Prize winners are either first-generation immigrants or else their offspring. But immigrants and their offspring are as rare among Japanese scientists as they are among the Japanese population in general. That relationship between immigration and Nobel Prizes is not surprising when one reflects that the willingness to take risks and to try something drastically new is a prerequisite both for emigrating and for innovating at the highest level.

In the short run, Japan is presently unwilling to solve these problems by immigration. In the long run, it's unknown whether Japanese people will continue to suffer from these problems, or will instead choose to solve them by changing their immigration policy, or will figure out some yet-unknown solutions other than immigration. If Japan does decide to re-evaluate immigration, a model palatable to Japan might be Canada's policy, which stresses evaluating applicants for immigration on the basis of their potential value to Canada.

———

Japan's next neglected big problem, after immigration, is the effect of Japan's wartime behavior towards China and Korea on its current relations with those countries. During and before World War Two, Japan did horrible things to people in other Asian countries, especially China and Korea. Long before Japan's "official" declarations of war on December 7, 1941, Japan was carrying out a full-scale undeclared war on China from 1937 onwards. In that war, the Japanese military killed millions of Chinese, often in barbaric ways such as using tied-up Chinese prisoners for bayonet practice to toughen the attitudes of Japanese soldiers, killing several hundred thousand Chinese civilians at Nanking in December 1937–January 1938, and killing many others in retaliation for the Doolittle Raid of April 1942. Although denial of these killings is widespread in Japan today, they were well documented at the time, not only by Chinese but also by foreign observers, and by photographs taken by Japanese soldiers themselves. (You can see more than 400 such photographs in the book by Shi Young and James Yin *The Rape of Nanking: An Undeniable History in Photographs* [1999].) Japan annexed Korea in 1910, mandated that Korean schools use the Japanese language rather than the Korean language for 35 years of Japanese occupation, forced large numbers of Korean women and women of other nationalities to become sex slaves in Japanese military brothels, and forced large numbers of Korean men to become virtual slave laborers for the Japanese army.

As a result, hatred of Japan is widespread today in China and Korea. In the view of Chinese and Koreans, Japan hasn't adequately acknowledged, apologized for, or expressed regret for its wartime atrocities. China's population is 11 times Japan's, while the combined population of South and North Korea is more than half of Japan's. China and North Korea both have nuclear weapons. China, North Korea, and South Korea all have big, well-equipped armies, while Japan's armed forces remain minuscule because of the U.S.-imposed Japanese constitution reinforced by widespread pacifism in Japan today. North Korea from time to time fires missiles across Japan, to demonstrate its ability to reach Japan. Yet Japan is locked in territorial disputes with both China and South Korea over uninhabited tiny islands of no intrinsic value themselves but important because of fish, gas, and mineral resources within each island's marine zone. That combination of facts seems to me to spell big dangers for Japan in the long run.

For an Asian perspective on Japan's view of World War Two, here is an assessment by Lee Kuan Yew, a keen observer of people who as prime minister of Singapore for several decades became familiar with Japan, China, and Korea and their leaders: "Unlike Germans, the Japanese have not had a catharsis and rid themselves of the poison in their system. They have not educated their young about the wrong they had done. Hashimoto [a Japanese prime minister] expressed his 'deepest regrets' on the 52nd anniversary of the end of World War Two (1997) and his 'profound remorse' during his visit to Beijing in September 1997. However, he did not apologize, as the Chinese and Koreans wished Japan's leader to do. I do not understand why the Japanese are so unwilling to admit the past, apologize for it, and move on. For some reason, they do not want to apologize. To apologize is to admit having done a wrong. To express regrets or remorse merely expresses their present subjective feelings. They denied the massacre of Nanking took place; that Korean, Filipino, Dutch, and other women were kidnapped or otherwise forced to be 'comfort women' (a euphemism for sex slaves) for Japanese soldiers at the war fronts; that they carried out cruel biological experiments on live Chinese, Korean, Mongolian, Russian, and other prisoners in Manchuria. In each case, only after irrefutable evidence was produced from their own records did they make reluctant admissions. This fed suspicions of Japan's future intentions. Present Japanese attitudes are an indication of their future conduct. If they are ashamed of their past, they are less likely to repeat it."

Every year, my undergraduate classes at the University of California in Los Angeles include students from Japan, who talk to me about their schooling there and about their experiences on coming to California. They tell me that their history classes in Japanese schools devoted little time to World War Two ("because that war lasted just a few years in the thousands of years of Japanese history"), said little or nothing about Japan's role as aggressor, stressed the role of Japanese as victims (of the two atomic bombs that killed about 120,000 Japanese) rather than as responsible for the deaths of millions of other people plus several million Japanese soldiers and civilians, and blamed the U.S. for somehow tricking Japan into launching the war. (In all fairness, Korean, Chinese, and American schoolbooks present their own skewed accounts of World War Two.) My Japanese students are shocked when they join Asian student associations in Los Angeles, meet Korean and Chinese students, and hear for the first time about Japan's wartime deeds that still arouse hatred of Japan by students from those other countries.

At the same time, some of my Japanese students, and many other Japanese people, point to numerous apologies offered by Japanese politicians, and ask, "Hasn't Japan already apologized enough?" A short answer is: no, because the apologies sound contrived, unconvincing, and mixed with statements that minimize or deny Japanese responsibility. A longer answer is to compare Japan's and Germany's opposite approaches to dealing with their respective legacies of recent history, and to ask why Germany's approach has largely convinced its former enemies while Japan's approach has not convinced its main victims China and Korea. Chapter 6 described the many ways in which Germany's leaders have expressed remorse and responsibility, and in which German schoolchildren are taught to face up to what their country did. Chinese and Koreans might be convinced of Japan's sincerity by Japanese responses analogous to Germany's: for instance, if Japan's prime minister were to visit Nanking, fall on his knees before Chinese spectators, and beg forgiveness for Japan's wartime massacres at Nanking; if throughout Japan there were museums and monuments and former POW camps with photos and detailed explanations of Japanese wartime atrocities; if Japanese schoolchildren were routinely brought on school outings to such sites in Japan, and to sites outside Japan such as Nanking, Sandakan, Bataan, and Saipan; and if Japan devoted much more effort to depicting wartime non-Japanese victims of Japanese atrocities than to depicting Japanese victims of the war. All of those behaviors are non-existent and unthinkable in Japan, but their analogues are widely practiced in Germany. Until they are practiced in Japan, Chinese and Koreans will continue to disbelieve Japanese scripted apologies, and to hate Japan. And as long as China and Korea are armed to the hilt while Japan remains without the means to defend itself, a big danger will continue to hang over Japan.

———

All peoples depend for their existence on renewable natural resources, including trees, fish, topsoil, clean water, and clean air. All of those resources pose problems of management, about which scientists have already accumulated much experience. If the world's forests and fisheries were managed according to recommended best practices, it might be possible to harvest forest products and aquatic food for the indefinite future, in quantities sufficient to meet the needs of the world's current population. Sadly, though, much actual harvesting is still destructive and non-sustainable. Most of the world's forests are shrinking, and most fisheries are declining or have already collapsed. But no country is self-sufficient in all natural resources; all countries have to import at least some resources. Hence in most countries there are government agencies, branches of international environmental organizations (like World

Wildlife Fund and Conservation International), and local environmental organizations hard at work to solve these problems.

The problems are especially acute for Japan. Until 1853, while Japan was closed to the outside world and did negligible importing, it was self-sufficient in natural resources. Forced to depend on its own forests, and alarmed by their declines in the 1600's, Japan pioneered in developing scientific forestry methods independently of Germany and Switzerland, in order to manage its forests. Now, because of Japan's population explosion since 1853, rise in living standards and consumption rates, large population crammed into a small area, and need for raw materials essential for a modern industrial economy, Japan has become one of the world's biggest importers of natural resources. Among non-renewable resources, almost all of Japan's needs for oil, natural gas, nickel, aluminum, nitrates, potash, and phosphate, and most of its needs for iron, coal, and copper, have to be imported. Among renewable natural resources, Japan ranks variously as the world's leading or second- or third-leading importer of seafood, logs, plywood, tropical hardwoods, and paper and pulp materials.

That's a long list of essential resources for which Japan depends on imports. As any of these resources becomes depleted worldwide, Japan will be the first or one of the first countries to suffer the consequences. Japan is also the major country most dependent on imported food to feed its citizens. Japan today has the highest ratio (a factor of 20) of agricultural imports to agricultural exports among major countries. The next highest ratio, that for South Korea, is still only a factor of 6, while the U.S., Brazil, India, Australia, and quite a few other major countries are net food exporters.

Japanese thus have good reason to view their country as resource-poor. One therefore expects that Japan, as the developed country with the most extreme dependence on resource imports, would be driven by self-interest to become the world's leading promoter of sustainable resource exploitation. In particular, the rational policy would be for Japan to take the lead in sustainable exploitation of the world's fisheries and forests on which Japan depends.

Paradoxically, the reverse is true. As a director of World Wildlife Fund–U.S. and Conservation International, I hear a lot about the national policies of resource management with which these two organizations deal. I also hear a lot about Japan's policies in particular, from my Japanese friends and colleagues. Japan appears to be the developed country with the least support for and the strongest opposition to sustainable resource policies overseas. Japanese imports of illegally sourced and non-sustainably harvested forest products are much higher than those of the U.S. or of European Union countries, whether calculated on a per-capita basis or as a percentage of total forest product imports. Japan is a leader in opposing prudent regulation of ocean fishing and whaling. Here are two examples.

My first example involves Atlantic and Mediterranean Bluefin Tuna, which is especially prized and consumed in Japan as sashimi or sushi. A single big imported tuna fish recently sold in Japan for the stunning price of more than $1,000,000. Those tuna stocks are in steep decline from overfishing, and that's stimulating counter-efforts to preserve this valuable resource by agreeing on sustainable catches and by imposing fishing quotas. Incredibly, when those tuna stocks were proposed in 2010 for international protection (so-called CITES listing), Japan wasn't the initiator of the proposal. Instead, Japan viewed it as a diplomatic triumph to have succeeded in blocking the proposal.

My second example is that Japan today is the leading and most insistent whaling nation. The International Whaling Commission determines quotas for hunting whales. Every year, Japan legally circumvents those quotas by killing large numbers of whales for the supposed purposes of research, then publishes little or no research on those dead whales and instead sells them for meat. Yet Japanese public consumer demand for whale meat is low and declining, and whale meat is wasted for dog food and fertilizer rather than for human consumption. Maintaining whaling represents an economic loss for Japan, because its whaling industry has to be heavily subsidized by the government in several ways: direct subsidies to the whaling ships themselves; additional costs of more ships to escort and protect the whaling ships; and the hidden costs of so-called "foreign aid" paid to small non-whaling countries that are members of the International Whaling Commission, as a bribe in return for their pro-whaling votes.

Why does Japan pursue these stances? My Japanese friends suggest three explanations. First, Japanese people cherish a self-image of living in harmony with nature, and they did traditionally manage their own forests sustainably — but not the overseas forests and fisheries that they now exploit. Second, Japanese national pride dislikes bowing to international pressure. Japan especially does not want to be seen as giving in to the anti-whaling campaigns of Greenpeace and the Sea Shepherd, and to international pressure to regulate the Bluefin Tuna fishery. One could describe Japan as "anti-anti-whaling" rather than pro-whaling. Finally, awareness of Japan's limited home resources has led it for the last 140 years to maintain, as the core of its national security and a keystone of its foreign policy, its claimed right of unrestricted access to the world's natural resources. While that insistence was a viable policy in past times of world resource abundance, when supplies exceeded demands, the policy is no longer viable in today's times of declining resources.

To an outsider like myself, who admires Japan, its opposition to sustainable overseas resource use is sad and self-destructive. Efforts to grab overseas resources already drove Japan to self-destructive behavior once before, when it made war simultaneously on China, the U.S., Britain, Australia, New Zealand, and the

Netherlands. Defeat then was inevitable. Now, too, defeat is again inevitable — not by military conquest, but by exhaustion of both renewable and non-renewable overseas natural resources. If I were the evil dictator of a country that hated Japan and wanted to ruin it without resorting to war, I would do exactly what Japan is now doing to itself: I would destroy the overseas resources on which Japan depends.

———

Finally, let's consider what lies ahead for Japan in the light of our 12 predictive factors. As a mere academic exercise, we could just ask whether our factors predict that Japan is or is not likely to succeed in solving its current problems. More usefully, we can suggest how understanding of the predictive factors could be used by the Japanese to craft solutions, and to cut through some of the obstacles that they are now creating for themselves.

One cause for optimism is Japan's history of success at resolving crises (factor #8 in Table 1.2). Twice in modern times, Japan has provided outstanding national success stories of re-appraisal and selective change. The most drastic changes came with the Meiji Restoration beginning in 1868. The forced opening of Japan by Commodore Perry's fleet in 1853 raised the specter that Japan, like so many other non-European countries, might be taken over by Western powers. Japan saved itself by a crash program of selective change. It jettisoned its international isolation, its government by a shogun, its samurai class, and its feudal system. It adopted a constitution, cabinet government, a national army, industrialization, a European-style banking system, a new school system, and much Western clothing, food, and music. At the same time, it retained its emperor, language, writing system, and most of its culture. Japan thereby not only preserved its independence, but also became the first non-Western country to rival the West in wealth and power.

Again, after World War Two, Japan made further drastic selective changes, jettisoning its military tradition and its belief in its emperor's divinity, adopting democracy and a new constitution, and developing or reviving an export economy.

Another big cause for optimism is Japan's track record of patience and ability to recover from failure and defeat (factor #9), as acknowledged by Singapore's Prime Minister Lee Kuan Yew, whose criticisms of Japan I quoted previously: "In spite of my experiences during the Japanese occupation and the Japanese traits I had learned to fear, I now respect and admire them. Their group solidarity, discipline, intelligence, industriousness, and willingness to sacrifice for the nation make them a formidable and productive force. Conscious of the poverty of their resources, they will continue to make that extra effort to achieve the unachievable. Because of their cultural values, they will be lonely survivors after any catastrophe. From time to time they are hit by the unpredictable forces of nature — earthquakes, typhoons, and tsunamis. They take their casualties, pick themselves up, and rebuild.... I was amazed at how life was returning to normal when I visited Kobe in November 1996, one-and-a-half years after the [massive] earthquake. They had taken this catastrophe in their stride and settled to a new daily routine."

Other factors of my checklist in Japan's favor are the freedom of choice that Japan gains from being an island archipelago without neighbors sharing land borders (factor #12), offset by its overwater proximity to China and Korea; its strong national identity, pride, and cohesion (factor #6); the friendly support or at least benevolent neutrality that Japan receives from its many trade partners other than China and Korea (factor #4); and the available models that other countries offer for solving some of Japan's main problems, should Japan choose to draw on those models (factor #5: see below). Further major advantages of Japan are its economic strength, its human capital, its culture, and its environment as discussed in the first pages of this chapter.

Offsetting these advantages are three factors on my checklist. I mention them not in order to foster pessimism, but instead to focus attention on attitudes that Japan will have to change if it is to succeed in solving its current problems. One obstacle is a traditional core value that has now become inappropriate because of changed circumstances (factor #11): Japan's continued effort to secure unrestricted access to the world's natural resources as if they were superabundant, instead of leading international cooperative efforts to harvest dwindling resources sustainably. Another obstacle is Japan's narrative of World War Two that focuses on self-pity and viewing Japan as the victim, rather than on accepting Japan's responsibility for the war and for Japanese actions (factor #2). In national politics as in personal life, no progress can be made towards solving a problem as long as one denies one's own responsibility. Japan will have to follow Germany's example of acknowledging responsibility, if Japan wishes improvement in its relations with China and Korea.

The remaining obstacle is what appears to me a lack of honest, realistic self-appraisal in several key spheres (factor #7). Two examples are those just-mentioned issues of imported resources and World War Two narrative. Another example is Japan's mistaken belief in the supposed cardinal importance of preventing population decline. While a decline from the current 127 million to 20 million would indeed pose problems, I see no disadvantages in a decline to 80 million, and instead a huge advantage: namely, reduction of Japan's hunger for imported resources, which has cursed modern Japanese history. Japan is strong because of its many qualitative advantages discussed at the beginning of this chapter, and not because Japan's current population happens to be 127 million and equal to Mexico's rather than 81 million and equal to Germany's.

Still another area calling for self-appraisal is immigration. That's the method that many countries use to solve problems that Japan perceives as serious: especially, the declining ratio of young workers to older retirees, the few available options for child care, and the inadequate number of caretakers for older people. One option is for Japan to consider immigration modeled on Canada's highly successful immigration program, or on the experiences of Japanese emigrants themselves to the U.S. and to South America. An alternative option is for Japan to continue to say no to immigration and instead to put into practice some of the obvious alternatives: e.g., expanding the native Japanese workforce by removing the well-known obstacles keeping women out of the workforce, and greatly expanding the number of term visas issued to guest workers to serve as child-care providers, nurses, and caretakers for old people. There is no secret about these various possible solutions, each of which has its own advantages and disadvantages. What's required is to bite the bullet, reach consensus on one solution, and avoid the current continued paralysis.

How will all of these questions work themselves out for Japan in the next decade? Realistically, the problems that Japan now faces are less formidable than the ones that it faced when its long policy of isolation was abruptly ended in 1853, or when Japan lay shattered in defeat in August 1945. Japan's successes in recovering from those traumas give me hope that today, once again, Japan can selectively re-appraise its core values, jettison those values that no longer make sense, retain those that still do make sense, and blend them with some new values appropriate to changed modern circumstances.

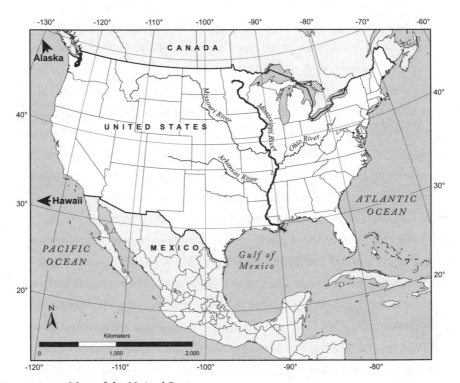

FIG. 8 *Map of the United States*

CHAPTER 9

WHAT LIES AHEAD FOR THE UNITED STATES? STRENGTHS, AND THE BIGGEST PROBLEM

The U.S. today — Wealth — Geography —
Advantages of democracy — Other advantages —
Political polarization — Why? — Other polarization

As of the moment that I write these lines, the U.S. is not experiencing an acute crisis comparable to that of Japan following Perry's uninvited visit on July 8, 1853. However, most Americans will agree that the U.S. does face serious problems. Many would agree that our current situation rates as a slowly unfolding crisis, like that of post-war Germany or Australia. Our problems include internal ones of American society and politics, as well as external ones of foreign relations.

For example, among our foreign relations problems, many Americans are concerned about the long-term threat to us from the rise of China, which already has the world's second-largest economy after that of the U.S. China's population is more than four times bigger than ours. China's economic growth rate for years has consistently exceeded not only ours but also the growth rate of every other major country. It has the world's largest number of soldiers and (after the U.S.) second-largest military spending. It has possessed nuclear weapons for half-a-century. It already outstrips the U.S. in some spheres of advanced technology (such as alternative energy generation and high-speed rail transport). Its dictatorial government can get things done much faster than can our democracy hobbled by two parties and by checks and balances. To many Americans, it seems only a matter of time before China overtakes us economically and militarily. We increasingly hear claims that the 21st century will become an Asian century — specifically, a Chinese century.

I agree that these concerns cannot be lightly dismissed. On the one hand, throughout my life, in each decade there have been reasons to consider that particular decade as posing the toughest problems that we Americans have ever faced — whether it was the 1940's with World War Two against Japan and Nazi Germany, the 1950's with the Cold War, the 1960's with the Cuban Missile Crisis and the Vietnam War that lacerated American society, and so on. But even when I tell myself that we should be suspicious because every decade has seemed at the time to be the one offering the most cause for anxiety, I still have to agree: the current decade of the 2010's really is the one offering the most cause for anxiety.

Hence it seems appropriate, after the previous chapter discussing what lies ahead for Japan, to consider in this chapter and the next one (Chapter 10) what lies ahead for the U.S. Just as in the case of my chapter on Japan, I'll avoid focusing one-sidedly on what's wrong with the U.S. Instead I'll first ask what are the U.S.'s long-term fundamental advantages. For each of those advantages, I'll briefly evaluate China in that same sphere, in order to assess the realism of our fears that time is on China's side and against us. Of course, other countries besides China — especially North Korea, Russia, and Afghanistan — pose problems for the U.S. But it's more useful for the purposes of this book to compare the U.S. with China than with those other countries, which pose more narrowly focused problems for the U.S. than does China. I'll then set out what I see as the U.S.'s current fundamental problems — not the problems of immediate concern for the 2020 elections, but the problems that I expect to remain at the forefront over the next decade. As in the preceding chapter on Japan, I'll discuss just problems specific to the U.S., and I'll save for Chapter 11 the broader world problems that also affect the U.S. Finally, I'll ask whether this book's dozen outcome predictors suggest what may help us or hurt us in solving those fundamental problems.

———

My assessment of the U.S.'s strengths starts with the reality that we are now, and have been for many decades, the world's most powerful country, and the one with the largest economy. (China's economy is close in size, and by some measures is already larger than ours.) To understand the basis for our large economy, let's remind ourselves of the fact mentioned in the previous chapter to help us understand the size of Japan's economy. A national economic output or income is the product of two factors: a country's population, multiplied by its average output or income per person. The U.S. is close to the world's highest-ranking country in both of those factors, whereas all other countries near the top for one of those two factors are low for the other.

As for population, the U.S.'s (currently around 330 million) is the world's third highest, behind only China and India. But those other two countries, and in fact 16 of the countries with the world's 20 highest populations, have low per-capita outputs or incomes, just 3%–40% of the U.S.'s. (The three other rich countries in the top 20 for population are Japan, Germany, and France, whose populations are still just 21%–39% of the U.S.'s.) The reason for the U.S.'s large population is its large area of fertile land. The only two larger countries, Russia and Canada, have much lower populations, because a large fraction of their area is Arctic, suitable only for sparse habitation and no agriculture.

My saying now that the U.S.'s large population is part of the reason for its large economy may seem to contradict my saying, in the previous chapter, that Japan's large population is not a benefit and possibly even a disadvantage for Japan. The reason for this apparent contradiction is that the U.S. is resource-rich, self-sufficient in food and most raw materials, and large in area, and has a population *density* less than 1/10th of Japan's. But Japan is resource-starved, heavily dependent on imports of food and raw materials, has an area less than 1/20th that of the U.S., and is crowded (population density more than 10 times the U.S.'s). That is, it's much easier for the U.S. to support its large population than it is for Japan.

The other factor contributing to the U.S.'s world-leading economic output or wealth is its high output or wealth per person, due to the geographic, political, and social advantages to be discussed below. The various alternative ways to measure per-capita output or income include GDP (gross domestic product) or else income per person, either corrected or uncorrected for differences in purchasing power parity (i.e., differences among countries in how much goods a dollar of income can actually buy in that country). In all of these alternative per-capita measures, the U.S. exceeds by a large margin all other populous countries with large economies. The only countries in the world with per-capita GDPs or incomes higher than the U.S.'s are either small (populations of just 2–9 million: Kuwait, Norway, Qatar, Singapore, Switzerland, and the United Arab Emirates) or tiny (populations of 30,000–500,000: Brunei, Liechtenstein, Luxembourg, and San Marino). Their wealth comes mainly from oil or finance, whose earnings are spread over few people, resulting in high GDP or income per person but a low rank in total national economic output (which equals output per person times population).

The fact that the U.S. has the world's largest economy enables it also to have the world's most powerful military. While China has many more soldiers in its army, the U.S.'s long-standing investment in military technology and ocean-going warships (Plate 9.1) more than counter-balances China's advantage in number of soldiers. For instance, the U.S. has 10 large nuclear-powered aircraft carriers capable of being deployed around the world; only one other country (France) has even a single one, and few countries have any aircraft carrier at all, nuclear-powered or not. As a result, the U.S. is today the world's sole global military power that can and does intervene around the world — a fact, whether one approves or disapproves of those interventions.

———

It is no accident that the U.S. has become economically rich and militarily powerful. The many reasons for this outcome, besides the advantages of large area and large population already discussed, are advantages of geography, politics, economics, and society. In case you come to feel, as you read the following pages, that I'm going chauvinistically overboard in touting the U.S.'s advantages, be forewarned: these pages will be followed by many more pages on the big problems that we face.

As regards geography, we are fortunate to be endowed with excellent real estate. The U.S.'s lower 48 states lie entirely within the temperate zones, which are the world's most productive zone for agriculture, and the safest from the perspective of public health. While China also lies largely within the temperate zones, much of southern China is subtropical, and part of it extends into the tropics. More seriously, China includes the world's largest and highest plateau, of low value for agriculture, plus a large area of high mountains (including five of the world's six highest mountains) offering no human economic value except mountain-climbing tourism and glaciers that supply water for rivers.

Temperate-zone soils are in general more fertile than tropical soils, due in part to the legacies of high-latitude Ice Age glaciers that repeatedly advanced and retreated over the landscape, grinding rocks and generating or exposing fresh soils. That happened not only in North America but also in northern Eurasia, contributing there to Eurasia soil fertility. But glaciation was especially effective in North America because of a peculiar North American geographic feature, unique among the world's continents. To appreciate that feature, just glance at a world map, and quickly describe to yourself the shape of each continent in one short sentence. You'd say that South America and Africa are both broadest near the middle and become narrow towards the South Pole, while Eurasia and Australia are broad both at high and low latitudes. But North America has a unique wedge-like shape, broadest towards the North Pole and becoming narrower at lower latitudes.

That shape had consequences for North American soils. Several dozen times during the Ice Age or Pleistocene Era, glaciers formed in the Arctic and marched south, both in North America and in Eurasia. Because of North America's tapering wedge shape, large volumes of ice forming in the broad expanse at high latitudes were funneled into a narrower band and became heavier glaciers as they advanced towards lower latitudes. In Eurasia, without that wedge shape, the volume of ice formed at high latitudes moved into an equally broad band at low latitudes. The continents of South America, Africa, and Australia all end far short of the Antarctic Circle, and couldn't generate ice sheets marching northwards. Hence creation of fertile young soils by the advance and retreat of glaciers originating in high latitudes was most effective in North America, less effective in Eurasia, and slight or non-existent in the three southern continents. The result was the deep fertile soils of the Great Plains that astonished and delighted immigrant European farmers, and that now constitute the world's largest and most productive uninterrupted expanse of farmland (Plate 9.2). Thus, North America's wedge shape and history of repeated past glaciations, combined with the moderate rainfall prevailing over most of the continent today, are the underlying reasons why the U.S. has high agricultural productivity and is the world's largest exporter of food. In contrast, China has less fertile soils much damaged by erosion, and an average human population density four times the U.S.'s, making China a net importer of food.

The other major geographic advantage of the U.S. is our waterways, both coastal and interior. They constitute a big money-saver, because transport by sea is 10–30 times cheaper than transport overland by road or by rail. The eastern (Atlantic), western (Pacific), and southeastern (Gulf) borders of the U.S. consist of long seacoasts, protected along the Atlantic and Gulf coasts by many barrier islands. Hence ships navigate the latter two coasts through an intra-coastal waterway partly sheltered by those islands. All three U.S. coasts have big indentations within which lie sheltered deepwater ports (Plate 9.3), such as Long Island Sound, Chesapeake Bay, Galveston Bay, San Francisco Bay, and Puget Sound. As a result, the U.S. is blessed with many excellent protected natural harbors: more on our East Coast alone than in all the rest of the Americas south of the Mexican border. In addition, the U.S. is the world's only major power fronting on both the Atlantic and Pacific Oceans.

As for interior waterways, the U.S. East Coast has many short navigable rivers. But our most important interior waterway is the huge Mississippi River system and its big tributaries (the Missouri and others), which drain more than half of our area, including our prime farmland of the Great Plains (map on page 324). Once barriers to navigation on those rivers had been engineered out of existence by construction of canals and locks, ships could sail 1,200 miles into the interior of the central U.S. from the Gulf Coast (Plate 9.4). Beyond the Mississippi's headwaters lie the Great Lakes, the world's largest group of lakes, and the group carrying more shipping than any other. Together, the Mississippi and the Great Lakes constitute the world's largest network of inland waterways. When one adds the intra-coastal waterway to the Mississippi / Great Lakes system, the U.S. ends up with more navigable internal waterways than all the rest of the world combined. For comparison, Mexico has no large navigable river at all, and the whole African continent has only one navigable to the ocean (the Nile). China has a much shorter coastline (only on its east side), not as good ports, a much lower fraction of its land area accessible to navigable rivers, and no big lake system comparable to our Great Lakes. All of those waterways join together much of the U.S., and connect the U.S. to the rest of the world, by means of inexpensive water transport.

The other advantage of our sea-coasts is as protection against invasion. It may seem contradictory that, just after I've gotten through praising sea-coasts as the ideal way to deliver freight, I should now dismiss them as a sub-ideal way to deliver troops. The reason, of course, is that it's cheaper and safer to make deliveries from a ship off the coast than from a vehicle on land only if the people awaiting you on land welcome your planned delivery. Delivery by sea is expensive and unsafe if the people awaiting you are shooting at you. Amphibious landings have always ranked among the most dangerous forms of warfare: just think of the 58% casualties suffered by the Canadian troops who raided Dieppe on the French coast in August 1942, or the 30% casualties suffered by the American marines who captured Tarawa atoll in November 1943. The U.S. was further protected from attack by our annexations of Hawaii and Alaska controlling the approaches to our Pacific Coast. The portions of our borders that don't consist of sea-coasts are our land borders with Mexico and Canada, both of which have much too small populations and armies to threaten us (although we fought a war with each during the early 19th century).

Hence the U.S. is virtually immune to invasion. None has even been attempted in our history as an independent nation; the U.S. has not been involved in a war on our mainland with a foreign power since the 1846–1848 Mexican War, which we ourselves initiated. Even mere raids on the U.S. mainland have been negligible: just a British raid on Washington during the War of 1812, Pancho Villa's raid on Columbus in New Mexico in 1916, one shell fired by a Japanese submarine in World War Two onto the U.S. coast at Santa Barbara, and six American civilians killed by an explosive-laden balloon launched from Japan also during World War Two. In contrast, all other major nations have either been invaded (Japan, China, France, Germany, India), occupied (Japan, Italy, Korea, Germany), or threatened with imminent invasion (the United Kingdom) within the last century. Specifically, China was not only massively attacked from the sea and extensively occupied by Japan in 1937–1945, but was also attacked from the sea by the United Kingdom, France, and Japan in the previous century; has recently fought Russia, India, and Vietnam across its land borders; and frequently in the past was attacked by Central Asian armies, two of which (the Mongols and the Manchu) succeeded in conquering all of China.

———

Those are the geographic advantages of the U.S. Now, let's consider our political advantages, which begin with the fact that our government has been a democracy uninterruptedly for the 230 years of our national existence. In contrast, China has had non-democratic dictatorial government uninterruptedly for the 2,240 years of its national existence.

What really are democracy's advantages — or at least its potential advantages? (I emphasize "potential" because, as we'll see, our supposedly democratic American government is losing some of those potential advantages by deviating from actual democracy.) Today, it's increasingly easy to get disillusioned with democracy, and Americans sometimes envy China's dictatorship for its ability to decide and implement good policies quickly. There's no doubt that decisions and their implementation take longer in democracies than in dictatorships, because the essence of democracy is checks, balances, and broad-based (hence time-consuming) decision-making. For instance, China's adoption of lead-free gasoline took just one year, whereas that policy required a decade of debates and court challenges in the U.S. We envy China's quickly outstripping us in its construction of networks of high-speed rail transport, city subway systems, and long-distance energy transmission. Skeptics about democracy can also point out examples of disastrously harmful leaders who came to power through democratic election.

Those disadvantages of democracy are real. But dictatorships suffer from a far worse, often fatal, disadvantage. No one, in the 5,400-year history of centralized government on all of the continents, has figured out how to ensure that the policies implemented with enviable speed by dictatorships consist predominantly of good policies. Just think of the horribly self-destructive policies that China also implemented quickly, and whose consequences were unparalleled in any large First World democracy. Those self-destructive policies included China precipitating the large-scale famine of 1958–1962 that killed tens of millions of people, suspending its system of education, sending its teachers out into the fields to work alongside peasants, and creating later the world's worst air pollution. If air pollution in the U.S. became even half as bad as it now often is in many large Chinese cities, American voters would complain and throw out the government then in power at the next election. Think also of the even more self-destructive policies implemented in the 1930's without broad-based decision-making by dictatorial governments in Germany and Japan, which launched those countries into wars that killed millions of their own citizens (not to mention more than 20 million citizens of other countries). That's why Winston Churchill quipped, in response to someone expounding to him the usual complaints about democracy's disadvantages, that democracy is indeed the worst form of government, except for all of the alternative forms that at one time or another have been tried.

The advantages of democratic government are numerous. In a democracy, citizens can propose and debate virtually any idea, even if the idea is initially anathema to the government then in power. Debate and protests may then reveal the idea to be the best policy, whereas in a dictatorship the idea would never have gotten debated and its virtues would never have become accepted. The prime example in recent American history, because our government was so tenacious in pursuing a policy that revealed itself to be bad, and because the protests against that policy were so vigorous, was our government's eventual decision to end its policy of making war in Vietnam (Plate 9.5). In contrast, Germans in 1941 did not have the opportunity to debate the folly of Hitler's decision to invade the Soviet Union and then to declare war against the U.S. while already being at war against Britain.

Another basic advantage of democracy is that citizens know that their ideas are getting heard and debated. Even if their ideas are not adopted now, they know that they will have other opportunities to prevail in future elections. Without democracy, citizens are more likely to feel frustrated, and to conclude correctly that their only option is to resort to violence, and even to try to overthrow the government. Knowledge that peaceful outlets for expression exist reduces the risk of civil violence. A cynical but politically astute friend remarked to me, "What counts in democracy is the *semblance* of democracy." By that, my friend meant that the semblance of democracy may suffice to dissuade citizens from resorting to violence, even if (as is now true in the U.S.) democracy is actually being thwarted in not-so-visible ways.

A further basic advantage of democracy is that compromise is essential to its operation. Compromise reduces tyranny by those in power, who might otherwise ignore opposite viewpoints. Conversely, compromise also means that a frustrated minority agrees not to paralyze government.

Still another basic advantage of democracy is that, in modern democracies with universal suffrage, all citizens can vote. Hence the government in power has an incentive for investing in all citizens, who thereby obtain opportunities to become productive, rather than those opportunities being reserved for just a small dictatorial elite.

In addition to those advantages of democracies in general, the U.S. derives further advantages from its particular form of democracy, namely, federal government. In a federal system important functions of government are reserved for regional democratic units and aren't the prerogative of a single centralized national government. The U.S. version of a federal system consists of 50 states, which in practice often means 50 competing experiments that test different solutions to the same shared problem, and that may thereby reveal which solution works best. For instance, American states variously permit (Oregon) or ban (Alabama) assisted suicide, and variously levy high (California) or low (Montana) state taxes. As another example, while I was growing up in the northeastern U.S. state of Massachusetts, the first Californian whom I met explained to me that California had become the only U.S. state to adopt a law permitting cars to make right turns on a red light at an intersection, after coming to a full stop. In the U.S. such traffic laws are the prerogative of individual American states, not of the national government. To my fellow Massachusetts citizens of the early 1960's, and to the citizens of all other American states, that seemed an insanely dangerous idea that only those crazy freaked-out Californians would even dream of trying. But when California did try the experiment, it proved safe, other states were able to learn from California, and all states eventually adopted the same law (Plate 9.6).

You may object that being permitted or forbidden to turn right on a red light after a full stop isn't important enough to convince you of the advantages of our federal system. A more consequential experiment carried out recently was that Governor Brownback of the American state of Kansas maintained that cutting state taxes was more important to the well-being of Kansas citizens than was a well-funded system of public education. Hence, beginning in 2012, he reduced state tax income to the point where drastic cuts in public education became necessary in Kansas. Other U.S. states watched the outcome of this experiment with interest. By 2017, results from Kansas convinced even Kansas legislators belonging to the same political party as Governor Brownback that cutting public education was not a good idea, and so they voted to raise state taxes again. But our federal system permitted one state to test that idea by itself, and let the other 49 states learn from what happened in that one state.

Those are some of democracy's big advantages that the U.S. enjoys, and that China doesn't. The lack of those advantages is in my opinion the biggest single disadvantage that will prevent China from ever catching up with the U.S. in average income per person — as long as the U.S. remains democratic and China remains non-democratic. That reminds me to reiterate: a nominally democratic country loses those advantages if its democracy is seriously infringed; more on that below. I also acknowledge that democracy isn't necessarily the best option for all countries; it's difficult for it to prevail in countries lacking the prerequisites of a literate electorate and a widely accepted national identity.

I'll briefly mention two other political advantages of the U.S. besides democratic government. The U.S. has had uninterrupted civilian control of our military throughout our entire history. That's not true for China or for most Latin American countries, and it was disastrously untrue for Japan in the period from the 1930's until 1945. The U.S. has relatively low overt corruption by world standards, though in that respect it lags behind Denmark, Singapore, and two dozen other countries. Corruption is bad for a country or for a business, because decisions become influenced by what's good for corrupt politicians or business people, even though the decision may be bad for the country or the business as a whole. Corruption also harms businesses because it means that they can't count on contracts being enforced. That's another huge disadvantage of China, which has much overt corruption. But the U.S. does have much *covert* corruption, because Wall Street and other rich entities and individuals influence U.S. government policy and actions by means of lobbying and election campaign contributions. While those money outlays are legal in the U.S., they achieve results similar to those achieved illegally by corruption. That is, legislators or officials adopt policies or actions harmful to the public good, but beneficial to the donor of the money, and sometimes beneficial to the legislators or officials as well.

———

The next-to-the-last U.S. advantages that I'll mention are the most familiar ones, which most Americans would cite before thinking of the fundamental geographic and political advantages that I have been discussing so far. The U.S. has been characterized (at least until recently — more about that in Chapter 10) by high socio-economic mobility. Our ideal and reality of rags-to-riches mean (or meant) that able hard-working people who are born poor or arrive poor may achieve wealth. That's a big incentive driving people to work hard, and means that the U.S. has made good use of much of its potential human capital.

The U.S. is preeminent in the ease with which even young people can found successful businesses. (Think of Amazon, Apple, Facebook, Google, Microsoft, and innumerable less spectacular but still profitable new companies.)

We have a long history of federal, state, and local government investment as well as private investment in education, infrastructure, human capital, research, and development. (China has only recently been catching up in investments in those areas.) As a result, the U.S. leads all the rest of the world combined in every major field of science, as measured by articles published or Nobel Prizes won. Half of what are generally considered the world's top-10 scientific research universities and institutions are American. For almost a century-and-a-half, we have held a big competitive advantage in inventions, technology, and innovative manufacturing practices — as exemplified by Eli Whitney's mass production of interchangeable parts for muskets; Henry Ford's assembly-line factories; the Wright brothers' powered airplanes; Thomas Edison's alkaline storage battery, incandescent light bulb, motion picture equipment, and phonograph (Plate 9.7); Alexander Graham Bell's telephone; and, more recently, the Bell Telephone Laboratories' transistor, men on the moon, cell phones, the internet, and e-mail.

Our last advantage to be mentioned is one that, nowadays, many Americans don't consider an advantage at all: immigration (Plate 9.8). Of course it creates problems, which now weigh on our minds. But the reality is that every single American today is either an immigrant or else descended from immigrants. The vast majority immigrated within the last four centuries (my own grandparents, in 1890 and 1904). Even Native Americans are descended from immigrants who arrived beginning at least by 13,000 years ago.

To understand the fundamental benefits of an immigrant population, imagine that you could divide the population of any country into two groups: one consisting on the average of the youngest, healthiest, boldest, most risk-tolerant, most hard-working, ambitious, and innovative people; the other consisting of everybody else. Transplant the first group to another country, and leave the second group in their country of origin. That selective transplanting approximates the decision to emigrate and its successful accomplishment. Hence it comes as no surprise that more than one-third of American Nobel Prize winners are foreign-born, and over half are either immigrants themselves or else the children of immigrants. That's because Nobel Prize–winning research demands those same qualities of boldness, risk tolerance, hard work, ambition, and innovativeness. Immigrants and their offspring also contribute disproportionately to American art, music, cuisine, and sports.

———

Everything that I have described so far in this chapter can be boiled down to saying: the U.S. enjoys enormous advantages. But countries can squander their advantages, as has Argentina. There are warning signs that the U.S. may be squandering its advantages today. High among those warning signs are four interlinked features that are contributing to the breakdown of American democracy, one of our historical strengths. I'll devote the remainder of this chapter to the first, and most serious, of those four sets of problems. The following chapter (Chapter 10) will discuss the "other" three sets of problems, which are serious. They rate as "other" only because they are eclipsed by our biggest problem.

The first, and also in my opinion the most ominous, of the fundamental problems now threatening American democracy is our accelerating deterioration of political compromise. As I previously explained, political compromise is one of the basic advantages of democracies as compared to dictatorships, because it reduces or prevents both tyranny by a majority and its converse of paralysis by a frustrated minority. The U.S. Constitution sought to create pressure for compromise by devising systems of checks and balances. For instance, our president leads government policy, but Congress controls the government's budget, and the Speaker of the House (Congress's lower chamber) sets the House's agenda for acting on presidential proposals. If, as regularly happens, our representatives in Congress disagree among themselves, and if backers of one view cannot muster sufficient votes to impose their will, a compromise must be reached before the government can do anything.

Naturally, fierce political struggles have been frequent, and majority tyranny or minority paralysis occasional, in American history. But, with the conspicuous exception of the breakdown of compromise that led to our 1861–1865 Civil War, compromises have usually been reached. A modern example is the relationship between Republican President Ronald Reagan and Democratic Speaker of the House Thomas (Tip) O'Neill between 1981 and 1986 (Plate 9.9). Both men were skilled politicians, strong personalities, and opposite to each other in their political philosophies and in many or most questions of policy. They disagreed and fought politically on major issues. Nevertheless, they treated each other with respect, acknowledged each other's constitutional authority, and played by the rules. While O'Neill disliked Reagan's economic agenda, he recognized the president's constitutional right to propose an agenda, scheduled House votes on it, and stuck to that scheduled agenda. Under Reagan and O'Neill, the federal government functioned: it met its deadlines, budgets were approved, government shutdowns were non-existent, and threats of filibusters were rare. Major pieces of legislation on which Reagan and O'Neill and their followers disagreed, but on which they nevertheless succeeded in reaching compromises, included lowering taxes, reforming the federal tax code, immigration policy, social security reform, reduction of non-military spending, and increases of military spending. While Reagan's nominees for federal judgeships were usually not to Democrats' tastes, and Democrats blocked some of those nominees, Reagan nevertheless was able to appoint more than half of federal judges, including three of the nine Supreme Court judges.

But political compromise in the U.S. has been deteriorating from the mid-1990's onwards, and especially from around 2005. Compromise has been breaking down not only between our two major political parties, but also between the less moderate and more moderate wings of each party. That's especially true within the Republican Party, whose more extreme Tea Party wing has mounted primary election challenges against moderate Republican candidates for re-election who had compromised with Democrats. As a result, the 2014–2016 Congress passed the fewest laws of any Congress in recent American history, was behind schedule in adopting budgets, and risked or actually precipitated government shutdown.

As an example of our breakdown of compromise, consider filibusters and blocked nominations of presidential nominees. A filibuster is a tactic admissible in the U.S. Senate under Senate rules (not specified in the Constitution), whereby a minority of senators (or even just one senator) opposed to a motion talks non-stop (or threatens to do so in a so-called phantom filibuster) in order to force a compromise or else withdrawal of that motion. (The record

PLATE 6.1. German civilians and Allied soldiers in the rubble of a German city.

PLATE 6.2. Allied aircraft bombing Cologne. The city was destroyed by bombing along with most other major German cities. Visible are a destroyed bridge over the Rhine River, and Cologne Cathedral, miraculously still standing.

PLATE 6.3. The notorious wall erected by the East German government between East and West Berlin, supposedly to protect East Berlin from West German infiltrators, and actually to prevent East Germans from fleeing to the West.

PLATE 6.4. The German student protest of 1968, West Germany's year of generational change.

PLATE 6.5. A key moment in modern German history: West Germany's Chancellor Willy Brandt spontaneously falling on his knees during a visit to Poland's Warsaw Ghetto, acknowledging Nazi war crimes and their millions of victims, and asking Poles for forgiveness.

PLATE 6.6. The flat North European Plain, without geographic obstructions, across which German armies (shown here) invaded Poland in 1939, and across which non-German armies throughout history have invaded what is now Germany.

PLATE 7.1. Australia's overwhelmingly white population in the mid-1900's.

PLATE 7.2. Australia's landscape of desert and kangaroos, very unlike a European landscape.

PLATE 7.3. Australia's mixed racial population today.

PLATE 7.4.1 and 7.4.2
Australia's flag (above)
consists of the British flag
(the Union Jack, below)
framed by the constellation
of the Southern Cross.

PLATE 7.5. ANZAC (Australia and New Zealand Army Corps) troops fighting in defense of their British motherland, by charging Turkish lines half-way around the world at Gallipoli in 1915. The anniversary of the Gallipoli landings, April 25, is a major Australian national holiday.

PLATE 7.6. The British battleship *Prince of Wales,* sinking after being bombed by Japanese planes on December 10, 1941, during Britain's vain attempt to defend its naval base at Singapore.

PLATE 7.7. Surrender of British troops on February 15, 1942 at Britain's large naval base of Singapore, leaving Australia exposed to Japanese attacks.

PLATE 7.8. Fires and smoke from the Japanese bombing of the Australian city of Darwin on February 19, 1942.

PLATE 7.9. Millions of Australians lined Australian streets to welcome the visit of Queen Elizabeth of the United Kingdom in 1954.

PLATE 7.10. Sydney Opera House, Australia's most famous building, and one of the most famous new buildings of the modern world, designed by a Danish architect and opened in 1973.

PLATE 9.1. American aircraft carriers, a type of military ship of which the U.S. has more than all other countries combined.

PLATE 9.2. The large flat expanse of the U.S.'s Great Plains, the world's most productive expanse of farmland.

PLATE 9.3. The port of Los Angeles, one of many sheltered deep-water ports on the coast of the U.S.

PLATE 9.4. Ship traffic on the Mississippi River, the largest of the U.S.'s many interior waterways that provide inexpensive water transport.

PLATE 9.5. Protests against the U.S. government's policy of making war in Vietnam—eventually recognized to be a bad policy and abandoned, but such anti-government protests are possible only in a democracy.

PLATE 9.6. An advantage of the U.S. federal system. Individual states can adopt laws that initially seem crazy to other states, but that eventually prove sensible and become adopted by all of the states—such as California's becoming the first state to permit right turns on a red light after a full stop.

PLATE 9.7. Thomas Edison, the best known of the U.S.'s inventors and innovators.

PLATE 9.8. Members of a Harvard College graduating class, many of them recent immigrants.

PLATE 9.9. When political compromise still functioned in the U.S.: Republican President Ronald Reagan and Democratic Speaker of the House Tip O'Neill (1981–1986), who often disagreed but nevertheless compromised and collaborated productively to pass much major legislation.

PLATE 9.10. U.S. Senator J. Strom Thurmond, who set a record for length of a filibuster speech used by a political minority to force a political majority to compromise.

Modern Gerrymanders

These newly drawn congressional districts are among the most contorted in the nation. In some places, their appendages are not much wider than a highway.

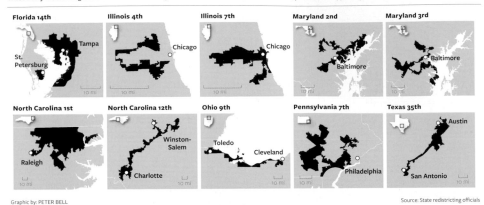

Graphic by: PETER BELL   Source: State redistricting officials

PLATE 9.11. Gerrymandered congressional districts in U.S. states, re-drawn by the party in power solely so as to ensure an exaggerated number of elected representatives. The name is derived from the resemblance of one such district's shape to the shape of a salamander.

PLATE 10.1. The Rodney King riots of 1992 in my city of Los Angeles: a result ultimately of economic inequality and feelings of hopelessness within American society.

PLATE 10.2. The response of some rich, powerful Americans to broad problems of American society: not to try to solve those problems, but instead to try to escape them by converting abandoned underground missile silos at great expense into luxurious defended bunkers for themselves.

PLATE 11.1. One of the major problems facing the world today: the risk that nuclear weapons will be used.

was set in 1967 by a non-stop speech lasting more than 24 hours: Plate 9.10.) Senate rules permit a filibuster to be ended by a "cloture" vote not of a simple majority of senators but of a supermajority (60 out of 100 senators). In effect, a filibuster permits a determined minority that would otherwise be outvoted to force a compromise, while cloture permits a determined supermajority to refuse to compromise.

Despite the obvious potential for abuse — i.e., for filibusters to introduce paralysis, and for cloture to introduce tyranny — this system has worked throughout most of our history. Minorities as well as supermajorities have recognized the potential for abuse, and resorted only rarely to filibusters and even more rarely to cloture. Under our first 43 presidents and our first 220 years of constitutional government, our Senate opposed a total of only 68 presidential nominees for government positions by filibusters. But when Democratic President Obama was elected in 2008, Republican leaders declared their intent to block anything that he proposed. That included blocking 79 Obama nominees by filibusters in just four years, more than in the entire previous 220 years. Democrats responded by abolishing the supermajority requirement for approving presidential nominees other than Supreme Court justices, thereby making it possible to fill government jobs but also reducing the safety valve available to a dissatisfied minority.

A filibuster is merely the most extreme and least frequent method to prevent confirmation of presidential nominees. In President Obama's second term of office from 2012 to 2016, the Republican-controlled Senate confirmed the lowest number of presidentially nominated judges since the early 1950's, and the lowest number of appeals court judges (the court level immediately below the Supreme Court) since the 1800's. The most frequent tactic used to block nominations was to refuse to schedule a Senate committee meeting to consider the nomination; next most frequent was to refuse to schedule a full Senate vote on a nomination approved by the relevant Senate committee. For instance, one nominee for an ambassadorship never got to serve because he died while waiting more than two years for a confirmation vote that still hadn't happened. Even the filling of jobs much less controversial or powerful than a position as judge or ambassador has been blocked. One friend of mine, nominated to a second-level position in the National Oceanic and Atmospheric Administration, withdrew his candidacy when he still hadn't been confirmed after a year of waiting.

———

Why has this breakdown of political compromise accelerated within the last two decades? In addition to the other harm that it causes, it's self-reinforcing, because it makes people other than uncompromising ideologues reluctant to seek government service as an elected representative. Two friends of mine who had been widely respected long-serving U.S. senators, and who seemed likely to succeed once again if they ran for re-election, decided instead to retire because they were so frustrated with the political atmosphere in Congress. When I have asked elected representatives, and people experienced in Congress's workings, about the causes of the trend, the explanations that they suggest include the three following ones.

One suggested explanation is the astronomical rise in costs of election campaigns, which has made donors more important than in the past. While some candidates for high office succeed in funding their campaigns by scraping together many small donations, many or most other candidates are forced to rely on a small number of large donations. Of course those large donors give because they feel strongly about specific goals, and they give to candidates who support those goals. They don't give to middle-of-the-road candidates who compromise. As one disillusioned friend wrote me after retiring from a long career in politics, "Of all the issues that we face, I think that the skew of money in our political system and our personal lives has been by far the most damaging. Politicians and political outcomes have been purchased on a grander scale than ever before... the scramble for political money saps time and money and enthusiasm... political schedules bend to money, political discourse worsens, and politicians do not know each other as they fly back and forth to their districts."

That last point raised by my friend is a second suggested explanation: the growth of domestic air travel, which now offers frequent quick connections between Washington and every American state. Formerly, our representatives served in Congress in Washington during the week; then they had to remain in Washington for the weekend because they couldn't return to their home state and back within the span of a weekend. Their families lived in Washington, and their children went to school in Washington. On weekends the representatives and their spouses and children socialized with one another, the representatives got to know one another's spouses and children, and the representatives spent time with one another as friends and not just as political adversaries or allies. Today, though, the high cost of election campaigns puts pressure on representatives to visit their home state often for the purpose of fund-raising, and the growth of domestic air travel makes that feasible. Many representatives keep their families in their home state, where their children go to school. The children don't play with the children of other congressional representatives, the representatives don't get to know one another's spouses and children, and they see one another only as politicians. At present, about 80 out of the 535 members of Congress don't even maintain an apartment or house in Washington, but instead sleep on a bed in their office during the week, then fly back to their home state for the weekend.

Still a third explanation that I hear to account for the breakdown of compromise involves the practice termed "gerrymandering." That means redrawing the geographic outlines of a state's congressional districts so as to favor one party, by assuring that party a proportion of elected representatives higher than the whole state's proportion of voters choosing that party. This is not a new practice in American politics. In fact, it derives its name from Governor Elbridge Gerry of Massachusetts, whose administration already in 1812 redrew the state's districts for the sole purpose of increasing the number of elected representatives belonging to Gerry's party. The resulting districts had geographically weird shapes, one of them resembling a salamander and thereby giving rise to the term "gerrymander" (Plate 9.11).

Nowadays, after each 10-year national census that reapportions the number of House seats among the states, each state legislature may redraw House district boundaries in that state. Increasingly, especially Republican-controlled state legislatures have been redrawing boundaries so as to concentrate as many likely Democratic voters into the smallest possible number of overwhelmingly Democratic districts (usually urban ones) — thereby leaving all the remaining likely Democratic voters spread around as many districts as possible with likely modest but reliable Republican majorities (often rural districts). The U.S. Supreme Court recently rejected a redistricting plan devised by North Carolina's Republican-controlled legislature, noting that the district boundaries made no geographic sense but had evidently been drawn "with surgical precision" so as to inflate the number of Republican representatives at the expense of Democratic ones.

The consequence of gerrymandering for political compromise is that it makes it clearer in advance which parties and which policies a majority of each district's voters is likely to favor. Hence candidates are likely to be defeated if they take a middle-of-the-road position appealing to voters of both parties. Instead, candidates know that they should adopt a polarized platform appealing only to the party expected to win in their particular gerrymandered district. But while gerrymandering does seem to make some contribution to current political polarization, there are several reasons why it's not the whole explanation: gerrymandering can't explain polarization in the Senate (because states are divided into electoral districts for House but not for Senate elections, but senators are now as uncompromising as are House members); gerrymandering fails to explain polarization in districts that haven't been redrawn; and much polarization even in the redrawn districts already preceded the gerrymandering.

However, all three of those theories about the polarization of American politics — fund-raising, domestic air travel, and gerrymandering — seek to explain only the polarization of that tiny group of Americans who are our politicians. But the actual problem is much broader: Americans as a whole are becoming polarized and politically uncompromising. Just look at a map of the outcome of the 2016 presidential election, depicting as red or blue the states that voted Republican or Democratic, respectively. You'll thereby remind yourself that our coasts and big cities are now overwhelmingly Democratic, and our interior and rural areas are overwhelmingly Republican. Each political party is becoming increasingly homogenous and extreme in its ideology: Republicans are becoming more strongly conservative, Democrats more strongly liberal, and middle-of-the-roaders are declining in both parties. Surveys show that many Americans of each party are increasingly intolerant of the other party, see the other party as a real danger to the U.S.'s well-being, wouldn't want a close relative to marry a supporter of the other party, and want to live in an area where other people share their own political views. If you are an American reader of this book, you can test this pulling-apart of

America on yourself: how many people do *you* personally know, and count among your friends, who told you that they were voting for the other party's presidential candidate in the 2016 election?

Thus, the question to answer isn't just why our politicians are becoming more uncompromising, independently of their constituents. We also need to understand why American voters themselves have become more intolerant and politically uncompromising. Our politicians are merely obeying their voters' wishes.

As for that political polarization of American society as a whole, one explanation frequently suggested is "niche information." When I was a teenager, cable TV didn't exist; the first TV program of any sort didn't come to my city of Boston until 1948; and for years thereafter, we Americans got our news from just three big TV networks, three major weekly newsmagazines, and newspapers. Most Americans shared those same sources of information, none of which was clearly identified with conservative or liberal views, and none of which slanted its information heavily. Now, with the rise of cable TV, news websites, and Facebook, and with the decline of broad-market weekly print newsmagazines, Americans choose their source of information according to their pre-existing views. Looking at my monthly cable TV bill, I see that I can choose among 477 channels: not only Fox News or MSNBC depending on whether I prefer a conservative or a liberal slant, but also channels devoted to Africa, Atlantic Coast college sports, cooking, crime, France, hockey, jewelry, Jewish life, Russia, tennis, weather, and myriads of other narrowly defined subjects and viewpoints. I can thereby choose to remain strictly tied to my current interests and views, and not be distracted by other subjects and unwelcome views. The result: I lock myself into my political niche, I commit myself to my own set of "facts," I continue to vote for the party that I've always preferred, I don't know what's motivating the supporters of the other party, and of course I want my elected representatives to reject any compromise with those representatives who don't agree with me.

Most of the U.S. population now uses social media, such as Facebook and Twitter. Two unrelated friends of mine, one of whom happens to be a Democrat and the other a Republican, explained to me separately how their Facebook account serves as their main information filter. The Democrat (a young man) posts news items and comments to his Facebook friends, who in turn post items of their own, and whom he has selected in part because they share his views. When someone posts an item with a Republican point of view, he "unfriends" that person, i.e., drops her from his list of Facebook friends. The people whom he unfriended included his aunt and uncle, whom he also stopped visiting in person because of their Republican views. He checks his Facebook account on his iPhone frequently throughout the day, and uses it to identify and read on-line newspaper articles aligned with his views, but he doesn't subscribe to a print newspaper or watch television. My other friend, who happens to be Republican, gave me a similar account, except that the acquaintances whom she unfriends are those who post items with a Democratic point of view. The result: each of my friends reads only within his or her already-determined niche.

———

But even this broadening of our question about political polarization in the U.S. today — from asking just about polarized views of our politicians, to asking about polarized views of our whole electorate — is still too narrow. It frames the question as being about polarization only in the political sphere. However, the phenomenon is even broader: polarization, intolerance, and abusiveness are also increasing in other spheres of American life besides the political sphere. Those of you American readers over the age of 40, please reflect on changes that you've seen yourself in American elevator behavior (people waiting to enter an elevator now less likely to wait for those exiting the elevator); declining courtesy in traffic (not deferring to other drivers); declining friendliness on hiking trails and streets (Americans under 40 less likely to say hello to strangers than Americans over 40); and above all, in many circles, increasingly abusive "speech" of all sorts, especially in electronic communication.

I've experienced these trends even in American academic life of scholarly research, which I entered in 1955. American academic debates have become more vicious today than they were 60 years ago. Already at the beginning of my academic career, I found myself involved in scholarly controversies, just as I am now. But I formerly thought of the scientists with whom I disagreed on scientific matters as personal friends, not as personal enemies. For example, I recall spending a vacation in Britain after a physiological conference, touring ruined Cistercian monasteries with a nice and gentle American physiologist with whom I had strongly disagreed about the mechanism of epithelial water transport at the conference. That would be impossible today. Instead, I've now repeatedly been sued, threatened with lawsuits, and verbally abused by scholars disagreeing with me. My lecture hosts have been forced to hire bodyguards to shield me from angry critics. One scholar concluded a published review of one of my books with the words "Shut up!" Academic life mirrors American life in general, just as do our politicians, our voters, our elevator riders, our car drivers, and our pedestrians.

All of these arenas of American life are facets of the same widely discussed phenomenon: the decline of what is termed "social capital." As defined by political scientist Robert Putnam in his book *Bowling Alone*, "...social capital refers to connections among individuals — social networks and the norms of reciprocity and trustworthiness that arise from them. In that sense social capital is closely related to what some have called 'civic virtue.'" It's the trust, friendships, group affiliations, helping, and expectation of being helped built up by actively participating in and being a member of all sorts of groups, ranging from book clubs, bowling clubs, bridge clubs, church groups, community organizations, and parent-teacher associations to political organizations, professional societies, rotary clubs, town meetings, unions, veterans associations, and others. Participation in such group activities fosters generalized reciprocity: i.e., doing things for and with other people, trusting them, and counting on them and on other members of the group to do things for you. But Americans have been decreasingly involved in such face-to-face groups, while becoming increasingly involved in on-line groups in which you never meet, see, or hear the other person.

One explanation that Putnam and many others have suggested for social capital's decline in the U.S. is the rise in non-face-to-face communication at the expense of direct communication. The telephone appeared in 1890 but didn't saturate the U.S. market until around 1957. Radio rose to saturation from 1923 to 1937, and TV from 1948 to 1955. The biggest change has been the more recent rise of the internet, cell phones, and text messaging. We use radio and TV for information and entertainment, and the telephone and those more recent electronic media for those same purposes plus communication. But, before the invention of writing, all human information and communication used to be face-to-face, by people either talking to each other or else watching/hearing performers together (speakers, musicians, and actors). While the motion picture theaters that arose after 1900 didn't provide face-to-face entertainment, they at least got people out of their houses into social groups, and were often enjoyed with friends as a straightforward extension of enjoying live speakers, musicians, and actors with friends.

Today, though, many of our entertainments — our smart-phones, iPods, and video games — are solitary rather than social. They are individually selected niche entertainment, like individually selected niche political information. Television, still the commonest form of entertainment for Americans, keeps Americans at home, and only nominally even with other members of our household. Americans spend three to four times more time watching TV together than talking with one another, and at least one-third of all TV viewing time is spent alone (often on the internet rather than in front of a TV set).

Consequences are that heavy TV viewers trust other people less, and join fewer voluntary organizations, than do people who are not heavy TV viewers. Before blaming TV-viewing for those behaviors, one might object: which is the cause and which is the result, or are the two sets of phenomena just correlated without either being the cause of the other? An unintended natural experiment in Canada illuminates this question. In a Canadian valley were three otherwise similar towns, one of which happened to be out of reach for the TV transmitter serving the area. When that town did gain reception, participation in clubs and other meetings declined compared to participation in that same town before TV arrived, down to levels comparable to participation in the other two towns already served by TV. This suggests that TV-viewing *caused* the decline in participation; it wasn't the case that people who were already non-participants then chose to watch TV.

In the remote areas of New Guinea where I do fieldwork, and where new communication technologies haven't yet arrived, all communication is still face-to-face and full-attention — as it used to be in the U.S. Traditional New Guineans spend most of their waking hours talking to one another. In contrast to the distracted and sparse conversations of Americans, traditional New Guinea conversations have no interruptions to look at the cell phone in one's lap, nor to tap out e-mails or text messages during a conversation with a person physically present but receiving only a fraction of one's attention. One American missionary's son who grew up as a child in a New Guinea village and moved to the U.S. only in his high school years described his shock on discovering the contrast between children's playing styles in New Guinea and in the U.S. In New Guinea, children in a village wandered in and out of one another's huts throughout the day. In the U.S., as my friend discovered, "Kids go into their own houses, close the door, and watch TV by themselves."

The average American cell-phone user checks his or her phone on the average every four minutes, spends at least six hours per day looking at the screen of a cell phone or a computer, and spends more than 10 hours per day (i.e., most waking hours) connected to some electronic device. The result is that most Americans no longer experience one another as live humans whose faces and body movements we see, whose voices we hear, and whom we get to understand. Instead, we experience one another predominantly as digital messages on a screen, occasionally as voices over a cell phone. We tend to have strong inhibitions about being rude to a live human who is two feet away from us, and whom we can see and hear. But we lose those inhibitions when people are reduced to words on a screen. It's much easier to be rude and dismissive towards words on a screen than towards a live person looking you in the face. Once we've thus gotten accustomed to being abusive at a distance, it's an easier next step to being abusive also to a live person.

However, that explanation of American breakdown of political compromise, and of polite behavior in general, faces an obvious objection. Non-face-to-face communication has exploded not just in the U.S. but around the whole world, especially in affluent countries. Italians and Japanese use cell phones at least as much as do Americans. Why hasn't political compromise declined, and social nastiness increased, in other affluent countries as well?

I can think of two possible explanations. One is that, within the 20th century, electronic communication and many other technological innovations became established first in the U.S., from which they and their consequences then spread to other affluent countries. By that reasoning, the U.S. is merely first, not forever unique, in its breakdown of political compromise, which will join telephones and television in spreading elsewhere. In fact, British friends tell me that personal abusiveness is greater now in Britain than it was when I lived there 60 years ago, while Australian friends tell me that non-compromise has been increasing in Australian political life. If this explanation is correct, then it will be only a matter of time until other affluent countries develop political gridlock to the degree that the U.S. has already reached.

The other possible explanation is that, already in the past, the U.S. for several reasons had, and still has today, less social capital to oppose the arrival of the impersonalizing forces of modern technologies. The U.S.'s area is more than 25 times greater than that of any other affluent country except Canada. Conversely, U.S. population density — people divided by area — is up to 10 times lower than in most other affluent countries; only Canada, Australia, and Iceland are more sparsely populated. The U.S. has always placed a strong emphasis on the individual, compared to European and Japanese emphasis on the community; only Australia exceeds the U.S. in ratings of individualism among affluent countries. Americans move often, on the average every five years. The much greater distances within the U.S. than within Japan or any Western European country mean that, when Americans do move, they are likely to leave their former friends much farther away than do those few Japanese and Europeans who move. As a result, Americans have more ephemeral social ties, and high turnover of friends instead of lots of lifelong friends living nearby.

But the U.S.'s area, and distances within the U.S., are fixed, and not about to decrease. Americans are unlikely to give up cell phones, or to move less often. Hence if this explanation linking that decline in American political compromise to the factors underlying our low social capital is correct, political compromise will remain at greater risk in the U.S. than in other affluent countries. That doesn't mean that we are inexorably doomed to worse and worse political gridlock. It does mean that it's going to require more conscious effort on the part of American political leaders and American voters to halt our gridlock than in other countries.

———

This book has already discussed two countries — Chile and Indonesia — where breakdown of political compromise led to one side imposing a military dictatorship whose explicit goal was to exterminate the other side. That prospect still seems absurd to most Americans. It also would have seemed absurd to my Chilean friends when I lived there in 1967, if anyone had expressed fears then of that possible outcome. Yet it did happen in Chile in 1973.

Americans may object, "But the U.S. is different from Chile!" Yes, of course the U.S. is different from Chile. Some of the differences make the U.S. less likely than was Chile to degenerate into a violent military dictatorship — but some of the differences make the U.S. more likely. Factors making that bad outcome less likely in the U.S. include our stronger democratic traditions, our historical ideal of egalitarianism, our lack of a hereditary land-owning oligarchy like Chile's, and the complete absence of independent political actions by our military throughout our history. (The Chilean army did intervene briefly in politics a couple of times before 1973.) On the other hand, factors making a bad outcome more likely in the U.S. than in Chile include far more private gun ownership in the U.S., far more individual violence today and in the past, and more history of violence directed against groups (against

Afro-Americans, Native Americans, and some immigrant groups). I agree that the steps to a military dictatorship in the U.S. would be different from the steps that were taken in Chile in 1973. The U.S. is very unlikely to suffer a take-over by our military acting independently. I instead foresee one political party in power in the U.S. government or in state governments increasingly manipulating voter registration, stacking the courts with sympathetic judges, using those courts to challenge election outcomes, and then invoking "law enforcement" and using the police, the National Guard, the army reserve, or the army itself to suppress political opposition.

That's why I consider our political polarization to be the most dangerous problem facing us Americans today — far more dangerous than competition from China or from Mexico, about which our political leaders obsess more. There is no way that China or Mexico can destroy the U.S. Only we Americans can destroy ourselves. We'll return to this issue in the next chapter, after we've considered the other fundamental problems facing the U.S., and the factors favoring or opposing our making selective changes that would prevent that grim scenario.

CHAPTER 10

WHAT LIES AHEAD FOR THE UNITED STATES? THREE "OTHER" PROBLEMS

Other problems — Elections — Inequality and
immobility — So what? — Investing in the future —
Crisis framework

T he previous chapter began with the good news about the United
States today. The U.S. did not become the world's richest and
most powerful country by accident, but because of a combination
of many advantages: demographic, geographic, political, historical,
economic, and social. The remainder of the chapter presented the
bad news: the current breakdown of political compromise that I
regard as the most serious problem among the ones specifically facing the U.S. (as distinct from worldwide problems also threatening
the U.S.).

This chapter will now discuss three "other" big problems, starting with our problems associated with voting. I lump these issues
under the seemingly dismissive term "other problems" only
because they don't hold as much immediate potential for undermining American democratic government as does the breakdown
of compromise. But they still are serious. Readers wanting to learn

more will enjoy Howard Friedman's book *The Measure of a Nation*, which includes dozens of graphs comparing the U.S. to other major democracies with respect to many of the variables discussed below. Of course, my list of U.S. problems isn't exhaustive. Problems that I don't discuss include race relations and the role of women, both of which are improved compared to 50 years ago but remain blights on American society. The four that I did select for discussion — the one of the previous chapter, and the three of this chapter — have unquestionably gotten worse in recent decades, and in my opinion constitute the most serious threats to American democracy and economic strength today.

——

Elections are the essence of any democracy. If a country has a constitution or laws specifying democratic government but the country's citizens don't or can't vote, such a country doesn't deserve to be called a democracy. By that standard, the U.S. is barely half-deserving of being called a democracy. Nearly half of American citizens eligible to vote don't vote even for our most important elected office, that of president. In each of the four most recent presidential elections the number of eligible Americans who haven't voted has been about 100 million. The percentage of citizens who don't vote for lesser elected offices is much higher. For instance, my city of Los Angeles (LA) is one of the U.S.'s major cities, and LA's most important elected official is our mayor. Nevertheless, in our most recent election for mayor of LA, 80% of eligible LA residents didn't vote.

There are several alternative ways to express voter turnout for elections. One way is to report the percentage of *residents* old enough to vote who did vote. Another measure, yielding a slightly higher number, is to report the percentage of *eligible* voters who did vote. (In the U.S. only 92% of residents old enough to vote are eligible to vote; the ineligible 8% consists mainly of resident non-citizens, prison inmates, and convicted and released felons.) A third measure, yielding a still higher number, is to report the percentage of *registered* voters who did vote; quite a few eligible voters aren't registered to vote, for reasons that I'll discuss below.

All three measures yield the same conclusion: among affluent democracies (so-called OECD nations), the U.S. ranks at the bottom in voter turnout. To set the context, average turnouts of registered voters in elections in other democratic countries are 93% in Australia, where voting is compulsory by law; 89% in Belgium; and 58%–80% in most other European and East Asian democracies. Since Indonesia resumed free democratic elections after 1999, Indonesian voter turnout has fluctuated between 86% and 90%, while Italian turnout since 1948 has ranged up to 93%.

For comparison, U.S. turnout of eligible voters for our national elections averages only 60% for years of presidential elections, and 40% for years of midterm congressional elections. The highest turnout ever recorded in modern American history, for the 2008 presidential election, was only 62%, far below even the lowest recent turnout in Italy or in Indonesia. When registered American voters are asked why they don't bother to vote, their commonest answers are that they don't trust our government, they have no faith in the value of voting, or they aren't interested in politics.

But there's another reason why many Americans eligible to vote don't do so: they can't, because they are not registered to vote. That's a distinctive feature of American democracy that calls for explanation. In many democracies, eligible citizens don't have to do anything to "register" to vote: the government does it for them by generating a list of people automatically registered, from government lists of drivers' licenses, taxpayers, residents, or other such databases. For instance, in Germany all Germans over the age of 18 automatically receive a card from the government notifying them that an election is coming up for which they are eligible to vote.

In the U.S. it's more complicated. It's not enough to be an American citizen eligible to vote by virtue of being over 18 years old, and not in prison or a convicted ex-felon: one still has to register to vote. The U.S. has had a long history of preventing whole groups of age-eligible citizens from registering. The largest such group was American women, who could not vote until 1919. Other groups, notably African-Americans, plus other minorities and immigrant groups, were prevented from registering by obstacles such as poll taxes, literacy tests, and "grandfather clauses." (I.e., you can't register to vote if your grandfather couldn't vote.) Of course it wasn't stated explicitly in the law that those measures were aimed to prevent African-Americans from voting. Nevertheless, everybody understood that the intended purpose and achieved effect of obstacles such as grandfather clauses were to make voter registration impossible for African-Americans.

In case you're inclined to dismiss such obstacles as a vanished feature of the remote past, in the state of Florida in the year 2000 about 100,000 potential voters, the vast majority of them Democrats, were pruned off the list of registered voters. That pruning had an enormous effect on tipping the Florida 2000 presidential vote, hence the U.S. presidency, to George Bush over Al Gore — a much greater effect than did the subsequent well-publicized arguments over disqualifying mere hundreds of so-called chad ballots to which the election's outcome is commonly misattributed. The basic flaw in our American system of voter registration is that, in Florida and many other states, our registered voter lists and election procedures are controlled by partisan procedures at state and local levels, not by non-partisan procedures at the national level. Partisan electoral officials often seek to make voting difficult for citizens likely to prefer the opposite political party.

The biggest broadening of U.S. voter registration procedures in modern American history was the Voting Rights Act of 1965, which outlawed "literacy tests" for registration and gave the federal government oversight over voting districts with a previous pattern of obstructing registration. The result was that voter registration of African-Americans in southern U.S. states jumped from 31% to 73%, and the number of African-American officials elected nation-wide jumped from less than 500 to more than 10,000. Congress renewed that act nearly unanimously in 2006. But in 2013 the U.S. Supreme Court, by a 5-to-4 vote, overturned Congress's 1965 for-mula for identifying districts to be subject to oversight, on the grounds that it had supposedly become unnecessary because of progress in registering African-American voters. The result was a rush by state legislatures to adopt new obstacles to voter registra-tion, varying greatly among states. Until 2004, none of the 50 U.S. states required potential voters to show a government-issued photo ID in order to register or vote. Only two states had adopted such a requirement by 2008. But immediately upon the Supreme Court decision, 14 states adopted photo ID requirements (usually a driv-er's license or passport) or other such restrictions, and most states now have or are contemplating them.

Just as the earlier grandfather clauses did not specifically men-tion African-Americans but were instead successfully designed to disenfranchise them, modern voting restriction methods have simi-lar designs and successes. The percentage of potential voters who possess the required photo ID is considerably higher (depending on the age group, up to three times higher) for whites than for African-Americans or Latinos, and higher for rich people than for poor peo-ple. The reasons are banal ones with no direct relationship to deserving the right to vote: e.g., poorer people, and African-Americans in general, are more likely not to have a driver's license because they haven't paid a traffic fine. The state of Alabama closed its Department of Motor Vehicle (DMV) offices (the offices that issue driver's licenses) in counties with large African-American populations. In response to the resulting public outcry, Alabama re-opened those offices — but for just one day per month. The state of Texas maintained DMV offices in only one-third of its counties, forcing potential voters to travel up to 250 miles if they were determined to satisfy the photo ID requirement by getting a driver's license.

Other obstacles to registering and voting also vary among states. Some states are "voter-friendly" in that they permit voters to register on Election Day itself, or they permit voters to mail their ballots rather than having to appear in person at the polls, or they keep election offices open on evenings and on weekends. Other states are "voter-unfriendly" by requiring that voters register within a short time window before Election Day, or by opening election offices only during work hours or weekdays. But poorer people (including our largest minorities) can't afford to miss work and to wait in long lines to register or to vote.

All of these selective obstacles contribute to the fact that voter turnout is over 80% for Americans with incomes exceeding $150,000, but under 50% for Americans with incomes under $20,000. Those obstacles thereby influence the outcome not only of U.S. presidential elections, but also of many close congressional, state, and local election contests every year.

These limits on American voter participation, whether they result from voluntary choices by voters or else are imposed upon voters against their will, form the reverse side of the fundamental advantages of American democracy that I discussed in the previous chapter. Those advantages included: the opportunity for citizens to debate, evaluate, and choose any proposal; citizens knowing that they are being heard, and that they have peaceful outlets for expression; reduction of the risk of civil violence; incentives for compromise; and incentives to the government to invest in all citizens (ultimately, because they vote), rather than just in an elite fraction of citizens. Insofar as Americans choose not to vote, are ill-informed when they vote, or can't vote at all, those are the advantages that we are losing.

———

No discussion of modern American democracy would be complete without mention of its most frequently criticized feature: the explosion in costs of election campaigns, due especially to the shift from inexpensive print-media advertising to expensive TV-based advertising. Campaigns have become predominantly funded by wealthy interests. There has also been an explosion in duration of campaigns, which now run virtually continuously from one election to the next. As a result, American politicians must devote most of their time (one retired senator friend of mine estimated, 80% of his time) to fund-raising and campaigning rather than to the task of governing; well-qualified citizens are discouraged from running for government office; and campaign information is reduced first to 30-second sound bites, then to short Twitter tweets. In contrast, the famous debates between Abraham Lincoln and Stephen Douglas for election to the office of senator from Illinois in 1858 lasted up to six hours each. While of course only a fraction of Illinois voters physically attended the debates, they were widely disseminated in newspapers. No country approaches the U.S. in the expense and uninterrupted operation of our political campaigning. In contrast, in the United Kingdom election campaigning is restricted by law to a few weeks before an election, and the amount of money that can be spent for campaign purposes is also restricted by law.

———

Our next fundamental problem is inequality. Let's consider what Americans think about American equality or inequality, how to measure it, and how the U.S. ranks in inequality and in socio-economic mobility compared to other major democracies. And, if inequality is high — so what? That is, if it turned out that many Americans really are poor, and doomed to remain poor, that would of course be very sad for them as individuals, but — is that also bad for rich Americans, and for the U.S. as a whole?

When asked about equality or inequality in the U.S., Americans are likely to respond that equality is a core American value, as stated already in the second sentence of our 1776 Declaration of Independence: "We hold these truths to be self-evident, that all men are created equal...." Note, however, that the Declaration doesn't state that all men (and now, also women) actually *are* equal or deserve to have equal incomes. Instead, the Declaration next merely says that all men are endowed with certain inalienable rights. But even that modest assertion was a big deal by world standards in 1776, at a time when nobles and peasants and clergy in European countries had different legal rights and, if put on trial, would be tried before different courts. So, the Declaration of Independence really did enshrine *legal* equality as a core U.S. value, at least in theory. What's the reality about *economic* inequality in the U.S.?

Economic inequality within a country can be measured in several different ways. One question concerns what quantity to compare among people: their raw unadjusted gross incomes? Or their adjusted incomes, after deductions such as for taxes, and after additions such as of Social Security payments and food stamps? Or their wealth or total assets? Individual variation among each of those quantities can in turn be measured in different ways, such as by the so-called Gini coefficient; by comparing the income of the country's richest 1% with its poorest 1%; by computing the percentage of total national income belonging to the richest 1%; and by calculating the percentage of billionaires among the country's population.

Let's restrict our comparisons to major democracies, so that we're not making an apples/oranges comparison of democracies against dictatorships such as Equatorial Guinea, where one man (the president) possesses most of the national income and wealth. Among major democracies, there are differences with respect to which country is calculated to have the greatest *equality*, depending on how one measures equality. However, as for which major democracy has the greatest *inequality*, all quantities compared and all measures yield the same conclusion: the major democracy with the greatest inequality is the U.S. That's been true for a long time, and that inequality of ours is still increasing.

Some of those measures of rising American economic inequality have now become frequently quoted and widely familiar. For instance, the share of unadjusted national income earned by the richest 1% of Americans rose from less than 10% in the 1970's to over 25% today. Inequality is rising even within the ranks of rich Americans themselves: the richest 1% of Americans have increased their incomes proportionately much more than the richest 5%; the richest 0.1% have done proportionately better than the richest 1%; and the three richest Americans (currently Jeff Bezos, Bill Gates, and Warren Buffett) have combined net worths currently equal to the combined net worths of the 130 million poorest Americans. The percentage of billionaires in our population is double that of the major democracies with the next highest percentage of billionaires (Canada and Germany), and seven times that of most other major democracies. The average income of an American CEO, which was already 40 times the income of the average worker in the same company in 1980, is now several hundred times that of the company's average worker. Conversely, while the economic status of rich Americans exceeds that in other major democracies, the economic status of poor Americans is lower than that in other major democracies.

That growing skew between rich and poor Americans is due to a combination of American government policies and American attitudes. As for government policies, "redistribution" in the U.S. — i.e., government policies that in effect transfer money from richer to poorer people — is lower than in other major democracies. For instance, income tax rates, and social transfers and spending such as vouchers and subsidies for low-income people, are relatively low in the U.S. compared to most other major democracies. Part of the explanation is the belief, more widespread in the U.S. than in other countries, that poor people are poor because it's their own fault, that they would become rich if only they would work harder, and that government support for low-income people (such as by food stamps) is rife with abuse and makes poor people unjustly affluent (so-called "welfare queens"). Another part of the explanation is the restrictions on voter registration and voting, and the campaign financing costs, that I discussed on earlier pages. Those issues give disproportionate political power to rich people, by making it easier for them than for poor people to register, vote, and influence politicians.

Closely related to this issue of economic inequality that I've just been discussing is the issue of socio-economic *mobility:* i.e., the likelihood that individual Americans can overcome economic inequality, and that poor Americans can become rich. Americans, more than citizens of other countries, believe that their country is a *meritocracy*, in which people achieve the rewards that their individual abilities permit them to achieve. This is symbolized by the distinctively American phrase "rags to riches": we believe that a poor immigrant who arrives in rags can become rich through ability and hard work. Is this central belief of ours true?

One method by which social scientists have tested this belief is to compare, among different countries, the correlation coefficients between incomes (or income ranks within people of their generation) of adults and the incomes of their parents. A correlation coefficient of 1.0 would mean that relative incomes of parents and of their adult children are perfectly correlated: all high-income people are children of high-income parents, all low-income people are children of low-income parents, kids from low-income families have zero chance of achieving high incomes, and socio-economic mobility is zero. At the opposite extreme, if the correlation coefficient were zero, it would mean that children of low-income parents have as good a chance of achieving high incomes as do children of high-income parents, and socio-economic mobility is high.

The conclusion of such studies is that socio-economic mobility is lower, and family intergenerational correlations of incomes are higher, in the U.S. than in other major democracies. For instance, 42% of American sons whose fathers belong to the poorest 20% of their generation end up in the poorest 20% of their own generation, whereas only 8% of sons of those poorest fathers achieve rags to riches by ending up in the richest 20%. Corresponding percentages for Scandinavian countries are about 26% (below Americans' 42%) and 13% (above Americans' 8%).

Sadly, the problem is making itself worse: economic inequality has been increasing, and socio-economic mobility has been decreasing, in the U.S. over the course of recent decades. American governments at all levels are increasingly influenced by rich people, with the result that governments pass laws (such as voter registration rules and tax policies) favoring rich people, making it increasingly likely that candidates favored by rich people will win the next elections and pass more laws favoring rich people, with the result that American governments will be increasingly more influenced… with the result that… etc. That may sound like a bad joke, but it's a truth of recent American history.

In short, our American belief in the feasibility of rags to riches is a myth. The rags-to-riches path is less feasible in the U.S. than in other major democracies. The likely explanation is that wealthier American parents tend to be better educated, to invest more money in their children's education, and to provide more useful career connections to their children than do poorer parents. For example, children of wealthy American parents are 10 times more likely to complete college than are children of poor parents. As Richard Reeves and Isabel Sawhill wrote, "Pick your parents carefully!"

———

Now, let's return to the query that I posed at the beginning of this discussion of inequality. Granted that it's a huge moral problem, and that it's unfortunate for those individuals who happen to be poor — so what? Is it also an economic and security problem for the U.S. as a whole? Does it cause any harm to affluent Americans that they live surrounded by poor Americans?

I choke at posing that selfish question about harm. Isn't the moral problem alone sufficient reason to be concerned about inequality? But the cruel reality is that people are driven not just by moral considerations but also by self-interest. Many affluent Americans would be more concerned about inequality if they realized that it affects them personally, as well as being an abstract moral issue.

My wife and I received a personal answer to that question "So what?" on April 29, 1992, after we arrived at a Chicago hotel for a conference following an airplane flight from Los Angeles, where we had left our children with a baby-sitter. When we encountered friends in the hotel lobby, they told us, "Go back to your hotel room and turn on the TV. You won't like what you see." We did as we were told, turned on the TV, and saw that uncontrolled rioting, looting, fires, and killings (the so-called Rodney King riots) had broken out in poor minority districts of Central Los Angeles and were spreading along the streets into other neighborhoods (Plate 10.1). At that moment, we calculated that our children would be in a car with our baby-sitter, being driven home from school. We spent an anxious couple of hours until our baby-sitter phoned us to confirm that she and our children had gotten home safely. All that the vastly outnumbered LA police could do to protect wealthy areas of LA from rioters was to string up yellow plastic strips of police tape asserting the closure of major streets.

On that particular occasion, it happened that the rioters didn't attack wealthier districts, nor had they in LA's previous major riots, the 1965 Watts riots. (Both the Rodney King riots and the Watts riots were race riots, motivated by racial discrimination resulting in economic inequality and feelings of hopelessness.) But one can be sure that the future will see more riots in LA and other major American cities. With increasing inequality, persisting racial discrimination, and decreasing socio-economic mobility, poorer Americans will perceive correctly that the vast majority of their children have low chances of achieving a good income or even just of modestly improving their economic status. Within the foreseeable future, the U.S. will experience urban riots in which plastic strips of police tape won't suffice to deter rioters from venting their frustration on affluent Americans. At that point, many affluent Americans will receive their own personal answer to the question, "Does it cause any harm to rich Americans that they live surrounded by poor Americans?" One answer is: yes, it causes personal insecurity.

Even those affluent Americans who live at a safe distance from rioters will receive another answer to that question "So what?" — a less violent answer, but one that will still have a big effect on their pocketbooks and lifestyles. That answer involves the last of what I see as the four fundamental problems now facing the U.S.: the economic consequences of declining American investment in our human capital and other public purposes. Those consequences will be felt by all Americans, including affluent ones.

———

The necessity of investing in one's future, whether for individuals or for nations, is obvious. If one is rich today but just sits on one's money without investing it, or if one invests it unwisely, then it will be just a matter of time until one is no longer rich. Is that really a concern for the U.S. today?

One's first answer may be: of course not! Many people consider U.S. *private* investment to be high, bold, imaginative, and extremely profitable. It's relatively easy in the U.S., compared to other countries, to obtain funding to start a new business and to test an idea's commercial potential. The result has been Microsoft, Facebook, Google, PayPal, Uber, and many other U.S. businesses that were founded only recently but that have already become international giants. Through friends in the venture capital business, I've seen second-hand why U.S. private investments succeed so well. Venture capital funds raise millions (or hundreds of millions) of dollars, which they then divide into investments in many new start-up businesses. Most of those businesses will fail, but one or a few may succeed on a grand scale that brings big profits to the original investors. The ideas in which my venture capital friends make bold investments include not just variants on familiar financial technologies, but also far-out high-risk ideas. That ease of obtaining private start-up investment funding is a big reason for the U.S.'s world dominance among explosively growing new businesses.

To illustrate that ease, I'll now list eight ideas that I would have considered crazy and high-risk a dozen years ago. Two of those eight ideas (which I'll designate as category A) have now become successful and created businesses worth tens of billions of dollars; two (category B) have attracted wealthy backers but haven't yet been shown to work; two (category C) have been shown to work and have attracted venture capital funding but aren't (yet) big businesses; and two (category D) are hoaxes that I thought up myself just now and that haven't attracted any funding (as far as I know). The ideas are: 1. an electromagnetic shark repellent for swimmers;

2. a dog collar that electronically transmits your dog's activity and health as well as its GPS location; 3. DNA intra-uterine technology to enable your dog to give birth to a silver fox pup with valuable fur; 4. a social medium that posts your photos and texts on-line but automatically erases them in 24 hours or less; 5. a pod that transports people at airplane speed through a vacuum tube; 6. technology by which you can rent a room in your house to a complete stranger sight unseen, should you actually want to do so; 7. technology to freeze you quickly as soon as you die, so that you can be brought back to life some day in the future when doctors have figured out how to cure the disease that killed you; and 8. a chemical to spray on your skin that lets you "breathe" underwater for 15 minutes.

Can you assign these ideas correctly to categories A, B, C, and D? The answers are listed at the bottom of this page. I'll bet that few of you readers assigned all eight ideas correctly to the four categories. That illustrates how even ideas that initially sound crazy can attract start-up funding in the U.S., can get the chance to prove themselves, and (if successful) can expand around the world as multi-billion-dollar businesses.

Another reason for initially dismissing concerns about American investment in our future is the world dominance of American science and technology, which account for 40% of U.S. economic output: the highest percentage for any major democracy. The U.S. leads the world by far in output of high-quality science articles in every major area of science: chemistry, physics, biology, and earth and environmental sciences. Half of the top science and technology research institutions in the world are American. The U.S. leads the world in *absolute* spending on research and development (though not in *relative* spending: Israel, South Korea, and Japan all invest a

1C, 2C, 3D, 4A, 5B, 6A, 7B, 8D

higher percentage of their GDPs in science and technology than does the U.S.).

Offsetting those reasons to feel optimistic about the U.S.'s investment in our future is a reason to feel pessimistic: the decline of American *government* investment in public purposes, such as education, infrastructure, and non-military research and development; and our large government expenditures for economically unprofitable purposes. Increasingly large segments of the American populace today deride government investment as "socialism." On the contrary, government investment is one of the two oldest established functions of government. Ever since the rise of the first governments 5,400 years ago, they have served two main functions: to maintain internal peace by monopolizing force, settling disputes, and forbidding citizens to resort to violence in order to settle disputes themselves; and to redistribute individual wealth for the purpose of investing in larger aims — in the worst cases, enriching the elite; in the best cases, promoting the good of society as a whole. Of course, much investment is private, by wealthy individuals and companies expecting to profit from their investments. But many potential pay-offs cannot attract private investment, either because the pay-off is so far off in the future (such as the pay-off from universal primary school education), or because the pay-off is diffused over all of society rather than concentrated in areas profitable to the private investor (such as the diffused benefits of municipal fire departments, roads, and broad education). Even the most passionate American supporters of small government do not decry the funding of fire departments, interstate highways, and public schools as socialism.

The result is that the U.S. is losing its former competitive advantage that rested on an educated workforce, and on science and technology. At least three trends are contributing to this decline: the decreasing amount of money that we devote to education, the declining results that we get for the money that we do spend on education, and large variation among Americans in the quality of education that they receive.

As for government funding of education (especially higher education), that has been dropping since at least the turn of the century. Despite our growing population, state funding of higher education has grown at only 1/25th of the rate of state funding for prisons, to the point where a dozen U.S. states now spend more on their prison systems than they do on their systems of higher education.

A second trend concerns the declining performance of American students, by world standards. In math and science comprehension and test scores, American students now rank low among major democracies. That's dangerous for us, because the American economy is so dependent on science and technology, and because math and science education plus years of schooling are the best predictors of national economic growth. But our educational spending per student, although in decline, is still high by world standards. That means that we are getting a poor return on our educational investment. Why?

A big part of the answer is that, in South Korea, Finland, Germany, and other democracies, the teaching profession attracts the very best students, because teachers there are highly paid and enjoy high social status, which leads to low job turnover of teachers. South Korean applicants for training as primary schoolteachers have to score in the top 5% on national college entrance exams, and there are 12 teachers applying for every secondary school teaching job in South Korea. In contrast, American teachers have the lowest relative salaries (i.e., relative to average national salaries for all jobs) among major democracies. In the American state of Montana, where my wife and I spend our annual summer vacations, schoolteacher salaries are near the poverty level, and teachers have to take one or two additional after-hours jobs (e.g., working as box-packers in supermarkets) to make ends meet. *All* schoolteachers in South

Korea, Singapore, and Finland come from the top third of their school classes, but nearly half of American teachers come from the bottom third of their classes. In all my 53 years of teaching at the University of California (Los Angeles), a university that attracts good students, I have had only one student who told me that he wanted to become a schoolteacher.

The remaining trend contributing to the decline in our educated workforce is the great variation in American education, both among and within American states. In contrast to most other major democracies, where the national government funds education and sets standards, in the U.S. that responsibility falls on the individual states and local government. State spending per student on public higher education varies 11-fold among American states, depending on variation in state wealth, in tax revenues, and in political philosophies. Within the same state, it varies among districts: poorer districts and poorer states have less-well-funded schools. That fact tends to make geographic variation in poverty within the U.S. self-perpetuating, because education is so important for economic performance. Quality of education also varies enormously between private and public schools within the same district, because private schools that charge tuition attract children of wealthy parents, pay teachers better, have smaller classes, and provide a much better education. That's impossible in Finland, where the national government itself pays the salaries of teachers of private schools as well as the public schools and pays the same salaries to teachers at both types of schools, so Finnish parents (unlike American parents) can't buy a better education for their children by sending them to private school.

What's the takeaway message of declining American government investment in public schools, and of the great variation in educational opportunities available to American children? It means that the U.S. is stinting its investment in the future of most

Americans. While we have by far the largest population among wealthy democracies, most of that population is not being trained for the skills that are the engine of our national economic growth. But we are competing against countries like South Korea, Germany, Japan, and Finland, which invest in the education of *all* of their children. In case you take comfort in the fact that those countries have smaller populations than the U.S. — e.g., in case you feel reassured that 20% of American schoolchildren still slightly outnumber 100% of South Korean schoolchildren — remember that China, whose population is five times that of the U.S., is now embarked on a crash program to improve the educational opportunities of its children. That bodes ill for the future of the competitive advantage that the U.S. economy has hitherto enjoyed.

All of these facts raise a paradox. The United States is the world's richest country. Where is our money going, if it is not being invested by our government in our own future?

Part of the answer is that most of our money stays in taxpayers' pockets; our tax burden is low compared to most other wealthy democracies. The other part of the answer is that much of our tax money is going toward government expenditures on prisons, the military, and health. In all three of those categories, our expenditures far exceed those of other major democracies. No one could claim that our prisons, which emphasize punishment and deterrence rather than rehabilitation and retraining, constitute investments in our future. Granted, our military expenditures do constitute investments in our future: but why do we spend so much more on our military than does the European Union, whose population is nearly double ours, but whose costs of military protection to ensure its future are ultimately shouldered disproportionately by us? As for our expenditures for health, it would seem natural to consider them as investments in our future — until one examines their uses and outcomes. In health outcomes the United States ranks below all other major democracies, by measures such as life expectancy, infant mortality, and maternal mortality. That's because the U.S. has high health-related expenditures for purposes not leading to healthy outcomes, such as high insurance premiums charged by our for-profit health insurance companies, high administrative costs, high costs of prescription drugs, high costs of medical malpractice insurance and defensive medicine, and expensive emergency room care for our large uninsured population that cannot afford non-emergency care.

———

We began these two chapters about the U.S. with an account of my country's strengths. We then discussed what I see as our most serious problems now unfolding. Let's conclude these chapters by viewing those problems within this book's framework of crisis and change.

Of the dozen predictive variables listed in Table 1.2 of Chapter 1, which ones favor, and which ones impede, the prospects of the U.S. solving our problems by adopting selective changes? My motive in applying this framework to the U.S. is not just academic interest, but also the hope of offering Americans some guidance in our search for solutions. If we could clearly understand the factors obstructing our search, that awareness could help us focus our attention on finding ways to deal with those obstructions.

The factors favorable to a happy outcome include material or partly material advantages, and cultural advantages. One set of partly material advantages includes our demographic advantage of a large population; our geographic advantages of large area, temperate location, fertile soils, and extensive coastal and interior waterways; our political advantages of federal democracy, civilian control of the military, and relatively low corruption; and our historical advantages of individual opportunity, government investments, and incorporation of immigrants. Those are the main reasons why the U.S. is now, and has been for a long time, the world's most powerful country and biggest economy. The other set of wholly material advantages is the set of geographic ones that has given us the greatest freedom of choice (factor #12 in Table 1.2) of any country in the world: the wide oceans that protect us on two sides, and the land borders with non-threatening and much less populous neighbors that protect us on the other two sides. As a result, the U.S. is at no risk of invasion in the foreseeable future, whereas two of the six other countries discussed in this book (Germany and Japan) have recently been conquered and occupied, and two others (Finland and Australia) have been attacked. But intercontinental ballistic missiles, economic globalization, and the ease of uncontrolled immigration permitted by modern transportation now reduce our former freedom from geopolitical constraints.

As for our cultural advantages, one is our strong sense of national identity (factor #6 on our list). Throughout our history, most Americans have held that the U.S. is unique, is admirable, and is a country of which we are proud. Non-Americans often comment on the optimism and "can-do" attitude of Americans: we view problems as existing in order to be solved.

Another American cultural advantage is American flexibility (factor #10 on our list), which expresses itself in many ways. Americans change their homes on the average of every five years, much more often than citizens of the other countries that I discuss. National transitions of power between our two major political parties have been frequent, with nine transitions at the level of the president in the last 70 years. Our long history of maintaining the same two major political parties — the Democrats since the 1820's, and the Republicans since 1854 — is actually a sign of flexibility rather than of rigidity. That's because, whenever a third party started to become significant (such as Theodore Roosevelt's Bull Moose Party, Henry Wallace's Progressive Party, and George Wallace's American Independent Party), it soon faded because its program became partly co-opted by one of the two major parties. Flexibility as regards core values has also characterized the U.S. On the one hand, our claimed core values (factor #11) of liberty, equality, and democracy are not officially up for negotiation (although we do have blind spots in applying them). On the other hand, the U.S. in the last 70 years has jettisoned long-standing values that were acknowledged to have become outdated: our foreign political isolation was cast aside after World War Two, and our discrimination against women and our race-based discrimination have been in retreat since the 1950's.

Now, our disadvantages. The first steps for any nation in addressing any national crisis are to achieve a national consensus that one's country really is entering a crisis (factor #1); to accept responsibility for one's problems (factor #2), rather than blaming them on "others" (other countries or other groups within one's own country); and to undertake an honest self-appraisal of what is and what isn't working well (factor #7). The U.S. is still far from uniting around those first steps. While Americans are increasingly concerned about our country's condition, we still have no national consensus about what's wrong. Honest self-appraisal is in short supply. There isn't widespread agreement that our fundamental problems are our polarization, voter turnout and obstacles to voter registration, inequality and declining socio-economic mobility, and declining government investment in education and public goods. Large numbers of American politicians and voters are working hard to make those problems worse rather than to solve them. Too many Americans are seeking to blame our problems not on ourselves but on others: favorite targets of blame include China, Mexico, and illegal immigrants.

A trend for wealthy and influential Americans with disproportionate power is to recognize that something is wrong, but, rather than devoting their wealth and power to finding solutions, they instead seek ways for just themselves and their families to escape American society's problems. Currently favored strategies of escape include buying property in New Zealand (the most isolated First World nation), or converting American abandoned underground missile silos at great expense into luxurious defended bunkers (Plate 10.2). But there's only so long that a luxurious micro-civilization in bunkers, or even an isolated First World society in New Zealand, can survive if the U.S. outside is crumbling: A few days? A few weeks? Even a few months? This attitude is captured in the following bitter exchange:

QUESTION: When will the U.S. take its problems seriously?
ANSWER: When powerful rich Americans begin to feel
    physically unsafe.

To that answer, I'd add: when powerful rich Americans realize that nothing they do will enable them to remain physically safe, if most other Americans remain angry, frustrated, and realistically without hope.

Our other big disadvantage: among my dozen predictors of successful coping (Table 1.2), the one that most flagrantly does *not* characterize the U.S. is willingness to learn from models of alternative coping methods practiced by other countries (factor #5). Our refusal to learn is related to our belief in American "exceptionalism": i.e., our belief that the U.S. is so unique that nothing that any other country does could be applicable to us. Of course that's nonsense: while the U.S. is indeed distinctive in many respects, all human beings and societies and governments and democracies have shared features, permitting all of us to learn something from others.

In particular, our neighbor Canada is, like the U.S., a rich democracy with a large area, low population density, English as the dominant language, freedom of choice resulting from protective geographic barriers, rich mineral resources, and a population made up largely of immigrants who arrived since AD 1600. While Canada's world role is different from the U.S.'s, Canada and the U.S.

share universal human problems. Many of Canada's social and political practices are drastically different from those of the U.S., such as with regards to national health plans, immigration, education, prisons, and balance between community and individual interests. Some problems that Americans regard as frustratingly insoluble are solved by Canadians in ways that earn widespread public support. For instance, Canada's criteria for admitting immigrants are more detailed and rational than the U.S.'s. As a result, 80% of Canadians consider immigrants good for the Canadian economy — a far cry from the lacerating divisions in American society over immigration. But American ignorance of neighboring Canada is astounding. Because most Canadians speak English, live literally next door to the U.S., and share with the U.S. the same telephone system of area codes, many Americans don't even think of Canada as something separate. They don't realize how different Canada is, and how much we Americans could learn from Canadian models for solving problems that are frustrating us.

Americans' view of Western Europe is at first sight unlike our view of Canada. It's obvious to us that Western Europe is different from the U.S., in a way that it's not obvious to us for Canada. Unlike Canadians, Western Europeans are far from the U.S., require at least five hours of airplane travel to reach rather than a short car trip, mostly speak languages other than English as their first language, and have a long history not based on recent immigration. Nevertheless, Western European countries are rich democracies facing the familiar American problems of health care, education, prisons, and others, but solving those problems in different ways. In particular, European governments support health care, public transport, education, senior citizens, the arts, and other aspects of life by means of government investments in policies that Americans tend to dismiss as "socialist." Although per-capita income is somewhat higher in the U.S. than in most European countries, life expectancy and measures of personal satisfaction are consistently higher in Western Europe.

That suggests that Western European models may have much to teach us. But recent U.S. history offers few examples of American government missions sent to learn from Western European and Canadian models, as did Japan's government missions of the Meiji Era. That's because we are convinced that American ways are already better than Western European and Canadian ways, and that the U.S. is such a special case that Western European and Canadian solutions could have nothing relevant to suggest to us. That negative attitude deprives us of the option that so many individuals and countries have found useful in resolving crises: learning from models of how others have already resolved similar crises.

The two remaining factors constitute one minor disadvantage and one mixed message. The minor disadvantage is that Americans have not been steeled to tolerance of national uncertainty and failure (factor #9 in Chapter 1), which clashes with our "can-do" attitude and our expectation of success. Compared with the British, who coped with the humiliation of the 1956 Suez Crisis, and with the Japanese and Germans, who recovered from crushing defeat in World War Two (plus in World War One for Germans), Americans found failure in the Vietnam War divisive and hard to tolerate. The U.S. gets a mixed grade for previous experience of surviving crises (factor #8). We have not been defeated in war and occupied as have Japan and Germany, nor have we been invaded as has Finland, nor have we been threatened with invasion as have Britain and Australia. We have not undergone as massive a transformation as did Japan in 1868–1912, nor as did Britain in 1945–1946 and subsequent decades. But the U.S. did survive a long civil war that threatened our national unity, did climb out of the Great Depression of the 1930's, and did successfully switch from peaceful isolation to an all-out war effort in World War Two.

———

In the preceding paragraphs I've taken stock of my dozen predictor factors as applied to the U.S. The geographic features giving us freedom of choice, our strong sense of national identity, and our history of flexibility are factors suggesting a good prognosis. Factors that stand in the way of a good outcome are our current lack of consensus about whether we are indeed entering a crisis, our frequent blaming of our problems on others rather than recognizing our own responsibilities, the efforts of too many powerful Americans to protect themselves rather than working to fix their country, and our unwillingness to learn from the models of other countries. But these factors don't predict whether we *will* choose to solve our problems; they merely predict how *likely* we seem to choose to solve them.

What is going to happen to the U.S.? That will depend upon the choices that we make. The enormous fundamental advantages that we enjoy mean that our future can remain as bright as has been our past, if we deal with the obstacles that we are putting in our own way. But we are presently squandering our advantages. Other countries have previously enjoyed advantages that they, too, squandered. Other countries have previously faced acute or else slowly unfolding national crises at least as serious as our current one. Some of those countries, such as Meiji-Era Japan and post-war Finland and Germany, succeeded in painfully adopting big changes that went a long way towards eventually resolving their crises. It remains to be seen whether we Americans shall choose to build a fence (factor #3), not along the Mexican border but between those features of American society that are functioning well and those that aren't; and whether we shall change those features inside the fence that constitute our growing crisis.

CHAPTER 11

WHAT LIES AHEAD FOR THE WORLD?

The world today — Nuclear weapons — Climate change — Fossil fuels — Alternative energy sources — Other natural resources — Inequality — Crisis framework

The previous chapters discussed crises within the bounds of single countries. Readers from elsewhere will be able to think of possible crises in store for their own country. Now, let's consider the impending world crisis: What factors threaten human populations and standards of living around the world? In the worst case, what threatens the continued existence of civilization globally?

I identify four sets of problems with potential for worldwide harm. In descending order of dramatic visibility but not of importance, they are: explosions of nuclear weapons (Plate 11.1), global climate change, global resource depletion, and global inequalities of living standards. Other people might expand this list to include other problems, among which Islamic fundamentalism, emerging infectious diseases, an asteroid collision, and mass biological extinctions are candidates.

———

The Hiroshima atomic bomb of August 6, 1945 killed about 100,000 people instantly, plus thousands more who died subsequently from injuries, burns, and radiation poisoning. A war in which India and Pakistan, or the U.S. and Russia or China, launched most of their nuclear arsenals at each other would instantly kill hundreds of millions. But the delayed worldwide consequences would be greater. Even if bomb explosions themselves were confined to India and Pakistan, the atmospheric effects of detonating hundreds of nuclear devices would be felt worldwide, because smoke, soot, and dust from fireballs would block most sunlight for several weeks, creating winter-like conditions of steeply falling temperatures globally, interruption of plant photosynthesis, destruction of much plant and animal life, global crop failures, and widespread starvation. A worst-case scenario is termed "nuclear winter": i.e., the deaths of most humans due not only to starvation but also to cold, disease, and radiation.

The only two uses of nuclear weapons to date were the Hiroshima and Nagasaki bombs. Ever since then, fear of large-scale nuclear war has formed the backdrop of my life. While the end of the Cold War after 1990 initially reduced grounds for that fear, subsequent developments have increased the risk again. What scenarios might lead to the use of nuclear weapons?

My account that follows relies on information provided by William Perry in conversation and in his book *My Journey at the Nuclear Brink* (2015). Perry's career underlying his expertise about nuclear issues includes his analyses of Soviet nuclear capabilities in Cuba for President Kennedy each day during the 1962 Cuban Missile Crisis; serving as U.S. secretary of defense from 1994 to 1997; negotiating nuclear and other issues with North Korea, the Soviet Union / Russia, China, India, Pakistan, Iran, and Iraq; negotiating the dismantling of the former Soviet nuclear facilities in Ukraine and Kazakhstan after the dissolution of the Soviet Union; and much else.

One can identify four sets of scenarios culminating in the detonation of nuclear bombs by governments (first three scenarios) or by non-governmental terrorist groups (fourth scenario). The scenario most often discussed has been a planned surprise attack by one nation with a nuclear arsenal on another nation with a nuclear arsenal. The purpose of this surprise attack would be to destroy the rival nation's arsenal completely and instantly, leaving the rival without an arsenal with which to retaliate. This scenario was the one most feared throughout the decades of the Cold War. Because the U.S. and the Soviet Union both possessed the nuclear capacity to destroy each other, the only "rationally planned" attack would be a surprise attack expected to be able to destroy the rival's retaliatory capacity. Hence both the U.S. and the Soviet Union responded to that fact by developing multiple systems to deliver nuclear weapons, in order to eliminate the risk that all of their own retaliatory capacity could be eliminated instantly. For example, the U.S. has three delivery systems: hardened underground missile silos, submarines, and a fleet of bomb-carrying aircraft. Hence even if a Soviet surprise attack destroyed every single one of the silos — unlikely, because the U.S. had so many silos including deceptive dummy ones, hardened against attack, small, and requiring implausibly high accuracy for Soviet missiles to destroy every one of them — the U.S. could still respond with its bombers and its submarines to destroy the Soviet Union.

As a result, the nuclear arsenals of both the U.S. and the Soviet Union provided "mutual assured destruction," and a surprise attack was never carried out. That is, no matter how tempting was the goal of destroying the rival's nuclear capacity, both American and Soviet planners realized that a surprise attack would be irrational, because it was impossible to destroy all of the rival's delivery systems in order to prevent the rival from subsequently destroying the attacker. But these rational considerations offer limited comfort for the future, because there have been irrational modern leaders: perhaps Iraq's Saddam Hussein and North Korea's Kim Jong-Un, plus some leaders of Germany, Japan, the U.S., and Russia. In addition, India and Pakistan today each possesses only a ground-based delivery system: no missile-carrying submarines. Hence a leader of India or Pakistan might consider a surprise attack to be a rational strategy offering a good chance of destroying the rival's retaliatory capacity.

A second scenario involves an escalating series of miscalculations of a rival government's response, and pressure by each country's generals on their president to respond, culminating in mutual non-surprise nuclear attacks that neither side initially wanted. The prime example is the 1962 Cuban Missile Crisis, when the low opinion that the Soviet premier Khrushchev formed of U.S. President Kennedy at their 1961 Vienna meeting led Khrushchev to miscalculate that he could get away with installing Soviet missiles in Cuba. When the U.S. did detect the missiles, U.S. generals urged Kennedy to destroy them immediately (posing the risk of Soviet retaliation), and warned Kennedy that he risked being impeached if he did not do so. Fortunately, Kennedy chose less drastic means of responding, Khrushchev also responded less drastically, and Armageddon was averted. But it was a very close call, as became clear only later, when both sides released documents about their activities then. For example, on the first day of the week-long Cuban Missile Crisis, Kennedy announced publicly that any launch of a Soviet missile from Cuba would require "a full retaliatory response [of the U.S.] upon the Soviet Union." But Soviet submarine captains had the authority to launch a nuclear torpedo without first having to confer with Soviet leadership in Moscow. One such

Soviet submarine captain did consider firing a nuclear torpedo at an American destroyer threatening the submarine; only the intervention of other officers on his ship dissuaded him from doing so. Had the Soviet captain carried out his intent, Kennedy might have faced irresistible pressure to retaliate, leading to irresistible pressure on Khrushchev to retaliate further...

A similar miscalculation could lead to nuclear war today. For example, North Korea currently has medium-range missiles capable of reaching Japan and South Korea, and has launched a long-range ICBM (intercontinental ballistic missile) intended to be able to reach the U.S. When North Korea completes development of its ICBM, it might demonstrate it by launching one towards the U.S. That would be considered by the U.S. as an unacceptable provocation, especially if the ICBM by mistake came closer to the U.S. than intended. An American president might then face overwhelming pressure to retaliate, which would create overwhelming pressure on China's leaders to retaliate in defense of their North Korean ally.

Another plausible opportunity for unintended retaliation by miscalculation involves Pakistan and India. Pakistan terrorists already conducted a lethal non-nuclear attack on the Indian city of Mumbai in 2008. In the foreseeable future, Pakistan terrorists might stage a more provocative attack (e.g., on India's capital city New Delhi); it might be unclear to India whether the Pakistan government itself was behind the attack; India's leaders would be pressured to invade some neighboring portion of Pakistan, in order to eliminate the terrorist threat there; Pakistan's leaders would then be pressured to use their small tactical nuclear weapons "just" against the invading Indian army, perhaps miscalculating that India would consider such a limited use of nuclear weapons as "acceptable" and not requiring a full retaliatory response; but India's leaders would be pressured to respond with their own nuclear weapons.

Both of those situations that could lead to nuclear war by miscalculation seem to me likely to begin to unfold within the next decade. The main uncertainty concerns whether leaders will then pull back as happened during the Cuban Missile Crisis, or whether escalation will run to completion.

The third type of scenario that could culminate in a nuclear war is an accidental misreading of technical warning signs. Both the U.S. and Russia have early warning systems to detect a launch of attacking missiles by the rival. Once missiles have been launched, are underway, and have been detected, the American or Russian president has about 10 minutes to decide whether to launch a retaliatory attack before the incoming missiles destroy the land-based missiles of his country. Launched missiles can't be recalled. That leaves minimal time to evaluate whether the early warning is real or just a false alarm due to a technical error, and whether or not to push a button that will kill hundreds of millions of people.

But missile detection systems, like all complex technologies, are subject to malfunctions and to ambiguities of interpretation. We know of at least three false alarms given by the American detection system. For example, on November 9, 1979 the U.S. army general serving as watch officer for the U.S. system phoned then-Under-Secretary of Defense William Perry in the middle of the night to say, "My warning computer is showing 200 ICBMs in flight from the Soviet Union to the United States." But the general concluded that the signal was probably a false alarm, Perry did not awaken President Carter, and Carter did not push the button and needlessly kill a hundred million Soviets. It eventually turned out that the signal was indeed a false alarm due to human error: a computer operator had by mistake inserted into the U.S. warning system computer a training tape simulating the launch of 200 Soviet ICBMs. We also know of at least one false alarm given by the Russian detection system: a single non-military rocket launched in

1995 from an island off Norway towards the North Pole was mis-identified by the automatic tracking algorithm of Russian radar as a missile launched from an American submarine.

These incidents illustrate an important point. A warning signal is not unambiguous. False alarms are to be expected and still happen, but real launches and real alarms are also possible. Hence when a warning alert does come through, the U.S. watch officer and president (and presumably a Russian watch officer and president in the corresponding situation) must interpret the alarm in the context of then-current conditions: is the current world situation such that the Russians (or Americans) are likely to assume the horrible risk of launching an attack that will guarantee immediate mass-destructive retaliation? On November 9, 1979 there were no current world events motivating a missile launch, Soviet/U.S. relations were not acutely troubled, and the U.S. watch officer and William Perry felt confident in interpreting the warning signal as a false alarm.

Alas, that comforting context no longer prevails. While one might naïvely have expected the end of the Cold War to reduce or eliminate the risk of nuclear war between Russia and the U.S., the result has been paradoxically the opposite: the risk is now higher than at any time since the Cuban Missile Crisis. The explanation is the deterioration of relations and of communications between Russia and the U.S.: a deterioration partly due to recent policies of Russia's President Putin, and partly due to imprudent American policies. In the late 1990's the U.S. government made the mistake of dismissing the post–Soviet Union Russia as weak and no longer worthy of respect. In line with that new attitude, the U.S. prematurely expanded NATO to encompass the Baltic Republics that had formerly been part of the Soviet Union, supported NATO military intervention against Serbia over strong Russian opposition, and stationed ballistic missiles in Eastern Europe supposedly as a defense against Iranian missiles. Russian leaders understandably felt threatened by those and other U.S. actions.

U.S. policy towards Russia today ignores the lesson that Finland's leaders drew from the Soviet threat after 1945: that the only way of securing Finland's safety was to engage in constant frank discussions with the Soviet Union, and to convince the Soviets that Finland could be trusted and posed no threat (Chapter 2). Today, the U.S. and Russia pose a big threat to each other, from a possible misinterpretation leading to an attack not planned in advance — because they are not in constant frank communication, and they are failing to convince each other that they pose no threat from a possible attack planned in advance.

The remaining scenario that could result in use of nuclear weapons involves terrorists stealing uranium or plutonium or a completed bomb from, or being given it by, a nuclear power: most likely Pakistan, North Korea, or Iran. The bomb could then be smuggled into the U.S. or another target, and detonated. While preparing for the 2001 World Trade Center attack, Al Qaeda did seek to acquire a nuclear weapon for use against the U.S. Perhaps terrorists could steal uranium or a bomb without the help of the bomb-producing country, if security at the bomb storage site were inadequate. For instance, at the time of the dissolution of the Soviet Union, 600 kilograms of former-Soviet bomb-quality uranium remained in the Soviet republic that became newly independent Kazakhstan. The uranium was stored in a warehouse secured by little more than a barbed-wire fence and could easily have been stolen. But more likely, terrorists might obtain bomb material by an "inside job," i.e., with the help of bomb storage personnel or leaders of Pakistan, North Korea, or Iran.

A related risk often confused with that danger of terrorists acquiring a nuclear bomb is the risk of their acquiring a so-called "dirty bomb": a conventional non-nuclear explosive bomb whose package includes non-explosive but long-lived radioactive material, such as the isotope cesium-137 with a half-life of 30 years. Detonation of the bomb in an American or other city would spread the cesium over an area of many blocks that would become permanently uninhabitable, as well as having a big psychological impact. (Just think of the permanent consequences of the World Trade Center attack on U.S. mindset and policies, although no explosives or long-lived isotopes were used.) Terrorists have already demonstrated their capacity to explode bombs in cities of numerous countries, and cesium-137 is readily available in hospitals because of its medical uses. Hence it's surprising that terrorists haven't already added cesium-137 to their non-nuclear bombs.

Of these four sets of scenarios, the most likely is the one involving terrorists using a dirty bomb (easy to make) or a nuclear bomb. The former would kill just a few people, the latter "just" a Hiroshima-like death toll of a hundred thousand people — but both would have consequences far eclipsing those death tolls. Less likely, but still possible, are the first three scenarios that could kill hundreds of millions of people directly, and ultimately most people on Earth.

———

The next of the world's four big problems that will shape our lives in the coming decades is global climate change. Almost all of us have heard of it. But it's so complicated, confusing, and bristling with paradoxes that few people except climate specialists actually understand it, and many influential people (including lots of American politicians) dismiss it as a hoax. I'll now try to explain it as clearly as possible, with the help of a flow diagram of the cause/effect chain that can be used to follow my explanation.

The starting point is the world's human population, and its average impact per person on the world. (That latter expression

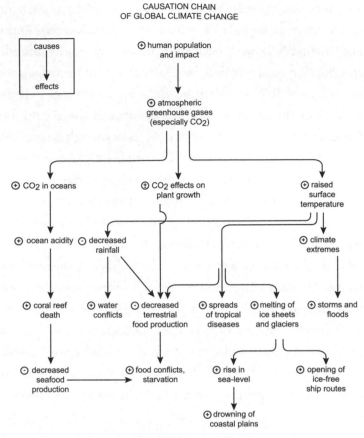

FIG. 9 *Causation Chain of Global Climate Change*

means the average amount of resources such as oil consumed, and of wastes such as sewage produced, per person per year.) All three of those quantities — the number of people, and an average person's resource consumption and waste production — are increasing. As a result, total human impact on the world is increasing: because total impact equals the increasing average impact per person, multiplied by the increasing number of people.

An important waste is the gas carbon dioxide (CO_2), which is constantly being produced by the respiration of animals (including us) and being released into the atmosphere. However, since the beginning of the Industrial Revolution and the consequent human population explosion, that natural CO_2 release has been dwarfed by CO_2 production resulting especially from human burning of fossil fuels. The next most important gas causing climate change is methane, which exists in much smaller quantities and is presently much less important than CO_2, but which could become important due to what is called a positive feedback loop: namely, global warming melting the Arctic's permafrost, which releases methane, which causes more warming, which melts more permafrost, which releases more methane, etc. etc.

The most discussed primary effect of CO_2 release is to act as a so-called greenhouse gas in the atmosphere. That's because atmospheric CO_2 is transparent to the sun's shortwave radiation, allowing incoming sunlight to pass through the atmosphere and warm the Earth's surface. The Earth re-radiates that energy back towards space, but at longer thermal infrared wavelengths to which CO_2 is opaque. Hence the CO_2 absorbs that re-radiated energy and re-emits it in all directions, including back down to the Earth's surface. The surface thus gets warm like the inside of a glass greenhouse, although the warming's physical mechanism is different.

But there are two other primary effects of CO_2 release. One is that the CO_2 that we produce also gets stored in the oceans as carbonic acid. But the ocean's acidity is already higher than at any time in the last 15 million years. That dissolves the skeletons of coral, killing coral reefs, which are a major breeding nursery of the ocean's fish, and which protect tropical and subtropical sea-coasts against storm waves and tsunamis. At present, the world's coral reefs are contracting by 1% or 2% per year, so they will mostly be gone within this century, and that means big declines in tropical coastal safety and protein availability from seafood. The other primary effect of our CO_2 release is that it affects plant growth, variously either stimulating or inhibiting it.

The most discussed effect of CO_2 release, though, is the one I mentioned first: to heat the Earth's surface and the lower atmosphere. That's what we call global warming, but the effect is so complex as to make the term "global warming" a misnomer; the term "global climate change" is a better one. First, cause/effect chains mean that atmospheric *heating* paradoxically ends up causing some land areas (including the southeastern U.S.) to become temporarily *colder*, even while most areas (including most of the rest of the U.S.) are getting warmer. For instance, a warmer atmosphere melts more Arctic Ocean sea ice, permitting more cold Arctic Ocean water to flow south and to cool some land areas downstream from those currents.

Second, rivaling the *average* warming trend in its importance for human societies is an increase in climate *extremes:* storms and floods are increasing, hot weather peaks are getting hotter, but also cold weather peaks are getting colder, producing effects like a snowfall in Egypt and a cold wave in the U.S. Northeast. That leads skeptical politicians who don't understand climate change to think that this disproves its reality.

A third complication is that climate change involves big time lags between causes and effects. For example, the oceans store and release CO_2 so slowly that, even if every human on Earth died tonight, or stopped breathing, or stopped burning fossil fuels, the atmosphere would still heat up for several more decades. Conversely, there are potential big non-linear amplifiers that could make the world heat up much faster than in current conservative projections that assume linear relations between causes and effects. Those amplifiers include permafrost and sea ice melting, and the possible collapse of the Antarctic and Greenland ice sheets.

As for the consequences of the world's average warming trend, I'll mention four. (At this point in my "clear explanation," you may be ready to agree that global climate change really *is* complicated!) The most obvious consequence to people in many parts of the world is drought. For example, my homeland of Southern California is getting drier and drier, and the year 2015 in particular was the driest year in the history of my city of Los Angeles since weather records began being recorded in the 1800's. The droughts caused by global climate change are uneven around the world: the worst affected areas are North America, the Mediterranean and Mideast, Africa, Australia's farmland in southern Australia, and the Himalayas. For instance, the Himalayan snow pack provides most of the water for China, Vietnam, India, Pakistan, and Bangladesh, and that snow pack and the resulting water supply that those countries have to share are shrinking, but those countries have a poor track record of peacefully settling their conflicts.

A second consequence of the average global warming trend is decreased food production on land, from the drought that I just mentioned, and paradoxically from increased land temperatures (e.g., because they can favor growth of weeds over growth of crops). Decreased food production is a problem because the world's human population, standard of living, and food consumption are in the process of increasing by a projected 50% over the next few decades, but we already have a food problem now with several billion people currently underfed. In particular, the U.S. is the world's leading food exporter, and American agriculture is concentrated in the western and central U.S., which are becoming uniformly hotter and drier and less productive.

A third consequence of the average warming trend is that tropical disease-carrying insects are moving into the temperate zones. The resulting disease problems so far include the recent transmission of dengue fever and the spread of tick-borne diseases in the U.S., the recent arrival of tropical chikungunya fever in Europe, and the spread of malaria and viral encephalitis.

The last consequence of the warming trend that I'll mention is rising sea levels. Conservative estimates of the average sea level rise expected during this century are 3 feet, but there have been past rises by up to 70 feet; the main uncertainty now involves possible collapses and melting of the Antarctic and Greenland ice sheets, which would dump a lot of water into the oceans. Even an average rise of just 3 feet, though, amplified by storms and tides, would be enough to undermine the livability of Florida and some other areas of the U.S. eastern seaboard, the Netherlands, lowland Bangladesh, and many other densely settled places — as well as damaging estuaries that serve as "nurseries" for ocean fish.

Friends sometimes ask me whether climate change is having any good effects for human societies. Yes, there are some, such as the prospect of opening ice-free shipping lanes in the far North as Arctic sea ice melts, and perhaps increased wheat production in southern Canada's wheat belt and some other areas. But most of the effects for human societies are big bad ones.

Is there any quick technological fix to these problems? You may have heard of various suggested geo-engineering approaches, such as injecting particles into the atmosphere, or extracting CO_2 from the atmosphere, in order to cool the Earth's surface. But there isn't any geo-engineering approach that is already tested and known to work; the proposed approaches are very expensive; and testing and implementing any such approach is certain to take a long time and likely to uncover unforeseen bad side-effects. For instance, when non-poisonous chlorofluorocarbon gases (CFCs) replaced the poisonous gases previously used in refrigerators until the 1940's, it seemed like a wonderful and safe engineering solution to the refrigerator gas problem, especially because laboratory testing had revealed no downside to CFCs. Unfortunately, lab tests couldn't reveal how CFCs, once they got into the atmosphere, would begin to destroy the ozone layer that protects us from ultraviolet radiation. As a result, CFCs became banned in most of the world — but only several decades later. That illustrates why geo-engineering would first require "atmospheric testing" — an impossibility, because we would have to ruin the Earth experimentally 10 times before we could hope to figure out how to make geo-engineering produce just the desired good effects on the 11th try. Hence most scientists and economists consider geo-engineering experiments as extremely unwise, even lethally dangerous, and deserving to be banned.

Does all this mean that climate change is unstoppable, and that our children are certain to end up in a world not worth living in? No, of course not. Climate change is being caused overwhelmingly by human activities, so all that we have to do in order to reduce climate change is to reduce those human activities. That means burning less fossil fuel, and getting more of our energy from renewable sources such as wind, solar, and nuclear.

———

The third big set of problems for the future of human societies around the world, besides nuclear weapons and global climate change, is the global depletion of essential natural resources. That's a formula for trouble, because some resources (especially water and timber) have imposed limits on past societies and caused them to collapse, and other resources (especially fossil fuels, minerals, and productive land) have motivated wars. Resource scarcities are already undermining societies or threatening to cause wars in many parts of the world today. Let's begin by considering one example in detail: the fossil fuels that we use primarily for energy, and also as starting materials for chemical synthesis of many products. (The term "fossil fuels" means hydrocarbon fuel sources formed long ago in the Earth's mantle: oil, coal, oil shale, and natural gas.)

Humans require energy for all of our activities, and we require especially large quantities for transporting and lifting things. For millions of years of human evolution, human muscle power was our sole energy source for transporting and lifting. Around 10,000 years ago, we began to domesticate large animals and harness them to pull vehicles, carry packs, and raise weights by systems of pulleys and gears. Then came wind power for driving sailboats and (later) windmills, and water power for driving waterwheels used for lifting, grinding, and spinning. Today, our most widespread energy source by far is fossil fuels because of their *apparently* low cost (more of that later), their high energy density (i.e., the large amounts of energy that a small quantity of fuel can deliver), and their ability to be transported for use anywhere (unlike animal, wind, and water power, which are available or can be maintained only in certain locations). That's why fossil fuels have been major recent drivers of wars and foreign policy, as exemplified by oil's role in motivating the U.S.'s and Britain's Mideast policies and Japan's entry into World War Two.

Already in ancient times, humans were using small quantities of oil and coal exposed on the Earth's surface. However, large-scale use of fossil fuels did not begin until the 1700's, with the Industrial Revolution. The exploitation of fossil fuels of different types and from different sources has gradually shifted with time. The first fuels used were those most accessible because they were available on or close to the surface, those easiest and cheapest to extract, and those whose extraction caused the least damage. As those first sources became depleted, we shifted to sources that were less accessible, deeper underground, more expensive to extract, or more damaging. Thus, the first industrial-scale fuel use was of coal from shallow mines, used to power steam engines for pumping water and then for powering spinning wheels, and (eventually in the 1800's) steamships and railroad engines. Industrial exploitation of coal was followed by exploitation of oil, oil shale, and natural gas. For instance, the first oil well that extracted oil from underground was a shallow well drilled in Pennsylvania in 1859, followed by progressively deeper wells.

There are debates about whether we have already reached "peak oil" — that is, whether we have consumed so much of the Earth's accessible oil reserves that oil production will soon start to decline. However, there is no debate about the fact that the cheapest, most accessible, and least damaging sources of oil have already been used up. The U.S. can no longer scrape up surface oil or drill shallow wells in Pennsylvania. Instead, wells have to be dug deeper (a mile deep or more), and not just on land but also under the ocean floor, and not just in shallow ocean waters but in deeper waters, and not just in Pennsylvania in the U.S.'s industrial heartland but far away in New Guinea rainforests and in the Arctic. Those deeper, more remote oil deposits are much more expensive to extract than were Pennsylvania's shallow deposits. The resulting potential for oil spills producing costly damages is higher. As costs of oil extraction increase, alternative but more damaging fossil fuel sources of oil shale and coal, and non-fossil-fuel sources such as wind and solar, are becoming more economic. Nevertheless, oil prices today still permit big oil companies to continue to be highly profitable.

I just mentioned the *apparently* low cost of oil. Let's pause to consider the *actual* cost of oil (or of coal). Suppose that oil sells for $60 per barrel. If it costs an oil company only $20 per barrel to extract and transport the oil, and if the company doesn't have to pay for anything else, selling oil at $60 per barrel means that the oil company makes a big profit.

But fossil fuels cause lots of damage. If those damages also got charged to the oil company, then the price of oil would increase. The damages produced by burning of fossil fuels include air pollution, which recently was serious in the U.S. and Europe and now is especially bad in India and China. That air pollution causes millions of deaths and high health costs every year. Other damages caused by fossil fuels are mediated by climate change, which costs us by decreasing agricultural production, raising sea levels, forcing us to expend money on barriers against those rising seas, and contributing to big damage by floods and droughts.

Here's an example to help you understand those indirect costs of fossil fuels, which fossil fuel producers at present don't pay. Suppose that you operate a factory that produces a type of doll called Happy Dolls. Suppose that it costs you $20 to make a ton of Happy Dolls, while other dolls cost $30 per ton to make, and that you can sell your Happy Dolls for $60 per ton. That profit margin of $60 minus $20 makes Happy Doll manufacturing very profitable, and lets it outcompete rival doll manufacturers.

Unfortunately, your manufacturing process to make Happy Dolls yields as a by-product lots of black sludge, which isn't a by-product of the manufacturing processes of rival dolls. You dump the black sludge onto the wheat fields of all of your neighbors, thereby decreasing their wheat production. Every ton of Happy Dolls that you produce costs your neighbors $70 of lost wheat income because of your black sludge.

As a result, your neighbors sue you and insist that you pay them $70 for the lost wheat income caused by each ton of your Happy Dolls. You object to your neighbors' demand, making many excuses: you deny that Happy Doll manufacturing produces black sludge, although your company's own scientists have been warning you of that by-product for decades; you say that black sludge hasn't been proven to be harmful; black sludge has been arising naturally for millions of years; more research is needed before we can judge how much of the black sludge on your neighbors' fields arises from your Happy Doll manufacturing plant; and Happy Dolls are essential to civilization and our high standard of living, so victims of black sludge should just shut up and stop complaining.

But when the lawsuit goes to trial, the judge and jury say that this case is a no-brainer: of course you have to pay $70 for every ton of your Happy Dolls, in order to compensate your neighbors for their diminished wheat production. The result is that your Happy Dolls have a true cost not of $20 per ton, but of $20 plus $70 = $90 per ton to manufacture. Happy Dolls are no longer a great profit machine: it isn't economical for you to manufacture them at $90 per ton if you can sell them for only $60 per ton. Now, your competitors' dolls costing $30 per ton to produce outcompete Happy Dolls, rather than vice versa.

Fossil fuels, like Happy Dolls in our hypothetical example, cause damages as well as yield benefits. The difference is that the CO_2 from fossil fuel burning is much less visible than is black sludge; and that fossil fuel producers and users don't yet have to pay the costs of the harm that they cause to other people, whereas our hypothetical doll manufacturers do. But there is increasing insistence that fossil fuel producers or users should be forced to pay up just like Happy Doll makers, e.g., by a tax on carbon emissions or by another method. That insistence is one factor behind the current search for alternative energy sources other than fossil fuels.

———

Some alternative sources appear to be virtually inexhaustible, such as wind, solar, tidal, hydroelectrical, and geothermal energy. All of those sources except for tidal are already "proven": i.e., they have been in use on a large scale for a long time. For instance, Denmark already gets much of its electricity from windmills in the North Sea, and Iceland's capital city of Reykjavík gets its heating from geothermal energy, while dams on rivers for hydroelectric energy generation have been in widespread use for more than a century.

Of course, each of these alternative energy sources is associated with its own particular problems. Large-scale solar energy generation here in my homeland of Southern California often involves converting areas of sunny desert habitat to solar panels, and that's bad for our already endangered population of desert tortoises. Windmills kill birds and bats and are resented by land-owners who complain that windmills spoil their view. Hydroelectric dams across rivers are obstacles to migratory fish. If we had other methods of energy generation that were cheap and that caused no problems, surely we wouldn't destroy desert tortoise habitat, kill birds and bats, spoil people's views, or block fish migration. But, as we've discussed, the alternative of fossil fuels is associated with its own big problems of global climate change, respiratory illnesses, and damages caused by oil and coal extraction. Since we thus don't have the option of choosing between a good solution and a bad solution, we have to ask: which of all of those bad alternatives is the least bad?

As an example of this debate, consider windmills. In the U.S. they have been estimated to kill at least 45,000 birds and bats each year. That sounds like a lot of birds and bats. To place that number in perspective, consider that pet cats that are allowed to wander in and out of their owners' houses have been measured to kill an average of more than 300 birds per year per cat. (Yes, more than three hundred: that's not a misprint.) If the U.S. population of outdoor cats is estimated at about 100 million, then cats can be calculated to kill at least 30 billion birds per year in the U.S., compared to the mere 45,000 birds and bats killed per year by windmills. That windmill toll is equivalent to the work of just 150 cats. One could thus argue that, if we are seriously concerned about U.S. birds and bats, we should focus our attention first on cats, rather than on windmills. In further defense of windmills over cats, please reflect that cats don't repay us for the damage they do to our birds by providing us with energy, unpolluted air, and relief from global warming, while windmills do provide all of those things.

This example illustrates how one can make a case for windmills, desert solar panels, and dams, despite the undoubted harm that they cause. They inflict less serious damage than do fossil fuels. Hence they could be considered to offer an acceptable compromise method for replacing fossil fuels as an energy source. One still often hears the objection that windmills and solar energy are not yet competitive with fossil fuels. But in some circumstances they already are, and the apparent economic advantage of fossil fuels is misleading; again the alternative methods would be much cheaper if we considered the big indirect costs (the Happy Doll costs) of fossil fuels.

By now, you are probably wondering about the obvious, and much-feared, alternative of nuclear energy generation. That's a subject to which most Americans, and many citizens of other countries as well, immediately close their ears. They do so for three reasons besides economic ones: fear of accidents, fear of diversion of nuclear reactor fuel to making nuclear bombs, and the unsolved problem of where to store spent fuels.

Our memories of the Hiroshima and Nagasaki atomic bombs lead many people instinctively to associate nuclear reactors with death, not with energy. In fact, since 1945 there have been two known events in which accidents at nuclear power stations did kill people: the 32 people killed immediately, and the large but uncertain number who died subsequently from radiation, as a result of the Chernobyl reactor accident in the former Soviet Union; and the Fukushima reactor accident in Japan. An equipment accident and human error damaged the Three Mile Island reactor in the U.S. in 1979, but no one was killed or injured, and escape of radioactive materials was minimal. However, the psychological effects of Three Mile Island were enormous: they led to a long suspension of ordering any new reactor for energy generation anywhere in the U.S. for many years.

The remaining fear associated with nuclear generation is the unsolved problem of where to dispose of the spent reactor fuel. Ideally, it should be stored forever, in a remote and geologically very stable area, deep underground and not at risk of fuel escape due to earthquakes or water penetration. The best candidate identified so far in the U.S. is a Nevada site that seems to fit the physical requirements. However, complete certainty about safety is impossible, and so the objections of Nevada citizens have succeeded in blocking the proposed site's adoption. As a result, the U.S. still doesn't have a site for the disposal of waste nuclear fuel.

Thus, just as we discussed for the problem of birds and bats killed by windmills, nuclear energy generation is not free of downsides. Even without those downsides, it wouldn't meet all of our major energy needs: e.g., one can't use nuclear reactors to power cars and airplanes. Our memories of Hiroshima and Nagasaki — reinforced by Three Mile Island, Chernobyl, and Fukushima — have paralyzed the thinking of most Americans and other peoples about nuclear energy generation. Again, though, we have to ask: what are the risks of nuclear power, and what are the risks of the alternatives? France has generated most of its national electricity requirements from nuclear reactors for many decades without an accident. It seems implausible to object that the French may really have had accidents and not admitted them: the experience of Chernobyl demonstrates that the release of any radioactivity into the atmosphere from a damaged reactor is easily detected by other countries. South Korea, Taiwan, Finland, and many other countries have also generated much electricity from nuclear reactors without any significant accidents. Hence we should weigh our fear of the *possibility* of a nuclear reactor accident against the *certainty* of the millions of deaths caused every year by air pollution resulting from

burning fossil fuels, and the enormous and possibly ruinous consequences of global climate change caused by fossil fuels.

For the U.S., the solution to these dilemmas will have to involve
two components. One is to reduce energy consumption per person
in the U.S.: ours is approximately double that of Europeans, despite
Europeans enjoying a higher standard of living than Americans.
Among the contributing factors are different government policies
in Europe and the U.S. influencing car purchases. Europeans are
discouraged from buying expensive big cars with high fuel consumption and low gas mileage, because the purchase tax on cars in
some European countries is set at 100%, doubling the cost of the
car. Also, European government taxes on gasoline drive gas prices
to more than $9 per gallon, another disincentive to buying a fuel-
inefficient car. Tax policies in the U.S. could similarly be used to
discourage Americans from buying gas-guzzling cars.

The second component of the solution to energy dilemmas for
the U.S., besides lowering overall energy consumption, will be to
get more of our energy from sources other than fossil fuels — i.e.,
from wind, solar, tidal, hydroelectric, geothermal, and perhaps
nuclear. After the 1973 Gulf oil crisis, the U.S. government offered
subsidies to developers of alternative energy generation, and U.S.
companies used those subsidies to develop efficient wind genera-
tors. Unfortunately, around 1980 the U.S. government ended
those subsidies for alternative energy, so the U.S. market for our
efficient windmills declined precipitously. Instead, Denmark, Germany, Spain, and other European countries improved on our
windmill designs and now use them to generate much of their
electricity needs. Similarly, China has developed long-distance
power lines to transmit electricity from wind-generating sites in
far western China to densely populated areas of eastern China;
the U.S. hasn't developed such long-distance electricity transmission systems.

Those are the problems associated with the depletion of one natural resource: fossil fuels, viewed in the broader context of the problem of our energy needs. Let's now discuss briefly the other major categories of natural resources, and their potential to pose difficulties for our future. Two of those categories were already introduced in Chapter 8, in connection with the problems that they cause specifically for Japan: forests, which provide our timber, paper, and crucial biological agents such as pollinators; and fisheries (mainly fish and shellfish from the ocean, also from fresh-water lakes and rivers), which provide a large fraction of the world's human need for dietary protein. The other categories are: many different elements and minerals used in industry (iron, aluminum, copper, nickel, lead, and others); fertile soil, essential for agriculture and for forestry; fresh water for drinking, washing, agriculture, forestry, and industry; and the atmosphere, in which all of us live. These various resources differ in four respects important for understanding their potential for creating problems for us: their renewability, and the resulting management problems; their potential for limiting human societies; their international dimensions; and the international competition that they provoke, including wars.

First, resources differ in their renewability. Like fossil fuels, minerals are inorganic (i.e., not biological and not renewable). That is, minerals don't regenerate themselves or produce baby minerals; the amounts available to us now on Earth are, for practical purposes, all that we shall ever have. In contrast, forests and fisheries are renewable biological resources: fish and trees do produce baby fish and baby trees. Hence in theory and often in practice, they can be exploited sustainably, by harvesting them at a rate lower than the rate at which new fish and new trees are produced, so that the population of fish and trees remains steady or even increases.

Fertile soil, although largely inorganic and only partly of biological origin, can also be considered a renewable resource because, while it can be eroded by human activities, it can also be regenerated by the action of earthworms and microorganisms. Fresh water is partly non-renewable (e.g., a drained aquifer), but partly renewable, because water evaporating from the ocean can end up as rain on land and generate new fresh water.

There is nothing that we can do to maintain the world's reserves of non-renewable resources (minerals and fossil fuels) by our management practices. But management practices have big effects on reserves of renewable biological resources. As mentioned already in Chapter 8, a lot is known about how to manage forests and fisheries sustainably. Some of the world's forests and fisheries, such as Germany's forests and the Alaska wild salmon fishery, are already well managed. Unfortunately, most aren't; they are being overharvested, with the result that their tree or fish stocks are shrinking or disappearing. Quick: when did you last eat Atlantic swordfish? Answer: not since many years ago, because it was overharvested and became commercially extinct. We also know how to manage topsoil, but sadly it too is often mismanaged and gets carried off into rivers and then into the ocean by erosion, or else its fertility and texture get degraded. In short, the world is currently mismanaging many or most of its renewable valuable biological resources.

Second, which natural resources could limit human societies? Answer: probably all of them, with the exception of atmospheric oxygen, which we show no signs of using up. Some minerals, especially iron and aluminum, are present in such huge amounts that they too seem unlikely to prove limiting — but I must temper this statement by acknowledging that the deposits that we have been exploiting have been the shallow, accessible, cheaply extractible ones. With time, we shall inevitably come to depend on deeper reserves that are more costly to extract, as is already the case for fossil fuels. Some other minerals important in industry are present in much smaller amounts, such that there are already fears of their reserves being limiting — for example, some so-called rare earths whose known reserves are concentrated in China. Perhaps you are inclined to view fresh water availability as unlimited, because there is so much salt water in the world's oceans that we could make essentially infinite amounts of fresh water by desalinizing ocean water. But that requires energy, and we are already hard pressed for energy and suffering huge costs from its overuse, so in practice fresh water is indeed available only in limited quantities.

Our next consideration is the international dimensions of world resource problems. Some resources, such as forests, don't move; each tree stays in the nation where it is now growing, so its management can in theory be dictated by that nation (although in practice there is an international dimension because other countries may buy or lease that resource). But international complications are unavoidable for resources lying in an international "commons," and for mobile resources that move across national boundaries.

The open ocean is a "commons": while ocean water within 200 miles of land is considered the territory of the nation to which that land belongs, ocean water beyond that 200-mile limit is owned by no one. (The name "commons" comes from a term applied to much pasture land in the Middle Ages: it was not owned by individuals but considered a "commons," available for use by the public.) Nations have the legal basis to regulate fishing within their 200-mile limit, but any fishing boat of any country can fish anywhere in the open ocean. As a result, there is no legal mechanism for preventing overfishing of the open oceans, and many ocean fish stocks are declining. Three other potentially valuable resources also lie in a commons beyond national limits: minerals dissolved in the ocean, fresh water in the Antarctic ice cap, and minerals lying on the sea floor. There have already been some attempts to exploit all three: after World War One the German chemist Fritz Haber worked on a process to extract gold from ocean water; at least one attempt has been made to tow an iceberg from Antarctica to a water-poor Middle Eastern nation; and efforts are far advanced to mine some minerals from the ocean floor. But none of those three exploitations of the commons has proved practical yet; our current commons problem is "just" open-ocean fisheries.

The other resources likely to cause international complications are mobile ones that move from one nation to another. Many animals are migratory and move across national boundaries: the ones most important economically are many commercially valuable ocean fish, such as tuna, and also some river fish and migratory land mammals and birds (like river salmon, Arctic reindeer, and African savannah antelope). Hence when a fishing boat of one country harvests an ocean migratory fish stock, it thereby depletes fish that might otherwise be available to another country. Fresh water is also mobile: many rivers flow between two or more countries, and many lakes are bordered by two or more countries, hence one country can draw down or pollute fresh water that another country wants to use. Besides those mobile useful natural resources already present in water or air, there are mobile harmful things that human activities add to water or air, and that can be carried by water currents and winds from one country to another. For example, smoke from Indonesian forest fires already seriously damages the quality of air blown to adjacent Malaysia and Singapore; dust from China and Central Asia gets blown to Japan and even to North America; and rivers carry plastic to end up in even the most remote oceans and beaches.

Finally, let's consider international competition for resources. That's a big problem, because if it can't be resolved amicably, countries may seek to resolve it by war. That has already happened in the case of international competition for oil, which was a major motive for Japan's entry into World War Two, and in the case of Chile's War of the Pacific (1879–1883) against Bolivia and Peru to control the rich copper and nitrate deposits of the Atacama Desert. Today, there is serious competition for fresh water in many parts of the world, such as for the water arising from melting of the Himalayan snow pack, which provides the water for the major rivers flowing through much of China, India, and all Southeast Asian countries. In the case of the Mekong and other rivers flowing through Southeast Asia, dams in upstream countries will block nutrient-rich sediments from reaching downstream countries. Competition for ocean fish off the coast of West Africa is occurring among fishing boats from the European Union, China, and West African nations. Other international "scrambles" over resources are underway for hardwoods of trees growing in tropical countries and coveted by temperate industrialized countries; for rare-earth elements used in industry; and for soil, such as China leasing agricultural land in Africa. In short, as world human population and consumption rise, we can expect many, many more conflicts caused by international competition for limiting resources.

———

Average per-capita consumption rates of resources like oil and metals, and average per-capita production rates of wastes like plastics and greenhouse gases, are about 32 times higher in the First World than in the developing world. For instance, each year the average American consumes about 32 times more gasoline, and produces 32 times more plastic waste and carbon dioxide, than does the average citizen of a poor country. That factor of 32 has big consequences for how people in the developing world behave, and it also has consequences for what lies ahead for all of us. That's the last of the four sets of problems that I see as threatening civilization and our species.

To understand those consequences, let's reflect on our concern with world population. Today, the world has more than 7.5 billion people, and that may rise to around 9.5 billion within this half-century. Several decades ago, many people considered population as *the* biggest issue facing humanity. But, since then, we have come to realize that population is just one of two factors whose product is what really matters. That product is total world consumption, which is the sum (over the world) of local consumptions, which are products of two terms: local population (number of people) times the local average consumption rate per person.

Population matters only insofar as people consume and produce. If most of the world's 7.5 billion people were in a cold-storage locker and not metabolizing or consuming, they wouldn't be creating a resource problem. The First World consists of about 1 billion people who live mostly in North America, Europe, Japan, and Australia, and who have relative average per-capita consumption rates of 32. Most of the world's other 6.5 billion people, constituting the developing world, have relative per-capita consumption rates below 32, mostly down towards 1. Those numbers mean that most resource consumption occurs in the First World.

Nevertheless, some people remain fixated on population alone. They note that countries like Kenya have population growth rates over 4% per year, and they say that that's a big problem. It is indeed a problem, especially for Kenya's 50 million people. But the much bigger problem for the world as a whole is we 330 million Americans, who outnumber Kenyans 6.6 to 1, and each of whom consumes as much as 32 Kenyans do. Multiply those two U.S.-to-Kenya ratios (6.6 to 1, and 32 to 1), and you'll see that the U.S. consumes 210 times more resources than Kenya as a whole. To take another example, Italy's population of 60 million consumes almost twice as much as do the 1 billion people who populate the whole continent of Africa.

Until recent times, the existence of all those poor people elsewhere didn't constitute a threat to First World countries. "They" out there didn't know much about our lifestyle, and if they did learn about it and got envious or angry, they couldn't do much about it. Many decades ago, American diplomats used to play a game of debating which of the world's countries were most irrelevant to U.S. national interests. Popular answers were "Afghanistan" and "Somalia": those two countries were so poor, and so remote, that it seemed that they could never do anything to create problems for us. Ironically, those two countries then became perceived as such threats to us that we sent troops into both of them, and American troops are still in Afghanistan.

The reasons why poor remote countries can now create problems for rich countries can be summed up by the word "globalization": the increased connections between all parts of the world. In particular, the increasing ease of communications and travel means that people in developing countries now know a lot about the big differences in consumption rates and living standards around the world, and that it's now possible for many of them to travel to rich countries.

Among the ways in which globalization has made differences in living standards around the world untenable, three stand out. One is the spread of emerging diseases from poor remote countries to rich countries. In recent decades, feared fatal diseases have often been carried by travelers to rich countries from poor countries where those diseases are endemic and public health measures are weak — cholera, Ebola, flu, (notably) AIDS, and others. Those arrivals will increase.

The spread of emerging diseases is an unintentional consequence of globalization, but the second of the three spreads made possible by globalization involves human intent. Many people in poor countries get frustrated and angry when they become aware of the comfortable lifestyles available elsewhere in the world. Some of them become terrorists, and many others who aren't terrorists themselves tolerate or support terrorists. Since the World Trade Center attack of September 11, 2001, it has become clear that the oceans that formerly protected the U.S. no longer protect us. We Americans now live under constant threat of terrorism. There will surely be more terrorist attacks against the U.S. and Europe, and probably against Japan and Australia as well, in the future — as long as that factorial difference of 32 in consumption rates persists.

Naturally, global inequality by itself isn't the direct cause of terrorist acts. Religious fundamentalism and individual psychopathology also play essential roles. Every country has its crazy angry individuals driven to kill other people; poor countries have no monopoly on them. The U.S. had its Timothy McVeigh who killed 168 people by a truck bomb in Oklahoma City, and its Theodore Kaczynski who mailed packages containing carefully designed bombs that killed three people and injured 23. Norway had its Anders Behring Breivik who killed 77 people and injured 319, many of them children, with a bomb and a gun. But those three terrorists remained isolated crazy individuals and did not receive widespread support, because most Americans and Norwegians aren't sufficiently desperate or angry. Only in poor countries, where much of the population does feel desperate and angry, is there toleration or support for terrorists.

The remaining consequence of that factor of 32, combined with globalization, is that people with low consumptions want to enjoy the high-consumption lifestyle themselves. They have two ways of achieving it. First, governments of developing countries consider an increase in living standards, including consumption rates, as a prime goal of national policy. Second, tens of millions of people in the developing world are unwilling to wait to see whether their government can deliver high living standards within their lifetime. Instead, they seek the First World lifestyle now, by emigrating to the First World, with or without permission: especially by emigrating to Western Europe and the U.S., and also to Australia; and especially from Africa and parts of Asia, and also from Central and South America. It's proving impossible to keep out the immigrants. Each such transfer of a person from a low-consumption to a high-consumption country raises world consumption rates, even though most immigrants don't succeed immediately in increasing their consumption by the entire factor of 32.

Is everybody's dream of achieving a First World lifestyle possible? Consider the numbers. Multiply current national numbers of people by national per-capita consumption rates (of oil, metals, water, etc.) for each country, and add up those products over the whole world. The resulting sum is the current world consumption rate of that resource. Now repeat that calculation, but with all developing countries achieving a First World consumption rate up to 32 times higher than their current ones, and no change in national populations or in anything else about the world. The result is that world consumption rates will increase by 11-fold. That's equivalent to a world population of about 80 billion people with the present distribution of per-capita consumption rates.

There are some optimists who claim that we can support a world with 9.5 billion people. But I haven't met any optimist mad enough to claim that we can support a world with the equivalent of 80 billion people. Yet we promise developing countries that, if they will only adopt good policies, like honest government and free market economies, they too can become like the First World today. That promise is utterly impossible, a cruel hoax. We are already having difficulty supporting a First World lifestyle even now, when only 1 billion people out of the world's 7.5 billion people enjoy it.

We Americans often refer to growing consumption in China and other developing countries as "a problem," and we wish that the "problem" didn't exist. Well, of course the so-called problem will continue: the Chinese and the people of other developing countries are just trying to enjoy the consumption rates that we already enjoy. They wouldn't listen if we were so silly as to tell them not to try to do what we are already doing. The only sustainable outcome for our globalized world that China, India, Brazil, Indonesia, African countries, and other developing countries will accept is one in which consumption rates and living standards are more nearly equal around the world. But the world doesn't have enough resources to sustainably support the current First World, let alone the developing world, at current First World levels. Does that mean that we are guaranteed to end up in disaster?

No: we could have a stable outcome in which the First World and other countries converged on consumption rates considerably below current First World rates. Most Americans would object: there is no way that we will sacrifice our living standards just for the benefit of those people out there in the rest of the world! As Dick Cheney said, "The American way of life is non-negotiable." But the cruel realities of world resource levels guarantee that the American way of life *will* change; those realities of world resources cannot be negotiated out of existence. We Americans certainly will sacrifice our consumption rates, whether we decide to do so or not, because the world can't sustain our current rates.

That wouldn't necessarily be a real sacrifice, because consumption rates and human well-being, while they are related, are not tightly coupled. Much American consumption is wasteful and doesn't contribute to high quality of life. For example, per-capita oil consumption rates in Western Europe are about half those in the

U.S., but the well-being of the average Western European is higher than that of the average American by any meaningful criterion, such as life expectancy, health, infant mortality, access to medical care, financial security after retirement, vacation time, quality of public schools, and support for the arts. When you finish reading this page of my book, just go out into a street in the U.S., look at the cars driving by, estimate their gas mileages, and ask yourself whether that wasteful American gas consumption contributes positively to any of those measures of quality of life. There are other areas besides oil in which consumption rates in the U.S. and in other First World countries are wasteful, such as the wasteful and destructive exploitation of most of the world's fisheries and forests already discussed.

In short, it's certain that, within the lifetimes of most of us, per-capita consumption rates in the First World will be lower than they are now. The only question is whether we shall reach that outcome by planned methods of our choice, or by unpleasant methods not of our choice. It's also certain that, within our lifetimes, per-capita consumption rates in many populous developing countries will no longer be a factor of 32 below First World consumption rates, but will be more nearly equal to First World consumption rates than is the case at present. Those trends are desirable goals, rather than horrible prospects that we should resist. We already know enough to make good progress towards achieving them; the main thing lacking has been the necessary political will.

———

Those are what I see as the biggest problems facing the world as a whole. From the perspective of our crisis framework, which factors favor, and which stand in the way of, humanity solving those problems?

There is no denying that we face formidable obstacles. Much

more than in the cases of the national crises faced by each of the seven individual countries discussed in the previous chapters of this book, world efforts to solve world problems force us onto unfamiliar terrain, with fewer precedents from the past to guide us. Just think of how the world as a whole differs from individual nations. The nations that we have discussed have coherent acknowledged national identities and national shared values, distinguishing that nation from other nations with different identities and different values. Our seven nations have long-established forums of national political debate, and national histories of coping from which to draw inspiration. All of our nations have benefitted from allied friendly nations offering material help, advice, and models to modify and adopt.

But our world as a whole lacks those and other advantages of nations. We aren't in contact with another inhabited planet from which we could seek support (factor #4 of Table 1.2), or whose society we could scrutinize for models to guide our own search for solutions (factor #5). Humanity lacks wide acknowledgment of a shared identity (factor #6) and shared core values (factor #11) contrasting with the identities and values prevailing on other planets. For the first time in history, we face truly global challenges; we lack past experience of such challenges (factor #8), and of failure to solve them (factor #9). Our precedents of previous success at worldwide coping are limited: the League of Nations and the United Nations have constituted the first two institutional attempts, and while they have achieved some successes, those successes have not yet been on a scale commensurate with the scale of world problems. There isn't worldwide acknowledgment (factor #1) of our world crisis, nor worldwide acceptance of responsibility (factor #2) for our current problems, nor worldwide honest self-appraisal (factor #7). Our freedom of choice (factor #12) is limited by severe constraints: the seemingly inexorable depletion of world resources, the rise of world CO_2 levels, and the worldwide scale of inequality leave us little room for experiment and maneuver. All of those cruel realities make many people feel pessimistic or hopeless about humanity's prospects for a decent future.

Nevertheless, there is already progress along three different routes towards solving world problems. One long-tested route consists of bilateral and multilateral agreements between nations. We know that there have been negotiations and agreements between political entities for at least as long as there has been writing to document them (over 5,000 years). Modern bands and tribes without writing also make agreements, so our history of political negotiation surely goes back through modern humans' tens of thousands of years of existence before the origins of state governments. In particular, all four of the world problems discussed in this chapter have been subjects of recent bilateral and multilateral negotiations.

I'll mention just one example, not because the problem that it solved was among the most pressing ones (it wasn't), but because it illustrates the possibility of reaching agreement even between nations otherwise locked in the most bitter enmity: Israel and Lebanon. Israel has invaded and partially occupied Lebanon. Lebanon has served as a base for launching rocket attacks into Israel. Nevertheless, bird-watchers of those two countries succeeded in reaching a milestone agreement. Eagles and other large birds migrating seasonally between Europe and Africa fly south from Lebanon through Israel every autumn, then north again from Israel through Lebanon every spring. When aircraft collide with those large birds, the result is often mutual destruction. (I write this sentence a year after my family and I survived the collision of our small chartered plane with an eagle, which dented but didn't bring down our plane; the eagle died.) Such collisions had been a leading cause of fatal plane accidents in Lebanon and Israel. That stimulated bird-watchers of those two countries to establish a mutual warning system. In the autumn Lebanese bird-watchers warn their Israeli counterparts and Israeli air traffic controllers when they see a flock of large birds over Lebanon heading south towards Israel, and in the spring Israeli bird-watchers warn of birds heading north. While it's obvious that this agreement is mutually advantageous, it required years of discussions to overcome prevailing hatreds, and to focus just on birds and airplanes.

Of course, an agreement between just two or even several countries falls short of an agreement for all 216 nations constituting the whole world. But it nevertheless constitutes a big step towards world agreement, because just a few nations make up the lion's share of the world's population and economy. A mere two nations (China and India) account for one-third of the world's population; another pair of nations (the U.S. and China) account for 41% of the world's CO_2 emissions and economic output; and five nations or entities (China, India, the U.S., Japan, and the European Union) account for 60% of emissions and outputs. China and the U.S. already reached an agreement in principle on CO_2 emissions. That bilateral agreement was then joined by India, Japan, and the European Union in the Paris agreement that came into force in 2016. Of course the Paris agreement wasn't enough, because it lacked a serious enforcement mechanism, and because the U.S. government in the following year announced its intention to pull out. But the Paris agreement is nevertheless likely to serve as a model or starting point for reaching an improved future agreement. Even if the world's 200 other nations with smaller outputs don't join such a future agreement, just a five-way agreement among the five biggest players could go a long way towards solving the emissions problem. That's because the five biggest players can then put pressure on the other 200, e.g., by imposing trade tariffs and carbon taxes on countries that don't adhere.

Another route towards solving world problems consists of agreements among a region's nations. There are already many such regional agreements for North America, Latin America, Europe, Southeast Asia, Africa, and other regional groupings. The most advanced set of regional agreements, with the widest range of institutions and agreement spheres and binding rules, is the set for the European Union (E.U.), currently comprising around 27 European nations. Of course, mention of the E.U. immediately makes one think of disagreements, back-sliding, Brexit, and other possible political exits. That's only to be expected, because the E.U. has constituted such a big and radical step forward, not just for Europe but for any world region.

But before you get overwhelmed by pessimism about the E.U., think of Europe's shattered condition in 1945 at the end of World War Two, and then think of what the E.U. has achieved. After several thousand years of nearly constant warfare, culminating in Europe's nations fighting the two most destructive wars in world history, no E.U. member has fought any war against any other E.U. member since the founding of the E.U.'s predecessors in the 1950's. When I first visited Europe in 1950, there was rigorous passport control at every national border; but restrictions on trans-border movements are now much more limited between E.U. nations. When I lived in Britain from 1958 to 1962, the number of British scientists holding permanent teaching and research jobs at universities on the European continent, and vice versa, was so minimal that I could name the few such individuals in my own field of research on the fingers of one hand. Now, a significant fraction of university positions in E.U. countries is held by non-nationals. Economies of E.U. nations are substantially integrated. Most E.U. nations share a common currency, the euro. For major world problems such as energy, resource use, and immigration, the E.U. discusses and sometimes adopts shared policies. Again, I acknowledge all the dissensions within the E.U. — but don't forget all the dissensions within any individual nation as well.

Other examples of more narrowly focused regional agreements include ones to eliminate or eradicate regional diseases. A major success was the eradication of rinderpest, a formerly dreaded cattle disease that inflicted huge costs on large areas of Africa, Asia, and Europe. Following a long regional effort that took several decades, there has now been no known case of rinderpest since 2001. Large-scale regional disease efforts currently underway in both hemispheres include ones to eradicate guinea worm and eliminate river blindness. Hence regional agreements constitute a second already-tested route towards solving transnational problems.

The third route consists of world agreements, hammered out by world institutions, and reached not only by the United Nations with its comprehensive world mission, but also by other world organizations with more specific missions — such as organizations devoted to agriculture, animal trafficking, aviation, fisheries, food, health, whaling, and other missions. Just as with the E.U., it's easy to be cynical about the United Nations and other international agencies, whose power is generally weaker than the E.U.'s, and much weaker than the power of most nations within their national boundaries. But international agencies already have many achievements, and they provide a mechanism for more progress. Major successes have been the worldwide eradication of smallpox in 1980; the 1987 Montreal Protocol to protect the stratosphere's ozone layer; the 1978 International Convention for the Prevention of Pollution from Ships (known as MARPOL 73/78) that reduced world pollution of the oceans by mandating separation of oil cargo tanks from water ballast tanks on ships, then by requiring that all transport of oil at sea be by double-hulled tankers; the 1994 Law of the Sea Convention that demarcated exclusive national and shared international economic zones; and the International Seabed

Authority that established the legal framework for seabed mineral exploitation.

Globalization both causes problems and facilitates solutions of problems. One ominous thing that globalization means today is the growth and spread of problems around the world: resource competition, global wars, pollutants, atmospheric gases, diseases, movements of people, and many other problems. But globalization also means something encouraging: the growth and spread of factors contributing to solutions of those world problems, such as information, communication, recognition of climate change, a few dominant world languages, widespread knowledge of conditions and solutions prevailing elsewhere, and — some recognition that the world is interdependent and stands or falls together. In my book *Collapse*, published in 2005, I compared the tensions between those problems and solutions to a horserace: a race between a horse of destruction and a horse of hope. It's not an ordinary horserace, in which both horses run at approximately constant top speed for the whole distance. Instead, it's an exponentially accelerating horserace, in which each of the two horses runs faster and faster.

When I wrote in 2005, it wasn't clear which horse would win the race. As I write these sentences in 2019, each horse has been continuing to accelerate for the last 14 years. Our problems, especially world population and world consumption, have increased markedly since 2005. World recognition of our problems, and world efforts to solve them, have also increased markedly since 2005. It still isn't clear which horse will win the race. But it is certain that fewer decades now remain until the race's outcome is settled, for better or for worse.

LESSONS, QUESTIONS, AND OUTLOOK

Predictive factors — Are crises necessary? — Roles of leaders in history — Roles of specific leaders — What next? — Lessons for the future

This last chapter will begin by summarizing how our dozen factors of Table 1.2, postulated at the outset as influencing the outcomes of national crises, actually apply to our sample of seven countries. Next, I shall use that sample to consider two general questions about crises that people often ask me: whether nations require a crisis-provoking acute upheaval to motivate them to undertake major change; and whether history's course depends heavily on particular leaders. I then suggest strategies for deepening our understanding of crises. Finally, I ask what lessons for the future we can draw from that understanding.

———

1. <u>Acknowledgment that one is in a crisis</u>. Acknowledgment is simpler for individuals than for nations, because in the former case one doesn't have to reach a consensus among many

citizens: there is only a single person who does or doesn't acknowledge that he or she is in a crisis. But, even for an individual, there may not be a simple yes-or-no answer. Instead, there are at least three complications: the person may initially deny that there is a crisis, or may acknowledge only part of the problem, or may downplay its seriousness. Eventually, though, the person may "cry for help." For practical purposes, that's the moment of acknowledging the crisis. National crises present the same three complications, plus a fourth one: a nation is composed of many people falling into different groups, as well as a few leaders plus many followers. Those groups, and the leaders and followers, often differ about acknowledgment.

Nations, as individuals, may initially ignore, deny, or under-estimate a problem, until that denial phase is ended by an external event. For example, already before 1853, Meiji Japan knew of the West's war of 1839–1842 against China, and the rising threat posed by the West to Japan. But Japan still didn't acknowledge a crisis and begin debating reform until Commodore Perry's arrival on July 8, 1853. Similarly, Finland received Soviet demands in the late 1930's, and knew that the Soviet Union was populous and had a huge army, but Finland still didn't take the threat seriously until the Soviet attack of November 30, 1939. When that happened, Finns reached virtually unanimous agreement overnight to respond by fighting. In contrast, while Perry's arrival did quickly produce Japanese agreement that their country faced an urgent problem, anti-shogun reformers disagreed with the shogun's government about how best to respond. That disagreement became resolved only 15 years later, when the reformers overthrew the shogun.

Some other cases of national crises yielded widespread agreement that the country did suffer from *some* big problem, but disagreement about what the problem was. In Chile, Allende and the political left saw the problem as Chilean institutions in need of reform, while the political right saw the problem as Allende and his proposed reforms. Similarly, in Indonesia the communists saw the problem as the Indonesian government in need of reform, while the Indonesian army saw the problem as the communists and their proposed reforms. In both cases the crisis was not resolved by the eventual reaching of a national consensus, nor by one group prevailing by force but sparing the lives and rights of their defeated adversaries. (Japan's last Tokugawa shogun was allowed to retire after his defeat, and he outlived the Meiji Restoration by 34 years.) In Chile and Indonesia the crisis was instead resolved by the victorious group exterminating much of the defeated group.

Both Australia and Germany after World War Two illustrate long denial of a growing crisis. Australia clung for a long time to its British and White Australian identities. Germany for a long time denied the widespread responsibility of many ordinary Germans for Nazi crimes, and the unpleasant permanent reality of Germany's territorial losses and Eastern European communist governments. Those issues became resolved in both Australia and Germany by the electorates slowly and democratically reaching enough of a national consensus to change government policies.

Finally, today as I write these pages, Japan and the U.S. are still practicing widespread selective denial of major problems. Japan currently acknowledges some problems (its large government debt and aging population), and incompletely acknowledges the issue of Japanese women's role. But Japan still denies other problems: its lack of accepted alternatives to immigration for solving its demographic difficulties; the historical causes of Japan's tense relations with China and Korea; and denial that Japan's traditional policy of seeking to grab overseas natural resources rather than to help manage them sustainably is now outdated. The U.S., as I write, is still in widespread denial of our own major problems: political polarization, low voter turnout, obstacles to voter registration, inequality, limited socio-economic mobility, and decreasing government investment in public goods.

2. **Accept responsibility; avoid victimization, self-pity, and blaming others**. The next step for resolving personal crises, after that first step of acknowledging the crisis, is to accept personal responsibility — i.e., to avoid wallowing in self-pity or focusing on oneself as the victim, and instead to recognize the need for personal change. That's as true for nations as it is for individuals, though with the same complications just discussed for national acknowledgment: that acceptance of responsibility and avoidance of self-pity are not a simple yes-or-no matter either for individuals or for nations; and that nations consist of diverse groups, and of leaders plus followers, who often differ in their views.

Our seven nations variously illustrate acceptance as well as denial of responsibility. Avoidance of self-pity is illustrated by Finland and by Meiji Japan. From 1944 onwards, Finland might have been paralyzed by self-pity, emphasized Finland's role as victim, and blamed the Soviet Union for invading Finland and killing so many Finns. Instead, Finland recognized that the Soviet Union had to be dealt with. Finland switched to constantly engaging in political discussions with the Soviet Union and winning its confidence, with many beneficial results: the Soviet Union evacuated its naval base at Porkkala near Helsinki, reduced the amount and extended the period of Finland's war reparations, and tolerated Finland's association with the European Economic Community and joining the European Free Trade Association. Even today, long after the Soviet Union's fall, Finland has made no effort to recover its lost province of Karelia. Similarly, Japan during the Meiji Era was exposed for decades to Western threats and unfair imposed treaties. But Japan didn't assume the role of victim; instead, it focused on its responsibility to develop its power to resist.

A counter-example, of a nation's viewing responsibility as falling on others rather than on itself, is Australia blaming British "treachery" for the fall of Singapore, rather than recognizing that Australia had failed in its responsibility to develop its own defenses before World War Two. Similarly, Australia initially blamed the United Kingdom as treacherous for applying for membership in the European Economic Community, before Australia eventually came to the painful recognition that the United Kingdom had to pursue its own interests. That blaming may have slowed Australia's development of economic and political ties with Asian countries.

An extreme and disastrous example of denying responsibility comes from Germany after World War One. A large segment of the Germany public accepted the false claim, made by Nazis and many other Germans, that Germany had lost that war because of a "stab in the back" by German socialists, rather than because Germany was in the process of being defeated militarily by overwhelming Allied forces. Nazis and other Germans focused on the gross unfairness of the Treaty of Versailles. They failed to acknowledge the long series of pre-war political mistakes by Emperor Wilhelm II and his government, leading to Germany entering the war under unfavorable military conditions, and then to the disaster of Germany's defeat and the imposition of the Treaty of Versailles. The result of Germans thus denying their own responsibility, and assuming the mantle of victimization and self-pity, was support of the Nazis, resulting in World War Two, which was even more disastrous for Germany.

A striking example of simultaneous contrasting approaches to accepting responsibility is provided by Germany and Japan after World War Two. Both countries' governments were responsible for initiating that war entirely by themselves; it was not the case, as it had been for Germany in World War One, that their opponents shared the responsibility for precipitating war. During World War

Two both Germany and Japan did horrible things to other peoples, and the German and Japanese peoples themselves suffered horribly. Germany's and Japan's approaches to those realities have been opposite. Germany's reaction might have been dominated by self-pity and a sense of victimization for the millions of Germans killed during the war (including all those killed by Allied bombing of German cities that would have been considered a war crime if the Allies hadn't won the war); for the million German women raped in the Soviet advance from the east; and for the loss of large German territories after the war. Instead, in Germany there has been widespread acknowledgment of Nazi crimes, teaching in schools about them and about German responsibility, and the establishment of better relations with Poland and other countries victimized by Germany in the war. In contrast, Japan largely continues to deny its responsibility for initiating the war; a widespread Japanese view is that the U.S. somehow tricked Japan into bombing Pearl Harbor and thereby initiating the war, ignoring the fact that Japan had already begun a major undeclared war against China four years earlier. Japan also continues to deny its responsibilities for Japanese crimes against Chinese and Korean civilians and against Allied prisoners of war. Instead, Japan focuses on self-pity and on its role as victim of the atomic bombs, without frank discussion of the worse things that would have happened if the bombs had not been dropped. That embrace of denial, victimization, and self-pity continues to poison Japan's relations with its powerful Chinese and Korean neighbors, and thereby poses a big risk for Japan.

3. **Building a fence/selective change**. All six countries that I discussed in Chapters 2–7 as having dealt with their crises adopted selective changes. The two countries for which I discuss changes underway (Japan and the U.S.) are doing so now, Japan more than the U.S. All of those countries changed, or are

debating changing, only certain specific policies; other national policies are not under discussion. Especially instructive, because of the contrast between what did change and what didn't, are again the cases of Meiji Japan and Finland. Meiji Japan westernized in many areas: political, legal, social, cultural, and others. But, in each area, Japan didn't slavishly copy the West; it instead sought out which of the numerous available Western models was most suited to Japan, and modified that model to suit Japanese circumstances. At the same time, other basic aspects of Japanese society remained unchanged, including emperor worship, kanji writing, and many aspects of Japanese culture. Similarly, Finland changed by conducting constant discussions with the communist Soviet Union, sacrificing some freedom of action, and shifting from being a predominantly rural country to a modern industrial country. At the same time, Finland has remained a liberal democracy in other respects, and has retained far more freedom of action than have other European countries neighboring on the former Soviet Union (now Russia). The resulting seemingly glaring inconsistencies in Finnish behavior were heavily criticized by non-Finns, who failed to recognize the cruel realities of Finland's geographic location.

4. Help from other nations. This theme of help from others, which is important in individual crises, has played either a positive role or a negative role in the resolution of most of the national crises that we have discussed. Western help of many kinds, ranging from sending advisors to Japan and receiving Japanese missions abroad to building a prototype battle-cruiser, was important for Meiji Japan in its selective Westernization. Economic help from the U.S. was important for Chile's and Indonesia's military governments' strengthening their countries' economies after the 1973 and 1965 coups, respectively, and for Japan's and

Germany's rebuilding after the destruction suffered during World War Two. Australia looked first to Britain, then to the U.S., for military protection. On the negative side, Allende's government of Chile was destabilized by U.S. withdrawal of help and erection of barriers to the Chilean economy; and Germany's Weimar Republic after World War One was destabilized by British and French extraction of war reparations. For Australia, the shocks of the failure of British military protection after the fall of Singapore, and of Britain's withdrawal of Australia's preferential tariff status as a result of Britain's EEC negotiations, contributed to Australia's seeking a new national identity. Our outstanding example of lack of help from friends is Finland during its Winter War against the Soviet Union, when all of Finland's potential allies couldn't or chose not to deliver the hoped-for military assistance. That cruel experience became the foundation of Finland's post-1945 foreign policy: the recognition that Finland could not expect help in case of a renewed conflict with the Soviet Union, and instead had to develop a working relationship with the Soviet Union that preserved as much Finnish independence as possible.

5. **Using other nations as models**. Just as models are often valuable in resolving individual crises, they have also been significant, positively or negatively, for most of our countries. Borrowing and modifying Western models was especially important in the transformation of Meiji Japan, and to a lesser extent for Japan after World War Two when Japan again borrowed with modification (or had imposed on it) some American models of democratic government. Chile's and Indonesia's military dictatorships borrowed American models (or what they imagined to be American models) of free-market economies. Australia for most of its history before World War Two borrowed heavily from British models, then increasingly rejected them.

Conversely, our countries also provide two examples of actual or presumed lack of models. For Finland, there is no model of another neighbor of the Soviet Union that succeeded in preserving its independence while satisfying Soviet demands; that was the essence of Finland's policy of Finlandization. Finns' recognition of the uniqueness of their situation was the basis of the saying by their President Kekkonen, "Finlandization is not for export." An example of presumed lack of models is provided by the U.S. today, for which belief in American exceptionalism translates into the widespread belief that the U.S. has nothing to learn from Canada and Western European democracies: not even from their solutions to issues that arise for every country, such as health care, education, immigration, prisons, and security in old age — issues about which most Americans are dissatisfied with our American solutions but still refuse to learn from Canadian or Western European solutions.

6. **National identity**. Of the dozen outcome predictors for individual crises, some translate readily into predictors of national crises. One that doesn't readily translate is the individual characteristic of "ego strength," which instead serves as a metaphor to suggest a related national characteristic: sense of national identity.

What is national identity? It means shared pride in admirable things that characterize one's nation and make it unique. There are many different sources of national identity, including language, military accomplishments, culture, and history. Those sources vary among countries. For example, Finland and Japan both have unique languages that are spoken in no other country, and that are viewed with pride. Chileans, on the contrary, speak the same language as most other South and Central American countries, but paradoxically turn that into a unique identity: "We Chileans are different from all of those other Spanish-speaking Latin American countries, in our political stability and democratic traditions. We are more like Europeans than Latin Americans!" Military accomplishments contribute heavily to the national identity of some countries: Finland (the Winter War), Australia (Gallipoli), the U.S. (World War Two), and Britain (many wars, most recently World War Two and the Falkland Islands War). In many countries national pride and identity focus on culture: for example, Italy's historical preeminence in art and modern preeminence in cuisine and style, Britain's in literature, and Germany's in music. Many countries feel pride in their sports teams. Britain and Italy illustrate pride in memories of their history and world importance — in Italy's case, memories of the Roman Empire 2,000 years ago.

Of our seven countries, a shared sense of national identity is strong in six of them. The exception is Indonesia, where national identity is weaker. This is no criticism of Indonesians: it just reflects the obvious fact that Indonesia didn't come into existence as an independent country until 1949, and wasn't effectively unified even as a colony until around 1910. Hence it's no surprise that Indonesia has experienced secession movements and rebellions. However, Indonesian national identity has recently been growing rapidly, spurred by the spread of the unifying Indonesian language, and by the growth of democracy and citizen involvement.

National identity has been an important contributor to crisis resolution in all of our older countries. Sense of national identity held Meiji Japanese and Finns together, gave those countries the courage to resist powerful external threats, and motivated their citizens to survive privations and national humiliations and to make personal sacrifices in the national cause. Finns even turned in their gold wedding rings to help Finland pay its war reparations to the Soviet Union. National identity enabled post-1945 Germany and Japan to survive crushing military defeat and subsequent occupation. In Australia, national identity has been the focus of Australian reassessment and selective change, revolving around the question: who are we? Sense of national identity contributed to Chilean leftists behaving with restraint when they returned to power after Pinochet's fall: even as fear of the Chilean army receded, Chilean leftists in power, while continuing to hate Pinochet's supporters, adopted a conciliatory policy of building "a Chile for all Chileans," including right-wing admirers of Pinochet as well as left-wing admirers of Allende. That's a remarkable achievement. In contrast, in the U.S. today one hears much emphasis on subgroup identity and less on broad national identity.

Nations' peoples and governments regularly seek to reinforce national identity by recounting history in a way so as to foster national pride. Such recountings of history constitute "national myths." I don't use the word "myth" in its pejorative sense of "a lie," but instead in its neutral sense of "a traditional story, ostensibly with a historical basis, but serving to explain some phenomenon or to promote some purpose." In reality, national myths, told and retold for political purposes, encompass an entire spectrum from truthful recountings to lies.

At one extreme are accounts of the past that are factually accurate, and that do focus on the most important thing happening to that nation at that time, but the recounting is still for political purposes. Examples include the fostering of British and Finnish national pride by accounts of British history during the summer of 1940 that focus just on the Battle of Britain, or accounts of Finnish history during the period December 1939–March 1940 that focus just on the Winter War. Yes, one can argue that those were indeed by far the most consequential things happening in Britain and Finland at the time, *and* those events are still recounted over and over again today for political purposes.

An intermediate stage is an account of the past that is factually correct as far as it goes, but that focuses on just one out of multiple things happening at that time in the history of that country, and that omits other important things. Examples include histories of the early 19th-century U.S. that emphasize the Lewis and Clark transcontinental expedition and other stages in white European exploration and conquest of the West, but that omit killings and displacements of Native Americans and enslavement of African-Americans; histories of Indonesia's independence struggle that describe the battles of the Indonesian Republic against the Dutch, but that don't mention the large groups of Indonesians themselves fighting against the republic; and histories of early 20th-century Australia that recount only Gallipoli, and omit killings and displacements of Aboriginal Australians.

The opposite end of the continuum is accounts of the past that rest heavily on falsehoods. Examples include German accounts attributing Germany's defeat in World War One to German civilian treachery, and Japanese accounts minimizing or denying the Rape of Nanking.

Historians debate whether exact knowledge of the past is possible, whether history inevitably involves a plurality of interpretations, and whether all those alternative interpretations deserve to receive equal weight. Whatever the answers to those questions, the fact remains that national identities get reinforced for political purposes by national myths, that national identities are important to nations, and that the myths supporting them vary in their historical basis.

7. **Honest self-appraisal**. A totally rational visitor from Outer Space who knew nothing of humans and our societies might naïvely assume that, whatever factors lead to failures of human individuals and nations to resolve crises, lack of honest self-appraisal wouldn't be among them. Why, our rational extraterrestrial visitor might reason, would any individual or nation of those admittedly strange humans ruin itself, by choosing to be dishonest with itself?

In fact, honest self-appraisal requires two steps. First, an individual or a nation must possess accurate knowledge. But that can be difficult to acquire; failure to respond successfully to a crisis may be because of lack of information, rather than because of the moral vice of dishonesty. The second step is to evaluate knowledge honestly. Alas, any human familiar with nations or with other individual humans knows that self-deception is common in human affairs.

The most easily understood cases of national honest self-appraisal, or of its absence, involve strong leaders or dictators. In those cases the nation either does or doesn't undertake honest self-appraisal, insofar as its leader does or doesn't. Well-known internationally are the contrasting cases among modern German leaders. Bismarck, an outstanding realist, succeeded in the difficult goal of unifying Germany. Emperor Wilhelm II, an emotionally labile unrealist, needlessly made enemies for Germany and blundered into World War One, which Germany lost. Hitler, far more clever but far more evil, undid his initial successes by unrealism in attacking the Soviet Union and needlessly simultaneously declaring war on the U.S. while already at war with the Soviet Union and Britain. More recently, Germany was fortunate in being led for several years by another realist, Willy Brandt, who had the courage to recognize the need for a painful but honest policy in Eastern Europe (recognizing East Germany and the loss of German territories beyond East Germany), and thereby achieved prerequisites for Germany's re-unification 20 years later.

Less well-known in the West, but equally striking as a contrast between successive leaders, is the case of Indonesia. Its founding president, Sukarno, deluded himself that he was uniquely capable of interpreting even the unconscious wishes of the Indonesian people. While neglecting Indonesia's own problems, he involved himself in the world anti-colonial movement, and he

ordered the Indonesian army to try to take over Malaysian Borneo, against the wishes of its population and over the skepticism of
his own army officers. Unfortunately for Sukarno, army general
Suharto, who became Indonesia's second president, was (until late
in his political career) an outstanding realist whose style was to
proceed cautiously and to act only when he could be confident of
success. In that way, Suharto slowly succeeded in pushing Sukarno
aside, abandoned Sukarno's world pretensions and Malaysian
campaign, and concentrated on Indonesian affairs (albeit often in
evil ways).

The next three cases involve nations that were not dominated by a powerful leader, but that reached national consensus
based on honest self-appraisal. Meiji Japan confronted the painful
truth that the hated Western barbarians were stronger, and that
Japan could gain strength only by learning from the West. Meiji
Japan then acquired accurate knowledge of the West by sending
many government officials and private Japanese citizens to Europe
and the U.S. In contrast, Japan's disastrous entry into World War
Two occurred partly because young but powerful Japanese army
officers in the 1930's lacked first-hand knowledge of the West and
its power. Finns similarly confronted the painful reality that Finland would continue to receive almost no support from potential
allies, and that Finland's policy towards the Soviet Union instead
had to depend on Finland earning Soviet trust and understanding
the Soviet point of view. Finally, Australia reached a national consensus by facing up to the reality that Britain's former economic
and military importance for Australia had faded, and that Asia and
the United States had become more important.

Our last two cases involve the lack of honest self-appraisal
in two nations today. As already mentioned, Japan today does recognize some of its problems, but is currently failing to be realistic
about others. The U.S. is also deficient in honest self-appraisal

today: particularly in that not enough American citizens and politicians take our current major problems seriously. Many Americans also delude themselves by blaming other countries rather than ourselves for our current problems. Skepticism about science is increasingly widespread in the U.S., and that's a very bad portent, because science is basically just the accurate description and understanding of the real world.

8. <u>Historical experience of previous national crises</u>. Confidence derived from having survived previous crises is an important factor for individuals dealing with a new personal crisis. A corresponding factor at the national level is significant for several of the nations that we consider in this book, and for other nations as well. An example is modern Japan, with confidence derived from the extraordinary achievement of Meiji Japan in changing rapidly and gaining sufficient strength to resist the risk of dismemberment by the West, and eventually to defeat two Western powers (Russia in 1904–1905, and German colonial troops in 1914). Meiji Japan's success is all the more impressive when one contemplates the simultaneous failure of the much larger and apparently much stronger Chinese Empire to resist Western pressure.

Finland provides another case of national self-confidence derived from previous successes. For Finns, the pride gained from fighting off Soviet attacks during World War Two is so important that the hundred-year anniversary in 2017 of Finland's independence focused on the Winter War as much as on Finland's independence. Among countries that are not the focus of this book, another example is the United Kingdom, with its history of success in eventually defeating Hitler in World War Two with the U.S. and Soviet Union as allies; even more, fighting entirely alone against Hitler for the year from the fall of France in June 1940 until Hitler's invasion of the Soviet Union in June 1941; and especially from the

Battle of Britain, in which the British air force (the RAF) in the latter half of 1940 defeated the German air force (the Luftwaffe) in air battles over Britain, thereby thwarting German plans to invade Britain. Whatever difficulties Britain has faced from 1945 to the present day, the British often reflect: nothing could be more difficult than was the Battle of Britain; we succeeded then, so we can succeed against anything else now.

Past successes also contributed to American self-confidence. The successes on which we look back include the outcome of the American Revolution; our acquisition, exploration, and conquest of the entire width of the North American continent; holding the U.S. together in a long civil war that still remains the bloodiest war with the highest casualties in American history; and U.S. military successes simultaneously against Germany and Japan in World War Two.

Finally, Indonesia, as the youngest country discussed in this book, has the shortest history of successful coping from which to derive confidence. But, as I saw in the lobby exhibit in my Indonesian hotel in 1979, Indonesians still retell the success of their independence struggles against the Dutch in 1945–1949, and of their take-over of Dutch New Guinea in 1961. Those successes play a big role in Indonesian national self-confidence.

9. Patience with national failure. Even more than individual problems, national problems don't lend themselves to quick solutions, or to guaranteed success on the first try at solving them. Whether the problems are national or individual, crises tend to be complex, to require trying a series of possible solutions before identifying one that works, and thus to call for patience and for toleration of frustration, ambiguity, and failure. Hence even if national decisions were made by just a single absolute dictator, they would require patience. But most national decisions instead involve negotiations between groups with divergent interests. Thus, national crisis-solving requires extra patience.

Most of the countries that we have discussed have been steeled to patience by the experience of failure and defeat. That was especially true for Meiji Japan, Germany, Finland, and modern Japan. It took more than 50 years from Perry's 1853 uninvited visit ending Japan's isolation before Japan was able to fight and win its first war against a Western power. It took 45 years, after Germany's de-facto partition in 1945, for Germany to achieve re-unification. For decades after the end of Finland's Continuation War against the Soviet Union in 1944, Finland was constantly re-assessing its policy towards the Soviet Union, and trying to figure out which Soviet pressures it could safely refuse, and which independent actions it could safely adopt without provoking yet another Soviet invasion. Japan since World War Two has had to survive American occupation, decades of material and economic rebuilding, chronic economic and social problems, and natural disasters such as earthquakes, typhoons, and tsunamis. All four of those countries (counting Japan twice) experienced frustration, but resisted the pitfall of acting quickly and foolishly. Patience proved essential to their eventual successes.

The exception to these stories of patience is the modern U.S. Of course one can object: Americans have indeed tolerated initial failure, shown patience, and persisted through setbacks at many times in our history: notably, during the four years of the Civil War, the dozen years of the Great Depression, and the four years of World War Two. But the U.S. has not been steeled to crushing defeat and occupation, as have Germany, Japan, France, and many other countries. Having won all four of our foreign wars from the Mexican War of 1846–1848 to World War Two, Americans found it hard to come to terms with the effective stalemate ending the Korean War, to swallow defeat in the Vietnam War, and to tolerate protracted military stalemate in Afghanistan. In these first decades of the 21st century the U.S. has been struggling with complex internal social, economic, and political problems that do not lend themselves to quick solutions. They instead require patience and compromises that we have not yet displayed.

10. <u>Situation-specific national flexibility</u>. Psychologists use the dichotomy of flexibility versus rigidity for characterizing people. Personal flexibility means that a person is receptive to considering different new approaches to a problem. Personal rigidity means that a person believes that there is only one approach to any problem. That dichotomy has proved important in understanding differences among individuals in their success in resolving crises by devising new approaches. While any individual may be flexible in one area and rigid in another area, psychologists also recognize a trait of flexibility or rigidity that may pervade a person's character, that varies among individuals, and that is influenced especially by childhood upbringing and life experiences.

When we turn from individuals to nations, convincing examples of pervasive national flexibility or rigidity seem to me rare. The sole example that is familiar to me, and for which there are understandable reasons why the nation came to be that way, is a nation not otherwise discussed in this book: historical Iceland. During the centuries when Iceland was governed by Denmark, Icelanders frequently frustrated Danish governors by their apparent rigidity and hostility to proposed changes. Whatever well-intentioned suggestions for improvement the Danish government offered, Icelanders' response was usually, "No, we don't want to try something different; we want to continue doing things in our traditional way." Icelanders refused Danish suggestions about improving fishing boats, fish exports, fishing nets, grain agriculture, mining, and rope-making.

That national rigidity is understandable when one considers Iceland's environmental fragility. Iceland lies at high latitudes, with a cool climate and short growing season. Icelandic soils are fragile, light, formed by volcanic ash, susceptible to erosion, and slow to regenerate. Iceland's vegetation is easily stripped off by grazing or by wind or water erosion, and then is slow to regrow. In the early centuries of Viking colonization, Icelanders tried various subsistence strategies, all with disastrous results, until they eventually devised a set of sustainable agriculture methods. Having devised that set, they didn't want to consider changes in their subsistence methods, or in other aspects of life, because of their painful experience: having finally devised one strategy that worked, whatever else they tried made things worse.

Perhaps there are other countries besides historical Iceland that can be characterized as flexible or rigid in many respects. But it seems much more common to find that national flexibility is situation-specific: a country is flexible in some spheres but rigid in other spheres. Finns have adamantly refused to compromise on their country being occupied, but have been extraordinarily flexible in compromising on what other nations consider inalienable rights of a democracy — such as not permitting other nations to change the rules for a presidential election in one's own country. Meiji Japan refused to compromise on the role of the emperor and traditional Japanese religion, but was extraordinarily flexible in compromising on political institutions. Australia for a long time refused to compromise on its British identity, while simultaneously developing a society much more individualistic and egalitarian than Britain's.

The U.S. poses interesting questions with respect to flexibility. Americans can be characterized as flexible as individuals, based for example on their frequent house moves, on the average once every five years. The history of American politics has

441

been marked by signs of national flexibility, such as our frequent transitions of federal government control between the major political parties, and our major parties frequently co-opting programs of nascent new parties and thereby aborting those parties' development. Conversely, though, American politics for the last two decades have been characterized by increasing refusal to compromise.

Hence I expect that it usually won't be profitable for social scientists to generalize about a nation as being uniformly either flexible or rigid. Instead, it may prove worth considering whether nations can be classified as variously flexible or rigid independently along multiple axes. That question remains a challenge for the future.

11. National core values. Core values for individuals underlie a person's moral code, and often constitute what a person is willing to die for. For individuals, core values may make it either easier or else harder to resolve crises. On the positive side, core values can provide clarity and a position of strength, from which one can contemplate changing other aspects of one's life. On the negative side, people may cling to core values when they have become no longer appropriate under changed circumstances, and when they thus interfere with a person's solving a crisis.

Nations also have core values that are widely accepted by a nation's citizens, and that in some cases its citizens are willing to die for. Core values are related to national identities, but there are differences. For example, Finland's national identity is related especially to its unique language and cultural achievements, but the core value for which so many Finns died in their war against the Soviet Union was Finnish independence; that, rather than the Finnish language, was what the Soviet Union sought to destroy. Similarly, German national identity revolves around the

German language and culture and the shared histories of Germanic peoples. But German core values include what many Americans decry as "socialism," and what most Germans view as admirable: government support of public benefits; restriction of individual rights in order to favor the common good; and not letting important public benefits depend on selfish private interests that may or may not see pay-off in supporting them. For example, the German government provides large-scale funding for the arts (including opera companies, symphony orchestras, and theaters), provides good medical care and financial security in old age for all Germans, and enforces the maintenance of traditional local architectural styles and woodlands; those are among modern Germany's core values.

Just as true for individuals, core values of nations can make it either easier or harder for a nation to adopt selective change. Core values of the past may continue to be appropriate in the present, and may motivate citizens to make sacrifices in defense of those values. Core values motivated Finns to die in the successful defense of their country's independence, Meiji Japanese to make big efforts to catch up to the West, and Germans and Japanese after World War Two to work hard and to put up with privation in order to rebuild their shattered countries. But national core values of the past may also prove inappropriate today, and clinging to such outdated values may prevent a nation from adopting necessary selective changes. That was the central issue in Australia's slowly unfolding crisis after World War Two: Australia's role as an outpost of Britain made less and less sense, and it proved painful for many Australians to abandon that role. Another example is provided by Japan after World War Two: while core values of Japanese culture and respect for the emperor give Japan strength, Japan's clinging to its former policy of unlimited exploitation of overseas natural resources is hurting Japan.

   12. **Freedom from geopolitical constraints**. For individuals, external constraints restricting one's ability to adopt selective changes include financial constraints, the burden of responsibility for other people, and physical danger. Nations also face constraints on their freedom of choice, but the types are different from those limiting individuals: especially, geopolitical ones resulting from powerful neighbors, and economic limitations. Among our 12 factors, this is the one *historically* exhibiting the widest variation among our sample of nations. The U.S. has been outstandingly unconstrained; four nations (Meiji Japan, Chile, Indonesia, and Australia) have been constrained in some respects and relatively free in others; and two (Finland and Germany) have been extremely constrained. I'll discuss below how geopolitical constraints today differ from the historical ones that I'll summarize first.

   The U.S. has been historically unconstrained because of isolation by wide oceans on two sides, land borders with unthreatening neighbors on the two other sides, natural advantages of geography within the U.S., and large population and wealth. More than any other country in the world, the U.S. has been free to do as it pleases within its own borders. At the opposite extreme, Finland and Germany are both severely constrained. Finland has the misfortune to share Europe's longest land border with Russia (formerly the Soviet Union). Recent Finnish history has been dominated by the dilemma of how to preserve as much freedom of choice as possible despite this severe constraint. Germany has the misfortune to lie in the center of Europe, and to be exposed to more neighbors (several of them large and powerful) across land and sea borders than any other European country. German leaders who ignored this basic fact of geography (Emperor Wilhelm II and Hitler) plunged Germany into disaster twice within the 20th century. Germany twice required exceptional gifted leaders (Bismarck and

Willy Brandt) to negotiate the minefield of geopolitical constraints upon Germany.

Our other four countries furnish a mixed picture. Meiji Japan, despite being an island nation, was seriously threatened by prowling Western powers. Chile, protected by the Andes on the east and by deserts in the north, now faces no significant threats within South America; but the Chilean economy was still weakened by pressure from the distant U.S. during Allende's presidency. Indonesia is geographically protected by oceans and no nearby threatening neighbors, but had to struggle for independence against the Netherlands located half-way around the world. Indonesian governments since independence have been constrained by Indonesia's internal problems of poverty and rapid population growth. Finally, Australia, despite being remote and geographically protected by oceans, was nevertheless threatened and bombed by Japan in World War Two. All of these countries have thus experienced intermittent constraints on their freedom of action, but not as serious and chronic as the ones constantly operating on Finland and Germany.

Geopolitical constraints have obviously changed globally in recent millennia. In the remote past, local human populations were largely self-sufficient, received and sent goods and information over relatively short distances, and faced military threats only from immediate neighbors. Within the last five centuries, communications and economic and military connections have become global. Military threats by sea arrived from around the world: the Dutch began to occupy Indonesia around 1595, and Commodore Perry's American fleet breached Japan's isolation in 1853. Japan formerly was economically self-sufficient, with negligible imports and exports; now Japan's industrial economy is severely limited by natural resources and dependent on imports and exports. The U.S. is also a major importer and exporter. Chile depended on U.S. capital and technology to develop its copper mines. Chile's President Allende, and to a lesser extent Indonesia's President Sukarno, were subjected to U.S. economic pressure and U.S. support for their domestic opponents. Three of this book's seven nations were bombed by planes from enemy aircraft carriers originating thousands of miles away: the U.S. by Japan's Pearl Harbor raid of December 1941, Australia by Japan's Darwin raid of February 1942, and Japan by the U.S.'s Doolittle Raid of April 1942. Germany and Japan suffered massive attacks by land-based bombers during World War Two. The first rocket attacks were by German V-2s on Britain, France, and Belgium in 1944 and 1945, launched from 200 miles away. Now, ICBMs are capable of hitting targets anywhere in the world across the widest ocean barriers.

All of these developments mean that historical geopolitical constraints have been greatly weakened. Does that mean that geography is now irrelevant? Of course not! Finland's foreign policy is still dictated by its long land border with Russia. Germany's foreign policy is still dictated by its nine land neighbors, and by the eight other nations that it faces across the Baltic and North Seas. Chile's deserts and high mountains ensured that it has never been invaded in the two centuries since its independence; it is unlikely to be invaded in the foreseeable future. The U.S. could be hit by missiles but remains prohibitively difficult to invade and conquer, and Australia nearly as difficult. In short, Finland's motto "Our geography will never change" continues to apply to every country.

———

That summarizes what we've learned about the question that initially motivated this book: the relevance of the dozen factors suggested by outcomes of individual crises to the outcomes of national crises. Let's now consider two questions that were not my initial motive for this study, but that have proved to be the questions that people most often ask when we get into a conversation about national crises. Those two questions concern the role of crises as a driver of national policy change, and the role of leaders.

Do countries require a crisis to motivate them to act, or do nations ever act in anticipation of problems? The crises discussed in this book illustrate both types of responses to this frequently asked question.

Meiji Japan avoided dealing with the growing danger from the West, until forced into responding to Perry's visit. From the Meiji Restoration of 1868 onwards, however, Japan did not require any further external shocks to motivate it to embark on its crash program of change: Japan instead changed in anticipation of the risk of further pressure from the West.

Similarly, Finland ignored Soviet concerns until it was forced to pay attention by the Soviet attack of 1939. But from 1944 onwards, the Finns did not require any further Soviet attacks to galvanize them: instead, their foreign policy aimed at constantly anticipating and forestalling Soviet pressure.

In Chile, Allende's policies were in response to Chile's chronic polarization, and not in response to a sudden crisis, so Allende was anticipating future problems as well as addressing current ones. In contrast, the Chilean military launched their coup in response to what the military perceived as the acute crisis provoked by Allende's declared intention to turn Chile into a Marxist state.

In Indonesia, both types of responses were at play. Communist-sympathetic elements in the Indonesian military launched their coup in anticipation of actions that they feared from an anti-communist Council of Generals. The rest of the Indonesian military apparently reacted in response to the crisis of the October 1, 1965 coup, but there are reasons to suspect that the military had anticipated that coup and had already prepared their response.

Post-war Germany offers two of modern history's outstanding

examples of nations acting in anticipation of, rather than responding to crises. Chancellor Konrad Adenauer's program of setting up the European Coal and Steel Community, then setting up economic and political structures leading to the European Common Market and the European Union, was adopted explicitly to anticipate a crisis and to prevent it from ever happening (Chapter 11). After the horrors of World War Two, Adenauer and other European leaders sought to avoid a World War Three, by integrating Western Europe so that Western European countries wouldn't want to and couldn't attack one another. Similarly, Willy Brandt's Ostpolitik was not launched in response to an immediate crisis in Eastern Europe (Chapter 6). Brandt faced no urgent need to recognize East Germany or other Eastern European communist governments, nor to acknowledge Germany's loss of its eastern territories. Instead, Brandt did so in order to anticipate opportunities in the distant future, and to create stable conditions for the re-unification of Germany whenever that became possible — as finally proved to be the case.

Japan today is struggling with its seven major problems, without taking decisive action to address any of them. Will Japan succeed in solving these problems by slow change as did post-war Australia, or will it require a sudden crisis to motivate Japan to act vigorously? Similarly, the U.S. today is not taking decisive action in response to our big problems, except for our quick response to the World Trade Center attack by invading Afghanistan, and our response to the supposed presence of weapons of mass destruction in Iraq by invading Iraq.

Thus, the governments in four of the cases discussed in this book required crises to galvanize them into action, and in two cases today are not taking decisive action in the absence of galvanizing crises. Once crises struck, however, Meiji Japan, Finland, Chile, and Indonesia all set out on programs of change that required years or decades, without requiring further crises to keep motivating them. But our nations do provide examples of pre-emptive actions to prevent crises from materializing (Indonesia and Germany) or getting worse (Chile). Of course, all governments are constantly taking actions for the future to deal with less urgent current or anticipated problems.

Hence the answer to the question "Does it require a crisis to galvanize a nation into adopting major selective change?" is similar to the answer for individuals. We as individuals act constantly to deal with current or anticipated problems. Occasionally, we foresee a big new problem coming at us, and we try to head it off before it hits us. But, for nations as for individuals, there are much inertia and resistance to overcome. Something big and bad suddenly happening motivates us more than do slowly developing problems, and also more than the prospect of something big and bad happening in the future. I'm reminded of Samuel Johnson's saying: "Depend upon it, sir, when a man knows he is to be hanged in a fortnight, it concentrates his mind wonderfully."

——

Do leaders make a difference? The other question that people often raise when they and I fall into conversation about national crises concerns the long-running historical debate as to whether national leaders have a significant effect on history, or whether history would have unfolded in the same way regardless of who was a country's leader at a particular time. At the one extreme is the so-called "Great-Man" view of the British historian Thomas Carlyle (1795–1881), who asserted that history is dominated by the deeds of great men, such as Oliver Cromwell and Frederick the Great. Similar views are still common today among military historians, who tend to emphasize the decisions of generals and wartime political leaders. At the opposite extreme was the author Leo Tolstoy, who maintained that leaders and generals had minimal influence on the course of history. To make his point, Tolstoy included in his novel *War and Peace* fictitious accounts of battles in which generals issue orders, but the orders are irrelevant to what is actually happening on the battlefield.

That view, that history's course depends upon lots of details rather than on policies or decisions of great men, is now common among historians. They often argue that a leader appears to be influential only because he (or she) pursues policies resonating with views already held by his or her countrymen; that otherwise unimpressive politicians may appear to become great because of the opportunities that they enjoy at the time, not because of their personal qualities (examples often suggested are the American presidents James Polk and Harry Truman); and that leaders can only choose from a limited set of options determined by other factors of history. A view intermediate between the Great-Man view and the leaders-don't-matter view is exemplified by the German sociologist Max Weber (1846–1920), who maintained that certain types of leaders, so-called charismatic leaders, could sometimes influence history under some circumstances.

This debate remains unresolved. Each historian tends to hold some a priori general view based on principle rather than on some valid method for assessing empirical evidence, and to apply that view to individual case studies. For example, all biographies of Hitler have to recount the same key events of his life. But proponents of the Great-Man view relate those events while asserting that Hitler was an unusually effective and evil leader who caused developments in Germany to turn out differently from how they would have turned out under some other leader. Opponents of the Great-Man view relate those same events while portraying Hitler as a voice reflecting widespread features of German society at the time. The debate is impossible to resolve by narratives and individual case studies.

Instead, a promising approach comes from recent analyses that combine three characteristics: a large sample of many historical events, or of all historical events of some defined type; using "natural experiments of history," i.e., comparing otherwise-similar historical trajectories in which a certain perturbation did or did not occur (I'll give two examples in the following paragraphs); and measuring the outcomes quantitatively. Two outstanding such papers have been published by Benjamin Jones at Northwestern University and Benjamin Olken of the Massachusetts Institute of Technology.

In their first paper, Jones and Olken ask: what happens to the national economic growth rate when a leader dies in office from natural causes, as compared to what happens at randomly selected times when a leader doesn't die in office from natural causes? This comparison offers a natural experiment to test the effect of a change in leadership. If the Great-Man view is correct, then a leader's death should be more likely to be followed by changes of economic growth rates — either decreasing or increasing, depending on whether the leader's policies really made a difference by being good or bad, respectively — than after random moments when a leader doesn't happen to die. For their database, Jones and Olken took every instance in the world of a national leader dying from natural causes while in office between 1945 and 2000. They succeeded in assembling 57 such cases: mostly deaths due to heart attacks or cancer, plus a few plane crashes, a drowning, a fall from a horse, a fire, and a broken leg. Those events really do constitute a random perturbation: a leader's economic policies don't affect the likelihood that that leader will accidentally drown. It turned out that economic growth rates were much more likely to change following a leader's natural death than following random moments when a leader didn't die. That suggests that, averaged over many cases, leadership does tend to affect economic growth.

In their second paper, Jones and Olken ask: what happens when a leader is assassinated, instead of dying of natural causes? Of course, assassinations are not at all random events: they are more likely to be attempted under some conditions (e.g., if citizens are dissatisfied with low economic growth) than under other conditions. Hence Jones and Olken compared *successful* assassination attempts with *unsuccessful* attempts, when the bullet missed. That really is a random difference: national political conditions may have influenced the frequency of assassination attempts but don't affect the assassin's aim. The database consisted of all 298 assassination attempts on national leaders from 1875 to 2005: 59 of them successful, 239 unsuccessful. It turned out that successful attempts were more likely than unsuccessful attempts to be followed by a change in national political institutions.

In both studies the effect of a leader's death was stronger for deaths of autocratic leaders than for those of democratic leaders — and stronger for autocrats with no constraints on their power than for autocrats constrained by legislatures or by political parties. That's as we'd expect: strong leaders with unlimited power can have more effect (whether for good or for bad) than leaders with only limited power. Thus, these studies agree on a general conclusion: leaders *sometimes* make a difference. But it depends on the type of leader, and on the type of effect examined.

———

Let's now tie these natural experiments on the roles of leaders to the seven countries discussed in this book. My goal is to see whether our leaders fit the patterns recognized by Jones and Olken, and what further questions they pose for testing. The histories of our seven countries have suggested the following appraisals of their leadership to many historians:

In Meiji Japan, no single leader was dominant; several leaders shared similar policies.

In Finland, political leaders and citizens were virtually unanimous in their agreement that Finland should do its utmost to resist Soviet attack. (But it's sometimes suggested that Field Marshal Mannerheim's skills as military commander, and President Paasikivi's and President Kekkonen's abilities to win the trust of Soviet leaders after the war, affected Finland's fate positively.)

In Chile, Pinochet was considered (even by his fellow generals) decisive and unusual in his cruelty, his tenacity at holding on to power, and his choice of economic policy.

In Indonesia, Sukarno and Suharto are both considered decisive leaders, but subsequent presidents are not.

In post-war Germany, Willy Brandt is often suggested as having played a unique role in reversing previous West German government foreign policy, recognizing Eastern European communist governments and German frontiers, and thereby making possible Germany's subsequent re-unification. In earlier German history, Bismarck, Emperor Wilhelm II, and Hitler are regularly cited as examples of unique leaders who made a difference for better or for worse.

In Australia there has been no single clearly dominant leader. The closest possible example is Prime Minister Gough Whitlam and his crash program of change, but Whitlam himself acknowledged that his reforms were a "recognition of what has already happened."

In the United States, President Franklin Roosevelt is credited with gradually preparing the U.S. for World War Two against the will of American isolationists (who may initially have constituted a majority of Americans), and for his efforts to pull the U.S. out of the Great Depression. In 19th-century American history, President Lincoln is considered to have played a unique role in the course of the Civil War.

In short, our seven countries offer examples of nine leaders (six autocratic, three democratic) often rated as having made a difference. In addition, in countries other than the seven discussed in this book, the leaders most often argued to have made a difference in modern times include Winston Churchill in the United Kingdom, Lenin and Stalin in the Soviet Union, Mao in China, de Gaulle in France, Cavour in Italy, and Gandhi in India. Thus, we have a short list of 16 leaders commonly viewed as having made a difference. Of the 16, 11 were in autocratic regimes, five in democracies. At first sight, this outcome seems to conform to the conclusions of Jones and Olken about the greater effect of leaders in autocracies. But I haven't tabulated relative numbers of all autocratic and democratic leaders worldwide over this time span, so I can't say which, if either, type of leader is disproportionately represented.

Our small dataset does suggest two hypotheses worth testing by methods similar to those of Jones and Olken: by assembling a large dataset comprising a natural experiment, and measuring outcomes quantitatively.

One hypothesis stems from the observation that, of the four democratic leaders most often suggested as having been uniquely influential (Roosevelt, Lincoln, Churchill, and de Gaulle), at least three had their effects or their greatest effects in wartime. Almost all of Lincoln's presidency took place during the American Civil War. Churchill, Roosevelt, and de Gaulle served both in war and in peace, but two or all three are viewed as having had their most decisive effects in wartime (Churchill as wartime prime minister from 1940 to 1945 but not as peace prime minister from 1951 to 1955; de Gaulle as wartime general, then as president during the Algerian uprising of 1959–1962; and Roosevelt after the outbreak of World War Two in Europe in 1939 but also during the Depression). These outcomes fit the observation of Jones and Olken that leaders have more decisive influence, the fewer constraints on their power: democratic leaders exercise more concentrated powers in wartime.

The other hypothesis that our results suggest for testing is that leaders make the most difference under circumstances where they face strong opposition (whether in democracies or autocracies) from people espousing a very different policy, and where the leaders nevertheless eventually get their views to prevail, usually by cautious step-by-step efforts. The examples are: Piedmont's Prime Minister Cavour and Prussia's Chancellor Bismarck slowly achieving the unifications of Italy and of Germany respectively over strong opposition from foreign powers, from other Italians or Germans respectively, and even from their own kings; Churchill convincing an initially closely divided British war cabinet to reject Lord Halifax's proposal to seek a negotiated peace with Hitler, then persuading Americans to make their first priority the war against Germany rather than the war against Japan (initially the obvious priority for America after the Japanese attack on Pearl Harbor); Roosevelt slowly preparing the U.S. for World War Two over the opposition of American isolationists; de Gaulle slowly convincing both his countrymen and Algerians to reach a negotiated settlement of the Algerian struggle for independence; Suharto's slowly pushing aside Indonesia's beloved founding President Sukarno; and Willy Brandt persuading West Germans to swallow the bitter pill of renouncing much former German territory, over the fierce opposition of the CDU Party, which had until then ruled West Germany uninterruptedly for two decades.

———

This book has been an initial step in a program of comparative studies of national crises — an exploration of a small sample of nations, investigated by narrative methods. How can this study be extended so as to deepen our understanding? I suggest two extensions: a larger and more random sample, and a more rigorous analysis translating outcomes and hypothesized predictors from verbal concepts into operationalized variables.

First, the sample. My sample of nations is not only small, but also selected non-randomly. I selected these countries not because they offer a random subset of the world's 216 nations, but because they are drawn from the countries that I know best. As a result, they consist of two European nations, two Asian nations, one each from North America and South America, and Australia. Five of the seven are wealthy. All seven are currently democracies, although two were dictatorships during the period that I discuss. All except Indonesia have long histories of independence or (Finland) autonomy, and of strong institutions. Only one recently emerged from colonialism to independence. Missing are any African nations, any current dictatorship, and any very poor nation. All six for which I discussed past crises survived their crisis with some degree of success. None illustrates an unambiguous failure to respond to a crisis by means of appropriate selective changes. That's obviously a non-random sample. Hence it remains a challenge for the future to see what conclusions a broader sample of nations will reveal.

Second, the most important methodological challenge for the future is to extend my book's narrative, verbal, qualitative analysis by a more rigorous quantitative analysis. As I mentioned in my book's introduction, a recent trend in some of the social sciences, especially in economics and economic history and some areas of psychology, has been to replace narratives based on single case studies with approaches combining quantitative data, graphs, large sample sizes, statistical tests of significance, natural experiments, and operationalized measures. By "operationalized measures," I mean translating a verbal concept into something that can be measured by a series of operations on presumed correlates or expressions of that concept.

The two papers by Jones and Olken discussed earlier in this chapter are examples of that approach. They replaced single case studies of what some particular leader did or didn't do with an analysis of 57 or 298 leaders simultaneously. They took advantage of natural experiments in order to compare outcomes associated with the presence and the absence of a particular leader, by examining countries before and after a leader had died of a natural death, or else countries in which an assassination attempt had failed or succeeded. Finally, they expressed putative outcome variables operationally either by means of measurable numerical quantities (e.g., economic growth rates), or else by means of defined scales (e.g., a scale of governmental institutions ranging from autocracies with minimal constraints on a leader to democracies with maximal constraints on a leader).

In order to apply that approach to my study of national crises, we would need operationalized measures of the outcomes and of the postulated factors that I discussed, including "acknowledgment," "acceptance of responsibility," "national identity," "freedom from constraints," "patience at dealing with failure," "flexibility," "honest self-appraisal," "change or lack of change," and "success or failure at resolving a national crisis." Possible starting points for developing such operationalized measures include the data in social science databases, such as the World Values Survey led by Ronald Inglehart, the Economic Values Survey, the European Social Survey, the Economic and Social Survey of Asia and the Pacific, and books by Geert Hofstede, Michael Minkov, and others. I put effort into trying to use these data sources to devise operationalized measures for some of my variables, before reluctantly concluding that that would require a large project beyond the scope of this book's narrative survey, which already took me six years even without devising operationalized measures. Such quantitative approaches need to be developed not only for the national crises that are this book's focus, but also for the individual crises that I discussed in Chapter 1. While psychologists have operationalized and tested a few of the variables postulated in that chapter as affecting the outcomes of individual crises, much more remains to be done even for individual crises. Hence the same limitations of narrative style that apply to my study of national crises, and to most historical studies of leadership, also apply to most studies of individual crises.

———

What can we learn from history? This is a general question, of which a specific sub-question is: what can we learn from our seven nations' responses to the crises discussed in this book? A nihilistic answer is: nothing! History's course, say many historians, is too complicated, the outcome of too many independent uncontrolled variables and unforeseeable changes, to permit us to learn anything from the past. In June 1944, who could have predicted correctly the post-war map of Eastern Europe? It would have turned out to be very different, if the would-be assassin Claus von Stauffenberg had succeeded in pushing his briefcase carrying a time bomb 20 inches closer to Hitler on July 20, 1944, and if as a result Hitler had been killed rather than just been wounded on that date, when Soviet armies were still beyond Germany's frontiers, instead of Hitler's actual suicide on April 30, 1945, when Soviet armies had conquered Berlin and all of Eastern Europe and Eastern Germany.

Yes, of course much about history is unpredictable. Nevertheless, there are two sorts of lessons to be learned. But first, as background, let's consider corresponding lessons to be drawn from understanding of individual people, because (once again) there are parallels between the histories of nations and the lives of individual people.

What, if anything, can we learn from the life histories and biographies of individual people? Aren't people, like nations, so complicated, so different from one another, and so subject to unforeseeable events that it's difficult to predict the behavior of one person, let alone to extrapolate from one person's behavior to the behavior of another person? Of course not! Despite the difficulties, most of us still find it useful to devote a large fraction of our lives to trying to anticipate the likely future behavior of individuals close to us, based on our understanding their personal life histories. In addition, training enables psychologists, and "people skills" enable many of us laypeople, to generalize our experience of people whom we already know, so as to anticipate the behavior of new people whom we encounter. That's why it's instructive to read biographies even of people whom we can never encounter, and thereby to broaden our database for understanding human behavior.

I write these lines just after spending an evening with two women friends, one of them a psychologically naïve optimist in her 20's, the other a perceptive person in her 70's. The younger woman was devastated by the recent break-up of her relationship with a fascinating man who had seemed so caring, but who suddenly, after several years, cruelly and without warning abandoned the woman. But as the younger woman related her story, even before reaching the devastating denouement, the older woman (without having met the man) recognized the warning signs that the man was a charming but destructive narcissist, of whom she had come to understand quite a few. That illustrates why experience of a wide range of people, and reflecting on them, are useful. There really are broad themes in human behavior, even though everyone differs in detail from everyone else.

What are corresponding types of lessons to be drawn from attention to human history? One type consists of specific lessons about the likely future behavior of a particular country, based on understanding the history of that country. For instance, Finland is a small democratic country that works hard to maintain good relations with its autocratic neighbor Russia, maintains a well-trained army, and doesn't count on other countries to protect it. The reasons for those Finnish policies become clear from Finland's recent history. Anyone ignorant of Finnish history is unlikely to understand why Finland pursues and will continue to pursue those policies — e.g., anyone like me when I first visited Finland in 1959, ignorant of Finnish history, and asked my Finnish host why Finland didn't stand up to Soviet pressure in the belief that the U.S. would protect Finland.

Another type of lesson to be drawn from history consists of general themes. Again, take Finland and Russia as an example. Along with features specific to Finland and Russia, their relationship exemplifies a general theme: the dangers hanging over small countries near aggressive large countries. There is no universal solution to that danger. It's the subject of one of the earliest, and still one of the most cited and most gripping, passages in written history: the pages of Book 5 of the history of the Peloponnesian War, composed by the Athenian historian Thucydides in the fifth century BC. Thucydides described how the citizens of the small Greek island of Melos responded to pressure from the powerful Athenian Empire. In a passage now known as the Melian Dialogue, Thucydides reconstructed the gut-wrenching negotiations between the Melians and the Athenians: the Melians bargaining for their freedom and their lives, attempting to convince the Athenians not to use force; and the Athenians warning the Melians to be realistic. Thucydides then briefly related the outcome: the Melians refused Athenian demands, just as the Finns two millennia later initially refused Soviet demands; the Athenians besieged Melos; the Melians resisted successfully for some time; but they eventually had to surrender; and — the Athenians killed all the Melian men and enslaved all the women and children.

Of course, the Finns did not end up massacred and enslaved by the Russians, illustrating that the Melian dilemma's outcome and the best strategy vary greatly from case to case. Nevertheless, there is a universal lesson: small countries threatened by large countries should remain alert, consider alternative options, and appraise those options realistically. While this lesson may seem so embarrassingly obvious as to be not worth mentioning, sadly it has often been ignored. It was ignored by the Melians; it was ignored by the Paraguayans, who waged a disastrous war against the combined forces of the much larger Brazil and Argentina plus Uruguay from 1865 to 1870, resulting in the deaths of 60% of Paraguay's population; it was ignored by Finland in 1939; it was ignored by Japan in 1941, when Japan simultaneously attacked the United States, Britain, the Netherlands, Australia, and China while Russia was hostile; and it was ignored by Ukraine in its recent disastrous confrontation with Russia.

If I've now persuaded you not to dismiss the possibility that we can learn something useful from history, what can we learn specifically from the histories of the national crises discussed in this book? Many general themes have emerged. One set of themes consists of the behaviors that have helped our seven nations to deal with crises. Those behaviors include: acknowledging when one's nation is in a crisis; accepting responsibility for change, rather than just blaming other nations and retreating into victimhood; building a fence to identify the national feature(s) needing to be changed, so as not to be overwhelmed with a sense that nothing about one's country is working adequately; identifying other countries from which to seek help; identifying other countries' models that have solved problems similar to the problems now facing one's own country; being patient, and recognizing that the first solution attempted may not work and that several successive attempts may be necessary; reflecting on which core values continue to be appropriate, and which are no longer appropriate; and practicing honest self-appraisal.

Another theme concerns national identity. Young countries need to construct a national identity, as Indonesia, Botswana, and Rwanda have been doing. For older countries, national identities may need revision, as may core values; Australia illustrates such revision in recent times.

Still another theme involves uncontrollable factors that influence crisis outcomes. A nation is stuck with its actual experience of previous crisis-solving, and with its geopolitical constraints. More experience can't suddenly be constructed, and constraints can't be wished away. But a nation can still take them realistically into account, as did Germany under Bismarck and Willy Brandt.

Pessimists may respond to these suggestions by protesting: "How absurdly obvious! We don't need Jared Diamond's book to tell us to practice honest self-appraisal, to look to other countries for models, to avoid retreating into victimhood, and so on!" No, we do need a book, because it's undeniable that those "obvious" requirements have so often been ignored, and are still so often ignored today. People who paid with their lives for ignoring "obvious" requirements in the past included all Melian men, hundreds of thousands of Paraguayans, and millions of Japanese. People whose ignoring of "obvious" requirements threatens their well-being today include my fellow several hundred million Americans.

A pessimist might also respond, "Yes, sadly we do often ignore the obvious, but a book can't change that blindness. Thucydides' Melian Dialogue has already been available to us for over two millennia, yet nations still make the same mistakes. What good can yet another book do?" Well, there are encouraging reasons why we authors keep trying. More people are literate readers today than ever before in world history. We know far more about world history, and can make much better documented arguments, than did Thucydides. More countries are democracies, which means that more citizens can have political input, than at any time in the past.

While ignorant leaders abound, some national leaders read widely, and it's now easier for them to learn from history than in the past. I've been pleasantly surprised to encounter heads of state, and many other politicians, who told me of having been influenced by my own previous books. The whole world now faces global problems — but within the past century, and especially within recent decades, the world has been developing institutions for addressing global problems.

Those are among my reasons for not listening to the pessimists and giving up hope, but for continuing to write about history, in order that we'll have the option of learning from history, if we so choose. In particular, crises have often challenged nations in the past. They are continuing to do so today. But our modern nations and our modern world don't have to grope in the dark as they try to respond. Familiarity with changes that did or didn't work in the past can serve us as a guide.

Acknowledgments

I acknowledge, with pleasure and gratitude, the many friends and colleagues whose contributions made this book possible. They earned badges of heroism for their devoted efforts.

I owe the idea for the book to my wife Marie Cohen.

My editor Tracy Behar, and my agent John Brockman, shaped and shepherded my text from its conception to its completion. Eileen Chetti polished it as copy-editor, Betsy Uhrig as production editor.

Lynda and Stewart Resnick, Peter Kaufman, Sue and Keith Tibbles, Frank Caufield, Skip and Heather Brittenham, and Conservation International made this six-year project possible by their support.

My research assistants Michelle Fisher, Yuki Shimura, and Boratha Yeang tracked down information and references. Michelle typed and re-typed the manuscript, again and again. Yuki shared her understanding of Japan. Ruth Mandel tracked down all of the photographs. My cousin Evelyn Hirata found the cover art. Matt Zebrowski prepared all of the maps.

Several hundred UCLA undergraduate students who took my courses for the last six years, and my teaching assistants Katja Antoine, Katie Hale, and Ali Hamdan, helped me to explain and understand crises.

Eight friends heroically read all or most of my draft manuscript, and helped me to improve its ideas and its presentation. They are Marie Cohen, Paul Ehrlich, Alan Grinnell, Rebecca Kantar, Kai Michel, Ian Morris, Michael Shermer, and Sue Tibbles.

Dozens of other friends and colleagues commented on drafts of individual chapters, shared with me their experience, sent me articles or references, or did several or all of those things. They include: Eldon Ball, Barbara Barrett, Scott Barrett, Nicolas Berggruen, K. David Bishop, Heidi Borhau, Daniel Botsman, David Brown, Frank Caufield, Kamala Chandrakirana, Alejandra Cox, Sebastian Edwards, Ernst Peter Fischer, Kevin Fogg, Mikael Fortelius, Zephyr Frank, Howard Friedman, Eberhard Frömter, Nathan Gardels, Al Gore, James Green, Verity Grinnell, Karl-Theodor zu Guttenberg, Jeffrey Hadler, Yasu Hibi, Stefan-Ludwig Hoffmann, Antero Holmila, David Howell, Dian Irawati, Ivan Jaksic, Martin Jay, Benjamin Jones, Peter Kaufman, Joseph Kellner, Hiroshi Kito, Jennifer Klein, Matti Klinge, Sho Konishi, Markku Kuisma, Robert Lemelson, Hartmut Leppin, Tom Lovejoy, Harriet Mercer, Robin Miller, Norman Naimark, Monika Nalepa, Olivia Narins, Peter Narins, Tom Narins, Nathan Nunn, Benjamin Olken, Kaija Pehu-Lehtonen, William Perry, Louis Putterman, Johanna Rainio-Niemi, Geoffrey Robinson, Frances McCall Rosenbluth, Charly Salonius-Pasternak, Ken Scheve, Yuki Shimura, Chantal Signorio, Nina Sillem, Kerry Smith, Laurence Smith, Susan Stokes, Greg Stone, Mark Suster, Mak Takano, Jurist Tan, Spencer Thompson, Sirpa Tuomainen, Julio Vergara, Gary Waissi, D. A. Wallach, Stuart Ward, Tim Wirth, and Yoshinori Yasuda.

To all of these people, I express my heartfelt thanks.

Illustration Credits

Plate 0.1: AP Photo

Plate 2.1: Courtesy of Alexander Stielau

Plate 2.2: History Photo Collection, National Board of Antiquities
Collections, Helsinki

Plate 2.3: E. J. Reinikainen, National Board of Antiquities
Collections, Helsinki

Plate 2.4: Courtesy of St. Petersburg Travel Guide, www.guideto
petersburg.com

Plate 2.5: History Photo Collection, National Board of Antiquities
Collections, Helsinki

Plate 2.6: Library of Congress LC-DIG-ppmsca-18369

Plate 2.7: History Photo Collection, National Board of Antiquities
Collections, Helsinki

Plate 3.1: Wikimedia

Plate 3.2: Library of Congress LC-USZ62-110249

Plate 3.3: Takeo City Library and Historical Museum

Plate 3.4: Courtesy of Getty's Open Content Program

Plate 3.5: Waseda University Archive

Plate 3.6: Bain News Service, Library of Congress LC-DIG-ggbain-38442

Plate 3.7: Photo by Underwood & Underwood, Library of Congress LC-USZC2-6353

Plate 3.8: Courtesy of the Print Department of the National Library of Russia

Plate 3.9: ©SZ Photo / Scherl / The Image Works

Plate 4.1: Estate of Naúl Ojeda

Plate 4.2: Naval History & Heritage Command: Photographic Section, Naval Subjects Collection, L-53-41-1

Plate 4.3: © Chas Gerretsen, Nederlands Fotomuseum, Rotterdam

Plate 4.4: © Chas Gerretsen, Nederlands Fotomuseum, Rotterdam

Plate 4.5: Antonio Larrea / Fundacion Victor Jara

Plate 4.6: © Julio Etchart

Plate 4.7: © Rickey Rogers / Reuters Pictures

Plate 5.1: Historic Images, Inc. Press handout

Plate 5.2: Historic Images, Inc. Source unknown

Plate 5.3: State Secretariat of the Republic of Indonesia

Plate 5.4: Bettmann / Getty Images

Plate 5.5: © Hans Tanawi

Plate 5.6: Gunawan Kartapranata, CC Attribution-Share Alike 3.0 Unported License

Plate 5.7: Courtesy of Muhamad Taufiq Hidayat

Plate 6.1: U.S. Army Center for Military History

Plate 6.2: Courtesy of www.b24.net

Plate 6.3: U.S. Information Agency / National Archives & Records Administration (NARA)

Plate 6.4: © Barbara Klemm
Plate 6.5: © 51/1970 Der Spiegel
Plate 6.6: National Digital Archives of Poland (NAC)
Plate 7.1: From the collection of the National Archives of Australia
Plate 7.2: © Johncarnemolla / Dreamstime
Plate 7.3: Leonard Zhukovsky / Shutterstock.com
Plate 7.4.1: Lachlan Fearnley, Wikimedia CC Attribution-Share Alike 3.0 Unported license
Plate 7.4.2: Edward Orde, Wikimedia CC Attribution-Share Alike 4.0 International license
Plate 7.5: National Archives and Records Administration, NAID 533108
Plate 7.6: Australian War Memorial
Plate 7.7: Source unknown
Plate 7.8: Australian War Memorial
Plate 7.9: From the collection of the National Archives of Australia
Plate 7.10: Knödelbaum, Wikipedia. Creative Commons Attribution-Share Alike 3.0 Unported license
Plate 9.1: U.S. Navy photo by Mass Communication Specialist 2nd Class Ernest R. Scott / Released
Plate 9.2: © Tyler Olson / Shutterstock.com
Plate 9.3: Courtesy of the Port of Los Angeles
Plate 9.4: Bob Nichols / United States Department of Agriculture (USDA)
Plate 9.5: Lyndon Baines Johnson Library photo by Frank Wolfe / NARA
Plate 9.6: Courtesy of Alan Chevat
Plate 9.7: Thomas Edison National Historical Park
Plate 9.8: © Jim Harrison
Plate 9.9: Courtesy Ronald Reagan Library / NARA

Plate 9.10: Strom Thurmond Collection, Special Collections & Archives, Clemson University

Plate 9.11: Republished with permission of National Journal Group, Inc., from *National Journal,* March 30: 2012; permission conveyed through Copyright Clearance Center, Inc.

Plate 10.1: AP Photo / Paul Sakuma

Plate 10.2: Courtesy of Larry Hall

Plate 11.1: U.S. Department of Defense

Fig. 1: Matt Zebrowski

Fig. 2: Matt Zebrowski

Fig. 3: Matt Zebrowski

Fig. 4: Matt Zebrowski

Fig. 5: Matt Zebrowski

Fig. 6: Matt Zebrowski

Fig. 7: Matt Zebrowski

Fig. 8: Matt Zebrowski

Fig. 9: Matt Zebrowski

Further Readings

CHAPTER 1: PERSONAL CRISES

This chapter's references consist of recent books to illustrate the current status of the field of crisis therapy, plus older books, chapters, and journal articles to illustrate the field's development.

———

Donna C. Aguilera and Janice M. Messick. *Crisis Intervention: Theory and Methodology*, 3rd ed. (Mosby, St. Louis, MO, 1978).

Robert Calsyn, Joseph Pribyl, and Helen Sunukjian. Correlates of successful outcome in crisis intervention therapy. *American Journal of Community Psychology* 5: 111–119 (1977).

Gerald Caplan. *Principles of Preventive Psychiatry*. (Basic Books, New York, 1964).

Gerald Caplan. Recent developments in crisis intervention and the promotion of support service. *Journal of Primary Prevention* 10: 3–25 (1985).

Priscilla Dass-Brailsford. *A Practical Approach to Trauma*. (Sage Publications, Los Angeles, CA, 2007).

James L. Greenstone and Sharon C. Leviton. *Elements of Crisis Intervention: Crises and How to Respond to Them*, 3rd ed. (Brooks-Cole, Belmont, CA, 2011).

Charles Holahan and Rudolf Moos. Life stressors, resistance factors, and improved psychological functions: An extension of the stress resistance paradigm. *Journal of Personality and Sociopsychology* 58: 909–917 (1990).

Gerald Jacobson. Programs and techniques of crisis intervention. Pp. 810–825, in *Child and Adolescent Psychiatry, Socioculture and Community Psychiatry*, ed. G. Caplan. (Basic Books, New York, 1974).

Gerald Jacobson. Crisis-oriented therapy. *Psychiatric Clinics of North America* 2, no. 1: 39–54 (1979).

Gerald Jacobson, Martin Strickler, and Wilbur Morley. Generic and individual approaches to crisis intervention. *American Journal of Public Health* 58: 338–343 (1968).

Richard James and Burt Gilliland. *Crisis Intervention Strategies*, 8th ed. (Cengage, Boston, 2016).

Erich Lindemann. *Beyond Grief: Studies in Crisis Intervention*. (Jason Aronson, New York, 1979).

Rick A. Myer. *Assessment for Crisis Intervention: A Triage Assessment Model*. (Brooks Cole, Belmont, CA, 2001).

Howard J. Parad, ed. *Crisis Intervention: Selective Readings*. (Family Service Association of America, New York, 1965).

Kenneth Yeager and Albert Roberts, eds. *Crisis Intervention Handbook: Assessment, Treatment, and Research*, 4th ed. (Oxford University Press, New York, 2015).

———

Papers in the journal *Crisis: The Journal of Crisis Intervention and Suicide Prevention*. (Volumes 1–38, 1980–2017).

CHAPTER 2: FINLAND'S WAR WITH THE SOVIET UNION

It's common practice in scholarly books to devote dozens of concluding pages to footnotes. Those footnotes guide readers to specialty journal articles and other sources available in research libraries, and providing the basis for detailed statements in the book's text. That practice seemed appropriate for my earlier books (*The Third Chimpanzee; Guns, Germs, and Steel; Why Is Sex Fun?; Collapse;* and *Natural Experiments of History*), which made much use of articles on highly technical subjects for which most readers would have difficulty discovering sources — subjects such as the Neolithic distribution of large-seeded wild cereals, or the frequency of fish bones in medieval Greenland Viking garbage deposits. But the resulting proliferation of references increased considerably the length, weight, and cost of my books. One friend complained to me, "Jared, I liked your book, but it hurt my neck and arms to hold its weight over my head while reading it in bed at night. Please make your next book less heavy."

My most recent book (*The World Until Yesterday*) did save length, weight, and cost by relegating footnotes and references to an on-line website, rather than printing them at the back of the book. I thereby discovered how many readers actually consulted my footnotes and references: only one or two readers around the world each year.

This present book therefore tries something different: to provide references that readers may actually find useful and accessible. Most of my references now consist of books available in large general libraries, rather than articles in scholarly journals. Readers wanting to learn more about a country that I discuss will discover that many of those books are interesting and comprehensible. To guide me in deciding which type of references to provide for my next book, I shall be grateful to readers willing to write me about their own preference.

———

Seppo Hentilä, Markku Kuisma, Pertti Haapala, and Ohto Manninen. Finlandization for better and for worse. *Historical Journal/Historiallinen Aikakauskirja*. No. 2: 129–160 (1998).

Max Jakobson. *Finland Survived: An Account of the Finnish-Soviet Winter War 1939–1940*, 2nd ed. (Otava, Helsinki, 1984).

Eino Jutikkala and Kauko Pirinen. *A History of Finland*, 6th ed. (WS Bookwell Oy, Helsinki, 2003).

Sakari Jutila. *Finlandization for Finland and the World*. (European Research Association, Bloomington, IN, 1983).

Urho Kekkonen. *A President's View*. (Heinemann, London, 1982).

Tiina Kinnunen and Ville Kiviimäki, eds. *Finland in World War 2: History, Memory, Interpretations*. (Brill, Leiden, 2012).

Matti Klinge. *A Brief History of Finland*, 3rd ed. (Otava, Helsinki, 2000).

Walter Laqueur. *The Political Psychology of Appeasement: Finlandization and Other Unpopular Essays*. (Transaction Books, New Brunswick, NJ, 1980).

Ohto Manninen, Riitta Hjerppe, Juha-Antti Lamberg, Markku Kuisma, and Pirjo Markkola. Suomi — Finland. *Historical Journal/Historiallinen Aikakauskirja*. No. 2: 129–160 (1997).

George Maude. *The Finnish Dilemma: Neutrality in the Shadow of Power*. (Oxford University Press, London, 1976).

Johanna Rainio-Niemi. *The Ideological Cold War: The Politics of Neutrality in Austria and Finland*. (Routledge, New York, 2014).

Esko Salminen. *The Silenced Media: The Propaganda War between Russia and the West in Northern Europe*. (St. Martin's Press, New York, 1999).

William Trotter. *A Frozen Hell: The Russo-Finnish Winter War of 1939–40.* (Algonquin Books, Chapel Hill, NC, 1991).

Steven Zaloga. *Gustaf Mannerheim.* (Osprey, Oxford, 2015).

———

https://www.sotasampo.fi/en/cemeteries/list   This database for all of Finland's local war cemeteries gives not only the numbers of those buried and those missing, but also the names and dates and places of birth of each person buried.

www.sotasampo.fi   This database contains a massive amount of information on Finland and Finns during World War Two.

CHAPTER 3: THE ORIGINS OF MODERN JAPAN

Michael Auslin. *Negotiating with Imperialism: The Unequal Treaties and the Culture of Japanese Diplomacy.* (Harvard University Press, Cambridge, MA, 2004).

W.G. Beasley. *The Japanese Experience: A Short History of Japan.* (University of California Press, Berkeley, 1999).

Daniel Botsman. *Punishment and Power in the Making of Modern Japan.* (Princeton University Press, Princeton, NJ, 2005).

Takashi Fujitani. *Splendid Monarchy: Power and Pageantry in Modern Japan.* (University of California Press, Berkeley, 1996).

Carol Gluck. *Japan's Modern Myths: Ideology in the Late Meiji Period.* (Princeton University Press, Princeton, NJ, 1985).

Robert Hellyer. *Defining Engagement: Japan and Global Contexts, 1640–1868.* (Harvard University Press, Cambridge, MA, 2009).

Marius Jansen. *Sakamoto Ryōma and the Meiji Restoration.* (Princeton University Press, Princeton, NJ, 1961).

Donald Keene. *Emperor of Japan: Meiji and His World, 1852–1912.* (Columbia University Press, New York, 2002).

Kyu Hyun Kim. *The Age of Visions and Arguments: Parliamentarianism and the National Public Sphere in Early Meiji Japan*. (Harvard University Press, Cambridge, MA, 2007).

Hyoson Kiryaku. *Drifting Toward the Southeast: The Story of Five Japanese Castaways*. (Spinner, New Bedford, MA, 2003).

Ernest Satow. *A Diplomat in Japan*. (Seeley Service, London, 1921).

Ronald Toby. *State and Diplomacy in Early Modern Japan: Asia in the Development of the Tokugawa Bakufu*. (Princeton University Press, Princeton, NJ, 1984).

James White. State building and modernization: The Meiji Restoration. Pp. 499–559, in *Crisis, Choice and Change: Historical Studies of Political Development*, ed. G.A. Almond, S.C. Flanagan, and R.J. Mundt. (Little, Brown, Boston, 1973).

CHAPTER 4: A CHILE FOR ALL CHILEANS

Patricio Aylwin Azócar. *El Reencuentro de los Demócratas: Del Golpe al Triunfo del No*. (Ediciones Grupo Zeta, Santiago, 1998).

Edgardo Boeninger. *Democracia en Chile: Lecciones para la Gobernabilidad*. (Editorial Andres Bello, Santiago, 1997).

Erica Chenoweth and Maria Stephan. *Why Civil Resistance Works: The Strategic Logic of Nonviolent Conflict*. (Columbia University Press, New York, 2011).

Simon Collier and William Sater. *A History of Chile, 1808–1994*. (Cambridge University Press, Cambridge, 1996).

Pamela Constable and Arturo Valenzuela. *A Nation of Enemies: Chile under Pinochet*. (Norton, New York, 1991).

Sebastian Edwards. *Left Behind: Latin America and the False Promise of Populism*. (University of Chicago Press, Chicago, 2010).

Carlos Huneeus. *El Régimen de Pinochet.* (Editorial Sudamericana Chilena, Santiago, 2000).

Peter Kronbluh. *The Pinochet File: A Declassified Dossier on Atrocity and Accountability.* (New Press, New York, 2013).

Thomas Skidmore, Peter Smith, and James Green. Chapter 10. Chile: Repression and democracy. Pp. 268–295, in *Modern Latin America*, 8th ed. (Oxford University Press, Oxford, 2014).

Arturo Valenzuela. Chile. Pp. 1–133, in *The Breakdown of Democratic Regimes*, ed. Juan Linz and Alfred Stepan. (Johns Hopkins University Press, Baltimore, 1978).

Stefan de Vylder. *Allende's Chile: The Political Economy of the Rise and Fall of the Unidad Popular.* (Cambridge University Press, Cambridge, 1976).

Edwin Williamson. Chapter 4. Chile: Democracy, revolution and dictatorship. Pp. 485–510, in *The Penguin History of Latin America*, rev. ed. (Penguin, London, 2009).

CHAPTER 5: INDONESIA, THE RISE OF A NEW COUNTRY

Benedict Anderson. *Java in a Time of Revolution.* (Cornell University Press, Ithaca, NY, 1972).

Edward Aspinall. *Opposing Suharto: Compromise, Resistance, and Regime Change in Indonesia.* (Stanford University Press, Stanford, CA, 2005).

Harold Crouch. *The Army and Politics in Indonesia*, rev. ed. (Cornell University Press, Ithaca, NY, 1988).

Harold Crouch. *Political Reform in Indonesia after Soeharto.* (Institute of Southeast Asia Studies, Singapore, 2010).

R.E. Elson. *Suharto: A Political Biography.* (Cambridge University Press, Cambridge, 2001).

R.E. Elson. *The Idea of Indonesia: A History.* (Cambridge University Press, Cambridge, 2008).

Herbert Feith. *The Decline of Constitutional Democracy in Indonesia*. (Cornell University Press, Ithaca, NY, 1962).

George Kahin. *Nationalism and Revolution in Indonesia*. (Cornell University Press, Ithaca, NY, 1970).

George Kahin and Audrey Kahin. *Subversion as Foreign Policy: The Secret Eisenhower and Dulles Debacle in Indonesia*. (New Press, New York, 1995).

J.D. Legge. *Sukarno: A Political Biography*. 3rd ed. (Archipelago Press, Singapore, 2003).

Daniel Lev. *The Transition to Guided Democracy: Indonesian Politics 1957–59*. (Cornell University Press, Ithaca, NY, 1966).

Katharine McGregor. *History in Uniform: Military Ideology and the Construction of Indonesia's Past*. (NUS Press, Singapore, 2007).

Joshua Oppenheimer. *The Act of Killing*. (2012). [Documentary film].

Joshua Oppenheimer. *The Look of Silence*. (2014). [Documentary film].

Elizabeth Pisani. *Indonesia etc.: Exploring the Improbable Nation*. (Norton, New York, 2014).

M.C. Ricklefs. *A History of Modern Indonesia*. (Macmillan Education, London, 1981).

Geoffrey Robinson. *The Dark Side of Paradise: Political Violence in Bali*. (Cornell University Press, Ithaca, NY, 1995).

Geoffrey Robinson. *If You Leave Us Here, We Will Die: How Genocide Was Stopped in East Timor*. (Princeton University Press, Princeton, NJ, 2010).

Geoffrey Robinson. *The Killing Season: A History of the Indonesian Massacres, 1965–66*. (Princeton University Press, Princeton, NJ, 2018).

John Roosa. *Pretext for Mass Murder: The September 30th Movement and Suharto's Coup d'État in Indonesia*. (University of Wisconsin Press, Madison, 2006).

J. Sidel. *Riots, Pogroms, Jihad: Religious Violence in Indonesia.* (Cornell University Press, Ithaca, NY, 2006).

Bradley Simpson. *Economists with Guns: Authoritarian Development and U.S.–Indonesian Relations, 1960–1968.* (Stanford University Press, Stanford, CA, 2008).

CHAPTER 6: REBUILDING GERMANY

Neal Bascomb. *Hunting Eichmann.* (Mariner, Boston, 2010).

Jillian Becker. *Hitler's Children: The Story of the Baader-Meinhof Terrorist Gang,* 3rd ed. (Pickwick, London, 1989).

Gordon Craig. *The Germans.* (Putnam, New York, 1982).

Norbert Frei. *1968: Jugendrevolte und Globaler Protest.* (Deutscher Taschenbuch Verlag, München, 2008).

Ulrich Herbert, ed. *Wandlungsprozesse in Westdeutschland.* (Wallstein, Göttingen, 2002).

Ulrich Herbert. *Geschichte Deutschlands im 20. Jahrhundert.* (C.H. Beck, München, 2014).

Michael Hughes. *Shouldering the Burden of Defeat: West Germany and the Reconstruction of Social Justice.* (University of North Carolina Press, Chapel Hill, 1999).

Peter Merseburger. *Willy Brandt 1913–1992: Visionär und Realist.* (Deutsche Verlags, Stuttgart, 2002).

Hans-Joachim Noack. *Willy Brandt: Ein Leben, ein Jahrhundert.* (Rowohlt, Berlin, 2013).

Andreas Rödder. *Die Bundesrepublik Deutschland 1969–1990.* (Oldenbourg, München, 2004).

Axel Schildt. *Die Sozialgeschichte der Bundesrepublik Deutschland bis 1989/90.* (Oldenbourg, München, 2007).

Hanna Schissler, ed. *The Miracle Years.* (Princeton University Press, Princeton, NJ, 2001).

Gregor Schöllgen. *Willy Brandt: Die Biographie.* (Propyläen, Berlin, 2001).

Edith Sheffer. *Burned Bridge: How East and West Germans Made the Iron Curtain*. (Oxford University Press, Oxford, 2011).

Nathan Stoltzfus and Henry Friedlander, eds. *Nazi Crimes and the Law*. (Cambridge University Press, Cambridge, 2008).

Nikolaus Wachsmann. *KL: A History of the Nazi Concentration Camps*. (Farrar, Straus and Giroux, New York, 2015).

Hans-Ulrich Wehler. *Deutsche Gesellschaftsgeschichte*, vol. 5: *Bundesrepublik und DDR 1949–1990*. (C.H. Beck, München, 2008).

Harald Welzer, Sabine Moller, and Karoline Tschuggnall. *Opa war kein Nazi: Nationalsozialismus und Holocaust im Familiengedächtnis*. (Fischer, Frankfurt, 2002).

Irmtrud Wojak. *Fritz Bauer 1903–1968*. (C.H. Beck, München, 2011).

Alexei Yurchak. *Everything Was Forever, Until It Was No More: The Last Soviet Generation*. (Princeton University Press, Princeton, NJ, 2006).

CHAPTER 7: AUSTRALIA: WHO ARE WE?

Peter Brune. *A Bastard of a Place: The Australians in Papua*. (Allen & Unwin, Crows Nest, Australia, 2003).

Anthony Burke. *Fear of Security: Australia's Invasion Anxiety*. (Cambridge University Press, Cambridge, 2001).

James Curran and Stuart Ward. *The Unknown Nation: Australia after Empire*. (Melbourne University Press, Carlton South, Australia, 2010).

Peter Edwards. *Crises and Commitments: The Politics and Diplomacy of Australia's Involvement in Southeast Asian Conflicts 1948–1965*. (Allen & Unwin, North Sydney, Australia, 1992).

Marilyn Lake. British world or new world? *History Australia* 10, no. 3: 36–50 (2013).

Stuart Macintyre. *A Concise History of Australia*, 4th ed. (Cambridge University Press, Port Melbourne, Australia, 2016).

Neville Meaney. The end of "white Australia" and Australia's changing perceptions of Asia, 1945–1990. *Australian Journal of International Affairs* 49, no. 2: 171–189 (1995).

Neville Meaney. Britishness and Australia: Some reflections. *Journal of Imperial and Commonwealth History* 31, no. 2: 121–135 (2003).

Mark Peel and Christina Twomey. *A History of Australia*. (Palgrave Macmillan, Houndmills, UK, 2011).

Deryck Schreuder and Stuart Ward, ed. *Australia's Empire*. (Oxford University Press, Oxford, 2008).

Gwenda Tavan. The dismantling of the White Australia policy: Elite conspiracy or will of the Australian people? *Australian Journal of Political Science* 39, no. 1: 109–125 (2004).

David Walker. *Anxious Nation: Australia and the Rise of Asia 1850–1939*. (University of Queensland Press, St. Lucia, Australia, 1999).

Stuart Ward. *Australia and the British Embrace: The Demise of the Imperial Ideal*. (Melbourne University Press, Carlton South, Australia, 2001).

Frank Welsh. *Australia: A New History of the Great Southern Land*. (Overlook, New York, 2004).

CHAPTER 8: WHAT LIES AHEAD FOR JAPAN?

W.G. Beasley. *The Japanese Experience: A Short History of Japan*. (University of California Press, Berkeley, 1999).

Ian Buruma. *The Wages of Guilt: Memories of War in Germany and Japan*. (Farrar, Straus and Giroux, New York, 1994).

John Dower. *Embracing Defeat: Japan in the Wake of World War Two*. (Norton, New York, 1999).

Eri Hotta. *Japan 1941: Countdown to Infamy*. (Knopf, New York, 2013).

McKinsey Global Institute. *The Future of Japan: Reigniting Productivity and Growth*. (McKinsey, Tokyo, 2015).

David Pilling. *Bending Adversity: Japan and the Art of Survival*. (Penguin, London, 2014).

Frances McCall Rosenblugh, ed. *The Political Economy of Japan's Low Fertility*. (Stanford University Press, Stanford, CA, 2007).

Sven Steinmo. *The Evolution of Modern States: Sweden, Japan, and the United States*. (Cambridge University Press, Cambridge, 2010).

N.O. Tsuia and L.S. Bumpass, eds. *Marriage, Work, and Family Life in Comparative Perspective: Japan, South Korea, and the United States*. (University of Hawaii Press, Honolulu, 2004).

Lee Kuan Yew. *From Third World to First: The Singapore Story: 1964–2000*. (HarperCollins, New York, 2000).

CHAPTERS 9 AND 10: WHAT LIES AHEAD FOR THE UNITED STATES?

Larry Bartels. *Unequal Democracy: The Political Economy of the New Gilded Age*, 2nd ed. (Princeton University Press, Princeton, NJ, 2016).

Ari Berman. *The Modern Struggle for Voting Rights in America*. (Farrar, Straus and Giroux, New York, 2015).

Joseph Califano, Jr. *Our Damaged Democracy: We the People Must Act*. (Touchstone, New York, 2018).

Tim Flannery. *The Eternal Frontier: An Ecological History of North America and Its Peoples*. (Text, Melbourne, 2001).

Howard Friedman. *The Measure of a Nation: How to Regain America's Competitive Edge and Boost Our Global Standing*. (Prometheus, New York, 2012).

Al Gore. *The Assault on Reason*. (Penguin, New York, 2017).

Steven Hill. *Fixing Elections: The Failure of America's Winner Take All Politics*. (Routledge, New York, 2002).

Robert Kaplan. *Earning the Rockies: How Geography Shapes America's Role in the World*. (Random House, New York, 2017).

Jill Lepore. *These Truths: A History of the United States*. (Norton, New York, 2018).

Steven Levitsky and Daniel Ziblatt. *How Democracies Die: What History Reveals about Our Future*. (Crown, New York, 2018).

Thomas Mann and Norman Ornstein. *It's Even Worse than It Looks: How the American Constitution System Collided with the New Politics of Extremists*. (Basic Books, New York, 2012).

Chris Matthews. *Tip and the Gipper: When Politics Worked*. (Simon & Schuster, New York, 2013).

Yascha Mounk. *The People vs. Democracy: Why Our Freedom Is in Danger and How to Save It*. (Harvard University Press, Cambridge, MA, 2018).

Robert Putnam. *Bowling Alone: The Collapse and Revival of American Community*. (Simon & Schuster, New York, 2000).

Joseph Stiglitz. *The Price of Inequality: How Today's Divided Society Endangers Our Future*. (Norton, New York, 2012).

Sherry Turkle. *Reclaiming Conversation: The Power of Talk in a Digital Age*. (Penguin, New York, 2015).

CHAPTER 11: WHAT LIES AHEAD FOR THE WORLD?

Scott Barrett. *Environment and Statecraft: The Strategy of Environmental Treaty-making*. (Oxford University Press, Oxford, 2005).

Scott Barrett. *Why Cooperate? The Incentive to Supply Global Public Goods*. (Oxford University Press, Oxford, 2007).

Nick Bostrom and Milan Cirkovic, eds. *Global Catastrophic Risks*. (Oxford University Press, Oxford, 2011).

Jared Diamond. *Collapse: How Societies Choose to Fail or Succeed.* (Viking Penguin, New York, 2005).

Tim Flannery. *Atmosphere of Hope: Searching for Solutions to the Climate Crisis.* (Atlantic Monthly Press, New York, 2015).

Clive Hamilton. *Earthmasters: The Dawn of the Age of Climate Engineering.* (Yale University Press, New Haven, CT, 2013).

Michael T. Klare. *The Race for What's Left: The Global Scramble for the World's Last Resources.* (Metropolitan Books, New York, 2012).

Fred Pearce. *Confessions of an Eco-sinner: Tracking Down the Sources of My Stuff.* (Beacon Press, Boston, 2008).

William Perry. *My Journey at the Nuclear Brink.* (Stanford University Press, Stanford, CA, 2015).

Laurence Smith. *The World in 2050: Four Forces Facing Civilization's Northern Future.* (Dutton Penguin Group, New York, 2010).

Richard Wilkinson and Kate Pickett. *The Spirit Level: Why More Equal Societies Almost Always Do Better.* (Allen Lane, London, 2009).

EPILOGUE: LESSONS, QUESTIONS, AND OUTLOOK

Thomas Carlyle. *On Heroes, Hero-Worship, and the Hero in History.* (James Fraser, London, 1841).

Jared Diamond and James Robinson, eds. *Natural Experiments of History.* (Harvard University Press, Cambridge, MA, 2010).

Geert Hofstede. *Culture's Consequences: International Differences in Work-Related Values.* (Sage, Beverly Hills, 1980).

Geert Hofstede, Gert Jan Hofstede, and Michael Minkov. *Cultures and Organizations: Software of the Mind.* (McGraw Hill, New York, 2010).

Ronald Inglehart. *Modernization and Postmodernization: Cultural, Economic, and Political Change in 43 Societies.* (Princeton University Press, Princeton, NJ, 1997).

Benjamin Jones and Benjamin Olken. Do leaders matter? National leadership and growth since World War II. *Quarterly Journal of Economics* 120, no. 3: 835–864 (2005).

Benjamin Jones and Benjamin Olken. Hit or miss? The effect of assassinations on institutions and war. *American Economic Journal: Macroeconomics* 1/2: 55–87 (2009).

Michael Minkov. *What Makes Us Different and Similar: A New Interpretation of the World Values Survey and Other Cross-Cultural Data.* (Klasika I Stil, Sofia, Bulgaria, 2007).

Thucydides. *The Peloponnesian War.* Steven Lattimore, translator. (Hackett, Indianapolis, IN, 1988).

Leo Tolstoy. *War and Peace.* Ann Dunnigan, translator. (New American Library, New York, 1968).

Index

INDEX

Indonesia (cont.)
population of, 179, 183–84, 188, 208, 210, 445
power struggle in, 193–201
reconciliation and, 181
reconciliation in, 137–38, 176, 211
religions in, 208
revolution in, 137, 174
30 September Movement in, 194, 197
vs. U.S., 359
See also factors in outcomes
industrialization, 83, 144, 205, 317
in Japan, 103, 123, 128, 320
Industrial Revolution, 393, 398
inequality, 122, 368–69, 383, 418
in U.S., 338–39, 363–68, 378, 426
Inglehart, Ronald, 457
International Convention for the Prevention of Pollution from Ships (MARPOL), 421
International Monetary Fund (IMF), 190
International Seabed Authority, 421–22
International Whaling Commission, 318–19
Inuit, 48–49
Iran, 384, 390
Iraq, 384, 386, 448
Ireland, 271, 277
Ishiba, Shigeru, 310
Islam, 179, 182, 188, 204, 383
Israel, 227, 277, 285, 307, 371–72, 418–19
Itagaki Taisuke, 133
Italy, 74, 222, 281, 333, 353, 359, 411
Australia and, 277, 279
generational differences in, 230, 233
Germany and, 80, 243
leaders in, 454–55
unification of, 250
Ito Hirobumi, 117, 134
Iwakura Mission (1871–1873), 117, 124

Japan, 12, 100
homogeneity of, 133–34, 297, 309, 311
Japan, Meiji, 101–39, 441, 448
Australia and, 103, 126, 129, 289
daimyo in, 107, 109, 112, 114–15, 120, 122
external vs. internal pressures on, 18–19, 102, 138, 174, 432, 447
foreigners in, 112–13, 116, 134–35
foreign relations of, 119, 127–32, 138, 219
government of, 111n4, 115–21, 123–24

isolation of, 104–6
Korea and, 103, 105–6, 128
leaders in, 136–37, 175, 453
legal system in, 119, 122–23, 127, 132, 135
military of, 109–11, 114, 119–20, 127–28, 132, 134, 138–39, 320
modern period and, 16, 22, 293
reconciliation in, 137–38
reforms in, 115–20, 122–24, 126–27, 138
tradition in, 133–34
unequal treaties with, 110–12, 116, 119, 123–24, 426
the West and, 103, 105, 111–12, 134, 381
See also economy, Japanese; education, Japanese; emperor, Japanese; factors in outcomes
Japan, modern
aging population of, 294, 296–300, 303–9, 311–12, 317, 322–23, 327–28, 425
Australia and, 256, 265–66, 268–69, 272–79, 284, 287–89, 317, 319, 448, 461
author's experience of, 15, 100–102
birth rates in, 300, 304–6
environment of, 294, 297–98
foreign relations of, 127–32, 319–20, 322, 425
future of, 293–323, 398, 406, 409–10, 413, 462
generational differences in, 233
vs. Germany, 315–16
immigration in, 309–12, 323, 425
Indonesia and, 185–86, 189–90
Korea and, 239, 252, 310, 312–16, 321–22, 333, 425
marriage in, 305–6
Meiji period and, 16, 22, 293
military and, 313
military of, 296, 321
North Korea and, 387
nuclear weapons and, 386
reconciliation in, 239, 252
student revolts in, 230
vs. U.S., 325–28, 338, 353–54, 371–72, 377, 381
in World War Two, 52, 61, 80, 96, 129, 135, 163, 219, 310, 315, 333, 384, 428, 446, 455
See also economy, Japanese; factors in outcomes

494